Islands of the Dawn

Islands
of the
Dawn

The Story of Alternative
Spirituality in New Zealand

Robert S. Ellwood

University of Hawaii Press · Honolulu

Library of Congress Cataloging-in-Publication Data
Ellwood, Robert S., 1933–
  Islands of the dawn : the story of alternative spirituality in New
Zealand / Robert S. Ellwood.
     p.   cm.
  Includes bibliographical references and index.
  ISBN 0-8248-1487-8 (alk. paper)
    1. Sects—New Zealand.   2. Cults—New Zealand.   3. New Zealand—
Religion.   I. Title.
BL2615.E444   1993
291'.046'0993—dc20   92-38937
                                           CIP

University of Hawaii Press books are printed on
acid-free paper and meet the guidelines for permanence
and durability of the Council on Library Resources

Text design by Janet Heavenridge

Contents

Preface

THIS historical study of alternative spirituality in New Zealand is the tangible product of a Fulbright grant, supported jointly by the governments of the United States and New Zealand, which enabled my family and myself to spend the first six months of 1988 in Wellington while research was being carried out. The sponsor of my project was the Alexander Turnbull Library, the historical research facility of the New Zealand National Library.

It would be impossible to name all those who assisted my work in one way or another, who hosted me on visits to all the New Zealand universities and to several places of special interest in connection with my work, and who generally made the New Zealand months such a special and wonderful experience for all of us. I would, however, particularly like to thank Laurie Cox, executive director of the New Zealand-United States Education Foundation, who dealt with practical arrangements for our visit and my research with exceptional competence and consideration; and James Traue, director of the Turnbull Library, and his staff for their unstinting kindness and helpfulness in making the reading rooms and unequaled archival resources of this library, and other branches of the National Library, such a pleasant and invaluable workplace.

I wish to thank Peter Lineham, senior lecturer in history at Massey University, Palmerston North, and leading authority on New Zealand religious history, for reading the entire manuscript and making numerous helpful corrections and suggestions; Murray Bott, director of Mutual UFO Network (MUFON)—New Zealand, for extensive help with the section on UFO religion; Patrick Zalewski, author and magician, for generous assistance with the chapter on the Golden Dawn in New Zealand; and J. W. Graham for making available to me his fine private collection of materials on Spiritualist history. To the many others, both in academic circles and within the spiritual movements under consideration, who have earned my deepest gratitude, I can say only that I hope this book itself reflects the respect and indebtedness I feel toward them. At the same time, I want to state emphatically that the contents and judgments of this book are entirely my own.

A word about the scope of the study: *Islands of the Dawn* should be taken as primarily a historical examination of alternative spirituality within the European-descended (Pakeha) population of New Zealand. Although a number of current groups of this type are mentioned, particularly in appendix 2, it is not the purpose of this book to provide an up-to-date or comprehensive listing. For this, and for current addresses and other such information provided by the religions themselves, the reader is referred to the most recent edition of *Beliefs and Practices in New Zealand: A Directory,* published by the Department of Religious Studies, Massey University, an excellent handbook that I found invaluable to my work.

The present book also does not attempt to cover religious movements based primarily within the indigenous Maori community or other distinct ethnic groups. These are no less interesting and important than the Pakeha movements I have endeavored to trace, but for that very reason they deserve a book or books of their own—which to some extent they have received, although to the best of my knowledge most of the history in this book has never before been presented in a general study, if at all. (For this reason the present book does not contain the usual bibliography at the end. The scholarly monographs and articles, or original sources devoted principally to the topic at hand, are far too few to justify formal listing, and the primary or journalistic materials, plus scattered references in works of all sorts from which I have culled this story, can be easily ascertained from the notes.)

The historical, Pakeha scope of the study has meant that most of the focus has been on Spiritualism and Theosophy and their devolutions, and to a lesser extent on the Golden Dawn, the only New Zealand alternative spirituality traditions with deep roots in the European community extending back well into the nineteenth century. This has inevitably meant that a fundamental question raised by the study, one that may have broader application than New Zealand history alone, is, Why have movements like Spiritualism and Theosophy flourished particularly well in nineteenth-century British settler communities? Indications are that immigrant communities of other ethnic background, or those established chiefly before or after the Victorian heyday of those movements, have not shown quite the same proclivities. New Zealand, despite its great distance from the British homeland, is no doubt the clearest example of such a community and so may be of particular help in the search for answers. Some preliminary responses to this question are suggested in the concluding chapter, and others may occur to readers as they peruse the historical chapters of this book themselves.

Finally, I would like to underscore the high regard in which I hold the expressions of alternative spirituality that are the subjects of this study, both as human experiences and as fruits of the spiritual quest that seems to be an irreducible part of human nature. Occasionally it may be necessary also to point to human foibles in connection with them, but that should not be taken to suggest I see them as no more than human folly, as I hope other passages make clear. I am myself a member of the Theosophical Society, and I have the deepest respect for all human beings willing to undertake the spiritual quest with all its hopes and risks, both those who set foot on the well-traveled roads and those who strike out on fainter alternative trails or even do their own exploring.

I am also aware of the risks—and potential for folly—involved for one writing so fully of the spiritual history of a country not his own and to which he has been no more than a visitor. The possibility of error, or for misjudging the nuances of a people's consciousness and historical experience, are certainly there and have probably not been entirely avoided. I can say only that I hope these dangers are to some extent outweighed by the potential benefits of an outside perspective; to provide many scholars from many countries the opportunity to lend that perspective is the purpose of the program by which this research was supported.

1 From Nineveh to New Zealand
A Brief History of Alternatives

THE ALTERNATIVE spirituality tradition of the West, the tradition of alchemists and Rosicrucians, of nineteenth-century Spiritualists and Theosophists and twentieth-century New Agers, had a very long history before reaching New Zealand during the reign of Queen Victoria. Its tortuous and sometimes-obscure course can be compared to that of an underground river. Its sources stretch far back to ancient Chaldea and to Hellenistic times. Its route took it beneath the cathedrals and castles of medieval Europe. Surfacing decisively in the occultism of the Renaissance, it sank again under the rising mountain ranges of religion reformed and of the new science. But its waters have sparkled in the light subsequently in various times and places: as a counter to eighteenth-century Rationalism in the form of such persons as Cagliostro and Saint Germain; in the symbolism of Freemasonry; in Swedenborg, Mesmer, and their joint child, Spiritualism; in Theosophy and the Golden Dawn.

Almost from the beginning of large-scale British immigration to New Zealand in the 1850s and 1860s, such alternative spirituality has had high visibility and relative success in those islands so remote from the homeland. Spiritualism in the 1870s and 1880s, and Theosophy in the 1890s, though small in numbers of committed believers, were a favored subject of articles and ongoing correspondence in the newspapers and sometimes involved prominent persons. The first lodge of the Theosophical Society in the country, established in Wellington in 1888, included on its membership roll no less a person than the prime minister of the day, Sir Harry Atkinson.

In this chapter, a brief overview of the history of Western alternative spirituality is offered as a background to its course in New Zealand.

1

Before that story, however, a look at aspects of New Zealand history may facilitate an understanding of why the nineteenth-century colony was such an apt receptacle for new and unconventional spiritual movements like Spiritualism and Theosophy.

The New Zealand islands are islands of the dawn in more ways than one, not only because, by the convention of the international date line, they are among the first places in the world to receive the light of each new day. Before human footfall they supported a peculiar flora and fauna—cycads and conifers without flowers, birds and reptiles but no mammals except bats—which seemed almost to link these islands to the dawn of life, or at least more to the age of dinosaurs than to the Pleistocene and after. The New Zealand islands also were, with Iceland, the last large inhabitable place in the world to receive human settlement. They were also the last separate terrain to receive, subsequently, large-scale European settlement. Thus there is something dawnlike about life and culture in New Zealand. However old the cultures from which its various waves of settlers derived, in that land humanity is barely past sunrise. For some this has always suggested that here, if anywhere, the human race could mark a new beginning, start a new day under a new sun.

An early proponent of this view was Robert Pemberton (1788?–1879), who wrote *The Happy Colony* in 1854. Described by John Rockey as "the last of the self-confessed Owenites and the last of the World Makers," Pemberton believed in original human goodness and the inherent goodness of nature, in the tradition of Rousseau. Evil was the product of society, especially presenting itself when social classes were sharply divided. At the same time, Pemberton disliked individuality and favored group excellence rather than individual virtue. Education would reign supreme in his happy colony. Children would be trained for their first three years in an "Infant Temple" and then by "spirit teachers and trainers" who would be "artists of the soul" and perfect models. Pemberton believed in human perfectibility; social control would be exercised in the classroom rather than by the state. He tried to establish colonies near Mt. Egmont on the North Island, but unfortunately perfection eluded them and they did not survive.[1]

The colonization scheme of Edward Gibbon Wakefield and the New Zealand Association, though in the end depleted in its original form, attained relatively greater success on the ground—no doubt because his plan was better grounded in hard economic reality and had highly placed support. In brief, Wakefield, whatever his personal motives, claimed his scheme would alleviate destitution and unemployment in England, as well as provide investment opportunities for capital, through promoting emigration from Britain and the establishment of colonies. The colonies were to be intensively settled and worked agricultural communities, with land owned by the investors but with better wages paid labor than at home. This arrangement would attract and benefit labor, and at the same time alleviate the horror Wakefield felt toward too much independence and dispersal on the part of settlers. The New Zealand Association was founded in 1837 to implement his concepts in that place.

The first Wakefield colonists, dispatched by the association in the ship *Tory*, reached Port Nicholson (Wellington) in 1840, the year of annexation and of the Treaty of Waitangi between the Maori leadership and the crown. Wakefield's system also inspired later religiously based colonization efforts, the "Free Kirk" Presbyterian in Otago in 1848 and the Anglican in Canterbury (Christchurch) two years later.

Rising evangelical concern for the welfare of colonial natives must be added to this picture. The Aborigines Protection Society was founded in England in the wake of the abolition of slavery throughout the British Empire in 1833. Its view, like that of most missionaries and not a few British officials, was that colonial policy must include attention to the welfare of such indigene races as the Maori in New Zealand and must curb the exploitative greed of unscrupulous traders and settlers. These ideals were reflected in the 1840 Waitangi treaty, with its careful attention, on paper, to rights and responsibilities on both the government and the Maori sides.

On one hand, then, in New Zealand's background are exceptionally "modern," planned, and idealistic concepts of how to establish a new colony. The settlement would, to be sure, greatly expand the domain of the Anglo-Saxon race, but in a manner far removed from the crass fortune making of John Company's India nabobs or the brutality of Botany Bay. New Zealand was to be planted by the right people in prosperous, well-organized communities, democratic yet loyal to the queen. There was to be due regard for the good of the indigenes, who would have a worthy part in the rising society. Education, a cooperative spirit, and economic planning would work for the good of all. Surely the implementation, and it was seriously tried, of such a vision would mark a new dawn in human affairs.

On the other hand, there is the problem that none of this quite worked out: Settlers had a tendency to disperse out from the planned settlements, above all as wool quickly became the dominant product. Sheep require scattered shepherds. Despite Waitangi, relations between settlers and Maori soon degenerated into bloody wars and the pathetic decline—not unwelcome to some Europeans—of the indigenous race as the nineteenth century advanced.[2] Soon enough immigration was flowing into New Zealand in full spate, unguided by any plan or project but rugged individualism, and New Zealand society in most places was no better than any raw frontier.

Yet the original New Zealand dream or myth remained somewhere in the back of the collective national mind. It would seek embodiment again and again and find it, never perfectly but sometimes with sufficient effect to attract world attention, in socialist or welfare state reforms, in Plunket Society idealism, in antinuclear policy, in utopian literature starring New Zealand from Samuel Butler's *Erewhon* to Aldous Huxley's *Ape and Essence*.[3]

The role of religion in late-nineteenth-century New Zealand, as our story begins in the 1870s, reflects the ambiguity latent in this mix. A residue of missionary enthusiasm, including good intentions toward the natives, remained. So did a potent residue of the denominationalism of Otago and Canterbury. There was also disillusion as these projects lost their original character. A fundamental tension also existed between the religious impulse and the essentially secular, scientific nature of a planned colonization scheme, not to mention a utopia. Finally, religion was often simply overwhelmed by the influx from the 1850s on of predominantly male immigrants who by and large had little religious interest or who were in hearty reaction against church as they had known it at home.

Established religion was also confronted in the 1870s and 1880s by an upsurge in Rationalism, associated with, among others, a later prime minister, Sir Robert Stout. Although the heyday of Rationalism as an organized, burgeoning movement turned out to be brief, it had lasting effects, both on latent but deep-seated skeptical attitudes and in complex ways on new movements like Spiritualism.[4]

The Rationalist heyday corresponded, both in England and New Zealand, with the immense publicity and controversy generated by the 1877 trial, for publishing a book advocating birth control, of the British freethinker and (though initially not seated) member of parliament Charles Bradlaugh and his associate Annie Besant—who would later lecture in New Zealand in a new incarnation as a Theosophist.

Robert Stout (1844–1930) came to New Zealand in 1864. Settling in Dunedin, then the intellectual center of the new country, Stout taught, practiced law, and edited a newspaper, the *Echo*. Both the paper and his personal library (now at Victoria University) reflected a sympathetic interest in Spiritualism and later Theosophy but, although his wife was a Spiritualist, it is unlikely he was deeply convinced by either. Owing to the labors of Robert Stout, Rationalist societies, complete with lyceums, the free-thought equivalent of Sunday schools and church halls, appeared for a time throughout New Zealand. Although Stout was vigorously debated by another prime minister, Sir William Fox (1812–

1893), a fervent Christian and temperance advocate, it says much for the tolerance, or indifference, of New Zealand voters that a secularist as outspoken as Stout could attain high office.

Stout had in common with Sir Harry Atkinson, prime minister and member of the first Theosophical lodge in New Zealand in 1888, active participation in Freemasonry, though both became inactive in 1891 over a then-bitter issue dividing New Zealand Masonry. The antipodean brethren were torn by debate over uniting the variously affiliated New Zealand lodges—English, Irish, and Scottish—into one Grand Lodge most closely linked with the United Grand Lodge of England. Atkinson felt strongly this move was premature. Stout, allied in this cause with yet another Rationalist and sometime prime minister, John Ballance, wished to unite instead with the Grand Orient of France. Unlike the British lodges it did not require belief in a supreme being, which, for those two men, was a vital consideration. But for most Masons ties of kinship and patriotism were stronger than ideology, and the notion of a French connection garnered little further support. (However, it is interesting to note that the first recorded Masonic meeting in New Zealand was actually held under the aegis of the Grand Orient. In 1837 or 1838, the captain of the *Comte de Paris,* a French whaler, called a Masonic meeting in Port Levy and reportedly initiated three persons.)

Masonry under British auspices took root immediately on the annexation of New Zealand in 1840. Masons in regalia took part in the laying of the cornerstone of St. Paul's church in Auckland in 1841, and a lodge under the Irish constitution, sponsored by a Sydney lodge, was established in 1842. At first Masonry grew fairly slowly—there were only sixteen lodges thirty years later in 1871. But in the 1870s and 1880s the number grew rapidly, reaching sixty-seven by 1890. Those two decades were a period marked by continuing immigration, but even more by the slow, steady socialization of the largely male immigrant class of the previous decades, a cohort for whom the male bonding that Masonry sanctified was already a fact of life, but to which the lodge lent gentility, appropriate symbols, and purpose. It was no less a time when Freemasonry was at its peak throughout the English-speaking world, in the United States and the empire alike, as a conveyor of respectability and, slightly more subtly, of those contacts and acceptances that made for power in the commercial and political spheres.[5]

As New Zealand advanced toward political maturity within the empire, it is perhaps no coincidence that its ranks of governors and prime ministers were for a time, in the 1870s and 1880s, thick with Freemasons. Very indirectly, this could hardly help but impart a certain legitimacy to those movements, like Theosophy and the Golden Dawn, that had Masonic roots and borrowed Masonic terminology.

In New Zealand there were, and are, other men's organizations without the social cachet of Freemasonry that were nevertheless important on both spiritual and practical levels—those commonly known collectively as Friendly Societies. (Although they may be spoken of in the past tense, with reference to their Victorian prime, they continue to exist, even if many of their welfare responsibilities have now been assumed by government and other agencies. The high point of New Zealand Friendly Society membership was 107,167 in 1930; by 1960 it had declined to 66,347.) Here are a couple of the most prominent:

The Druids were reportedly founded in 1781 at Drayston, near Manchester, by "a party of congenial spirits" who met under the title of the Druids for the purpose of "jest and song." The name and activity apparently spread through early industrial England until it was organized as a benefit society in 1833. It came to Melbourne in 1849 with the immigration of a member named James Himer, declined, but was revived in 1861. The first New Zealand lodge was established in Christchurch in 1876, under the Grand Lodge of Australia.

By now the Druids had moved beyond conviviality to ceremony. Druidism was kept before the public eye by its spectacular pageants, torchlight processions, tableau, striking costumes, all bearing an air of the antique and the picturesque. The regalia included a purple velvet collar with a border of gold lace and fringe and embroideries of oak leaves and acorns for the Arch Druid and other officers.

Like all Friendly Societies, however, the Druids also met a serious social need. Officials called bards visited the sick, and the society gave its members and their families reasonably priced medical, death, and annuity plans. In an often-rootless pioneer society, before the days of the welfare state, benefits like these could be of desperate importance to working-class people. What is striking to contemporary observers, accustomed to gray, bureaucratic ways of meeting these requisites, is the combination in the Victorian heyday of the Friendly Societies of such practical, down-to-earth services with exuberant sociability and fantastic costume-play ritual, as though those three disparate elements were all part of a unity.[6]

The largest of the Friendly Societies was the Oddfellows, with over one million members worldwide by the end of the nineteenth century. The New Zealand branch was founded by the Manchester Unity Independent Order of Oddfellows, the first meeting being held on board an immigrant ship in 1841. A lodge was established the next year in Nelson, and soon the movement spread throughout the colony. Interestingly, the first Swedenborgian church meetings in New Zealand were conducted in the Oddfellows Hall in Christchurch. Although not as theatrical as the Druids, the Oddfellows also possessed their initiations and rituals and provided a range of social benefits.[7]

The Friendly Societies were, of course, only one facet of turn-of-the-century social history. They were indeed finally to be rendered obsolete in some of their functions by the ultimate fruits of another trend, the 1890s reformism that eventuated in the cradle-to-grave welfare state and its ideal of a planned, hygienic society. As W. H. Oliver has pointed out, these social welfare reforms may have had their Bismarckian paternalistic social control and efficiency dimensions and even a white, empire-building, racist element, as well as compassionate reasons.[8] But the view at the time, both in New Zealand and around the world, was of the new colony as an embryonic utopia.

The alternative spirituality community has by and large shared the utopian vision but insisted that it must be spiritual as well as material, and it has not seldom seen that its ideals are forcefully expressed ritually as well as in cold type or dry parliamentary enactments. In this respect groups from the Golden Dawn to the Liberal Catholic Church had a definite affinity to Freemasonry and the Friendly Societies. But even those, like Spiritualism, which were not highly ritualistic in the robes-and-chant sense, were well aware of being new movements in a new land that needed to carve out a spiritual as well as a political and historical identity for itself.

Finally, it must be emphasized that the Masonic lodges and Friendly Societies differed from the alternative spirituality community in another vital respect: the former were exclusively male, though sometimes possessing women's auxiliaries; the alternatives offered mixed meetings, frequently enjoyed female leadership, and were pioneers in promoting religious gender equality. They were far ahead of both the conventional churches and the lodges in this regard, and the spiritual equality of Spiritualist mediums and Theosophical women even anticipated the franchise equality New Zealand gave women in 1893, the first nation in the world to do so.

Alternative Spirituality Movements

The spiritual wave that washed ashore in New Zealand in the form of the movements discussed in this book came from elsewhere and have a long history. The effect of that wave in modern New Zealand cannot be understood without a glance at its vast journey across space and time. For, although the particulars have varied immensely, the underlying worldview and the nature of the experience represented by Spiritualism, Theosophy, and their kindred nonetheless possess a reasonably consistent set of principles and have held together as a clearly discernible entity within Western culture at least since Hellenistic times. Even the Asian religions, in their Westernized packaging for Western constituencies, have presented themselves in terms of much the same principles and experiences and have found a niche in the Western spiritual ecology alongside those descended from the ancient Hellenistic mix of East and West.

It is well known that the Hellenistic world, shaped by the conquests of Alexander and the Caesars, was rife with new and exotic spiritual movements supplementing the traditional cults of hearth and public square. The Orontes, it was said, flowed into the Tiber, for most of the new religions came ultimately from the East, from Nineveh or Nazareth or the banks of the Nile. Of those variegated faiths, Christianity was only the most successful in the end. Devotees also pursued mystery religions offering salvation through Orpheus, Isis, Mithra, or the frenzied rites of Cybele; intellectuals found solace in the schools of the Stoics, the Epicureans, or the more mystical Neoplatonists. Judaism was widespread as an urban faith as well as the religion of its homeland; the Gnostics, drawing from Judaism, Christianity, and other sources, appealed to alienated sophisticates with their talk of an unknown god and souls imprisoned in the tomb of matter.

The reasons for the Hellenistic spiritual pluralism were, at root, not so different from those that have encouraged the proliferation of religious alternatives today. It was a time of movement and change— whether as captured slave, conquering soldier, merchant for whom relative peace had opened roads to distant commodities and markets, or wandering seeker after truth, great numbers of peoples were uprooted from familiar grove and shrine and dispersed into the great polyglot Mediterranean cities. Cut loose from the family and community support systems of traditional religion, one is forced in a new way to undertake personal responsibility for one's own subjectivity. This was to be as characteristic of the nineteenth-century immigrant as of the ancient diaspora.

That new responsibility encouraged religious emphasis on personal behavior and subjective experience: on sin, salvation, karma, enlightenment. The cosmic and agricultural dimensions of collective faith, the sacred wells and harvest festivals, characteristic of the peasant community from which the wanderer or immigrant derived, lingered but as ghosts from another era. They were now far less important than individual guilt or rapture.

This freshly sharpened focus on human inwardness as the crucial religious arena led, in turn, to finding human images for the divine and as models of spiritual transformation. The ancient era of which we are speaking, Karl Jaspers' axial age, was the age in which the divine and human saviors, saints, and founders of the great religions—the deified human faces of Jesus or the Buddha—substantially replaced the sacred groves and shining gods of yore.

At the same time, a rising awareness of change in the world—one-way, irreversible change as empires rose and fell but nothing returned to what it had been—added to the new perception of what it meant to be human. The invention of writing and hence of chronicles to replace myth and legend as records of the past, the succession of pharaohs and emperors, all led to the crisis of the axial age and the "discovery of history," or more precisely the revelation that we humans live in historical as well as cosmic time.[9]

This discovery, actually of course an only half-conscious and still-uncompleted process of realization stretching over millenia, had several consequences for religion. A sense of uncertainty and hence insecurity about living in the realm of time was heightened. The discovery of irreversible, historical time, in which the new and unexpected could happen at any hour, was more often than not a dark revelation for ordinary people in a world wracked by famine, plague, and marauding armies. It therefore supported the compensatory religious trend favoring atemporal personal, subjective experience, whether of mystical union with the timeless or salvation out of the world of time into eternity. Simultaneously, religion's usual penchant for countering chaos with schemes of cosmic order exfoliated into tight patterns of meaning in history. Concepts of karma, fate, eschatology, apocalyptic and God acting in history are all examples.

The personal and historical dimensions of axial-age religious consciousness came together in the so-called founder religions—Buddhism, Christianity, Islam, Confucianism, and Taoism—which then arose, all boasting a historical figure whose life displayed a special divine intervention, or unique historical moment, at a pivotal point in the stream of time, a point at which "the hopes and fears of all the years are met."

Yet the axial age was a time when many new religions arose in addition to those that have come to be called the great religions. Axial age emphasis on the inward and the human naturally spotlighted the individualistic nature of religious needs and so suggested the possibility of individualistic answers. It encouraged, in other words, religious pluralism, and so it is not surprising there were claimants to the august role of religious founder other than those few whose faiths have drawn hundreds of millions over a score of centuries.

In the Hellenistic era, then, as in the modern era, which in certain ways is a recapitulation of it, religious responses to the discovery of history and the discovery of the personal moved, broadly speaking, in two directions.

The great monotheistic faiths—Judaism, Christianity, and Islam—were one response. They dealt with the historical crisis by stressing eschatology and the control of the historical process by God. They answered the personal subjectivity crisis by emphasizing a personal relationship to a personal God or savior and by means of codes of law and morality that made individual life meaningful, while regulating it. These religions accepted the alienation of the human being in the created world as it is but pointed to the prospect that one could have a transcendent relation to its Creator.

In a real sense the scientific worldview, which has lately flourished in societies religiously dominated by these monotheistic faiths, has perpetuated something of the same combination of alienation and transcendence. Despite bitter science-versus-religion debates, both sides have tacitly assumed some of the same fundamental definitions of the terrain. The human being is presumed by both to be a finite and individual center of thinking and feeling thrown into an essentially alien and inert universe, who nonetheless through faith and knowledge can transcend that condition sufficiently to establish a viable relation to the principles that underlie the unhuman universe and to bend them toward human good —whether through prayer or technology.

Aspects of Alternative Thought

However, an alternative mode of understanding the universe and the human place in it exists. In the West it is best represented by the Platonic and especially the Neoplatonic traditions. This alternative has at various times been influenced by Eastern thought, but it stands on its own as a Western strand of thought (or, better, of experience) reaching from Plato and his possible sources in Egypt and the Orphic mysteries, down to Swedenborg, Mesmer, and modern Theosophy. This mystical golden chain has certainly undergirded important exponents of Christian, Jewish, and Islamic mysticism, from Dionysius the Areopagite to the Rhineland mystics, and brilliantly links them with the kabbalah and Sufism. But the tradition has been most conspicuous on its own terms when it has tested the limits of orthodoxy, whether in respectable guise in Renaissance Platonism or New England Transcendentalism, or when in more marginal venues, such as occultism and magic.

First, in contrast to the majority Western religious and scientific outlook, this alternative view emphasizes continuity between the natural, the human, and the divine. The universe as a whole, like human beings, has a hidden spiritual nature prior to its material expression— call it God, the One, the Absolute—tightly linked to the soul within each human being; thus the spiritual unity of the universe and the occult laws by which it works are more basic than outer diversity. The tradition, speaking of God within and of consciousness as a substratum of nature, sees life where others might see only the creation swayed by natural law. Mystical experience, wherein the self simultaneously knows itself and God from inside, as it were, is of central importance to this tradition, as is faith to monotheism and observation to science.

Second, of no less importance is the alternative tradition's belief in the separability of soul and body. The soul comes from elsewhere and can have a separate destiny from its physical casement. Thus, the tradition generally accepts preexistence, including the soul's descent from higher realms into incarnation on earth and the possibility of many reincarnations. It also can accept out-of-the-body experiences (astral travel) here and a postmortem separate existence on spiritual planes and so can validate mediumistic communication with the dead. Some such disembodied, or only very subtly bodied, spirits may attain high status on the higher planes.

Third, as part of this vitalizing of the universe the alternative tradition tends to personify the great chain of being reaching from matter to the divine. Even as plants and animals stand between minerals and man, so between the human and ultimate-reality range shining hierarchies of superhuman beings: gods, angels, spirits, and ascended masters. In addition, the tradition characteristically inculcates hidden laws of nature, or more precisely laws on the boundary between nature and consciousness, which when mastered can give one access to psychic and even seemingly magical powers.

Fourth, closely related is the ancient concept of correspondences, the idea that special relationships obtain between aspects of cosmic and human nature. "As above, so below," according to the old hermetic tag. Zodiacal signs, planets, gemstones, and herbs may therefore bear a particular rapport with parts of the human body or human moods. Correspondences not only express philosophically an integralist view of the universe but also have obvious potential for exploitation in astrology, magic, or the traditional medicine with its bodily airs and humors. These practices, interpreted on many levels of sophistication, have been important sectors of the alternative tradition and as such have ended up in New Zealand, whether as the intellectual framework of Theosophy or the stuff of ritual magic in the Golden Dawn.

Fifth, knowledge of these things—of the origin and destiny of the soul, of the spiritual laws and planes of the universe—is seen as saving and liberating knoweldge. It is gnosis, difficult of access, transmitted only by often-obscure teachers and initiations, but all the more precious for its rarity; such wisdom is the true pearl of great price.

Sixth, for that reason the tradition typically makes central the role of a spiritual leader with unique ability to teach and initiate; he or she may be called a magus. Like the shaman of old, the magus is often said to be of mysterious background, to have undergone strange initiations in far places, to possess remarkable psychic skills, and even to have a crazy-wisdom side that may produce behavior sufficently bizarre to disconcert those who think of spiritual leadership only in conventional terms. But the magus, unlike the shaman, plies mystic arts in the context of literate and even advanced technological cultures and may be called a shaman in civilization.

Examples range from Pythagoras and Apollonius of Tyana to Blavatsky, the mediums of Spiritualism, and Gurdjieff or L. Ron Hubbard. The magus type of spiritual leadership has been described by Eliza M. Butler.[10] As one able to heal, divine, and communicate with gods and spirits, the ancient (and modern) magus is particularly associated with the ideas we have put on the alternative spirituality ledger: the separate destiny of soul and body, the ability to communicate with beings up and down the great chain of being, and the skill to manipulate the law of correspondences.

Yet, although both wise and charismatic, the magus is more a secretive wizard, or a sage amid disciples, than a great public preacher or institutional spiritual leader. He or she is a teacher rather than an evangelist; the group is a school and initiatory lodge rather than a congregation. Although his or her activity may well have a diffuse as well as intense influence, the inner circle is likely to be small but serious, like the journeymen of Gurdjieff or the Golden Dawn, and engaged in private study and self-transformative rituals rather than public services. These were, in ancient times, the supplicants of Isis or Mithra, or apprentices to the theurgic magic of esoteric Neoplatonism.

The same features were preserved in the medieval continuations of the Hellenistic spiritual worldview, whether kabbalah, ritual magic, or alchemy; and in certain heretical movements, like the Cathars who perpetuated ancient Manichaeism. These activities, too, had their magus-like teachers and bands of disciples and their transformative practices, as Carl Jung and Mircea Eliade have shown in the case of alchemy. The medieval forefather of chemistry, at least in its most idealistic phases, masked spiritual transformation behind the physical transmutation of metals.

Alternative Traditions in the Renaissance

It was in the Renaissance, however, that the alternative tradition received its first great modern expression, one that has affected its course ever since. By and large, later occultists have known the ancient mystics, astrologers, and hermeticists less directly than as they were relearned by the Renaissance.

As it rediscovered the magic as well as the philosophy of antiquity, the Renaissance favored the Platonists and Neoplatonists who best brought the two together, while they reacted against recently dominant Aristotle and the Scholastics. The Rationalism of the latter seemed now the petty computations of a cramped worldview. In a way comparable to the later Romantics, who were fraternal with the modern occult revival, the Renaissance occultists were expansive of mind, letting their thoughts flow backward in time and outward in space into an infinite universe beyond anything reason had emcompassed so far.

The *Corpus hermeticum,* brought to Florence as early as 1460 and incorrectly thought to be the oldest book in the world, the Christian kabbalah of Cornelius Agrippa, the magic and medicine of Paracelsus—all seemed at the time to offer daring speculation at the very edge of what could be known to mortals. The key to comprehending the heights and the depths, as Paracelsus in particular liked to assert, was imagination —not mere fantasy, but imagination disciplined and powerfully directed as a way of knowing the universe through its rapport with that which is within. Although much of Renaissance occultism may now seem quaint and outmoded, its supreme vision—a vision the world has since largely lost to its great deprivation—was of human subjectivity and science united in a single organ of perception, in a world in which the mystic and the technologist were not alien but mutually understanding friends.

The Renaissance worldview, under the effect of the alternative tradition, had three major pillars. (They are finely delineated for readers of English on many pages of Elizabethan literature.)[11] Those foundations are the earth-centered Ptolemaic astronomy; the great-chain-of-being concept of cosmic hierarchy linking heaven and earth and underlying both angelology and belief in high adepts or masters; and the idea of correspondences. The traditional medicine, making substantial use of correspondences, was related to this tradition. (So was the darker belief in witchcraft, especially in the jaundiced view of witch finders who extracted from their tortured victims confessions broadly based on the learned magical tradition as well as Christian doctrines of the devil. Some, including the Puritans, believed in witchcraft and harried witches because that black art was held to have scriptural affirmation, but rejected astrology and other forms of occultism as unbiblical.)

In the seventeenth and eighteenth centuries, this worldview underwent progressive decline before the rise of modern science and Age of Reason skepticism. Copernican astronomy, physiological discoveries like Harvey's of the circulation of the blood, and a growing mood of doubt concerning regular supernatural intervention in human life contributed to its failure. By the end of the eighteenth century few, if any, educated believers in the old cosmic order remained, and such matters as horoscopes and the calling up of spirits were subjects of ridicule or, at best, gothic romance.

Yet that was far from the end of the Neoplatonist current, that half-underground river that has often divided as it sought new channels, but has yet to run dry. As the Renaissance worldview decayed it also fragmented, so that a person might believe one tenet of it while denying another or combine its spiritual outlook with the physical perspectives of the new science. Benjamin Franklin made light of astrology but eloquently embraced the great chain of being with its implication that ill is a matter of scale. Others might merely transfer their allegiance to astrology from the Ptolemaic to the Copernican universe or find place for both the magic of healing stones and the circulation of the blood. Most important of all, there were those who wished to retain what they perceived to be the central spiritual values of the old worldview and who knew now they would have to organize effective rearguard action to do so.

The term "Rosicrucian," often employed to denominate those spiritual holdouts, came into use in 1614. In that year the town of Cassel in Germany was astonished by the appearance of a pamphlet titled *The Fame of the Fraternity of the Meritorious Order of the Rosy Cross,* or for short the *Fama fraternitatis.* It proposed that men of learning should band together to bring about a reformation of science comparable to that which religion had recently undergone in the Protestant Reformation and that this renovation should be done with the aid of a hitherto-hidden brotherhood of light—the Rosicrucians. The document told of a noble German knight, Christian Rosencreutz, who had lived from 1378 to 1484. In travels to Morocco and the Near East this worthy had received instruction from adepts and had undergone great initiations. Then, back in Germany, the learned noble lived out the remainder of his extraordinarily long life quietly with seven followers. Although the secret brotherhood and the story of Rosencreutz were probably allegories by which the anonymous author of the *Fama fraternitatis* (often thought to have been Valentin Andreae, a Lutheran pastor) hoped to advance the cause of wisdom, the name stuck. Ever since, it has been applied to individuals and groups dedicated to occult wisdom in the Western tradition.

Those persons who wished to hold at least to the spiritual value of the old worldview now had a name. What had once been simply the common wisdom—Ptolemaic astronomy, the great chain of being, correspondences, alchemy—was now given a party label that implicitly set it against the new science and an emergent new skepticism, not to mention the newly rigorous orthodoxies of Reformation and Counter-Reformation alike. Those who held to the old, and who were sometimes called Rosicrucians, did so less out of love for classical or medieval science, now acknowledged by the educated on almost every hand to be faulty, than because they contended that powerful spiritual qualities still effervesced within the old wineskins, and could be quaffed even as one discarded the outworn containers.

Correspondences, theurgic magic, and the great chain of being, exoterically correct or not, at least gave the inner message that human consciousness is immensely important and powerful, that the universe has patterns that fit together on the level of mind as well as matter, that latent forces exist whose mastery can give one hope, and finally that a path known to the wise has been charted, which one can follow to the full realization of all one's divine potential.[12]

Freemasonry

Ideas of this vibrancy had survival strength. As the Renaissance worldview seemed to collapse, and even Rosicrucianism showed signs of aging, its battalions were regrouping for a new surge forward under new banners. Some of Renaissance occultism was preserved in the unlikely guise of Freemasonry. Masonry was a surprisingly successful eighteenth-century assembly of bourgeois, liberal, and anticlerical elements, which chose, as tokens of its distinct spiritual identity, symbols drawn from the alternative as well as the craft-guild tradition. This fraternity borrowed also from the esoteric Near East where Christian Rosencreutz had allegedly attained initiation. Masonry's hierarchy of degrees suggested the initiations of the old wisdom, and the model of a lodge devoted to keeping ancient secrets alive in the modern world was to serve as a paradigm of many later, perhaps more intense, esoteric orders.

In the eighteenth century Masonry attracted colorful alchemists and occultists like Saint Germain and Cagliostro, intimates of the French court, and had links to such men as Saint-Martin and the Bavarian Illuminati, who allegedly conjoined esotericism with revolutionary fervor. In those days three causes that may now appear highly incongruous —enlightenment science, democracy, and occultism—could be effectively combined as one. All three stood against the great enemy of liberal thought, autocracy in church and state, and all three stood for an egalitarian world amenable to reason and the values of the rising middle business and professional classes who flocked to the fanes of Freemasonry.

The modern history of Freemasonry began in 1717, when the Grand Lodge of England was inaugurated. Many of the old craft guilds of

England had traditional rituals by which apprentices were initiated and then advanced to journeymen and masters. Often these rites inculcated moral and even spiritual values in the language of the trade. None essayed that task better than the Masons. The Grand Lodge commenced with the intentional initiation of several nonworking masons into the esoterica of Masonry. They underwent ornate and symbol-laden rites of passage in one of London's old Masonic guild halls. The new venture, masonic rites for other than professional masons, was under the obvious guidance of highly placed persons, including members of the freshly arrived house of Hanover.

The purpose was apparently to provide a relatively secular Whig counterweight to Tory high churchmanship and to find a means of transmitting values to an increasingly skeptical age weary of the sanguinary religious wars of the previous century. The movement spread with remarkable speed, clearly meeting some deeply felt eighteenth-century need. Within little more than a decade, there were lodges of the new Masonry throughout England, the continent of Europe, and the American colonies. In the process, Masonry came to carry more luggage than was perhaps originally intended.

The symbols and ideas of the old Rosicrucian type of occultism found a place in Masonry, though they were tempered by Deistic religion and Rationalistic ethics. Some lodges became quite taken up with secret wisdom and esoteric initiations. Especially on the continent, Masonry became a magnet for men of classes chafing under anachronistic autocracies; the secretive lodges easily became hotbeds of anticlericalism and talk of republicanism and democracy. But most significantly for the present study, Masonry offered a model for an initiatory lodge purveying rituals, symbols, and ancient spiritual wisdom outside the church.

Swedenborg and Mesmer

The two eighteenth-century men most important for our New Zealand history, however, were Emanuel Swedenborg and Anton Mesmer. Spiritualism, the first alternative spirituality movement to sweep the island nation, was at base little more than the Swedenborgian worldview crossed with the mesmerist trance, and Theosophy—the next great movement—that endeavor conjoined with the East and the Masonic lodge model.

EMANUEL SWEDENBORG

Emanuel Swedenborg (1688–1772) was the major link between the old Rosicrucian occultism and the Spiritualist séance in pioneer New Zealand. The son of a Swedish Lutheran court chaplain and bishop, this tall, austere, brilliant man began life as a mining engineer and scientist. He produced papers on several scientific topics that were well ahead of his time. In his search for the ultimate principles of the universe, however, he turned more and more to religion and mysticism.

Then, in 1743–1745, a profound change came over Swedenborg's life. He began to experience remarkable dreams, visions, and spiritual journeys. The spirits of the departed, and even God himself, appeared to him in fully visible form. The Swedish mystic was moreover taken on extensive tours of heaven and hell, where he perceived an afterlife made up of various schools and grades, with spirits able to graduate from one level to a higher. In 1757 he saw in a vision that the Last Judgment and the Second Coming of Christ commenced in the spiritual realms in that year. This "realized" eschatology may be seen as a precursor of later New Age or Aquarian Age talk, even as his accessible, pedagogical hereafter was the foundation of the Spiritualist "Summerland."[13] (Although strict Swedenborgians insist that their mentor's ability to converse with angels and spirits was a unique privilege granted him only, and not a warrant for general mediumship, many others were unwilling to accept that exclusivity.)

Theologically, Swedenborg drew heavily from both the occult tradition, especially "as above, so below," implemented through correspondences, and the Bible, which he read with great attention to the symbolic meaning of key words. Swedenborg believed in two realms, the spiritual and the material, with the latter a reflection of the former and requiring to be brought into exact correspondence with its spiritual prototype. Knowledge of the spiritual realm, beyond what was imparted to the sage himself through revelation, could be gained by a correct allegorical reading of the Scriptures.

But what, out of Swedenborg's prolific writings, most influenced popular religious culture was certainly the benign, educative picture of the afterlife in his *Heaven and Hell* (1758) and the relatively liberal views on sex and marriage that he, though celibate, propounded in his most controversial book, *Conjugal Love* (1768). In both, the therapeutic rather than forensic tone resounds with a strikingly modern ring and suggests why the Swedenborgian recovery of ancient wisdom was also a brisk step toward the advanced social and moral thinking for which many of his Spiritualist, Theosophical, and other progeny after the spirit were noted. The many mansions of this life and the life to come were all swept, garnished, remodeled, and brought up to date by the industrious Swede.[14]

Although Swedenborg himself did not found a church, some of his disciples in England established the Church of the New Jerusalem, commonly called the New Church or the Swedenborgian Church, in the

1790s to preserve and present his religious teachings in an ecclesiastical setting. The New Church first met in New Zealand in 1865, in Christchurch, and now has an edifice in Ellerslie, Auckland.

FRANZ MESMER

The Austrian doctor Franz Anton Mesmer (1733–1815), also well known and highly controversial in his day, gave his name to the word "mesmerism," which has come to mean hypnotism.[15] But Mesmer was not so much interested in hypnotism in the modern sense as he was in altered states of consciousness in which healing could be effected and in the occult worldview that, for him, accompanied his discoveries. He found that, when he put patients in a quiet, restful, trancelike state and made gentle suggestions, they often experienced healing.

Undoubtedly Mesmer had discovered anew the psychosomatic nature of much illness and the power of states of mind in which one is open to suggestion to counter it. However, Mesmer was persuaded he had found something else as well: He believed the cures were wrought by the influx of a universal energy or vitality transmitted from the healer to the patient, through a process called animal magnetism. At first Mesmer had tried to control the substance through actual magnets, or the famous séancelike sessions in which patients sat around a vat of dilute sulfuric acid while holding hands, or grasping iron bars in contact with the chemical. But in time Mesmer and his disciples learned that the healing energy could be conveyed even better by dim lights, stroking, the celebrated mesmeric passes, and verbal induction. Clearly, the state of mind—engendered by a powerful, suggestion-transmitting relationship between healer and patient—was the important thing, and here hypnotism and mediumship were both close at hand. Mesmer, in his *Memoir* of 1799, presented the opinion that animal magnetism could also awaken latent powers in humans to see past, present, and future, to develop extrasensory perception, and to penetrate the mysteries of the universe. Our minds, in other words, are in their own nature virtually unlimited in scope but are severely crippled by lack of access to powers locked within them. The key to that lock was now found.

Mesmer believed that the supernatural-seeming abilities attributed to the shamans and seers, the mystics and occultists, of the past were largely real and unfeigned, though not for the religious reasons usually put forward. Those wise ones had, instead, inadvertently stumbled on genuine but little-understood human potentials, powers that were remarkable but no less natural than the storms or eclipses also once credited to gods; now the time had come to give a scientific accounting of them. The Theosophical Society was only following Mesmer in listing as its third objective, "to investigate the hidden laws of nature and the powers latent in man." Helena Blavatsky later praised Mesmer lavishly, calling mesmerism the most important branch of magic. Indeed, for her it was the true base of what is called magical or miraculous, which she also imputed to arcane but natural laws and forces.[16]

Mention must also be made of Romanticism, the dominate literary and cultural mood at the end of the eighteenth century and the early decades of the nineteenth, which replaced the Enlightenment's faith in reason with a new faith, in some ways congruous with the alternative tradition, in the cognitive power of feeling and imagination. Romanticism, moreover, exalted the distant and the past for their appeal to imagination, and hinted at possible human transcendence of all limits, even the veil separating the living from the dead. All this helped shape the nineteenth-century reconstruction of the alternative tradition.

The Beginnings of Spiritualism

In the late 1840s, Swedenborg and Mesmer—with a dash of romance—fused to become Spiritualism. The first great manifestation of the new spiritual impulse was the publication in 1847 of *The Principles of Nature: Her Divine Revelation and a Voice to Mankind,* by Andrew Jackson Davis.[17] Delivered out of trance by an author of only twenty years, this tome of nearly eight hundred pages created a sensation.

Davis (1826–1910), the "Poughkeepsie seer," had experienced a poor and miserable childhood until he was apprenticed to the owner of a shoe shop in Poughkeepsie (New York) at sixteen. Soon after, he began studying Swedenborgianism and practicing mesmerism, in time leaving the shoe shop to support himself as a trance healer and stage hypnotist. By his own account, he also, at seventeen, underwent a powerful initiatory experience. Summoned by the voice of his mother—who had just died—he journeyed, apparently in some supernatural manner, into a place of icy mountains and deep valleys, where he met and was blessed by the shades of Swedenborg and the ancient physician Galen.[18] Soon after, he began dictating his *Principles of Nature* in the presence of a small circle (which sometimes included Edgar Allan Poe and the Fourierist Albert Brisbane); the amenuensis was William Fishbough, a Universalist minister.

Although only the first in a long series of publications by the prolific Davis, *Principles of Nature* well summed up the progressivist, optimistic spirit of Spiritualism even before the movement as such was launched. Davis remained the most important intellectual Spiritualist for decades. The book covers the creation of the world from liquid fire, the evolution of the solar system and the earth, and human history from a Deistic perspective that gives no special favor to Christianity. It presents well-disposed accounts of Swedenborg and the utopian writer Charles Fourier and describes the spiritual constitution of humanity and of the seven spiritual worlds around earth through which the soul evolves after death.[19] Above all, this treatise, with its passionate denunciation of social ills, including those of religion, and its youthful enthusiasm for a splendid, democratic future in which they would all be removed under a new spiritual influx, sets the sometimes naive but humane, forward-looking tone of the new faith. It is another reminder that early Spiritualism was a progressive social movement no less than a personal penchant for spirit contact.

But Davis was only the dawn before the spiritual sunrise of religious Spiritualism the next year. That revolutionary year, 1848, was the year of the famous Rochester rappings, when the young Fox sisters, Catherine ("Kate," 1839?–1892) and Margaret (1833?–1893), heard mysterious tappings in their impoverished rural home near Rochester, New York—rappings they later ascertained to be messages from the spirit of a deceased peddler. (An older sister, Leah, 1814?–1890, was not present at the time but soon became involved. The three constitute the Fox sisters of Spiritualist fame.) Widely reported in the press, scientifically investigated by a solemn academic committee, the case became a sensation and soon enough turned into a nationwide vogue for spirit taps, slate writings, table tiltings, and voice mediumship. Very dry tinder indeed had been prepared by Swedenborg, Mesmer, and Davis; it now took but the spark of the Fox sisters' farmhouse revelations to become a wildfire religious movement.[20]

It is worth noting that Spiritualism was launched the year after the invention of the telegraph and emerged in the same decades that advanced societies were first becoming truly literate and the press was first gaining a genuinely mass readership. The spirit faith was probably the initial significant religious movement to engage public attention primarily through the agency of modern mass media. This new-style creed soon benefited no less from new, modern means of rapid steam transportation. Hurtling railroad trains and ocean-conquering steamships carried expeditiously and in relative ease its lecturers and express-shipped books and magazines to far corners of the globe, including New Zealand.

Spiritualism was a new kind of religion for the new scientific age in another sense, too. It was the first to submit its claims regularly and from the beginning to empirical scientific tests and to make much of their objective verifiability, even as it also obviously met deep-felt religious needs. Although the results of this laboratory-type probing may have been mixed and in the end subjected the religion to as much ridicule as acclaim, the emergence of such a scientific cult in the mid-nineteenth century is of no small cultural significance.[21]

Spiritualism was introduced to Britain in 1852 when the American medium, Mrs. Hayden, gave demonstrations there. She was followed by others, and a brief craze for the religion swept Britain as it had the United States. Further impetus was given by visits of the remarkable Scottish-born, American-raised medium Daniel David Home in the 1850s and 1860s. But the main social vehicle of Spiritualism was, as in America, the "home circle." The home circle might consist of a congenial group who would gather, often in dim light, to experiment or, alternatively, to listen to the trance utterances of a favorite medium. Very successful mediums might also give demonstrations in public halls, and lectures by Spiritualist speakers, whether mediums or not, were popular.

When the movement waned as a popular enthusiasm, its more serious devotees formed societies that gave some institutional shape to the home circles. These in turn were eventually ecclesiasticized as Spiritualist churches. Perhaps significantly, outside of the London area Spiritualism, always plebeian in its roots, was most successful in the industrial and mining areas of Yorkshire and Lancashire. The first national organization was the British Association of Progressive Spiritualists, formed in Darlington in 1865. Although it collapsed in 1868, partly after attacks for being anti-Christian, it lent its name to the Victorian Association of Progressive Spiritualists, formed in faraway Australia in 1869 by W. H. Terry and friends. Lecturers from this body and Terry's periodical, *Harbinger of Light,* were soon very influential in New Zealand. In England, other national associations followed, including the Spiritualists' National Union in 1902, which still survives as the largest, and the more Christian-oriented Greater World Christian Spiritualist League in 1931. Both have affiliated churches in New Zealand.

The Theosophical Society

After Spiritualism, the next important development was the emergence of the Theosophical Society, established in New York in 1875. It may be considered a further product of the same spiritual wave that gave rise to Spiritualism. The original founders of Theosophy were sympathetic observers and participants in Spiritualism, drawing especially on its sense of communication with older and wiser denizens of the otherworld. But Theosophy also integrated into its system much from Masonry and from occultism East and West. Generally more intellectual than Spiritualism, the new movement quickly developed a distinctive style of teaching and institutional life.

Theosophy has had an important presence in New Zealand, suggested by the monumental buildings that house its lodges in some cities.

Within these imposing classical edifices, one is likely to be met by large framed portraits of the two principal founders of the Theosophical Society, Helena Blavatsky and Henry Steel Olcott. Blavatsky's squarish face, striking even after thickening with middle age, is set off by ringlets of dark hair. One's attention is drawn to the remarkable eyes—wide, smoldering, luminous, yet also oddly opaque, as if packed with mysteries this modern priestess of Isis could only begin to reveal. Her partner, Olcott, though equipped with a flowing white beard of ample Victorian proportions, bears no such mystic air. His steady, slightly downcast gaze recounts instead the sturdy yet bemused companion, a willing partner in an adventure that nonetheless ended up much greater than he at first intended.

These two, the Theosophical Twins, as Olcott liked to call them, first met in America in 1874. Their backgrounds were stunningly different. Blavatsky (1831–1891) was born in Russia of a family with high aristocratic connections.[22] Her father, of German descent, was an army officer. Her mother, a popular novelist whose stories inevitably involved women suffering at the hands of callous men, was of the ancient, princely Dolgoruky house, and Helena's maternal grandfather, with whom she lived much of her childhood, served as a provincial governor for the czar. By all accounts Helena was a willful and headstrong child, though possessing great imagination and intelligence.

Despite having often declaimed her opposition to conventional love and marriage, at eighteen she impulsively married N. V. Blavatsky, vice-governor of Erivan (Armenia) and a widower more than twice her age. She soon left him and for most of the next twenty-five years was on her own. According to her own later account, she spent this time wandering the world investigating magic, Spiritualism, and shamanism to learn their ultimate secrets, culminating her quest with initiations in Tibet in the late 1860s. Although, to say the least, questions have been raised about some of her tales, and she acknowledges in her books that she sometimes had to employ "blinds," there is no question she emerged as a singular person of much unusual learning.

In any event, Blavatsky surfaced in New York in 1874, having come, she said, as a pilgrim to study Spiritualism in its homeland like a Muslim going to Mecca. Before the year was out she was at Chittenden, Vermont, where the dour Eddy brothers were putting on nightly séances that had excited much publicity and numerous visitors. Among those present at the same time as Blavatsky was Olcott, a lawyer and journalist, who was preparing a series of newspaper articles on the phenomenon.

Olcott (1832–1907) was born into the solid American middle class in upstate New York. He had, however, some early contact with alternative spirituality. As a visitor to an uncle's farm in Ohio as a youth, he had dabbled in mesmerism and attended Spiritualist sessions. After serving the Union in the Civil War as an investigator of fraudulent military suppliers and receiving the rank of colonel, he made his way in postwar New York City as a rising lawyer, journalist, and convivial man-about-town. But by 1874 his marriage to a pious clergyman's daughter was failing, and apparently some deep need on his part for strange adventure, both inner and outer, remained unmet. That gap was soon filled by the exotic Russian woman, with her volatile personality, remarkable psychic phenomena, and accented talk of faraway mysteries.

Back in the city, they spent much time together, finally sharing an apartment (though not, Olcott made clear, a bedroom), and exploring the marvels of *Brahma Vidya* (Eastern Spiritualism), as far above Western Spiritualism, Olcott was assured, as the sky is above earth. Above all, Blavatsky spoke to him of the Masters of the Wisdom, adepts, or mahatmas, who though still living in this world in physical or subtle form, had attained high initiations. They constituted an inner directorate of the world and were prepared to accept serious students; Olcott began his training under the African Section of the Occult Brotherhood but later was transferred to the Indian branch.[23]

The New York apartments of Blavatsky and Olcott, one dubbed the Lamasery, understandably became a magnet for the city's coterie of seekers, esotericists, and bohemians. Fascinating conversation, exuberant parties, and lectures on Egyptian and other enigmas are reported in the first volume of Olcott's later reminiscences, *Old Diary Leaves*. The presence of the colorful, if sometimes razor-tongued, immigrant from Russia, perhaps by way of Tibet, dominated all, though she had no clearly defined role in the New World and refused to speak in public.

In 1875 the Lamasery crowd determined to form an organization for the study of the sort of borderline knowledge in which they were interested and that was so exceptionally manifested in Blavatsky and her lore. After some deliberation it was called the Theosophical Society.[24]

Olcott became the first president, and Blavatsky corresponding secretary. Although she was certainly a catalyst of the movement, that is the only formal office she ever held in it. Olcott gave a fine inaugural address, in which he spoke of the pretensions and limitations of both the religion and the science of the day and of the need to recover an older, more unified wisdom in which the roots of both intertwined; now, in the fresh atmosphere of American religious freedom, that task could finally be essayed.

However, the society prospered in its original form no more than a few months, but as it declined, Blavatsky, Olcott, and a few others turned their attention to another project, the compilation of a massive book, H. P. Blavatsky's first major work, *Isis Unveiled,* published in 1877. Unexpectedly successful, it brought new attention to the Theosophical movement and has remained one of its fundamental texts ever since.

At first, *Isis Unveiled* may seem to be little more than a rather disorganized collection of tales of magic and shamanism from around the world, mixed in with acerbic—but often telling—attacks on the dogmatisms of science and religion alike. But gradually a series of basic principles emerges, which remain essential to any intellectual understanding of Theosophy: nature is a subtle and complex intermixture of two substances, spirit and matter; the highest interaction of the two produces consciousness; and spirit can be somewhat detached and directed as something like the animal magnetism of Mesmer or the *prana* of yoga, producing seemingly magical (though actually natural, when understood) effects. These basic truths are reflected in the myths and religious symbols of the world; they constitute an ancient wisdom that underlies all exoteric religion and learning. This spirit-matter universe, moreover, is in a process of evolution. In Blavatsky's later great work, *The Secret Doctrine* (1888) we learn much more of that evolutionary process on both outer and inner planes.

After the publication of *Isis Unveiled,* the interests of Blavatsky and Olcott moved decisively in the direction of India. One factor was the Arya Samaj, the Hindu reform movement led by Swami Dayananda. Somewhat misled as to the nature of this organization and the doctrine of its conservative and reformist prophet, they considered it to be similar to their own Theosophy and wished to make a pilgrimage to its swami. That enthusiasm proved to be unreciprocated, but it did help the Theosophical Twins to get to the East.

So did, undoubtedly, a growing awareness that India, and beyond it mysterious Tibet, were the greatest living redoubts of the ancient wisdom they desired to present anew to the world. Apart from Dayananda, no specific place or person in India drew them so much as the idea of India itself. On their way to Bombay in 1879, they sailed through the Suez Canal, that modern wonder of the world whose construction only ten years before had been celebrated by Walt Whitman in his "Passage to India," which culminated in the lines

> Passage to more than India—
> Are thy wings plumed indeed for such far flights?

Certainly the Theosophical adventure was a vast exploration in space and time for which India was only a geographical way station and which indeed called for rare plumage.

Nevertheless, in India—at the high noon of the British raj—Theosophy received a reception positive enough to ensure that the movement would be no passing fad. Curiously, the viceroy of India at the time was the romantic imperialist Lord Lytton, son of Edward Bulwer-Lytton, whose occult novels had earlier inspired Blavatsky and others of esoteric bent. The enigmatic Russian and her confident American companion were greeted with both amazement and skepticism by the British community (in some circles she was thought to be a Russian spy), but they were undoubtedly long the talk of its famous dinner parties and clubhouse verandas, from Simla to Madras.

One important convert was A. P. Sinnett, an influential newspaper editor who subsequently devoted his talents to the new cause.[25] Sinnett was a recipient of celebrated and controversial Mahatma Letters—correspondence containing Theosophical instruction reputedly from unseen masters. The missives fell from the ceiling or arrived by other remarkable means, finally appearing regularly in the cabinet of a shrine room at Theosophical headquarters at Adyar, near Madras. The letters were the centerpiece of the greatest crisis the nascent society underwent: the investigation by Richard Hodgson, representing the Society for Psychical Research (SPR), of the shrine room and related alleged supernormal phenomena. His 1885 report, adverse to Blavatsky, did the movement much harm, though the debate continues.

The native Indian response to the Theosophists was, however, positive and often enthusiastic. In those days they were among the few Europeans to manifest much sympathy for Hindu religion and culture, or to stand with Hindus and Buddhists against aggressive missionaries and colonial overlords. Olcott's practical labors on behalf of Buddhists in Ceylon (Sri Lanka) and elsewhere were particularly noteworthy; he is still commemorated by a national holiday in that country. When most oppressed by the Hodgson affair, Blavatsky was cheered by crowds of Indian students.

She returned to Europe in 1885, where she completed *The Secret Doctrine,* and died in London in 1891. Despite schisms and further vicissitudes, Theosophy quickly established itself as a small but remarkable international movement, much in the news in those years. By early in the twentieth century, it had national organizations in most of the English-speaking world, many European countries, Latin America, and such then-colonial territories as Indonesia and Indochina.

During the first third of the twentieth century the worldwide Theosophical Society headquartered at Adyar was under the leadership of Annie Besant (1847–1933), who succeeded Olcott to the presidency in 1907. She worked in close association with the prolific Theosophical writer Charles Webster Leadbeater (1854?–1934). Together they developed what has often been called Neo-Theosophy or second-generation Theosophy, an interpretation of the teaching that stresses elaborate, diagrammatic descriptions of the hierarchy of masters; the inner planes; the occult evolution of the world; and psychic powers.

The apogee of Neo-Theosophy was its enthusiasm over Jiddu Krishnamurti (1895–1986), then a young Indian raised by Theosophists under the supervision of Besant and Leadbeater; the latter had determined by occult means that Krishnamurti was destined to play a messianic role as vehicle for a coming world teacher. But in 1929 Krishnamurti created consternation in the Theosophical world by renouncing all titles and membership in the society or any other organization, spending the remainder of his long life teaching a unique gospel of inner freedom through "choiceless awareness." Since then, Theosophy seems to have put its colorful, tempestuous youth behind it and to have settled down to a sedate but still influential middle age. It came to New Zealand as early as 1888—the same year the Hermetic Order of the Golden Dawn was founded in England, though the order did not reach New Zealand for some twenty-five years. This organization, inspired by Masonry, was a culmination of the widespread nineteenth-century occult revival.

Alternative spirituality movements have come and gone. Virtually by definition they lack the institutional stability of mainline churches. Yet the ideas they possess have shown survival value, and the needs they meet are no doubt perennially human. The impulses that shaped many of them in the past unquestionably will shape and reshape alternative spirituality in the future, putting old wine in new wineskins. For alternative, marginal spirituality is to the mighty institutional churches what the amoeba is to the whale, far smaller, more formless, yet in a real sense far more immortal.

2 Unbroken Circles
The Story of Spiritualism

On January 31, 1988, in Wellington, I attended my first New Zealand Spiritualist service. Following worthy precedent, the gathering met in an upper room, in this case an Oddfellows Hall above a Toyota dealership. About thirty-five people were present, a surprising number of them youthful. But the presiding officer was a man of some years, dressed with summery informality in shorts and knit shirt.

The service opened in conventional Protestant manner with a hymn, a prayer, and a lection—though the last was not from the Bible but from the teachings of White Eagle, a popular spirit mentor. Next the chief speaker came forward. He was a pleasant youngish man of partial Maori descent, a minister of a mainline denomination who is also an active Spiritualist. In a brief sermon, he talked about an example of driftwood sculpture he had recently been given. It was a rather curious piece of work, bearing in relief enigmatic faces pointing in opposite directions. Apparently with the aid of a typical Spiritualist reading, he sensed that the wood had been found on the west coast of the South Island and had been carved by a young couple near Nelson. The preacher then alluded to his Maori mother, who had possessed clairvoyance though she would have used not that term but rather a Maori expression meaning depth of sight. The Maori people, he said, unlike most others save Spiritualists, spoke easily and naturally of those who had gone ahead on the path of life and addressed them as companionably as the faces we see around us.

The clergyman then moved into what is the eagerly awaited high point of any Spiritualist service, the clairvoyant readings. He successively asked five or six attenders whether he could come to them and then told each of portents he saw around their earthly forms—a trip, change of jobs, a visit to the country, moderate hassles that could be overcome. Nothing, so far as I could tell, was remarkably veridical, but many of the comments evoked a nod of recognition and were undoubtedly significant to the receiver.

In addition to this sort of divining, which can be practiced either within or apart from services, Spiritualists engage in mediumship. A medium is one who, going into a trance state, presents direct-voice communication from the other side; the communicators may be departed loved ones or high Spirit Teachers like White Eagle or even deceased prime ministers of New Zealand. Séances at which voice mediumship is exclusively presented are today generally separate occasions from Spiritualistic church services. In the nineteenth and early twentieth centuries séance phenomena also included such celebrated demonstrations as table turning, rappings, trumpet messages, and the visible manifestation of spirits. In New Zealand, as elsewhere, these are much less common today. But the fundamentals of Spiritualism, clairvoyance and voice mediumship, remain firmly in place in Spiritualist churches throughout New Zealand—where they draw a following proportionately much greater than in Britain or in the United States.[1]

The Early Nature of Spiritualism

These churches have roots in New Zealand's nineteenth-century origin as a settler society planted in the very decades when the new religion was a much-discussed vogue in Europe and America. The nineteenth century was interested, often passionately, in psychic and Spiritualistic phenomena. It reacted to these extraordinary claims sometimes with fervent faith, sometimes with acerbic skepticism. But it is the very passion of the debate that is telling, for it reveals how deeply felt were the issues raised by accounts of ghosts and messages from beyond the tomb, not least in New Zealand, where newspaper debates and sermon sequences on the topic could be sustained for weeks. Beneath the gossamer of apparitions and the murky dark of the séance room lurked some of the most awkward issues with which the Victorian mind had to contend.

Science versus religion, the argument that agitated and divided thinking Victorians perhaps more than any other, caught Spiritualism in a vise and gave it several turns. As various lights fell on the upstart faith, it was forced to appear the extreme case in several contradictory categories. On the one hand, Spiritualism claimed to be the most scientific of religions, based on empirical evidence rather than the dead hand of scriptural or ecclesiastical authority. That evidence impressed scientists like Sir William Crookes, though not others such as Michael Faraday, who claimed to have debunked the table-tilting vogue. To skeptics like him, Spiritualism was hardly the most scientific of religions, but rather the most ridiculously credulous, a prime example of faith, the will to believe, taken to the nadir of absurdity.

On yet another margin, Spiritualism clearly addressed a residue of unmet personal, human concerns in a civilization many felt wholly given over to Blake's "number, weight, and measure" or to religious institutions whose rites and theological squabbles were so much dead-weight, wholly out of touch with the times. Amid those vast spaces, impersonal natural laws, and professional religionists, was there a place for plain human life, for love, for wonder unsnared by even the last enemy? In a world whose science prided itself on its cool objectivity and whose religion seemed ensconced in cathedrals and clerics hardly less cold, many were more aware of what had been lost than of what had thus far been gained by a new age.

Not a few shared Edgar Allan Poe's deep disquiet (in his "Sonnet— To Science") as he addressed science, "Who alterest all things with thy peering eyes." For with those peering eyes the intrusive new craft's hard gaze perceived only "dull realities" and had

> dragged Diana from her car
> And driven the Hamadryad from the wood.

So, for that matter, had Swinburne's "pale Galilean" and his joyless churchmen centuries before. But now, in Spiritualism, in the form of revenants whose nocturnal walks were clocked and chalked by doctors of the uncanny or whose mediumistic utterances were tested against names and dates, wonder might survive even an age of dull realities and empirical checks.

Indeed, the whole Romantic mood, of which it was certainly an off-shoot, can be sampled in Spiritualism. Like the larger weltanschauung, on its own scale Spiritualism shaped its era while in revolt against many of its ostensible values. Romanticism, with its cults of the feelings and the imagination as more creative and cognitive than mere reason, of the individual and the heroic against the mass, of the aesthetic and the nat-ural, or the utopian and the traditional, against ugly banality all around, inspired revolutionaries and reactionaries alike with its restless energy yearning for otherness. Spiritualism, though a popular religion touched perhaps by the Victorian sentimentality that was Romanti-cism's sticky lower level, in its own terms offered enhancement in all the Romantic categories. Not only did it offer personal immortality to those caught in the cogwheels of a materialistic, industrializing society; it also led them on trails of wonder outside the one-dimensionality of the present to forge living links with the past and an envisioned paradisal future. (It was not uncommon for such past worthies as Plato or Elijah to speak again in the séance room or for spirit advocates to foretell a splendidly democratic and abundant future of progress without end.)

Spiritualism also encapsulated, and in some respects paradigmed, the century's increasingly bitter liberal-versus-conservative battles in religion. Although claiming to be the oldest religion in the world, one with the faith of the paleolithic shaman, and sometimes proclaiming Jesus and the prophets as great mediums, the spirit faith displayed no high reverence for contemporary religious institutions. Instead, it anticipated issues and perspectives soon to be raised in more respectable circles by modernism: universalism, religious empiricism, insistence that scripture be examined critically and reinterpreted to harmonize with current scientific and social realities.

It must be emphasized that, in its own time and terms, Spiritualism was a strongly liberal movement both religiously and socially. It saw itself on the side of progress and reform in virtually all the great causes of the day: abolition of slavery, women's rights, universal suffrage, and opposition to privilege—whether in church or state. As early as the 1870s New Zealand Spiritualism was in uneasy but definite alliance with the burgeoning Rationalist movement. Both mediums and freethinkers opposed the ignorance and superstition of the past. Spiritualists even called their educational centers lyceums like the Rationalists to contrast them with the Christian Sunday schools.

The Arrival of Spiritualism in New Zealand

Spiritualism came to New Zealand after it had already experienced its earliest rise and fall in the United States and in Britain. It first appeared in the late 1860s in Otago, the intellectual center of the new colony. Indeed, in 1869 debate on Spiritualism in the *Otago Daily Times* was transcended only by the vociferous correspondence concerning the new Church of England Bishop of Dunedin, Henry Jenner.[2] But by 1870 the novel spirit faith was the most burning religious issue in Dunedin and was provoking among other responses the establishment of a Spiritual Investigation Society.[3] This was in the context of rapid immigration, the establishment of Otago University (among the first in the world that women were allowed to attend, just as Spiritualism was among the few faiths in which women then exercised leadership), and vigorous discussion of the relation of the colony to the home government. (There were voices in favor of virtual independence, or even of transfer of allegiance from Queen Victoria to the United States of America, and much discontent with the current colonial status.)

On May 28, 1870, an article in Robert Stout's Dunedin *Echo* presented Spiritualism as growing and gaining converts worldwide in the millions. Fifteen years ago, readers were told, Spiritualists were laughed at, but "now who laughs at them?" This observation was followed on June 11 by a piece borrowed from *Queen* (England) titled "Extraordinary Spiritual Phenomena," about the celebrated medium D. D. Home and his alleged levitation perceived by Lord Adare; the tone hovers evenhandedly between belief and skepticism. But on June 15 notice was given in the *Echo* that five or six spirit circles were meeting in Dunedin with successful results; these were countered with accounts of lectures by ministers against Spiritualism. The Spiritualist camp, however, benefited from the publication ten days later of an article by Emma Hardinge (later Hardinge-Britten), the famous Anglo-American Spiritualist who was subsequently to visit New Zealand and write about the faith there. Her June 25, 1870, contribution was, "Rules to Be Observed When Forming Spiritual Circles."

The rules were apparently well received, for shortly after, on July 9, the same paper reported, "[Spiritualism] still monopolises a large share of public attention, and nothing is heard of but the formation of 'Spirit Circles.' " An amusing incident took place at one such circle formed by some young gentlemen. The table they were trying to tilt would not move, notwithstanding a strict compliance with Emma Hardinge's rules. Every participant except one had asked it to be good enough to stir, but the piece of furniture remained immobile. The one recalcitrant gentleman was, it seems, a skeptic. But at last he was prevailed on to ask the table to oblige him by moving. Then suddenly—from whatever cause—that object abruptly lunged forward with violent, abrupt motion. This so shocked the skeptic that he fainted and had to be restored by his friends. The same issue of the *Echo* also contained news of the controversial Davenport brothers, whose stage-magic Spiritualist performances were arousing much interest, and much debunking, in both Europe and America.

On July 30 the *Echo* noted sympathetically the appearance of the third issue of a sister publication, the *Day Star,* which contained articles on natural theology, women's rights, and Spiritualism, together with "strictures on the clergy of Dunedin." This eclectic collection of interests was typical not only of the company that Spiritualism kept but also of the man behind the *Echo,* Robert Stout. Stout was then an energetic young editor, and soon would become both an outspoken Rationalist and an important political figure. One suspects he gave Spiritualism such vivid publicity less out of personal faith than to keep his paper lively, and no doubt also because the subject annoyed the orthodox churchmen he loved to bait.

Stout was clearly fascinated by Spiritualism. His book and pamphlet collection (now in the Beaglehole Room of the Victoria University

Library, Wellington) offers a treasury of early Spiritualist works. But there is no evidence here that he was ever seriously convinced, even though he was later to marry the Spiritualist daughter of a couple famous in Spiritualist history. Yet it says much for the level of religious tolerance and ferment in the colony that he could, as it were, get by with both Rationalism and open-minded sympathy toward Spiritualism, while retaining enough popularity to send him to parliament and later to the premiership.

Other Dunedin journalists evidenced less enthusiasm for the high-spirited new faith. A series of pieces in the *Otago Witness* in 1870 treated the burgeoning Spiritualist lectures and phenomena to light-hearted satire. But an account on August 13 of a speaker who treated of Christianity, socialism, Positivism, Darwinism, Spiritualism, and Mormonism —all in one lecture—indicated that the remote outpost was alert to the issues facing the intellectual world in the 1860s and 1870s. In the past, listeners were told, Christianity had often been assailed but few substitutes were proposed, but now Spiritualist tracts—as well as those of Mormons, socialists, and the rest—could be seen everywhere.

The lifeblood of Spiritualism itself, in this pluralistic society, was the visiting lecturer. An early example was James Smith, who came over from Australia to Dunedin in April or May 1872. Smith (1820–1910) had emigrated from England to Melbourne in 1854 and became a Spiritualist about 1870. He contributed to *Harbinger of Light,* founded in 1870, the long-influential Australian Spiritualist journal.[4]

In 1873, the year following his New Zealand visit, Smith predicted the imminent destruction of the world. This prediction led to his condemnation by the Victorian Association of Progressive Spiritualists; the controversy caused many defections. Smith later attracted mixed attention with his alleged attempts to educate his children by transmitting the wisdom of deceased scholars "magnetically" to their receptive minds. In 1872, however, Smith was in high form, lecturing in New Zealand not only on Spiritualism but also on Shakespeare and Venice. His Spiritualism generated heated debate but apparently won friends; at a farewell function on May 13, the Australian was given a purse of fifty sovereigns.[5]

Peebles and Dunn

Even more excitement was produced the following year, 1873, by the arrival of two Americans, J. M. Peebles and "Dr." E. C. Dunn. The *Otago Daily Times* (January 29, 1873) limned Peebles as "an elderly gentleman, of intellectual countenance and patriarchal mein" and added, "we will not say that he is an eloquent speaker, but he is fluent, earnest, and impressive."[6] Another account made him "an elderly gentleman, rather tall, somewhat eccentric—wearing long hair and beard," with a "distinct and fluent utterance."[7] (This characterization may be compared to Alfred Deakin's portrayal of Peebles as "a very amiable, composed, kindhearted and truthful man.")[8]

The Reverend Mr. Peebles, a sometime Universalist minister, had like several others of that denomination moved on to Spiritualism in the 1850s. Characteristically, he combined a wide set of progressive activities with his already liberal Universalism and Spiritualism; his admiring biographer says that he was "an earnest and unflinching friend and apostle of temperance" and that he also espoused "the anti-slavery reform, Oddfellowship, the dress-reform, and woman's rights."[9] Support for causes like these was typical of Spiritualists generally, whether in the United States, Britain, or New Zealand.[10]

Even as he aligned himself with the righteous on earth, Peebles also acquired the patronage of a notable band of spirit communicators, including Mozart, several Native Americans, a sister of Louis XIV, and John the beloved disciple of Jesus. After some vicissitudes, including several church ministries and a brief term as U.S. consul in the exotic city of Trebizond, he fell into a world-wandering career as itinerant lecturer. He possessed a this-worldly traveling companion in the form of Dr. E. C. Dunn. Although Peebles was married to a Bostonian art teacher, one gets an impression that relationship was less than ardent, and it was Dunn who joined the Spiritualist advocate on his wide-ranging expeditions.

According to Peeble's biographer, the frontier-born Dunn had been kidnapped at an early age by a band of thieves who trained him as their servant and scout. But he escaped and subsequently worked in a circus as a ventriloquist. He later settled in Battle Creek, Michigan, where Peebles was Universalist minister. Dunn then had a reputation as a wild and "dissipated" youth. But Peebles, seeing him perform as the subject in a traveling hyponotist's show in 1858, recognized remarkable mediumistic talent and determined to cultivate the hulking, uncouth young man. Under the minister's tutelage, Dunn reportedly reached remarkable heights of clairvoyant ability. Despite considerable community criticism of the relationship, Peebles then took him in as a companion and coworker in the ministry. As the Universalist minister moved into itinerant Spiritualism, Dunn served in his benefactor's demonstrations as medium and healer, while Peebles took the role of teacher and interpreter of the phenomena.

So it was in Dunedin, where Dunn exhibited his mediumship, while Peebles was content mainly to lecture and display the trance skills of his colleague, though he also did some healing as a specialist in the magnetic passes popular in mesmeric circles. Dunn received negative comment from one letter writer in the *Otago Daily Times* for his "Yankee twang" and bad grammar, and his professional credentials—allegedly from an Eclectic College of Medicine in Cincinnati—occasioned some skepticism on the part of other correspondents.[11] Finally, the *Otago Daily Times* seemed to find it necessary to vouch for this spiritual pair that "their relations were those of acquaintances, friends, and traveling companions—nothing more."[12]

The *Otago Daily News* announced a typical Peebles lecture in this manner:

> Notice: Spiritualism
> A Lecture on the Above Subject
> will be delivered in the
> Lower Hall of the Atheneum
> by the Rev. J. M. Peebles
> This evening, Tue., 28 Jan. [1873], at 8 o'clock
> Admission 1*s*

This address was reported the next day at considerable length in the press. "Delivered before a crowded and most respectable audience," it dealt with "the origin of the present Spiritual Wave, and the rapid dissemination of the principles of Spiritualism." The lecturer spoke of the modern wave as " 'new' to our conceptions and experiences," yet also as old, for it is but a new scientific perspective on phenomena as ancient as human records: "prophecy, premonitions, dreams, visions, angel visitations, and spiritual gifts." Peebles learnedly presented a host of witnesses, commencing with Zoroaster and Socrates and climaxing in the then-recent Rochester rappings and the spirit explosion they incited.

Peebles and Dunn maintained their popularity. At a farewell soiree for them in March, some two hundred men and women were present, the hall was eloquently decorated with evergreens and flowers, and the two Americans were presented the sum of one hundred pounds, plus "a greenstone pendant, mounted in gold" for each. In his remarks, Peebles referred to Dr. Dunn's "levitation and immunity while in a trance state." Peebles said he had seen Dunn "lying on a sofa entranced, and saw him raised by some unseen force or power, and floating in the atmosphere."[13] On this note they set sail.

A response to the visiting Spiritualists worth mentioning is a quite insightful article in the *Otago Daily News,* January 30, 1873, on current trends in religion. It perceived a broad falling away from orthodoxy worldwide, gauged by the growth of Positivism and Scientism, but also saw almost-sectarian responses to the loss of consensus orthodoxy in such conservative movements as Anglican ritualism and Roman Catholic papalism (this was of course the age of Pius IX, and just after the first Vatican council had defined papal infallibility), and another sort of response to the crisis of faith in Spiritualism.

Orthodoxy was far from defanged, however. A further consequence of the Peebles-Dunn visit was the ecclesiastical trial of one John Logan, a deacon of Knox Presbyterian church in Dunedin, who was hauled before the church session for appearing on the platform with the visiting Spiritualists and for thus countenancing an occasion where "blasphemy was being uttered against Christianity." It was one thing, the clergyman preferring charges said, to go to such an event only to listen "for the purpose of learning what was said," thereby the better "to oppose what was advanced," but in this case the errant believer was "on a platform backing up one who attacked the very foundations of their faith."[14] But Robert Stout, in an editorial titled "A Heresy Hunt in Otago," made clear his contempt of the whole matter.[15]

Logan was convicted and excommunicated but not forgotten. In her classic account of Spiritualism around the world, *Nineteenth Century Miracles,* the formidable Emma Hardinge-Britten—who traveled to New Zealand in 1879 and met the Logans—spared nothing to paint the embattled deacon as a victim of benighted bigotry against the faith of the future. Logan's wife was at his side during the trial, Hardinge-Britten relates, but to her poignant plea, "Is there no one here to speak a word for John Logan?" the churchmen's only answer was stony silence. Not surprisingly, after this ordeal both Logans became active Spiritualists, Mrs. Logan developing mediumship though she had showed little interest in spirit communication before.[16]

Emma Hardinge-Britten

Emma Hardinge (1823–1899) was born in England but came to the United States in 1855, where she performed as a singer for ten years and also became active in the new Spiritualist religion. She returned to her homeland at the end of the Civil War but was back in America in 1869 and married an American Universalist minister, William Britten, in 1870, the same year her famous rules for a spiritual circle were published in Dunedin. She was a founding member of the Theosophical Society in 1875, but Spiritualism remained her main commitment and her relations with Helena Blavatsky were not always smooth. (Both of these determined women, however, dramatized the power of the new faiths to liberate persons of their sex for careers in the realms of the spirit on a global scale, a possibility scarcely then imaginable in the conventional churches.)

Hardinge-Britten and her husband lectured widely on behalf of Spiritualism in the late 1870s, including the Australia–New Zealand visit of 1878–1879 in which she met the Logans. She settled permanently in England in 1881. Deakin described her as a woman "of large proportions, excellent appetite and unshakeable self-confidence." She was "theatrical," and though possessing "a large share of egotism, was also a sincere believer in spiritualistic principles."[17]

Hardinge-Britten's 1879 visit was the next major event in New Zealand Spiritualism after Peebles and Dunn, one that is exceptionally significant because it became the basis of a chapter in her *Nineteenth Century Miracles,* with its survey, drawn largely from her own travels, of Spiritualism around the globe. The New Zealand chapter begins with a look at spirit phenomena in Maori shamanism, an important move not only because of Spiritualism's general role as a revitalization within civilization of such primordial religious motifs but also because New Zealand was (from the European perspective) a new country in which both the primordial and the revitalized faced each other. There might be hope for a fresh level of mutual understanding between the most archaic and the most recent efflorescences of the human spirit. This was not entirely a forelorn expectation.

Mrs. Hardinge-Britten's Dunedin lectures were in the Princess Theater on Sunday evenings, and at the Atheneum on weekdays. They aroused heated controversy in the isolated colony over the several months of her stay. The combination of Mrs. Hardinge-Britten's imposing presence, her new religion with its sensational new claims, and her high-spirited challenge to Otago's well-entrenched and always-combative conservative Christians obviously set the city on its ear. In a day before the competing diversions of film or automobile, seeing the champions of rival sects having a go at each other was clearly prime entertainment.

Hardinge-Britten writes that no sooner had she begun her lecture-hall skirmishes than "the irrepressible M. W. Green," a "minister of the Church of Christ," arrived from Melbourne with a sheaf of counterlectures. It was not the first match between these two combatants, for Britten tells us that her rival disembarked "just in time to hurl his javelin once more at Spiritualism, in the height of its success and popularity." Now the gauntlet was down, and the halls were packed with hooting and stamping supporters of both sides, as though at a sporting event.[18]

Spiritualism and Rationalism

But Spiritualism was not the only sword the devil had to wield against Otago's embattled orthodoxy, and the question was whether two seemingly disparate blades could be forged into one. Hardinge-Britten's lectures were under the auspices of the Free Thought Committee chaired by Robert Stout, who by then was also an M.P., attorney general, and in conspicuous opposition to the use of the Bible in government schools. This clear-cut alliance of Spiritualism with Rationalism was of great, and revealing, importance to Mrs. Hardinge-Britten. She wrote, "The day has never come—and heaven grant that it never may! —when sharp lines of demarcation will be drawn, for the purpose of dividing the ranks of 'Freethinkers' and Spiritualists." Hardinge-Britten further observed that in 1881 when a Free Thought Association lyceum—that Rationalist, and Spiritualist, answer to the Sunday school —was dedicated in Dunedin, the silver trowel used to lay the cornerstone was donated by Mrs. Logan, Spiritualist and heretic's wife, and that Mr. Stout gave the address.[19] (Robert Stout married the Logan's daughter, Anna, a Spiritualist and ardent feminist. Anna was among the founders of the Society for the Protection of Women and Children, the Plunket Society. A Spiritualist source claims that she influenced her husband away from Rationalism toward the Spiritualist faith, but, if so, it is not clear that his support of his wife's faith was more than courteous.)[20]

The Spiritualist-Rationalist juxtaposition was not unique to New Zealand. The urbane Unitarian minister Moncure Conway, in an account of his 1883–1884 trip around the world, refers to the "friendly alliance between Freethinkers and Spiritualists" in Australia in those years.[21] But it must be added that the alliance in which Emma Hardinge-Britten placed such trust was not greeted with equal enthusiasm in the other camp. Even in the 1870s and 1880s, before the dust had entirely settled, Rationalists seemed unconvinced that Spiritualists were as rational as might be hoped. For example, the *Freethought Review* (Wanganui) for February 1, 1884, presents an interesting two-way argument, suggesting that the rise of Spiritualism is due to the decay of Christianity, and, though its own evidence is dubious, it deserves "at least the credit of a failure in the right direction." Then, with characteristic downrightness, the Rationalist writes, "Spiritualism is either true or false. If true, it must directly replace Christianity. If false, it is a strong logical argument against Christianity put in a most practical form, for it is obvious that if millions of intelligent persons have in our own day been the victims of a delusion, there is no reason whatever for assuming that the Christian belief is not the result of a similar delusion."

A year later, the same elegant but short-lived freethinking periodical spoke again to cite the good Spiritualism had done in helping "many to throw off the nightmare of orthodoxy" but predicted that its ghosts would dissolve before materialistic explanations.[22] (On the other hand, the Dunedin Freethought Association, founded in 1878 to include "Theists, Atheists, Agnostics, Pantheists, Unitarians and Spiritualists," is said by one source to have "collapsed in 1893 due largely to the influence of Spiritualism.")[23]

W. C. Nation

Many more ghosts were to haunt New Zealand before the last had flittered away, much less dissolved. The *New Zealand Mail* (Wellington), with an avid Spiritualist in the person of J. Chantry Harris as editor, was a veritable gallery of ghosts in those days, and fascinating reading his paper is.[24] In early 1884 Harris gave a series of lectures on Spiritualism in Freethought Hall, Wellington, and undoubtedly churned up within himself, whatever the effect on his audience, even greater enthusiasm for his subject than before. After the lectures were reported in the March 7 issue of his paper, more and more attention is given Spiritualism. The climax was undoubtedly the issue of May 30, 1884. As hors d'oeuvres it contains an indifferent poem, "Modern Spiritualism," written "under inspiration" by E. S. Watson, and a review of *Spirit Teachings* by M. A. Oxon. (Although not there stated, this was the pseudonym of Stainton Moses, an Anglican clergyman who became a practitioner and widely read advocate of the spiritual religion.)

But the major bombshell was a long account of remarkable phenomena in the Wairarapa reported by W. C. Nation. Although attributed to a country editor who signed himself Henry Anderson, the many-columned narrative is clearly based on the words of Mr. Nation, then editor and proprietor of the *Wairarapa Standard*. Nation lived in Greytown with his wife and four daughters, ranging in ages from eight to eighteen. This was the opening appearance on the stage of Spiritualism of a person who was subsequently destined to serve for many years as editor of New Zealand's leading Spiritualist paper and to die at a ripe age as his faith's grand old man.

The phenomena had begun a little more than a year before, in March 1883, when one of the daughters, Bertha, age ten, was noticed to possess the power to cause a small round table or a chair to move across the room by "mere contact of the hand—sometimes with one finger only." This was the beginning of manifestations of the table tilting so celebrated in the annals of nineteenth-century Spiritualism. (It then appeared so easy, a mere first step, but is now so incomprehensible. Were all those spirit circles, in their murky candle-lit or gas-lit rooms, sitting amid the heavy drapes and the antimacassared armchairs, simply deluded as the furniture tipped and spun about and even rose up into the air, or was some force actually in play for a few decades back then that has now exited earth? No one to my knowledge has any very good answer to this question.)

Here is more on the Nations' experience: "In a little while they discovered that there was an intelligent force at work. If Mr. Nation said, 'Move the table towards the door,' the table straightway made the required movement. 'I then,' says Mr. Nation, 'arranged that when the answer should be 'yes,' the table should tilt slightly three times, according to the number of letters in the word, and tilt twice for 'no.' "

That experience led to intriguing experiments, the table "finding" hidden persons and answering all sorts of questions with its intelligent tilts, or even scurrying through the house on its own to locate concealed family members in a sort of supernatural hide-and-seek. Mr. Nation reported stealing away to the parlor and crouching behind an armchair. But Bertha gave the command, "Find Papa," and the table slid across the dining room, down the hall, and into the parlor, where it closed on the suspicious armchair and turned over to point the claw of one leg toward the skulking parent. By the time of the reporter's visit to this extraordinary household:

> A circle was formed of five persons, who laid their hands lightly on the top of a heavy dining table, the hands of any one person not touching those of another. In a couple of minutes the table began to oscillate, and then to move round slowly. The movement soon became quicker, until the table spun round as fast as those forming the circle could move with it. The table was a heavy one, with large solid centre support, and it was impossible to suppose that it could have been moved by the exertion of muscular force on the part of those whose hands rested lightly on its top.

It was not long before the spiritual presences had moved on to more varied and subtle manifestations. One of the Nation daughters, Bella, perfected slate mediumship, writing communications on the board while in trance and sometimes, as a test, blindfolded. On another occasion, an unnamed female medium produced a cloud of beautiful light that moved to the center of the séance circle.

On the evening of Good Friday, two families of children gathered at the Nation residence to receive three separate communications from the spirit realm, apparently from three different communicators. One spoke of little children as the angels of earth, and the "links between this world and that which is to come," but warned that lessons must be learned here or they will have to be learned in "spirit land." The second message, from an "Annie Hansen," related further of "the beauties of the spirit land," where "you want nothing—your mind is a creation in itself."

But the third supernatural communiqué suggested both the intimacy and the problematics raised by the incursion of spirit into the earth plane of New Zealand. It went like this:

> No. 3. I am "Amy." Ellen wishes me to say that she is with you. Her heart is filled with love which she wishes to express. She prays that God will shower upon you all love, joy, and peace. She has been controlling Jessie. Bertha must give up entirely for a while. The power is withdrawn from her for a wise purpose, because it withdrew a certain amount of force. On any special occasion let her help me. She must be obedient to her parents and go to bed at an earlier hour. She is an excitable little body, and can't be still— she is all hop, skip, & jump. An excitable temperament throws off more force. I shall withdraw the power for a time, though we shall always be about her. . . . God has prepared a place of joy and rest, where we shall be united as one family. Trust in God's love. Dear little children, we love you all, and we try to induce you to look upwards. Good night.

It was Bertha, of course, who had begun the whole process a year earlier by supernaturally moving tables and chairs, and it was also through Bertha's pen and pad that "Amy" had first come as a communicator. Now, however, Bertha is to give up mediating the spiritual force for a spell. It is not stated who the medium of this message is; perhaps the slightly older Bella, elsewhere in the article identified as a "wonderful medium."

Some Aspects of Spiritualism

It is worth noting that in the Greytown narratives the mediums and psychics are all female, usually young girls. W. C. Nation himself, though to become the leading figure in New Zealand Spiritualism over several decades, was no more than the reporter or, as in the hiding incident, the butt, of spiritual experiments carried out by the womenfolk. The alternative religion gives prominent place to the other sex, not only in terms of leadership but on a subtler plane, one senses, in terms of the style of intimate communication and sensitivity the messages unveil.

The feminine focus of Greytown Spiritualism is reinforced by an episode described as occurring later when the Nation group was operating what is known as a rescue circle. A female spirit in great distress because she had, in life, killed her infant, received help via a medium from the compassionate departed soul of a Catholic Sister of Mercy. Of interest is the fact that this concern was entirely womanly both in origin and in resolution. A suffering female spirit, communicated through a female medium, was aided by the shade of a member of an order of women.[25]

A second feature of great interest, after the feminine preeminence, is the relation of Wairarapa Spiritualism to the Maori. On a couple of reported occasions, one during a session of the land court, groups of Maori observed the phenomena and were duly impressed by the table turnings, the rapping, and above all by the production on the slate of names of their own ancestors presumably unknown by the Pakehas.[26] According to Anderson, "the natives were awestruck, and talked together in their own tongue, calling to remembrance what they had seen in their younger days. Before the missionaries came they always had communication with departed spirits; the missionaries, however, forbade it." Thus, just as in America, the Spiritualist movement established unexpected rapport between a settler society (or, rather, a few persons in it) and the shamanistic and spiritistic religion of the conquered indigenes.

Spiritualism was controversial in the Wairarapa as elsewhere. Anderson concluded his article with the observation that public opinion out there was much divided. But he hopefully noted that "hosts of people are devoting themselves to the investigation of the phenomena," and more and more spirit circles were springing up. Nor did the excitement in the *Mail* soon die down. Fervent letters pro and con debated the Wairarapa happenings. A Wesleyan minister who, according to the original article, had unsuccessfully tried to wrestle with a vigorously moving table, now sought to debunk the episode. Archdeacon Stock at St. Peter's preached on the subject in a composed, evenhanded Anglican manner; clerics of more fundamentalist bent ranted of Scripture denial and demonic possession.

A Roman Catholic priest with the resounding name of the Reverend Theophilus Le Menant des Chesnais, S.M., arguing that Spiritualist phenomena is real but must be the work of evil spirits, made the interesting point that it actually dealt a deathblow to free thought and Rationalism. Admit evil spirits, he said, citing such authorities as Bayle and Voltaire, and you admit the whole system of Christianity.[27] Some three years later, in Wellington, the Reverend John Alexander Dowie of the Free Christian Tabernacle, Melbourne, spoke on "Spiritualism Unmasked; or, The Doctrine of Devils." He was answered a week later by William McLean, president of the Wellington Association of Spiritualists. Both speeches were given in the Wellington Opera House to a "large and select audience."[28] As the Spiritualists struck back in lectures and pamphlets, they particularly played up the horrendous nature of traditional doctrines of hell and damnation and showcased against them their far more elevated picture of the afterlife.

The Continued Evolution of Spiritualism

As the spiritual winter 1884 wore on, the *Mail* continued its coverage. June 13 brought a piece on the Wellington Spiritual Investigating Association, probably identical with the Wellington Association of Spiritualists. It had, as of that date, been in operation only about two months, but applications for admittance to its Sunday-evening open meetings exceeded the capacity of the accommodations, and larger premises were envisioned. At the meeting last Sunday

> after singing two hymns and reading a portion of scripture, the medium was entranced, and then delivered a very impressive invocation. After the delivery of the invocation, an address on the subject of "Death" was given by the controlling spirit, who fully described the change called death, and related the experiences of several spirits and their entrance to the spirit world. The address, which lasted about forty minutes, was delivered in a most impressive manner. . . . At the conclusion of the address, the medium was controlled by a different spirit, who invited the audience to put questions on the subject just dealt with. . . .[29]

The future was adumbrated in a brief mention on June 27, adapted from *Harbinger of Light,* of the Theosophical Society of India and its mix of occultism and "transcendental Buddhism"; this is probably the first reference in New Zealand media to that later-important vehicle of alternative spirituality. There was material on the famous trial in England already mentioned, of the radical freethinkers Charles Bradlaugh and Annie Besant. A notice appeared of a lecture by Moncure Conway, the genial Unitarian minister and world traveler. Conway's address in Wellington on June 6 was in opposition to corporal punishment of children. Another article exploited the vast nineteenth-century interest in bizarre states of consciousness and their consequence. It concerned a man in New York who killed his fiancée while trying to mesmerize her into doing his will. He had endeavored to administer the hypnotic shock by first pointing a pistol at her he wrongly thought was not loaded and then pulling the trigger.

All this time, the Wellington Association of Spiritualists continued to hold open meetings every Sunday night at seven in its chambers of Ingestre Street. Admission for gentlemen was two shillings, for ladies one shilling. Addresses were "by Spirit controls and others"; private circles could be held during the week in various rooms.[30] In a Sunday-evening address reported in the *Mail* (June 27, 1884), a spirit who revealed that his name on earth was John Mackey gave a discourse on "Criminals and Their Management," which vividly illustrates both the physical features of mediumship and the characteristic association of Spiritualism, and the spirits, with liberal humanitarian social ideas. After hymns and scripture reading:

> The medium, while seated at the table, gave one or two little spasmodic shudders similar to those which are premonitory symptoms in the cases of persons suffering from epileptic fits, and with closed eyelids remained in this position until the hymn was concluded. His corporeal frame was then presumed to have been taken possession of by the controlling spirit, which in this instance was stated to be that of the late departed John Mackey, and in his trance the medium rose and delivered a short prayer, after which he gave a short address relative to the treatment of criminals in the various prisons. The controlling spirit deprecated the present system of treating criminals, who were looked upon more like beasts than human creatures. It should, he said, be recollected that these men were but invalid spirits, who were capable of being taught and elevated to something better.

The reforming spirit went on to insist that "beginners in crime" should not be herded in with hardened criminals, that those who care for prisoners should not themselves be "of a repulsive character," that women prisoners should be under the care of women, and that solitary confinement should be substituted for capital punishment, which the ghostly visitor felt the state had no right to impose. In all, the generous Spiritualist vision of all humans as of ultimately equal spiritual nature, of life here and beyond as an exercise in moral education, and of all religions as containing truth, is apparent. The communicator ended by saying that "true religion consisted in the love of God, no matter whether they were Christian, Buddhist, or Mahommedan [*sic*]."

In the meantime the Greytown phenomena continued unabated. Late word from that sector on August 15 told of a trance sitting in which no fewer than twenty unseen intelligences communicated over an "entrancement" of two and three-quarters hours. (One of the "controls" tried to speak in "Swiss," but no one understood; the editor of the *Mail* felt constrained to point out this was undoubtedly because there is no such thing as a Swiss language, the good people of that nation speaking German, French, or Italian.) We are also told of a remarkable new medium in Greytown, a young married woman named McLennan, who was able to see distinct spirit forms. Another group was meeting twice a week to develop materialization and hoped by the end of the summer to succeed. Progress appeared on the horizon: a "light vapory form is just discernible at times even now."

By 1888, however, a changing attitude toward Spiritualism could be discerned in the closely written pages of the *New Zealand Mail*. On September 7 of that year a review was reprinted, from *The World* (London) of June 13, of the memoirs of the widow of D. D. Home, the celebrated "physical medium" who in mid-century had amazed patrons in the highest reaches of European society, including the courts of Napoleon III of France and Alexander II of Russia.

The review began with the astounding line, "Nothing has been heard of spiritualism for some considerable time." Then, although the reviewer treats the widow's reminiscences kindly, as a pleasant recall of days that are no more, he does not hide his view that Spiritualism—so much alive only four years before in the Wairarapa if not in the courts of Europe—is today as much a thing of the past as those now-dead emperors. Although there may be some Spiritualists still around in hole-and-corner séance rooms, he concedes, "not much more is now known about them than about the Irvingites, or the Sandemanians, or the Brownites, or any other of the obscurer and less obtrusive of contemporary religious sects."

This review may not have set well with New Zealand's Spiritual loyalists, but it cannot be denied that for the moment their numbers seemed to be declining and their faith weakening. An item in the *Mail* (September 28, 1888), tells us that the Wellington Association of Spiritualists, meeting in its Ingestre Street hall, received the resignations of officers "tendered in consequence of the passing of a resolution at a previous meeting to eliminate the quasi-religious element from the Sunday meetings." A further resolution was adopted to term the association the Wellington Psychological Institute, "and it was arranged that no proceedings likely to conflict with existing sects be permitted in connection with the Institute, but that its energies be devoted strictly to psychic research."

A later item (December 11, 1891), after Chantry Harris had sold the *Mail* to Captain Baldwin, noted that the Wellington Association of Spiritualists, after an existence of eight years, was defunct. Yet that was hardly the end of the Spiritualist or of the alternative spirituality saga. It may be significant, at least symbolically, that 1888, the year of those discouraging reports, was also the year of the first foundation of the Theosophical Society in New Zealand, also in Wellington. Theosophy had definite historical roots in Spiritualism but presented itself as a deeper and more universal embodiment of the occult worldview, one that (on a more mundane level) could appeal to classes of society more sophisticated than was often the case with Spiritualism.

Spiritualism's various first-generation circles and investigative societies were ill defined as to their religious or scientific nature. Here lay a
tension that could not forever be sustained. The 1890s were a time of
sifting in Spiritualism around the world, including New Zealand, when
circles increasingly either became frankly denominational and for real
believers or cast their lot with scientific work of the sort associated with
the new Society for Psychical Research. Otherwise, they found that
time had passed them by. Groups like the Wellington Association of
Spiritualists, mortally weakened by an inability to decide whether they
were sects or psychological research organizations, fell away. But then a
new generation of leaders arose to found real Spiritualist churches, with
ministers and services, in the 1890s. This was the direction religious
Spiritualism was to take; academic "psychical research" or parapsychology set out on a separate course.

Around the same time, Spiritualism also had to undergo a new
Calvary of unfavorable publicity, something that may have had a part
in its move toward separatist denominationalism. Beginning June 21,
1894, the *Mail* devoted much attention to the sensational account of the
trial, opening May 25, of James and Priscilla Hackett, brother and sister, charged with "exercising enchantment" and with fraud in connection with staged Spiritualist séances for which substantial fees were
charged. (The first article was titled "The Medium and His Methods:
Spiritualists in Court.") The séances involved the appearance of manifest spirit forms. It is worth noting that the alleged spirit controls and
materializations of the Hacketts included Maoris. Lengthy testimony
was produced and recorded in the paper regarding the materialized
forms, the possible use of muslin and phosphorescence, and the character of the defendents. In the end—obviously to the surprise of the newspaper and the disgruntlement of the judge—the jury acquitted Priscilla
Hackett and was hung regarding James; His Honor dismissed the case,
though permitting himself the observation that in his view the Hackett
spirits were a matter of "pure deception" and advising the prisoner
either to leave the country or to abstain from such practices in the
future. In the same month, the *Mail* also reported trials concerning the
practice of palmistry and fortune-telling—in all of which the jury also
returned verdicts of not guilty! Yet something was clearly different in
the atmosphere around Spiritualism from 1884 or from the epic Dunedin debates of the 1870s.[31]

Jane Elizabeth Harris

That beclouded atmosphere, however, did little to daunt New
Zealand Spiritualism's next great protagonist. Even as titillating spirit-

ual scandal was dancing through the daily papers, a new force as honest and devoted as any of the bygone Spiritualist reformers was rising in the form of a small, valiant woman, Jane Elizabeth Harris (later Harris-Roberts), known affectionately to a generation of New Zealand Spiritualists as "The Mater."

She was born in St. John's Wood, London, in 1852 and came to New Zealand in 1866, where she married Thomas Harris, a farmer near Thames, in 1873. In 1887 she was widowed with six children. She went to Australia for nine years, where the interest she and her husband had already developed in Spiritualism deepened. About 1897 she returned to New Zealand, where she commenced an active—indeed, virtually apostolic—ministry of lecturing, traveling, and founding churches on behalf of Spiritualism.

It is worthwhile to present something of her life story in her own words, for they record inimitably both her frank and vital personality, and something of what Spiritualism could mean to people in her day. Substantial portions of her autobiographical writings, from sources in the private Spiritualist history collection of Mr. J. W. Graham of Auckland, are transcribed in appendix 1. Here is a remarkable portrait of the power of Spiritualism in a New Zealand life and the power of that life for New Zealand Spiritualism. There is the young, overburdened farm wife's dread of Spiritualist ideas and phenomena. Then the religion takes hold, and with it grows her strength of character and her ability to cope with the many problems and sorrows that beset her, both all too typical of the Victorian widow of slender means. There are happy midlife days in the Spiritualist churches of Australia. (These Australian churches of the 1890s were actually among the very first full-fledged Spiritualist churches in the world, in contrast to the earlier circles and research societies such as those in which Mrs. Harris had participated more informally back in New Zealand in the 1880s. The passages give a sympathetic picture, from the church side, of the previously mentioned split between the scientific and religious wings of the movement. They help us understand the effect of religious Spiritualism in the life of someone like Mrs. Harris, the way the churches came into being, and incidentally the considerable extent to which visiting lecturers and mediums from around the world sustained them.)

On her return to New Zealand, Mrs. Harris, obviously inspired by the wonderful experiences she had in the Australian churches, moved with remarkable power and energy to replicate them throughout New Zealand.[32] Our impression that Spiritualism was at a low ebb there by the mid-1890s is confirmed by her; the societies had not resolved the science-religion schism satisfactorily, and scandals like that of the Hacketts had undoubtedly given Spiritualism a poor image. But Mrs. Harris set about to remedy the decline.

All her experience and instincts clearly put Jane Harris on the religion side of the science-religion bifurcation of Spiritualism, and she threw herself wholeheartedly into rescuing Spiritualism from the doldrums by undergirding its religious expression with solid ecclesiastical institutionalization. These young churches offered settings where Spiritualism's wondrous religious experiences could be regularly tasted, and testimonials to its truth publicly presented. Her churches are the foundation of Spiritualism's relative strength in New Zealand to this day.

In a narrative that reminds one of nothing less than the Apostle Paul's intrepid missionary journeys, we read of The Mater's whirlwind travels around the island nation under direction from her spirit guides, establishing churches, leaving them when ready in competent local hands, writing with love and blessing to her far-flung disciples. Not a few of those successors to the apostle, like the apostle herself, were women. It is here as much as anywhere that clues to the faith and life of Jane Elizabeth Harris can be sought.

Certain of Harris' surviving writings provide important insights into her mind, revealing vividly the relation of Spiritualism to her identity as a woman who not seldom felt herself in a position of powerlessness before society and an often-cruel fate. Paradoxically but dramatically intertwined with her feelings of inadequacy and weakness before the world was an obvious extraordinary capacity for prophetic spiritual leadership waiting to be unleashed. Already using the pseudonym "Jenny Wren," she published in 1884—at thirty-two and apparently about a year before becoming a Spiritualist—a pamphlet, "Woman's Work and Destiny," originally a "paper read before the Thames Mutual Improvement Association."[33] This was presumably one of the few gatherings of progressive thinkers before whom she had spoken prior to her move to Australia.

With the sharp radical vision that was ever to characterize her social writings, as it did much of early Spiritualism's, Harris opens by speaking of the hopelessness of the laboring class, yet herself voices a hope that "Land and Labor" would "shake themselves free from the bondage of Wealth and Power." But, in seeking to realize this hope, she asks herself, "What was I?—Only a woman!" "To what purpose was my life, with its ceaseless round of care and toil?" Then she beheld a vision of a beautiful land, but dominated by a city full of suffering "because wealth rather than love rules the world—and woman hides her aching heart beneath a silken robe, content to suffer thus at the hands of him she fondly calls 'her hero.' " Then, after this indictment of current evil, the speaker heard the voice of "Thought," who, after citing John Stuart Mill on the equality of the sexes, made a powerful statement on what today would be called the relation of sexism and economic oppression, including reference to the horrors of child labor. Thought further proclaimed that the answer must include Woman rising up to exert all her influence on the side of justice and human love. Here, just as in her later Spiritualist writing and speaking, is a strongly feminist and reformist theme, and at the same time the need—eloquent at once of both weakness and strength—to express those passionately felt ideas through the mediumship of another. Here it is the allegorical Thought, then came the pseudonym "Jenny Wren," and finally arrived the doubtless more satisfying actual spirit beings of her new faith. In all cases Jane Harris is, of herself, "only a woman," merely appalled by the immense evils of the world; with the help of a greater overshadowing presence she becomes a voice powerfully engaged against them.

After proceeding to Australia, Jenny Wren published a book of poems, *Leaves of Love,* in 1890, dedicated to "The Hon. Judith S. M. Carrington, youngest daughter of Lady Carrington, by the latter's gracious permission."[34] The verses are less than memorable as poetry but reflect obvious deep feeling. A recurring theme is of woman awakened by social distress, unappreciated by man, but able to overcome evils by her special capacity for labor and love. Not a few poems treat of the oppression of workers and the poor, and of the beauty of the land despite the ill-treatment "by the hand of Mammon" of those who labor on it. In one poem, heaven is eulogized as a place where there is no sorrow, no parting and—"no Rent to pay." Clearly drawing on personal experience, Jenny Wren writes much on the death and heavenly experiences of children and parents alike. But, no doubt because of the attitude of her patroness as reported in the autobiography, nothing in this book is distinctly Spiritualist; at the most there are only broad poetic references to the abiding spirits of departed loved ones.

Lectures Given by Mrs. T. Harris at the Opera House, Wellington, was published in 1897 and reflects a mature version of her Spiritualism and social views, combined with a very liberal Christianity.[35] The lectures are said to have all been given "under inspiration," a phrase that has a definite Spiritualist meaning. She speaks of the development of man from "primitive cave dweller without even fire" up to the dawning of the "divine idea" and finally the unveiling of the "divine image." Jesus was a "divinely inspired Socialist" as well as "divinely inspired medium," and through him surged healing for body, mind, spirit, and society. Mrs. Harris rejected original sin and bondage to creeds and called for a new religion of Christian love and worship of the universal Father. She vehemently attacked with her usual prophetic fire the double-dealing of Sunday church Christians whose weekday lives did not conform to their profession. At the end of the first lecture in the volume, she says, "If Spiritualism has a message more to one than another, it is to the woman soul of humanity." The diction here is a bit shaky, as is the relation of this sentence to the context, but that shakiness makes it only more likely the line is an outburst from deep within Harris' life experience. The import is clear and sums up that experience: the world is full of cruel evils; women with their special capacity for love and labor can heal them; and women can be empowered by Spiritualism.

Mr. Graham's Spiritualist history collection contains also a handwritten account by the Reverend Gertrude Brooks of Mrs. Harris-Roberts' funeral on September 22, 1942, at a little chapel on Khyber Pass Road, Auckland. Mrs. Richards, a Spiritualist minister, conducted the service. Mrs. Brooks records that during the rites a beautiful light appeared around the remains and above them something like a violet cloak suspended in space, signifying divine love and protection; golden and white rays beamed from the altar cross to the casket. These signs and wonders set an impressive seal on The Mater's long ministry, as did the fact that all three ministers—the deceased, the officiant, and the recorder—were women.

The Formal History of New Zealand Spiritualism

Early Spiritualism was a matter of informal circles or only quasi-religious associations like the Wellington, or societies like the Auckland Society for Spiritual Progress. They offered facilities for lectures and mediumship but were not quite ecclesiastical bodies. Full-fledged Spiritualist churches and denominations came into being in New Zealand, as in Australia, England, the United States and elsewhere, around the turn of the century.

In New Zealand it was certainly the apostolic labors of Mrs. Harris, after her return from Australia in 1897, that sparked the founding of churches even though at that moment she, too, was first content with circles and societies. The first churchly meetings, following her lectures, were held in 1900 in Wellington on Cambridge Terrace, and the city almanac first lists a Spiritualist church in Auckland in 1900. In 1901 Mrs. Harris lectured in Christchurch. A church organization was set up a couple of years later. According to J. W. Graham's historical materials, the earliest church organization in Christchurch, with Sunday services and a treasurer's report, was established in 1903 in the Hobbs Building in Cathedral Square, later moving to Druid Hall, Worcester Street, where lectures and demonstrations were regularly reported. Among speakers listed, without definite dates, in a manuscript chronicle were Susannah Harris, a "trumpet medium," and three visiting Australians whose names will be familiar to cognoscenti of the era's esoterica: Mrs. Praed, a novelist of some popularity, who later, in a book called *The Soul of Nyria,* was to present herself as the reincarnation of an aristocratic Roman lady; Charles Bailey, an "apport" medium whose ability to produce an incredible array of items in the séance room—from live birds, snakes, and fish to Babylonian cuneiform tablets—puzzled and impressed Arthur Conan Doyle and Horace Leaf as he had earlier Jane Elizabeth Harris, though he was widely considered fraudulent;[36] and Vivian Deacon (who came about 1920), "a fine speaker."[37]

Shortly after her Christchurch labors, Mrs. Harris worked in Dunedin with William Rough—he who, she reported in her autobiography, could carry live coals in his hands—to establish a church there.[38] A little later Dunedin (later Masterton) became the locus of the famous Blue Room, where the youthful Pearl Judd practiced clairvoyance. Through the guidance of her uncle, Clive Chapman, who later wrote a book about her, this teenage girl developed into one of the most celebrated of New Zealand mental and physical mediums.[39] Another Spiritualist book of the era includes standard Spiritualist messages transmitted through the medium Thomas McBride and others from no less than three former New Zealand premiers (Ballance, Seddon, and Massey), a Roman Catholic bishop, and Lord Northcliffe, of whose postmortem activities more later—despite the eminence of these persons, the communiqués emphasize that no titles are used in the otherworld.[40]

Message of Life

In 1903 the *Message of Life,* long New Zealand's major Spiritualist periodical, was founded. W. C. Nation, who had fruitlessly endeavored to escape detection by a self-propelled table, emerged nearly twenty years later as its editor. The paper survived until shortly after Nation's death in 1930. To dip into its now-rare files is to evoke the spirit world of an era. The September 1907 issue, for example, offers "A Vision of Paradise" by H. M. Boucher, describing the life of the pure souls in the blessed realm. "Some wear forms of lightest blue, transparent as though made of glass, and clear as any crystal ere yet seen by mortal man. Flawless, clear, and most ethereal are their shapes, to harmonise with their most pure and sinless souls." Elsewhere in the same issue this Mr. Boucher "is creating a most favourable impression, and his addresses at the Spiritualists' church (in Christchurch) are largely attended." In the same church, on August 9 "a progressive euchre party was held, when a number of members and friends assembled." On another note, Mr. William McLean of Wellington, president of the National Association of Spiritualists and an M.P., "had an interview with the Minister concerning the provisions of the Bill to suppress tohungaism." (This was a point of concern with Spiritualists because of fear that their own mediumistic practices might be seen—perhaps rightly—as no more than a European version of the same shamanism.)

Moving ahead, the issue for November 1, 1917, spoke anew of spirit life in the next world, observed that the Theosophist Annie Besant had been released from restraint in India for her home-rule work and reported trouble with fraudulent mediums.

October 1, 1926, presented a Maori translation of an article, "The Life after Death." Although Christian, it emphasized that "there are great Maori souls in the spirit world. . . ." Old-time Maori, it said, like Native Americans, talked to the Great Spirit through *tohungas* (shaman-priests) who could be trusted. This look backward was complemented by Mrs. Harris-Roberts' "The Religion of the Future," chracteristically ebullient, liberal, and socially progressive, The Mater calling for "a larger grasp of God's great plan" and living "the higher life."

A year representing a high point in the Theosophical movement as the Krishnamurti enthusiasm within it climaxed, 1927, brought to the *Message of Life* a couple of negative references to Spiritualism's now-rivalrous daughter. On August 1 "Theosophy and Spiritualism" contended that Theosophy offered only vague theories and that Spiritualism advanced proof of its claims. On October 1, Mrs. Besant and the Liberal Catholic Church were treated to biting satire. This issue, like many others, however, shared with the reader reflections on the pagan origins of Christian practice, a theme much developed by Spiritualist, Theosophical, and Rationalist writers alike.

On another topic, the May 1, 1928, issue cited a wartime letter from the association to the (acting) prime minister, James Allen, of January 1917, noting that Spiritualists in the armed forces were often not able to register as such, though they served alongside those of other faiths and the first Victoria Cross for New Zealand was won by a Spiritualist, "young Bassett, of Auckland." It was also complained that "census papers give no indication that Spiritualists could register as such," mentioning instances of difficulty with census takers who did not recognize the denomination.

Sad news came on June 1, 1929, with announcement of the death on November 28, 1928 of Charles Cecil Nation, son of the editor. Charles had been active in Spiritualism as a printer and had a weekly circle in his home where his wife served as medium. The same issue, on a brighter note, referred to a March 6 article in the *Waikato Times* about a remarkable new materialization medium, Mrs. Lily Hope, who was tied by strings while the visible manifestation of several spirits took place; as a result Spiritualism was said to be growing rapidly in the area.

July 1, 1930, was a memorial issue for the grand old man of New Zealand Spiritualism, W. C. Nation, himself. The man who had been a mainstay of the faith since the Greytown phenomena back in 1883, when he was a youngish father in a houseful of spirited and spiritualistic daughters, had died at the age of ninety on May 29. Much praise was justifiably given his near half century of faithful work, yet the continuation of problems was evidenced by the exposure of false trumpet mediums and faked psychic photos reported in the same issue.

The Institutional Development of Spiritualism

It remains to say something about the institutional development of Spiritualism in these years. In 1907 the National Association of Spiritualists of New Zealand (NAS) was formed; the first president was the parliamentarian William McLean, with W. C. Nation as vice president. In 1914, reflecting the growing ecclesiasticization of Spiritualism, this body became the National Association of Spiritualist Churches of New Zealand (NASC), with membership limited to churches rather than also accepting individual members as before. The trend was further reified in 1923 when the name was changed again to the Spiritualist Church of New Zealand (SCNZ). This body now sought incorporation analogous to that of other religious bodies from parliament; the Spiritualist Church of New Zealand Incorporation Bill was introduced and passed in 1924. However, the majority of New Zealand Spiritualist churches then as now remained independent of the SCNZ. A few are affiliated with the National Spiritualist Union or the Christian-oriented Greater World Spiritualist League, both based in England.

Incorporation did not end legal problems for Spiritualists. Mediums could be and sometimes were brought into court under the Crimes Act and Police Offenses Act (copied from ancient British legal codes, including the notorious Witchcraft Act of 1735) to face charges of witchcraft, fortune-telling, or fraud. Spiritualists, arguing that for them mediumship was a sacred religious practice, long strove to have these statutes removed. A special committee of the SCNZ was formed to that end, and lobbying campaigns were mounted in Wellington in 1965 and 1973. But, despite repeal of the Witchcraft Act in Britain in 1951, nothing happened in New Zealand until, in the new Summary Offenses Act of 1981, the old fortune-telling section was finally removed in favor of one that penalized only "acting as a medium with intent to deceive" or one who "with intent to deceive, purports to act as a Spiritualist medium. . . ." Spiritualists appear quite happy with this statute, especially because it seems to imply that there is such a thing as an honest, nondeceiving Spiritualist medium whose status is to be protected from fraudulent imitations.[41]

However, even more than is the case with most religious traditions, the legal and institutional history of Spiritualism is not the important story in the twentieth century. Just as in the nineteenth, the pulse of the movement was to be gauged by the effect of visiting speakers and, increasingly, the national visibility of native Spiritualist stars, so also was Spiritualism affected by the tides of world events in this troubled century. The First World War, with its anxiety and tragic loss of life, especially among the young, fostered yearnings to pierce the veil separating this world and the next. In New Zealand as elsewhere, Spiritualism was in the news during the decade or so following the Great War.

Sir Arthur Conan Doyle

No figure brought it more into the news, or better epitomized what might be called the silver age of Spiritualism, the 1920s, than Sir Arthur Conan Doyle, creator of Sherlock Holmes, and an avid writer and speaker on behalf of the spirit faith after the war. A lecture he gave immediately following the armistice at a London "National Memorial Service for War Dead in England under the Auspices of the National Spiritualist Union" linked the war and renewed interest in the spirits with Doyle's robust yet reflective British patriotism. In the presence of thousands the celebrated author attacked ignorance about his faith and the levity with which it was regarded in some circles. He evoked the dead soldiers present in their celestial divisions, with the eye of faith seeing them drawing near for joyful reunions with those loved ones who have hearts to understand. He recalled how Admiral Togo during the Russo-Japanese War had summoned his slain seamen. "When we have got to the level of Japan in psychical civilization, it will not be ignorant civilians like ourselves but the great chiefs of the Army and Navy who lead these men in battle who will welcome and thank them for their services."[42]

In 1920 Doyle made a lecture tour of Australia and New Zealand, duly recorded in his *The Wanderings of a Spiritualist*.[43] Not all hearers were convinced, but the famous writer generally spoke to sold-out halls, his well-known name, warm and articulate platform style, and sensational subject matter assuring him a tumultuous response. Like earlier Spiritualist visitors to the antipodes, he was preceded and followed by lengthy newspaper articles, alarmed sermons, and much letter-to-the-editor activity. Sir Arthur gave two lectures, on successive evenings, in each of the four major New Zealand cities. The first was always on the theory of Spiritualism, reinforced by personal accounts of Spiritualistic phenomena he had witnessed, and climaxing in a dramatic and poignant report of communication with his son Kingsley, who had died of war wounds. In 1920 many in his audiences undoubtedly shared with Doyle the pain of similar, still-fresh losses to the demons of battle. The second lecture consisted of an astonishing magic lantern display, with narrative, of alleged spirit photography.

The *Otago Daily Times* for December 1920 presented the reader an interesting sequence of articles. On December 11, a piece appeared— unrelated to the Doyle visit but in remarkable coincidence with it— about the "faith healing" of Tahupotiki Wiremu Ratana, the Maori prophet, whose doctrine had some similarities to Spiritualism which New Zealand Spiritualists themselves appreciated. Flourishing no mean scholarship, the writer alluded to such earlier healers as Mesmer, Fludd, Paracelsus, and the Christian Scientists, as well as Spiritualists, in endeavoring to understand the Ratana phenomena, but in the end assessed it as merely hypnotism. On December 13, reports reached the southern city of Doyle's Wellington lectures. The house was full, and "the lecturer had the audience in the grip of his earnestness throughout." It was announced he would give two lectures in Dunedin, "Death and the Hereafter: The New Revelation," followed by a presentation the next day of forty psychic photographs.

The following issue boasted an article on Doyle himself. He was "stated to have altered the point of view of many hundreds of people who have attended the lectures he has already given throughout Australia, and in Auckland and Wellington." More than twenty years ago, it was said, a Mr. R. S. Smythe first approached Sir Arthur with the suggestion he visit the two dominions, but a very busy life precluded that adventure until now. Doyle, the article said, is an active man of many interests, not reclusive, with a "healthy and broad outlook" and a "genial, sane philosophy of life." He has been interested in psychic phenomena since he was a medical student in Edinburgh. (Doyle was always at pains to emphasize that his Spiritualism was long-standing and not the product of some sudden conversion.) On another page was an account of a sermon against spiritism by a minister in the Tabernacle and a more moderate call by the Reverend Hector McLean in St. Andrew's for fairness and courtesy amid the discussion and excitement Sir Arthur's impending visit was arousing. However, the Presbyterian feared that Doyle himself was an extremist not given to reserve or true scientific temper in his judgments. On the other hand, a local Spiritualist contended that one of the greatest signs of the advancement of his faith was the alarm it was creating in the orthodox churches.

On December 15 letters to the editor on Spiritualism began to arrive.

In general they called for a fair hearing, speaking of prejudice against Spiritualism by those who have not really investigated it. Another article on Doyle reiterated his interest in psychic phenomena since his student days and claimed that he approached the subject in a sober mood, being neither dazzled by it nor discouraged by charlatans. On December 16, word of packed lectures in Christchurch was in. By December 18 the lecturer was heralded by paeans to the breadth of mind with which he approached his subject: "He has none of the hysteria of the youthful convert, none of the fanaticism of the man anxious to convert all to his point of view" but, with a "big, clear voice . . . states only facts he can prove from his own experience."

By the time he finally spoke in Dunedin on December 20, it is not surprising to learn that the auditorium was nearly full, despite rain; reportedly a number of the clergy were in attendance. The *Times* editorial on December 22, the issue in which the spirit-photography presentation was reported, called for more psychical research. It opined that, although Doyle may err in the direction of dogmatism with his Spiritualism, he is fair; the right response would be more scientific research on the phenomena he brings to our attention. (Once again, the science-religion split in what is considered an appropriate response to the Spiritualistic phenomena lurks in the background. The bemused editorialist can think of nothing better to do than to call for more study; Doyle has clearly, for all intents and purposes, gone over to religion as he genuflects before what he calls "the new revelation.") Then came the postlecture letters and sermons. These were in all varieties, supporters ranging from believing Spiritualists to those who, like the editor, at least favored serious psychical research, critics dividing between Bible-quoting Christians muttering of demonolatry, and unbelieving skeptics of all miracles and mysteries.

The second lecture with its spirit photographs, however, strained the credulity of all but the most devout Spiritualists. Even those prepared to be open-minded toward trance mediumship found these pictures, with their superimposed spirit faces or ghostly forms, disturbingly suggestive of developing-room foolery. Doyle did not help matters by refusing to allow a delegation of professional Auckland photographers to examine the puzzling prints and by saying that only an expert in psychic photography—of which there were evidently none in New Zealand—would be qualified to do so. Nor did he reassure doubters by letting fall widely reported confidences that he had with him, though was not yet ready to show publicly, other photographs in which authentic images of fairies were visible. These were the celebrated Cottingley Fairy Photos, subsequently published by Doyle in *Strand* magazine and his book *The Coming of the Fairies*.[44] Many shook their heads wondering whether the perspecuity of Sherlock Holmes had totally abandoned the great detective's maker.

Undoubtedly Doyle was taken in a good deal more than he should have been, or than Holmes would have stood for. But a look at the man and his milieu makes him at least a bit more understandable and sheds a certain light on the epoch. Sir Arthur Conan Doyle was, like so many late Victorians, an amateur enthusiast for an adopted cause. Men of his type disdained professionalism, whether in politics, sports, religion, or the arts, believing that service out of sheer affection for the cause, or sheer sense of duty, was an ideal that better suited the gentleman. Moreover, the labor of love afforded an independent perspective supposedly denied the trained and contracted jobholder, however undemanding—and the cost of this laxity was not always appreciated—amateur status may have been toward intellectual rigor.

Doyle was a gifted amateur par excellence in an age of gifted amateurs. He practiced the profession for which he was trained—medicine—consistently only for a few years and then turned to writing, in which he was fundamentally an amateur though a well-remunerated one. He then moved into his second amateur enthusiasm, Spiritualism. Although he had an interest in the psychic since medical school and had given up his natal Roman Catholic faith in the 1880s, Spiritualism took on a central and religious meaning for him only amid the traumas of world war.

There are varying accounts of exactly what happened during the war to produce that effect. Here are a couple of examples: In 1915 the Doyles were caring for a young woman, Lily Loder-Symonds, suffering from a prolonged and serious illness. Psychic, she entertained herself by doing automatic writing. Sir Arthur and his wife received these communications with mild skepticism until one day she came out with: "It is terrible. Terrible. And will have a great influence on the war." A few hours later the *Lusitania* was reported sunk, with its terrible loss of life and its pronounced influence on the United States' later entry into the war. Also in 1915, after Doyle's brother-in-law Malcolm Leckie was killed at Mons, Lily Loder-Symonds produced automatic writing that Doyle believed to be in Leckie's hand and that he reported conveyed precise information about a private conversation unknown to anyone else, not even to his wife, they had held before the war. From then on, by this account, Sir Arthur was convinced of survival and spirit communication, and in 1918 he published the first of a series of Spiritualist books, *The New Revelation*.[45]

But—if I may be permitted to digress a bit longer on Holmes' inventor as Spiritualist—it is important again to note carefully the amateur enthusiast nature of Doyle's commitment. Doyle—like Sherlock

Holmes—was an irregular, neither an official investigator nor formal judge of the phenomena he described and interpreted. He was neither a medium nor, by his own admission, even psychic. Much less was he a Spiritualist minister or other professional. Rather, like Holmes, he looked for evidence on his own and was willing to share his findings with the world. Also like Holmes, he took for granted that the prior findings of official, professional researchers could well be wrong, in large part because of their inability to give credence to those tiny incongruities, those obscure and easily overlooked clues, that actually proclaim what lies behind the mystery to be no conventional state of affairs, criminal or otherwise, but a totally unexpected, almost unbelievable, reality. Thus, precisely as his master sleuth exploded the pedestrian theories of prosaic policemen, so the Spiritualist saw in his pursuance of spirit clues often petty but unmistakable signs of a transcendent reality quite different from that of either dogma-blinkered churchmen or flat-footed Rationalists.

Doyle was, then, to his own satisfaction an honest investigator, honestly announcing the wonderful truths he found following out-of-the-way footprints most of the world had ignored amid the din of battle and the clash of creeds. He was a gentleman in every sense of the word, full of savoir faire and by all accounts a warm, large-hearted, and composed person who met without rancor the barrage of scorn and ridicule his last enthusiasm brought him. Yet, like his best-known creation, he remained an outsider, less a scientist than a celebrant—one might even say a self-ordained missionary priest—of the spirit world, much as Holmes was of the arcana of crime.[46]

In any case, Doyle liked New Zealand, even calling it "the most wonderful place in the world" and remarking in *The Wanderings of a Spiritualist* that the reception he received from the press in that country was conspicuously more cordial and fair than in Australia, where the distinguished visitor was greeted with venomous attacks from some of the leading papers.

Horace Leaf

Two years later, in 1922, Australia and New Zealand welcomed a Spiritualist protégé of Doyle, Horace Leaf. In 1923 his account of the journey, with a preface by Sir Arthur, was published as *Under the Southern Cross*.[47] His narrative, a bit more leisurely than his predecessor's, offers interesting insights into New Zealand Spiritualism in the 1920s. The account begins on a note of disappointment. The later traveler is compelled to observe that the effects of Doyle's mission had partly been spoiled by charlatans and incompetents endeavoring to take advantage

of the excitement the great man had generated. Leaf immediately recognized that he faced an uphill task but set about it diligently and was
able to report that audiences gradually increased. He visited Maori
communities and spoke highly of them and their *tohungas* who, like
Spiritualists, communicated with the souls of the departed; he mentioned also Ratana, the "Maori healer, and the large *huis* (meetings) he
was holding. He called on W. C. Nation, by now "the Grand Old Man
of Spiritualism in the Dominion, a kindly, thoughtful gentleman of well
over eighty years of age, but looking much younger."

Horace Leaf was pleased to note that in Wellington a well-built Spiritualist church seated four hundred near the center of the city, and that
the Reverend Wyndham Heathcote, the Unitarian minister in the capital, was also a Spiritualist who believed that the two liberal faiths should
combine forces. In Dunedin, on the other hand, he found Spiritualists,
under the leadership of W. S. Logan, "keen but not widespread," and
the press—as usual in that southern city—eager to debate the issue.

Other Voices

To get a further sense of New Zealand Spiritualism in the late
1920s and early 1930s, let us first return to the *Message of Life*. A few
new voices were beginning to be heard in it. In April 1932, Violet May
Cottrell, of whom more later, began publishing "Zonia scripts,"
inspired messages from her control of that name, the first being "The
Pursuit of Happiness." That title was an appropriate choice, for more
than those of an older generation Cottrell's spirits were ready to take
ordinary happiness as a good and to address the earthier components of
its makeup, including marital and sexual issues. But she also retained
something of the old vision: the April 1933 issue contained an ad for her
"Children in the Summerland: Psychic Scripts."

1933 also brought a long series of articles by J. A. Moyle on "Spiritualism Overseas," describing séances in England and the United States
he had experienced on an extended tour.[48] News of October 1, 1933,
reported V. May Cottrell and H. S. Cottrell as active in the Napier
church, sometimes speaking; May energetically played the piano. She
also was noted as an "internationally known writer of clairaudient
script," and indeed it was said that a paper by her was read at the World
Spiritualist Conference in Chicago, September 1933. January 1934
brought "Tohunga Tales" on Maori Spiritualism and a penultimate
article, so far as the *Message of Life* was concerned, by Violet May Cottrell, "A New and Better World." For the magazine was terminated
with its August issue of that year, apparently a victim of the loss of its
guiding star and the world depression; it bore a valediction by Cottrell

on genius. (Its place has subsequently been taken by the *N.Z. Psychic Gazette*, published in Auckland by Ron W. Gibbs beginning in 1979, and *The Communicator*, published by the Spiritualist Alliance [Auckland], affiliated with the Spiritualist National Union in the United Kingdom.)

Another periodical of those days that devoted considerable attention to Spiritualism was *Aquarius*, edited by Bertha Sinclair Burns, herself a medium. (One version of Jane Elizabeth Harris' memoirs was published in this magazine in 1939.) A major event for which Mrs. Burns was responsible was the first exhibition of psychic art held in Auckland in April 1924. A number of the works were drawn through her mediumship; some were later accepted for hanging by the New Zealand Academy of Fine Arts.[49]

The Search for the Lost Airmen

Now a curious incident of 1928, not apparently reported in the *Message of Life* though well known to the secular press, must be revealed. On March 13, 1929 (alongside an account of the "staggering" new marvel of "talkies," talking motion pictures, as yet only accessible overseas), headlines in *The Sun* (Auckland) screamed: "Into Mountain Wilds—Spiritualists' Strange Pilgrimage—Search for Lost Airmen." Intrigued by these grabbers, the reader continues:

> Told by spirits from the Beyond that the airmen, Hood and Moncrieff, had crashed in the Puketoi Ranges, Mr. and Mrs. J. Lawson, of Eden Terrace, Auckland, took a crystal-gazing seeress with them and plunged into the bush country to find the plane and the bodies.
>
> The amazing story of their 71-day trek into the wilderness is now told for the first time. How they gave up their business; how they suffered untold hardships through cold and hunger; and how they returned penniless from their strange pilgrimage into the mountain wilds, makes a fantastic story. They still maintain the airplane is lying in the heart of the Puketois.

The background of the adventure, for those whose memories do not reach back to the 1920s, is the attempted trans-Tasmanian flight of two New Zealanders, Captain George Hood and Lieutenant J. R. Moncrieff. They took off from Sydney for their homeland on January 10, 1927, in a Ryan monoplane. Radio signals were received until about seven hours later, when they would have been halfway across the water and then ceased. Nothing was heard from them again, and no trace of the plane was found.

The Lawsons, then living in Wellington, were Spiritualists. Mrs. Lawson reported to *The Sun* that she had always had "psychic gifts" and the ability in "semi-trance" to communicate messages from those who had "passed over." Mr. Lawson, on the other hand, said, "Before my marriage I was anything but a Spiritualist. I was a hard-boiled sceptic and took a lot of convincing. But after sitting in a circle for two nights I was completely cured of rheumatic trouble of 27 years' standing. That convinced me definitely."

At the time of the aviators' disappearance, Mrs. Lawson recounted, she was shown a "vision" of the place where they had fallen—not in mid-ocean, as most presumed, but in New Zealand near Pongaroa. Then on February 8, 1928, the couple was visited by a crystal reader, Mrs. Elizabeth Watson, who said she had received a similar vision and been miraculously guided to the Lawson home. The threesome first persuaded a party of young men to search for the fallen plane near Pongaroa, but they were unsuccessful. Then they went themselves, spending seventeen fruitless days, February 14–March 2, in the wild until returning because "we held a trance circle in our camp, and we were told to go home as a fierce storm would sweep the country. Later this proved accurate. A storm raged over the East Coast and did a lot of damage to shipping."

Undaunted, the party left again on April 19 after Lawson had sold his business to raise funds. Now they spent fifty-four days tramping some three hundred miles through untamed bush country under harsh conditions of cold and rain. Heavy winds required they lash the tent down night after night to keep it from blowing away. Of that tangled scrubland Lawson said, "Only those who have been in it know what it is like." Eventually they had to abandon the search, though still affirming that the downed plane, and the bodies, were somewhere in the dense heart of the Puketoi ranges of Hawke Bay. (These fifty-four days and the seventeen of the first expedition make up the seventy-one of the newspaper article.)

The Alexander Turnbull Library has obtained the diary of the expedition kept by John Lawson, and it is fascinating reading that offers remarkable insight into the Spiritualist minds of these pilgrims. This book of 108 pages, some only partly filled, is inscribed in a legible penciled hand. It commences with the setting out of the first venture: "Left Wellington 14th February 1928 to find the airmen that flew the Tasman." Later entries give names, and often confirmatory signatures, of persons met and who sometimes joined them for séances. Thus an entry for an early evening:

> Circle held at Maori House on Wednesday night at 8 o'clock.
> Conditions splendid. Maori spirits all around hundreds of them.
> Medium *Stella* [Mrs. Lawson]

Persons present

John Lawson

Keepa Tainguru

E. Pehikore

The Spirit says that we are with the right people. Lovely power lovely people will get great results. Little Star (meaning girl) went to heaven. Kanaaha pleased he say I bring them all here. All coming tonight. All coming through. You have great results. God guide you safely. Kanaaha lead you to his tribe. Bless all people. You soon will be satisfied. No danger go straight ahead. I go and let someone else through. . . . Success too. Hurry up and sing. . . .

Thurs. Morning. The spirits are all still with us. & helping us wonderfully. Spirits say we walked 22 miles. Too far.

Friday— . . . two Maories and the dog are quite well & in good spirits & they are both Ratanas so they are the same as us Spiritualists. I think we know more than the people give us credit for.

The main spirits the Lawson party dealt with were called Red Eagle, Little Bear, Marie, Kanaaha (an old-time Maori), and Yem Sing, who seemed to specialize in healing, giving advice for a bad throat and the like. We immediately note here names suggesting three categories of entities: the first two, the native American guides who, though redolent of modern Spiritualism's homeland, have traveled quite well as the faith has moved through the world; then a little girl spirit, a standby of the old-fashioned séance; then a Maori who, together with the hundreds of spirits of his race earlier reported, suggest that at least in New Zealand the Native Americans can be supplemented by supernatural helpers of that equally shamanistic people; finally, the Chinese-sounding Yem Sing reminds us that a sage of his venerable nation is also an ornament of many prestigious bands of spirit helpers, for most Spiritualists are nothing if not broad-minded regarding the world's many creeds and colors.

That admirable quality is pressed home more forcefully in the reference to the Ratana faith, for it must be remembered that in the 1920s the new faith that Tahupotiki Wiremu Ratana, known as Te Mangai, (mouthpiece of god), had founded on the basis of visions beginning in 1918, was strongly opposed. Newspapers, not to mention many clerics, denounced the prophet as a megalomaniac whose faith healings resulted in much suffering and death from lack of proper medical attention and whose sociopolitical activities were even more suspect. The Ratana movement, with its obvious overtones of Maori self-affirmation, drew immense crowds and in time gained a lock on the four Maori parliamentary seats. The Ratana church is definitely if rather unconventionally a Christian sect and is not really Spiritualistic. Ratana oppposed the traditional *tohungas* and their spiritism.

Yet, like many other such nativist movements, Ratana has offered symbols of psychological continuity with the pre-Christian spiritual world of its people. In Ratana this feature has taken the form of a cult of the faithful angels *(nga anahera pono),* who undoubtedly served a bridge-building function by reminding traditional Maori of the warmly familiar and ever-present ancestral and tutelary spirits of old. But the addition of these angels to the baptismal and healing formulas of Ratana was too much for New Zealand's Anglican bishops, who charged polytheism and in 1925 threatened to excommunicate any churchmen who joined the sect, in effect forcing the movement into a separatist stance. Nor was Ratana's role as mouthpiece (medium?) of God congenial to the Pakeha mind. It is therefore significant that our coterie of white New Zealand Spiritualists, themselves believers in an often-ridiculed religion and on a quest bound to appear absurd to the world, should celebrate their communion with the Ratana brethren.[50]

Indeed, the apparent futility of the search had to be faced by the end of May, as wintry conditions grew wilder and wilder. On May 20, John Lawson wrote in the diary that the group was "played out" and would have to give up because of the weather. Yet he added defiantly that he knew some people would call them "cranks and mad people and sorts of other things but we don't mind as we are going to show them that we are perfectly sane & know what we are talking about." Other alternatives for showing them were there. On May 16 the spirits were still very encouraging: Red Eagle said the flying machine was there, and he would give information about it shortly, but that spirit "also told us that the Great Master would show himself to Mrs. Watson through the crystal when we had finished the plane business."

Finally, with those promises no doubt in mind, the party came out of the wilderness in June, the plane undiscovered. So the adventure ended —or perhaps not quite: An unindentified 1956 newspaper clipping stuck in the diary says that a Miss E. E. Barren is looking for the airmen and the plane and claims a psychic said they were above high white cliffs. . . .

Violet May Cottrell and the Return of Doyle

The next great adventure in New Zealand Spiritualism involves Violet May Cottrell, who had been a rising young star of Spiritualistic journalism and who had published a series of articles in the final issues of the *Message of Life* and had played the piano in the Napier church. But there is much more to this memorable woman than that. First, this very prolific writer also published in the famous Australian Spiritualist publication, *Harbinger of Light.* Second, she was not unknown to the great Arthur Conan Doyle.

Doyle, in one of his last books, *The Edge of the Unknown,* spoke of a curious 1920s mediumistic phenomenon, the channeling of Lord Northcliffe, the dynamic and notoriously short-tempered British press magnate who had died in 1922. Hannan Swaffer, an editor of one of Northcliffe's papers, early in 1925 announced his conversion to Spiritualism and proclaimed his former chief's continuing dispatches at a public meeting in Queen's Hall, London. Swaffer soon after published the bombastic old man's postmortem ruminations as *Northcliffe's Return.* But the editor was not alone in receiving Northcliffe from the other side. Doyle, after reference to Swaffer in *The Edge of the Unknown,* goes on to speak of "a single long article, said to be dictated by Northcliffe, and coming through the hand of a lady living in New Zealand, and quite ignorant of her control's personality, or of his methods of thought and expression."

Then, after several quotes from this dictation, which contain typical outbursts of Northcliffean rage—now directed not at dilatory copywriters but at those who doubt the value of spirit communication—Doyle expostulates: "Can anyone imagine that these forceful words, which can be matched in unpublished communications from the same source in England, could really have come from the mind of the lady in far New Zealand?"[51] Not long after, the same question would be asked of the New Zealand lady and the English writer himself.

On July 8, 1930, word of the death of Arthur Conan Doyle was flashed around the world from London and reported the same day in New Zealand papers. Among the stories published in connection with the celebrity's passing was an item from the *Daily Express* claiming that he and Lady Doyle had a secret code between them, by which the one that embarked first for the other world would try to communicate with the other, and so the genuineness of the message by the code would be guaranteed. However, it appears that the shade of the deceased writer and Spiritualist, rather than attempt the intricacies of that cypher, made straight for New Zealand with a speed hardly less than that of the cabled news of his demise. There he straightway introduced himself into the home, and mind, of the same Napier woman whose earlier readings from Northcliffe he had so highly commended. For the *Daily Telegraph* of that city for July 10 excitedly tells us: "Sir Conan Doyle Speaks to Napier Medium. Mrs. H. S. Cottrell Receives Message."

Interviewed, Mrs. Cottrell revealed to the paper that mediums are "a type of human wireless set," which picks up messages from the spiritual world as a radio transmits programs. Unfortunately, as is not seldom the case in such communications, the Doyle message itself was rather less stunning than the fact of its prompt delivery. Sir Arthur spoke of "feeling sad at leaving all my dear ones," even though he knew he would get in touch with them presently. He was having to adjust to "changed conditions," and, although Spiritualism had helped greatly to prepare him for what he found over there, he was still "very unsettled." But, he added, "I will be very happy soon, I know, and am busy as ever, but in the meantime it is nice to have a chat with an understanding person still in the flesh." Doyle was also able to rejoice in the warm welcome he had received in spirit land and was especially gratified at seeing once again the face of his son.

Not all were convinced. A July 15 article, "Spiritualists Sceptical. Napier Claims Doubted in Dunedin," reported that Cottrell's coreligionists in the southern city opined dourly that her claims "should be subject to the closest investigation." There was much prickly sentiment that communication should have been first to Lady Doyle via the famous code, or that, if New Zealand had been favored, communication ought to have arrived through the much-discussed Blue Room, the Spiritualist receiving station established in Dunedin and later moved to Masterton.

Violet May Cottrell

Be that as it may, the Napier report led to an uncommon outburst of interest in Spiritualism and, in the Hawke Bay area, in Violet May Cottrell. She was forty-three at the time, and a photograph reveals a youngish, fair-featured and attractive woman whose pale intense eyes, full lips and inconoclastic tilt of the head suggest a person at once haunted, sensual, and independent. Beginning July 11, the *Daily Telegraph* published a remarkable series of interviews with her, revealing how this Napier housewife and mother became a sibyl of such audacity.

In an article of July 12, May Cottrell says that her psychic adventures began in simple experiments with her sister-in-law. When the latter was visiting on vacation from college, they tried doing divination by means of a ring suspended over a glass half filled with water. As the ring swung and tapped against the side of the glass, they asked it questions that they thought were answered through an alphabet code. At first it seemed a light and harmless game. But when May later had recourse to the ring alone, she found herself asking it more and more serious queries and became convinced that a real intelligence was forming its answers. She finally learned that the mind behind the talking ring was that of a man whom she had once known slightly and who had died in the great flu epidemic a couple of years before. This information was followed by communication from other guides.

By then tapping had come to be an awkward means of reception for the novice medium. In response to the suggestion of her spirit mentors, she switched to automatic writing. "The messages came with surprising ease and rapidity, from all sorts and conditions of people."

Among those were her own parents. Their case, in fact, indicates that her years of spiritual unfolding were by no means sunny.

> Both my parents had recently died, under very tragic circumstances within three months of each other. They were both over seventy, and their last years were full of mental and physical suffering, which with the painful nature of their going, so preyed upon my mind that I was in a shockingly nervous condition. I was bitterly resentful also, and more than a little included to curse God and life. My attitude towards life was gloomy in the extreme, so much so, in fact, that I got little joy out of my little daughter, who was then about one year old.
>
> My father, knowing this—for our loved ones on the other side do know what is happening to us here—most earnestly desired to help me back to health and happiness. Both he and my mother have written through me many times since then and have succeeded in removing much of the old bitterness from my heart. Their love and understanding have helped me over many difficult places, and the teaching I have received from my spirit guides has completely changed my attitude towards life.

Violet May's mate showed an initial aversion to the practices, a distaste clearly related to his awareness of her mental state: "Horace, my husband, was, at first, very averse indeed to my having anything to do with these spirit tappings and writings. I was in a very run-down, nervous condition, the victim of innumerable fears, forebodings and that black depression which a lack of nervous vitality produces." In time, however, Horace came to realize that Spiritualism was having more a therapeutic than unwholesome effect on his wife's condition, and he also became somewhat interested in the content of her communications. When she wrote "Children in the Summerland," he was impressed and said, "Well, even if this is only a fantasy, born of your own imagination, I am sure it has real literary merit."

Others, however, were less well affected. May Cottrell's fourth newspaper column was devoted to the negative response, often accompanied by impassioned warnings, which certain members of the clergy gave her "psychic radio." But the fifth and final installment told of the coming of "Zonia," her last and loftiest guide. Zonia was reportedly the spirit of an Arab who had lived at the time of the pharoahs and who delivered discourses on religious and moral topics. These scripts, which at first came to her while her two small children slept, were the Cottrell writings most widely published in Spiritualist journals. Zonia's very presence near her, she said, radiated peace and kindness, and love flowed "from him to his fellows in an unbroken stream."

Behind these accounts seems to be a woman of strongly alternating moods, who is reeling between confident exuberance and shattering self-doubt. *Harbinger of Light,* in publishing some of her Zonia material in 1930, introduced her as full of energy and humor, a fun-loving individual who had discovered her gifts fewer than ten years before and who would still rather be outdoors than taking messages.[52] The *Message of Life* around the same time (1933) depicted her lively piano playing in the Napier Spiritualist church. Yet her own words betray how one-sided these characterizations were. The woman of the interviews lay bare anguish and hours of black despair, so much so one almost wonders whether the extroverted side some apparently took for the whole person was no more than the frenetic energy that can be born of desperation. She herself was much later to present that frenzied activity as a constructive attempt to cope with inner darkness. Now, it appears Spiritualism was also a way, though not a wholly unambivalent way. Spiritualism could help to alleviate those gray descents, yet it could also aggrevate them when the creative Zonia or Doyle euphoria wore off and her faith was challenged by modern witch-hunters.

For all that, however, hers was a curious and bold new Spiritualist talent. The obscure New Zealander's claim to be the first to transmit no less a giant of the faith than Doyle was not the only example of her sauciness. In an article of September 1, 1930, "Clothes in the Spirit World," she faced head-on a Spiritualist conundrum.[53] Put starkly, the dilemma is, Why do we see ghosts clothed rather than naked? For as the old bromide has it, If ghosts have clothes, then clothes must have ghosts. But even those willing to concede that Uncle Henry's revenant could limn the facial features known to his loved ones (or enemies) might have trouble postulating that the shades of his boots or overalls had followed him to the Summerland. Yet spooks are generally clothed, if only in vaporous drapes, and Cottrell argues that this is because their garb reflects the thoughts of the apparition and thus the way it conceives of its own appearance.

She was, in fact, willing to sweep a lot of cobwebs out of the séance room. A May 2, 1936, article from *The Progressive Thinker,* a Chicago Spiritualist publication (apparently this was a paper she had given in absentia at the aforementioned Spiritualist conference there) was called "The Dawn of a New Knowledge Concerning Love and Marriage" and subtitled, "Sex Is an Essential Factor of Existence; as Real and Tangible beyond the Veil as It Is Here." This piece, said to be "by clair-audient dictation from the Zonia Scripts," affirms quite an open and positive attitude toward the sexual drive in this and any other world, though asserting it needs to be joined by love and a sense of intimacy. (Although early Spiritualism in America and England had significant links to Free Love and other radical social movements, by Cottrell's time the movement had long since fallen into a rather prim though fustian style, suggesting more a Victorian throwback than a voice of the radical 1930s.)

At the same time, Cottrell in the 1930s was becoming a widely published author on a variety of subjects. Pieces by her in New Zealand papers opposed tight-money policies, defended modern dancing, and discussed geysers, birds, international patriotism, and Maori life. Her article on the great 1931 Napier earthquake and its effects was widely reproduced around the English-speaking world. She was to publish more than seven hundred articles over a long career. She advertised cards with her poems on them. Her husband, employed by the *Napier Telegraph* 1931–1936, helped her market her writings and handled the business aspects of her burgeoning career. When she died in 1971 at the age of eighty-four she was among the best-known and best-loved citizens of Napier—and the Spiritualism of forty years before was apparently then little known and less regarded.

Her most famous poem, "Pania of the Reef: A Maori Legend," was the inspiration of the statue of Pania on the Napier waterfront, a local landmark. Its Hiawatha-like cadences well evoke emergence from darkness to light:

> Pania, beautiful sea maiden,
> Coming from dark depths mysterious,
> From the ocean's strange, weird caverns,
> Dwelt alone upon the shore.

> Well she loved the golden sunlight,
> Glinting, flashing on the waters;
> Gloried in the noontide splendour
> And the rosy glow of sunsets. . . .

Much of what she wrote about, in fact, was of local Napier interest—the gannets of Cape Kidnapper's, the Hawke's Bay Maori. Very little relating Cottrell to Spiritualism is found in the general press since about the time of the Napier earthquake, though as we have seen her Zonia scripts and other articles appeared in obscure Spiritualist publications through the 1930s. The *Weekly News* (Auckland) of October 4, 1939, in telling of the acceptance by a London publisher of her one book, a children's novel *(The Lost Cave of Pukeragi),* speaks of her *earlier* ("now some time ago") writing of "the occult." After the war, there is virtually nothing Spiritualist by her. In an article in *Woman* (May 20, 1950), Cottrell tells us frankly—or somewhat frankly—of overcoming ill health, fear, despair, and "nervous disorders" early in her married life through activity—dance, theater, tennis, and the like, and making herself do these things whether she felt like it at the moment or not. These are the same complaints of which she had spoken twenty years before in her psychic-radio interviews after the Doyle transmission. But now there is no mention of Spiritualism.

So also in her obituary. It speaks of her prolific writing, her love of Maori legend, and her close association with the Hukarere Maori Girl's College near her home in Napier. It mentions that she was a keen bowler, and tells us that her only son, Spence—one of the two small children around her feet in the days of Doyle and Zonia—was killed during active World War II service as a bomber pilot in the Royal New Zealand Air Force. Her funeral was out of St. Paul's Presbyterian church, not the tiny Spiritualist church where she had once played the piano.

What had happened? Had the spirits failed to foretell the great earthquake? Or the war in which a son was shot down from the sky? Violet May Cottrell had written much and revealed much about herself over many years. But she also took secrets with her into the Summerland.[54] The least that can be said is that, like Jane Elizabeth Harris, May Cottrell was a woman in whom inner zeal jousted with profound self-doubt. For both women the guidance of spirits wiser than themselves provided early resolution. The older stayed with the spirits and the Spiritualist cause that had done so much for her and for which she in turn did much. But in Cottrell's case, as the Napier writer found a publishable voice of her own, the otherworldly voices were quietly retired. As she harvested adequate communitywide recognition in her own right, the sectarian Spiritualist milieu probably seemed unnecessary, if not stifling.

Whether, as she went through these apparent changes, she felt loss or guilt or further self-doubt or good-riddance, one will never know, for she chose to remain silent about the disposition of what was once, in what must later have seemed almost another incarnation, the pivot of her inner life.

Later Events in Spiritualism

Spiritualism continued in New Zealand—between 1939 and 1954 the Psychic Research Society of Wellington held meetings that seemed to combine a spiritual and scientific interest in the subject. Lecture topics ranged from "Spiritual Gifts and Their Development," to St. Paul as one of the greatest occult initiates, to the parapsychological work of J. B. Rhine. On one occasion Mrs. Cottrell (who lived in Wellington in the 1940s, when her husband was employed there with Inland Revenue), showed slides of the Himalayas. A Mr. Singh spoke on yoga. Other lecturers dealt with Ratana, mystic evolution, and hermetic forces. In the postwar atmosphere of April 29, 1946, a discussion asked what psychic research could do for the great problems of the world: war, overpopulation, hunger, and insanity. The response was that the duty of the psychic is to put before people a vivid picture of life after death, and to give perspective and to make clear the object of life is to "build the mind."[55]

Mary Manson Dreaver

An important Spiritualist figure of those days was Mary Manson Dreaver (1887–1961), journalist, speech teacher, artist, and Labour Party activist. She was a member of the Auckland City Council in 1938–1944 and 1953–1961, M.P. for Waitemata 1941–1943, and a member of the Legislative Council, the now-discontinued parliamentary upper house, 1946–1950, the only woman ever to serve in that body. Mary Dreaver was also a Spiritualist minister. *Aquarius,* "The New Zealand Psychic Magazine," October 21, 1939, has on the back cover an advertisement for the Spiritualist church on Alma Street, Newmarket, Auckland, listing her as minister. She was moreover president of the SCNZ, as another box on the same page indicates.[56] A leading medium in the postwar era was Beatrice Swaby (b. 1905, in England), of the Petone Spiritualist church in the Hutt Valley, north of Wellington.[57]

Mary Fry

The Petone church was also frequented by two of the best-known New Zealand Spiritualists of the 1980s, Mary and Warwick Fry. Here it was that I first saw them on a rainy night in 1988. Warwick presided and delivered the address; Mary served as clairvoyant. Although the church was crowded, she picked me out as one of the half dozen or so people to give a reading, and to my surprise—because, although we later became acquainted, to the best of my knowledge she had no way of knowing who I was that night—she noted that I was "not a Kiwi," and said one or two accurate things about my house back in the United States.

Raised as an Anglican in the far reaches of the South Island near Invercargill, Mary Fry had psychic experiences as a child, playing with spirit children who were as real to her as her physical friends. She became a Spiritualist after a very difficult first marriage. During this time of great distress, she reported, Spiritualist ministers and services gave her more help and comfort than anyone else. She took up mediumship after a bad back, the result of polio in the 1950s, made employment difficult. "Then I made a decision," she said in an interview, "that I

wanted to be used. I placed myself in God's hands to be used as a channel, only so I wouldn't be using my physical strength, because that
would be depleting, nor my own intellect, because I'd be working in
areas I have no knowledge of. When I talk to people I'm in a completely
relaxed state. Sometimes I'm asked if I get very tired. No way."[58]

Her articulate manner and warm, dynamic personality quickly led to
success as a medium in personal consultation (for which she asked no
fee) and Spiritualist lecturing. Although she deeply believes in Spiritualism, her honesty and self-discipline in its practice are refreshing. In
1983–1985 she attained national prominence for a twice-monthly 2ZB
radio program. People would call in for Mary's psychic responses to
their queries, which were often in the form of mediumistic messages
from deceased relatives of the caller. The program became immensely
popular, generating many rings of the phone and much mail, often
from persons with serious problems with which the medium dealt as
best she could in her sincere, caring way. It also, inevitably, produced
controversy. Persons and groups on the attack against pseudoscience
and psychism questioned the propriety of Radio New Zealand sponsoring such a show. Although the station denied that this opposition was
the reason and acknowledged that letters and calls supporting the popular program greatly outweighed those opposing, Mary Fry's contract
was not renewed after two years, and she went off the air.[59]

Undoubtedly, Mary's presence and program had much to do with the
growth of Spiritualism reported in the 1980s censuses. She can be seen
as only the most recent in the list of colorful print, platform—and now
electronic media—personalities who have periodically reinvigorated
New Zealand Spiritualism, bringing it back to life whenever it seemed
likely to wither in insular isolation. Peebles, Hardinge-Britten, Doyle,
Leaf, Cottrell, Dreaver, and now Fry—more than anything else, the
Spiritualist story has been the story of names like these. Chances are
good that further names will be added to this register in the twenty-first
century.

3 Powers of the Air
UFO Religions and Other
Companions of Spiritualism

CONTACT WITH the spirit world through trance communication is a broader phenomenon than the Spiritualism begun with the Fox sisters. That religious lineage revived in the modern civilized world the practice known to shamans of old, as they roused the ancestral spirits, of hearing again the voices of the departed. But the ancient shamans and sibyls had another forte as well, channeling the speech of gods and angels. This, too, has been restored in the modern shamanism of the Spiritualist tradition. Modern Spiritualism has always communicated messages from high teachers of lofty wisdom, not seldom biblical, as well as the ordinary departed. But some groups distinctive from the regular Spiritualist churches have focused exclusively on communiqués from exalted teachers, generally one or a particular cluster of wise guides.

Gordon Melton has made a useful distinction by using the term "Teaching Spiritualism" for groups and movements centered on the teachings of one or a few such lofty beings.[1] In some cases their information has been transcribed in modern "bibles": the *Oahspe* or the *Urantia Book*. In any event, the important point about Teaching Spiritualism is the instruction, together with the implicit metaphysical correlate, that between the human plane and ultimate reality lies an intermediate plane redolent with wonder and wisdom, the realm of near-perfect yet individualized consciousnesses able to guard and guide struggling humanity: spirit teachers, masters, godlike UFO beings. It is worth noting that the teaching more often than not shows similarity to that of Theosophy, a widely employed source for alternative spirituality wisdom; significantly, the masters of Theosophy were ostensibly contacted through endeavors to deepen Spiritualism and align it with the lore of occultism East and West. Those beings, though communicating more through writing (the Mahatma Letters, their assistance to Helena Blavatsky in her literary work) than voice mediumship in original Theosophy, are certainly modern prototypes of the type.

The Culdian Trust

A native New Zealand example is the Culdian Trust, based on the Coromandel Peninsula. Its work commenced November 12, 1980, when a small group of people meeting to expand their spiritual awareness began to receive instruction from a high sacred mentor, Gwineva. Those teachings were published the following year as *The Book of Gwineva*.[2] *Culdee* is an ancient Celtic term for "priest" or "wise one," and together with the name of the teacher, the title "Culdian Trust" indicates a Celtic bent. Culdians indeed describe themselves as following "an enlightened and progressive form of mystic Christianity based broadly on the beliefs of the Ancient Culdees, the original pre-Augustinian Church in Britain."[3] Yet Culdianism is much more than a return to a romantic past. Gwineva is now "spirit being," though of Celtic background, and as a spirit teacher for today speaks of the "New Age" and what will come after it, the "Celestial Age." The latter will be "born out of the trials and travail of the New Age," and in it "humanity will fulfill its cosmic destiny and discover its universal place."

The Book of Gwineva speaks of the current New Age as a time when humanity is looking for a new spiritual orientation. We want something beyond political and economic change, the text says, as vital as that may be. We are prepared to make spiritual advances as well, realizing that the universe is the creation of the supreme spirit from which came the great design. Gwineva also imparts wisdom on human problems and affirms, for example, traditional male-female roles but insists they are spiritually equal ("complementary sexes"). Males should be strong and silent holders of wisdom; females are intuitive. On race, the Maoris are like the Celts, a dispossessed people. Both need to keep their cultures alive and so are entitled to some separateness. All the while, Culdians insist that their movement can embrace a wide variety of beliefs and perspectives and that it is not a cult.

The Culdian Revival Trust, the legal entity controlling the movement, announces that group and general public meetings are held at the center in Thames (The Thames Wholistic Centre, with books and candles for sale, a lending library, and appointments available for healing).[4] Members also attend attunement ceremonies. Nonetheless, it appears that the teachings are spread primarily through publications, whether *The Book of Gwineva,* assorted pamphlets, or a metaphysical correspondence course.

Faithists

An older new bible is *Oahspe,* transmitted through the American medium J. B. Newburgh (1828–1891), and first published in 1882.[5] Believers in the teachings of *Oahspe* are called Faithists and, though small in number, have long been active in America, England, and elsewhere. The movement is represented in New Zealand by Ken Mills of Auckland. He reports that, although there is no organized activity in the country, he has been surprised at the number of people who have the book or have expressed interest in it, in response to his ads in Spiritualist and New Age publications. Like many Faithists, he is also a Spiritualist, Mills acknowledges that the 844-page scripture, ponderous in style and riddled with strange names and terms, is heavy going, but he continues to send out tracts and sell the *Oahspe* book to serious inquirers.

Oahspe, also presented as the Kosmon Bible, relates that humanity entered the Kosmon Age in 1848, the revolutionary year modern Spiritualism started. In this New Age, carnal mindedness, with its wars and violence and perverted truth, will finally be abolished. A major feature of past eras has been the setting up of false religions, including theological Christianity though not the gospel of Jesus himself. The false faiths were fabricated by lower gods and even entail pseudoheavens. But throughout all ages there have been pure ones, like the modern Faithists, who worship the true supreme spirit, Jehovih (sic), and listen to authentic mediums and prophets who communicate words from him, or from his righteous spokesmen in the angelic realm.

Despite, or perhaps because of, its extreme dualism, *Oahspe* is a strangely moving bible in places. Those whom it exalts are the gentle, hidden ones of all ages, who eat only fruits and vegetables, are nonviolent to the point of martyrdom, live communally but take no part in earthly governments or wars. More of heaven than this mottled earth, these faithful ones commune with God and his angels while shunning the brutal ways and corrupt creeds of the great majority. But they have seen the future and know it works.

The Urantia Movement

A second massive modern scripture (2,097 pages) is the *Urantia Book,* first published in 1955 though reportedly transcribed in the 1930s by unnamed human receptors of messages from high in the cosmic hierarchy.[6] These revelations concern the spiritual and material superuniverse and universe of which we are a part, the history of our planet, Urantia, and the life of Jesus with special emphasis on his hidden years.

A small group in New Zealand actively supported by Mr. Dennis Clampitt of Auckland, who imports copies of the *Urantia Book,* meets regularly to discuss it. The world Urantia movement is headquartered in Chicago.

The White Eagle Lodge

Another movement with Spiritualist roots is the White Eagle Lodge. It began in England in the work of Grace Cooke, a medium and friend of Mary Conan Doyle, Sir Arthur's daughter. A principal communicator of Cooke's was a high teacher called White Eagle (a native American name), who spoke through her from the early 1930s until her death in 1979. Like May Cottrell, Grace Cooke received instruction from Arthur Conan Doyle after his death in 1930, as reported in a book by her husband, Ivan Cooke, *The Return of Arthur Conan Doyle.* These revelations, and the explicit direction of White Eagle, led to the formation of the lodge in 1935. The group survived bombing of its London headquarters in World War II and, now well established in England, has started to spread overseas. Its growth is aided by a good list of spiritual publications. Some of these, especially its fine books for children, are of exceptionally high quality. Some are transcripts of White Eagle's teachings out of various incarnations of his, including Atlantean, Native American, and ancient Egyptian.

The doctrine is in the general Spiritualist-Theosophical traditions, including ideas like karma, the *cakras,* and astrology. But the White Eagle Lodge has come to be mainly involved in spiritual healing and the inculcation of a full personal spiritual life centered on meditation. Regular mediumistic contact with the departed and physical phenomena are not encouraged. All this gives the White Eagle work its distinctive atmosphere. Its meetings exude a very quiet, affirmative tone, reflective of the inspirational, optimistic, always gentle and never condemnatory quality of the extensive White Eagle transmissions themselves.[7]

In March 1988 about fifteen persons gathered at a White Eagle retreat in Paraparaumu for a quiet day in a beautiful home overlooking the grey waters of the Tasman Sea. The agenda consisted of readings from the White Eagle books, silent meditation to taped music, and a meditation guided by a slow, soft, taped voice that spoke of closeness to the strength of trees and the earth. There was healing, under a certified White Eagle healer who did *cakra* balancing and a closing discussion in which participants talked of their reasons for interest in the White Eagle work. One member had joined after a critical medical emergency. The movement's concept of karma, which emphasized crises like this as opportunity rather than retribution, had helped her to understand the purpose of the event in terms of spiritual development. Karma seemed a popular theme in this group generally. People were also attracted by the gentle, loving tone of the White Eagle texts, which employ many images of a maternal, enfolding nature. The White Eagle Lodge seemed to be growing in New Zealand.

UFOism: Technological Angels

Unidentified flying objects, or flying saucers, have become so much a subject of modern curiosity and folklore since the first sightings in the United States near Mt. Rainier in 1947. Although UFOs have been the focus of scientific and quasi-scientific investigation, they have also, for some, found a religious role well summed up in Carl Jung's phrase, "technological angels."[8] We have observed a similar schism between scientific and religious responses to identical phenomena in Spiritualism; this is one clue that it and twentieth-century UFOism belong in the same category. According to Jung, the UFO visitants have, in a "space age" nurtured on science fiction, played the part once taken by descending gods, angels, saintly apparitions, and heavenly saviors. Mysteriously appearing out of the heavens, they have contacted favored earthlings to deliver messages of warning, hope, or forthcoming apocalypse and to impart philosophical wisdom. The demonic role is also there, for not all UFO beings are benign. There are accounts of the sinister men in black who allegedly harrass observers of UFOs and harrowing tales—including one from New Zealand—of interstellar abductions and assaults climaxing in bizarre medical procedures or even cosmic rape.

I have put religious UFOism alongside Spiritualism on the grounds that it is essentially a marginal religion of the same type. Both presuppose an order of spiritually significant beings between the human and ultimate reality, with which one can have both a conversational and disciplic relationship. Whether spirits or space brothers, a relationship with them opens up a sense of expanded consciousness and cosmic wonder, quite apart from whatever words are actually communicated. In both there are physical phenomena, or traces, that serve to support belief but that for real believers are like "signs" in a religious sense, promoting salvific faith, as well as anomalies to be investigated scientifically. For both Spiritualism and UFOism, human commerce with the others begins with the experience of elect individuals. In both, this privileged exchange soon enough becomes the focus of informal circles or even minor institutions, in which messages from the invisible friends are transmitted mediumistically, in trances or through automatic writing. At the same time in both movements the groups tend to be loose and ephemeral. For interest to be sustained, they need powerful periodic injections of fresh visions or novel messages. In New Zealand at least, both Spiritualism and UFOism have required a series of highly visible lecturers, mostly from overseas, to keep enthusiasm at a high pitch.

UFOism may have other affinities as well. Links with Teaching Spiritualism and Theosophy have already been noted. Some of the wise among the extraterrestrials clearly fall into the teaching role, and their wisdom tends toward Theosophical concepts of karma, reincarnation, and spiritual evolution, though sometimes with more of an apocalyptic edge than their older fellow initiates would have thought fitting. Yet parallels abound, not only in teaching but also in the concept of an adept who is not simply a god self-existent from all eternity but who attained high cosmic rank by dint of effort, initiation, and acquired wisdom.

Some commentators have also perceived a remarkable similarity between UFOs and their occupants, and the traditional fairy folk amply affirmed by generation after generation of European peasants and by Theosophists like Geoffrey Hodson (who spent the last decades of his life in New Zealand) and E. L. Gardner (who first displayed the Cottingley fairy photographs publicized by Arthur Conan Doyle). Writers like Jacques Vallee have pointed to striking convergences between the two otherworldly little-men beliefs: the round saucer traces on the ground like fairy rings, the elfin or goblinesque appearance of the alien intruders, the abductions during which ordinary time dissolved as it did for those countrymen of yore taken into a fairy mound, the new-old whispers of changeling children and queer half-human pregnancies.[9]

The 1909 Sightings

These are all matters in which New Zealanders have shown interest, and it is not surprising to learn that New Zealand and UFOs have also long gone together. Decades before the postwar series of sightings that underlies recent UFO groups in New Zealand, an impressive UFO wave swept over the island state. In July–August 1909 hundreds of New Zealanders claimed to see airships of varying shapes and sizes moving about the sky. The episode was comparable to the great airship mystery of 1896–1899 in the United States, when reports of a large, well-lighted aerial vessel flowed in from across the country and received enthusiastic press coverage. (Later studies of this episode have concluded there was little behind the reports but hoaxes and urban folklore–type rumor published and republished.)[10] Similar airship stories surfaced in Britain in March–May 1909 (and were thought by some to be related to growing panic over possible invading German airships) just prior to the New Zealand flap, and appeared in Australia just after it, as though the mysterious vessel were circuiting the world by a zigzag, albeit English-speaking, route.

In New Zealand in 1909, six years after Kitty Hawk, there were no known airplanes, dirigibles, large balloons, or other physical objects that could account for reports of something navigating up there. The skies belonged to clouds, birds, and astronomical bodies. Nonetheless, in that year a number of people saw, as though by precognition, moving lights and floating metal above them such as would become familiar a few years later, as commerce and war took to the heavens. In winter 1909 crowds even gathered in the streets in hope of spotting the phantom airship.

The reports began at the southern tip of the South Island in July. The *Clutha Free Press,* of Balclutha, stated on July 13 that several people in nearby Stirling had seen a few nights before the lights of what could be only an aircraft. A couple days later the lights were again sighted at Kaka Point, not far away. On July 27 the rival *Clutha Leader* reported a Mr. George Smith's testimony that the lighted object was seen at the beach every evening during the week of July 18. He also averred that on July 24 some boys playing on the beach at Kaka Point had seen a huge lighted object "as big as a house." But further reports from Mr. Smith made it out to be more like a dirigible, with a dark superstructure and a powerful headlight plus two smaller lights at the sides. That impression was confirmed by the witness of a group of schoolchildren at Kelso, who said that on July 23 an airship had come down and hovered over their school for a few minutes. Interviewed and asked to draw the craft separately by an *Otago Daily Times* reporter, they all produced a dirigiblelike cigar-shaped craft with smallish stabilizing wings extending on the sides, a cabin below, and a large propeller. From then on the reports flooded in from the lower half of the South Island, from Oamaru, Timaru, and Geraldine. The intrusive metallic monster was even caught sailing over Knox College in Dunedin with a loud noise like a ship dragging its anchor up—a big black thing in the night sky with searchlights on. By August the vessel had reached Nelson and Blenheim, and there were even reports from Hawke Bay, though far fewer in the North Island than in the South. By the end of August reports had mostly ceased, only to blossom briefly in New South Wales.[11]

Interpretations of the mysterious phenomenon varied. Some thought the airship came from Mars—the canals-of-Mars excitement was then at its height. Others opined it was a German spy instrument, perhaps launched from a cruiser at sea. The most popular notion, though, was that the witnesses encountered the handiwork of some backcountry inventor—an aerial Captain Nemo? Others, then as later, considered the whole episode no more than mass hysteria fanned by story-hungry reporters.

Post–World War II Sightings

When UFO appearances commenced again after World War II, New Zealand once more was in the forefront. Among the most important early sightings in this series was that of Bruce Cathie in 1952. With several other witnesses, Cathie saw a strange craft over Manukau Harbor in Auckland. A pilot, Cathie developed an interest in UFOs that eventually led to a series of books, *Harmonic 33* (1968), *Harmonic 695: The UFO and Anti-Gravity*, (with Peter Temm; 1971), *The Pulse of the Universe: Harmonic 288*, (1977), and *The Bridge to Infinity* (1983). These works propound a complex theory that there are grids of force over the earth that link UFOs, volcanoes, earthquakes, and other violent and sometimes mysterious phenomena. Cathie believes that interplanetary beings are rebuilding a world grid system that they use for navigational purposes and from which they will be able to draw motive power. New Zealand seems to be a key matrix of this grid. Whether one follows Cathie's intricate calculations or not, the books provide an interesting and sometimes provocative discussion of many facets of the UFO problem. They are not, however, overtly religious in their approach.

A December 21, 1978, contact by sight, radar, and film with an unexplained light off the coast at Kaikoura by two New Zealand pilots is still considered by science-oriented UFO buffs as one of the best cases worldwide of serious evidence for the mysterious flying vehicles. Ten days later a television crew flew the same route and photographed more unusual lights. A couple of popular books resulted.[12]

Along with UFO science mushroomed what can only be called a popular-culture UFO movement, made up of amateur and professional investigators bitten by the bug, itinerant lecturers, open-membership UFO organizations producing newsletters and meetings, sensational books and media coverage, and not-seldom overtly religious contactees claiming to be channels for revelations from superior UFO entities. In their wake came groups specializing in reporting encounters and engaging in mediumistic communication with the cosmic friends.

Contactee-oriented UFO groups have, in fact, tended to outpublicize and outpace those devoted to serious scientific study of the aerial enigma, much to the distress of the latter. At one point this divergence of interest produced a major schism in New Zealand UFOism. In exactly the same way, religious Spiritualism and scientific psychic research have for all intents and purposes parted company, and there have been times when the religious wing, meeting spiritual needs that could not always wait, threatened to swamp in both publicity and numbers those dedicated to the slow, careful objective study of verifiable psychic phenomena. On the other hand, New Zealand's small number of quasi-scientific, noncontactee UFO groups have had greater longevity than most of the Spiritualistic ones. Like religious Spiritualism, religious UFOism must produce continuing signs and wonders to maintain an eager following, and they are even harder to come by from spacemen than from spirits.

The Beginning of the UFO Movement

The earliest beginnings of the New Zealand UFO movement were not especially spiritual in orientation, but war in heaven soon intervened to put the UFO experience in an ominous new light. The initial force was Harold Fulton, a Royal New Zealand Air Force sergeant who founded a group called Civilian Saucer Investigation (CSI) (New Zealand) in 1952, in correspondence with similar groups in Australia and the United States. Within a year or so Fulton's well-produced periodical, *Flying Saucers,* had some five hundred subscribers. CSI created a nationwide network of observers and reporters, produced a great amount of written material, and promoted the concept of extraterrestrial intelligence in the news media. One member of CSI, Ronald Murray, managed an Auckland UFO bookshop. Fulton was an energetic and effective organizer and lecturer. But, when he was posted overseas for two years in 1959 the magazine and group went into recess, to be superseded by others. Nonetheless Fulton remained a pillar of the movement until his death in 1986. In the 1960s and 1970s he was the New Zealand representative of the now-defunct APRO (Aerial Phenomena Research Organization, headquartered in Tucson, Arizona), and later was director of the New Zealand branch of the Texas-based MUFON organization—by the 1980s the strongest scientific UFO group in both countries.

THEY KNEW TOO MUCH ABOUT FLYING SAUCERS

Two episodes in the 1950s saucerian golden age demand special attention: the Gray Barker–Harold Fulton–John Stuart riddle and the visit to New Zealand of contactee George Adamski in 1959. In 1956 the late Gray Barker (1925–1984), then a young UFO enthusiast in West Virginia, published his first book, *They Knew Too Much about Flying Saucers,* a trailblazer in the exploration of demonic counterpoints to saucerian "technological angels."[13] The book is chiefly concerned with the story of one Albert K. Bender, of Bridgeport, Connecticut, who until

1953 was director of a UFO club called the International Flying Saucer Bureau. After allegedly penetrating the secret of the saucers, Bender was, by his own account, visited by three men dressed in black suits who silenced him with threats and led him to terminate the bureau and its publication abruptly. Barker's narrative then goes on to relate other appearances of the men in black. This fearsome threesome, dressed soberly as undertakers and possessed of an uncanny knowledge of who had seen what, with their odd clockwork gait and mechanical-sounding voices, were now revealed to have phoned or made calls on a fair number of UFO percipients. In each case they made very clear that life would not go well for those who knew too much, or worse said or wrote too much, about UFO matters that did not concern them.

These heavies of the saucer scene fast became a part of UFO folklore everywhere. Among Barker's alleged silencing episodes were two in New Zealand, one involving Harold Fulton, the other John Stuart and Doreen Wilkinson of Hamilton. Stuart and Wilkinson were the principals of Flying Saucer Investigators of Hamilton. John Stuart wrote Barker of an incident of 1952 or 1953 and gave him permission to publish it. Here is Barker's rendition:

> John went to bed early that night, around 9:30. He wasn't asleep, though, when the telephone rang at 11:30, for he was trying to finish a book he had purchased a few days before.
>
> It was rather late for a telephone call, and there was almost annoyance in his voice when he answered it.
>
> "Are you John Stuart?"
>
> Yes, he replied that was correct.
>
> "You are the John Stuart who is interested in what Earth men call flying saucers."
>
> The voice put it more like a statement than a question. John noted an odd monotone about the voice, as if some kind of machine had learned how to talk.
>
> "You are quite correct," John answered. "Just what can I do for you?"
>
> "I warn you to stop interfering in matters that do not concern you!"
>
> John got angry. He appreciated a good joke as well as anyone, but not at any hour of the night.
>
> "Who is this?" he demanded.
>
> "I am ———— from another planet."
>
> John couldn't remember the name, which sounded unpronounceable. He replied to the voice with the New Zealand equivalent of "You and who else?"
>
> "You have been warned," the voice said. Then a click and the "otherworldly" conversation was terminated.
>
> John got up and poured himself a drink. . . ."[14]

This was merely the beginning, and John could still respond with a certain degree of grit and humor. Later there would be more—doorbells ringing when no one was there, moccasins walking by themselves, shuffling footsteps on the porch with no one visible. Then a nightmarish encounter, and an event so horrible it would be years before John Stuart could bring himself to tell the story. Doreen Wilkinson perhaps would never tell it, for Barker—who in this book only hints at what happened —said she was led to flee, "her mind in confusion." Stuart found the courage to relate a little more. He said he had a piece of metal that fell from a flying saucer. But it was claimed by a visitor. John added, "I have learned a lot about UFOs from this lad—oh yes he told me a lot— too much maybe, for my own personal safety."[15] At this Stuart abruptly gave up flying saucer work. However, he did finally allow Barker to publish his terrible tale.

Harold Fulton's story in *They Knew Too Much about Flying Saucers* is more modest than Stuart's, but, if Stuart's narrative is understated, Fulton's may have actually involved less than meets the eye in Barker's telling. With characteristic melodrama, Barker puts it like this:

> This may have nothing to do with flying saucers.
> It is a tale of abominable stenches and eldritch bangings in the night.
> It is a true story.
>
> You are Harold H. Fulton.
> It is with reluctance that you relate these personal experiences from your confidential file. After all, they may have nothing at all to do with Bender and his troubles, but you feel the story will not be complete without them.
> It is late afternoon, July 21, 1953, and you are busy taking care of CSI administrative details. You are all wool gathered, and your Siamese cat persists in making that odd growling noise, a sound that seems to come from somewhere deep within her insides. You investigate. She is on the window sill, deeply disturbed by something outside the window.
> You look. There is nothing there.
> You say, "Look, silly," pick her up and are going to hold her outside the window. The cat becomes terrified, and you realize she will attack you if you persist.
> As far as you know, there is nothing strange or terrifying outside the window. Though, come to think of it, you did detect a strange odor.
> You forget about it.

But on August 18 the same odor was there again, stronger and more unpleasant, and the cat again panicked at the idea of going out. A few nights later Fulton and his wife were awakened by a loud pounding on the outside of the house. As they roused from sleep, his wife saw an orange-pink glow near the door and screamed in fright, but, when Harold investigated, there was nothing.

Fulton had carried on an extensive correspondence with Gray Barker, as he did with UFO aficionados around the world. No doubt he had given Barker the raw material for this dramatic set of anecdotes. But Fulton himself did not concur in any extraordinary interpretation of the events. In the files of Fulton's correspondence now held by Murray Bott of Auckland, his successor as director of the New Zealand branch of MUFON, there is a carbon copy of a letter Harold Fulton sent Gray Barker dated August 6, 1956, and written just after Fulton had received a copy of *They Knew Too Much.* Fulton treated the matter with remarkable tact: "Although you have dramatised here and there, altered and added too a little, to create perhaps better continuity, all round you have done a remarkable piece of 'Who Done It' reporting, extremely readable and to those not in the act at the time, a most tantalizing mystery."

For an article of September 2, 1958, on Gray Barker's book, the tabloid newspaper *N.Z. Truth* "took the story to Mr. Fulton personally and asked him whether it was true. He said it was, in the main."[16] But more to the point, the second quarter 1957 issue of the CSI magazine, *Flying Saucers,* published "An Apology," in which, among other things, "Mr. Fulton also wishes to state most definitely that he is not withholding any sinister or dark secrets as may be strongly implied to some readers of Gray Barker's book, 'They Knew Too Much About Flying Saucers'; otherwise the chapter devoted to himself is reasonably accurate."[17]

Returning to the letter of August 6, 1956, from Fulton to Gray Barker, the former went on to suggest that the weird events Stuart faced may have been due more to personal problems than to alien intrigue. Referring to his invisible visitants (the doorbell ringing of itself, footfalls on the porch, above all the caller who retrieved the saucer piece and gave him certain firm admonitions), Fulton commented to Barker: "I personally interviewed and listened for two hours or more to his story. I came away not too impressed. (I had previously every confidence.) . . . I did not keep a copy of my conversation with him, but I have a letter he wrote me telling me briefly about his experiences prior to the interview. Still have this on file. He doesn't tell me about his visitor in the letter, only reiterates almost the same words used by Bender, with apparent similar effects and future intentions."

Nonetheless, there is reason to think something happened to John Stuart and Doreen Wilkinson. Some correspondence from this period that I have been able to see, but that is not presently available for publication, documents clearly that John Stuart believed in 1955 and 1956 that a terrible atrocity involving UFO occupants had happened to him and the woman. He had at first been able to regard the telephone call as a hoax and revealed that the book he had been reading late that evening was George Adamski's *Flying Saucers Have Landed*. But at the time as well as later he considered what happened next as certainly no joke. One correspondent referred to the events in Spiritualist terms as poltergeist phenomena—thus reaffirming the links we have perceived between Spiritualism and UFOism. But whatever it was, the dark side of the supernormal was clearly at work.

So deeply was Stuart—like Doreen—affected that evidently it was some time before he could bring himself to commit the story to paper and print. But in 1963 Gray Barker's Saucerian Press published Stuart's finally revealed full account of the events, *UFO Warning*.[18]

This eighty-two-page mimeographed volume tells a bizarre tale indeed. In 1953–1954, Stuart and a young woman, Barbara Turner (clearly Doreen Wilkinson), as "Flying Saucer Investigators," probed deeply into the UFO mystery. Although Stuart was married to someone else, the demands of this research required that he spend nearly every evening with Barbara, often until as late as 3 A.M. Needless to say, he had repeated occasion to complain of "evil-minded" rumors about the relationship. But the pair persisted until even more serious consequences intervened. They made important UFO sightings over Hamilton, and Stuart received the strange threatening phone call reported by Barker, from a robot-voiced entity with an unpronounceable name warning him to quit UFO work. Yet there was more that Stuart earlier did not—perhaps could not or dared not—recount to anyone. There were moments when Barbara, in Stuart's view under alien influence, became wantonly seductive despite the purely collegial nature of their association. This was a sign, Stuart thought, that the aliens' interest in the human race was for breeding purposes. John and "Barbara" talked about the danger she, as a woman, might be in. Then it happened. One evening, just after a saucer had hovered overhead, the couple encountered something they would much rather have avoided directly in back of Stuart's house. It was a hideous, stinking, hairy, web-footed, and conspicuously male entity. His face was "appallingly lecherous," and he advanced toward Barbara with obvious intent, somehow controlling the minds of the two so that neither could move. Then, inexplicably, he stopped, retreated, and disappeared. Barbara fell moaning into John's arms.

A few nights later, lying alone and undressed on her bed, the same woman was intruded on and raped by an invisible but otherwise identical version of the monster. Its presence was announced by the stench as before, its skin was very rough, and, when she could finally arise, she was covered with little scratches. After the thing left, a couple of small brownish circles about the size of a U.S. dime appeared on her body—a curious note, because small circles have been reported in other UFO abduction cases, as well as on medieval witches and others allegedly intimate with alien evil. Following this terrible occurrence, Barbara left town to stay with her mother. Stuart—this time as the result of a conversation with another attractive young woman friend—decided to give up UFOs and went to his mother's home in Auckland. Although, as his letters show, he did resume his studies somewhat, his "heart was not with it." Before long he got down his UFO notebooks, marked them "closed," and had no more to do with that devilish science save to publish his "Warning."

Although one interpretation of this grotesque affair is the Spiritualist's, psychoanalysts may have another perspective. Gray Barker doubtless connected it with the men in black and the rest of the UFO demonology that was something of a specialty of his. If UFOism was apocalyptic religion in the making, it fits for it to find room for both the children of light and the children of darkness, here and throughout the universe's vast seas of stars and worlds.

George Adamski

The next great event in the New Zealand flying saucer world was the lecture tour of the inimitable George Adamski in January–February 1959. Adamski was definitely aligned with the children of light among cosmic visitors. But the encounter with him both galvanized and deeply divided the UFO community in New Zealand. Adamski (1891–1965) was Polish born but lived most of his life in the United States. He was the most famous of all the early contactees, for whom the beings riding the UFOs bore divine wisdom to their earthly disciples. Those privileged ones, like Adamski, in turn dispensed it in books and from the lecture platform, together with lively accounts of their interworldly meetings and often their journeys in the UFOs to distant planets.

At the time of his adventure Adamski resided on the road to Mt. Palomar, the site of the famous observatory. He claimed that on November 20, 1952, he saw a UFO land and met Orthon, a man from Venus, on the California desert. More contacts followed, together with tours in spaceships and elevated discussions with beings from from various planets. All this was reported in books, especially *Flying Saucers Have Landed* (with Desmond Leslie, who contributed learned material on UFOs through the ages), and *Inside the Space Ships*.[19] These works, all reportedly composed with considerable ghostwriter assistance, were quite successful and gave Adamski celebrity status and innumerable opportunities for lectures, interviews, and television appearances.

By 1954, a year after the initial publication of *Flying Saucers Have Landed,* the Adamski enthusiasm reached New Zealand. His book sold well and was serialized in magazines, and advertisements appeared inviting interested people to write the author in California. In late 1954 Fred and Phyllis Dickeson of Timaru inaugurated a long UFO career by establishing the Adamski Flying Saucer Group, later the Adamski Correspondence Group. At their request Adamski agreed to make tapes, which were played at meetings in Timaru and Christchurch. (The tapes originally made for Timaru by Adamski and Desmond Leslie later became part of his permanent stock and were distributed worldwide.)[20] In the meantime, the Adamski Correspondence Group became successful and competed with Fulton's CSI for membership. In 1957 the Dickesons arranged with a newly formed Henderson (Auckland) group, under the Dutch-born Henk Hinfelaar, to organize North Island work; Timaru continued to manage South Island activities. Henk and Brenda Hinfelaar had been members of CSI since 1954 and were experienced UFO activists but were clearly moving in an Adamskian direction. The Hinfelaars produced a small newsletter independent of CSI for North Island Adamski Correspondence Group people, and the Dickesons did a southern version of the same. All this helped prepare for Adamski's 1959 visit to New Zealand but also paved the way for disillusionment.[21]

Already Adamski's critics were numerous, though perhaps the extent to which he and his claims struck most levelheaded people as outrageous was not yet appreciated in faraway New Zealand. The farfetched tale, the dubious look of the UFO photographs that adorned his publications, the insouciant self-contradictions, and the lack of the most elementary astronomical knowledge in much of what he said, repelled many. Reports surfaced that this was not the man's first foray into the profitably mysterious. During the 1930s he had operated an esoteric school called the Royal Order of Tibet. The cosmic philosophy of his UFO contacts was allegedly no more than a rehash of what he had retailed as that occult lodge's instruction.[22] An obscure science-fiction book he published in 1949 contains many striking parallels to what, amid the UFO excitement, he was able to market much more successfully a few years later as fact.[23] Despite the rivalry with the Dickeson's overtly Adamskian groups, Harold Fulton's early reaction to the Californian was reasonably tolerant.[24] But as time went on, and especially after Adamski himself actually appeared on the scene, the tone was much more critical. In the September 1959 issue of *Space Probe* (as the CSI magazine was now called; this was the final issue before it went into recess), Harold Fulton presented devastating attacks on Adamski's claims. The contactee still had his enthusiasts, however, and in any event he made news. Let us look at the accounts of his New Zealand tour.

January 1959 was an interesting month for news. Fidel Castro triumphed in Cuba, Pope John XXIII called his epoch-making ecumenical council, the *Polaris* missile found the earth to be pear shaped. A Canterbury University professor was quoted as saying that there may be conscious beings on other worlds, though they would not be people like us, and we should be prepared to meet them. Tucked among these items were stories about the visit to New Zealand of a man who said he *had* met them and they *were* like us.

The *Evening Post* (January 21, 1959) headlined the story, "Mr. Adamski Alights in N.Z.—From Conventional Plane." He was here, readers were told, for a four-week lecture tour. The visitor was greeted by news of a letter found in a bottle that had just washed up. The decanter had allegedly been thrown to sea by the crew of the *Joyita,* a ship that had disappeared without a trace in 1955, and the missive reported that all hands had been forced on board "a strange circular metallic object." Although the note rather sounds like someone's idea of a hoax, Adamski took it seriously and said the account was feasible.

The contactee then went on to talk about Venusian culture and religion (a "science of life" without temples), their desire to communicate with us, at least "through our minds." "But they say earthmen are so preoccupied with our own thoughts we are unable to receive impressions when they do send them." On Venus, however, religion is conveyed in educational institutions rather than churches, has to do with the power of mind over the body and relations with the cosmos, and is put into daily practice rather than once a week.

Adamski had other thoughts as well about the space friends. To sold-out lecture halls in the major New Zealand cities, he spoke of the Venusians as "exactly like us," but once added, "I have not been to Venus. If I do I will not come back. The ladies there are too beautiful." The Venusians, he said, have come to earth to observe, not to support any political or religious movement, though they are concerned about negative developments on the third planet.[25]

The January 31 *Post* juxtaposed the running Adamski story with an article on Carl Jung's work, *Flying Saucers: A Modern Myth of Things Seen in the Sky.* As we have noted, the great analytic psychologist opined that the saucer vogue was due to deep-level fears engendered by the atomic bomb and the cold war and by a corresponding desire to be rescued by "technological angels," a modern version of the heaven-descended gods and saviors of old. UFOs give us "a golden opportunity to see how a legend is formed and how in a difficult and dark time for humanity a miraculous tale grows up of an attempted intervention by extra-terrestrial 'heavenly' powers."[26]

An editorial, "Visitors from Outer Space," was skeptical of Adamski's humanlike Venusians but liberal on extraterrestrials and UFOs generally. The tone was remarkably reminiscent of the *Otago Daily Times* editorial that four decades before had greeted another sensational lecturer from overseas, calling his own beliefs a bit excessive and dogmatic, but endorsing more open-minded research in the areas of which he spoke. It was therefore appropriate that this editorial, without apparently being aware of the parallel, ended with a quote from Arthur Conan Doyle: "The wisdom of man is small, and the ways of Nature are strange, and who shall put a bound to the dark things which may be found by those who seek for them?"[27]

On February 6 a Tokoroa man reportedly took a clear picture of a UFO and said he would probably forward the photo to Adamski, "who would no doubt be pleased to study it to determine whether or not it would add confirmation to his theories." On February 9 the picture was reproduced in the paper. It was slightly hazy but did look like a UFO. The *Post* asked, somewhat facetiously, if the flying saucer people are following Mr. Adamski around. Adamski himself avowed that they were in his own account of his New Zealand tour, found in his last major book, *Flying Saucers Farewell.* He said that UFOs were sighted over Lake Taupo during his visit, seen by a Mr. W. Miller, "the local leader of the George Adamski Group," just after he had parted from Adamski. The lecturer added, "The spacecraft sightings seemed always to come at the right time to awaken public interest. This was one of the reasons we enjoyed overflow crowds at all the New Zealand lectures." Like earlier spiritual visitors to New Zealand, Adamski showed interest in Maori legend and faith. At Napier he spoke of the Pania statue and story, which we referred to in connection with the Spiritualistic Mrs. Cottrell. Adamski was excited to learn that several Maori boys had been taken on a ride in a spacecraft. (The *New Zealand Herald,* however, claimed he had confusedly taken an old Maori legend for current fact.)

Adamski's reception was decidedly mixed. His films of spaceships were declared unconvincing, and he sometimes met frank laughter and only moderate applause. But, for whatever reason, halls continued to be packed until his departure. However, Adamski found his New Zealand tour more successful than subsequent efforts in Australia and the United Kingdom, which were troubled by debate and alleged efforts to stop the showing of his film. Like Doyle, Adamski contrasted his New Zealand reception favorably with the rougher treatment he got across the Tasman, and (also like his predecessor) put New Zealand number one among nations, saying, "If I were a young man, choosing a new land in which to live, I believe I would select New Zealand."[28]

For all its oddity, the Adamski script contains the essential elements of a viable UFO religious movement and indeed of standard new religions generally. As C. G. Jung recognized, for the spiritually minded, UFOs can represent age-old otherworldly hopes (or, as for John Stuart, terrors), now ensconced in gleaming metallic vessels. Like cargo cults, they are classic religious eschatologies revamped to meet the fears and dreams of the modern world. Adamski took pains to distinguish between his contact experience and psychic, mediumistic, or ouija-board communication with the UFOnauts. Both sides, however, were there, as they must be: the initial definitive revelation, the ongoing more subjective commerce with the supernatural reality it launches.

There is also in Adamskism the important religious theme of a link with the past, that shows that, though the new faith may appear frail and precarious, it is really legitimated by a rich lineage. Thus Desmond Leslie, in his chapters in *Flying Saucers Have Landed,* makes much of saucers in Atlantis, ancient India, and medieval Europe, often using Theosophical texts like *The Secret Doctrine* as resources. In the New Zealand context, Adamski does much the same in referring to Maori lore, however inappropriately. Finally, Adamski's vaguely utopian evocations of life on Venus and elsewhere and the cosmic philosophy that underlies it offers some semblance, at least, of a prophetic message for earthlings. What is missing—and this no doubt explains why Adamskism never became a real religion—is any regular rite or institutional structure to give the faith vehicles for the long haul. But other UFO religions, all more or less inspired by Adamski's hour in the sun, have created these requisites, most often in the form of Spiritualistic mediums and circles through which UFO messages are continually received. Certain of these groups continue in New Zealand to the present.

UFOism after Adamski

Adamski came and went, but New Zealand saucerism continued. The year of his visit and of Harold Fulton's departure, 1959, was however understandably a watershed year for the movement. First, after the Adamski tour the Adamski Correspondence Groups, apparently at the instigation of the much-disappointed Dickesons, changed their name to New Zealand Scientific Space Research Groups (NZSSRG). The Adamski tour at least benefited UFO study; by 1961 there were some twenty-five NZSSRGs, from Kaikohe to Invercargill.

However, in 1961–1962 a rift emerged between the Hinfelaars and the Dickesons, over allegiance to Adamski. The Timaru group produced evidence that the California contactee's alleged photographs of Venusian spacecraft had been faked. The Henderson Adamski loyalists rejected such heresy and suggested among other things that the Dickesons "had not taken the refractive properties of Venusian glass into account."

In a personal letter, Phyllis Dickeson explained the appeal and the consequences quite effectively. On June 11, 1988, she wrote to me:

> The War [World War II] had highlighted man's inhumanity to man. Suddenly the F/S furore spread from the United States to the rest of the world. The George Adamski crusade hit New Zealand. We were confronted with G.A. and Desmond Leslie's book in 1954 . . . wherein readers were told of beautiful space friends coming from other planets, and living in peace and harmony, with love and understanding. To us the concept sounded wonderful to say the least. (How gullible we were.) However apparently, as you well know, this book aroused world wide interest. It did stir the hearts of many like ourselves. . . .
>
> . . . [But] in 1962 we were instrumental in doing an exposure of George Adamski, because we found our research had taken a new direction. Rather shattering at the time, but it was necessary, as we wished to find only the TRUTH in all matters concerned. Glaring inconsistencies were suddenly detected, when we saw for the first time . . . past photographs of spacecraft included in his two books. Careful study set us wondering if indeed we had been too gullible and conditioned into believing and accepting all we had been told by G.A. as gospel truth. No. 18–19 of SATCU mags goes into great detail of scientific tests we carried out. Incidentally we had both been photographers in the RNZAF and experience had taught us many things. . . .

After the schism, the southern group changed its title to New Zealand Scientific Approach to Cosmic Understanding (SATCU) and slowly set out to build a UFO network based on a middle ground between hard science and the contactee enthusiasts. For a time the Henderson camp dominated the New Zealand UFO world. But, as the 1960s wore on, its uncritically pro-Adamski stance tried the credulity of many followers. For one thing, Adamski had forcefully maintained that the moon, Mars, and Venus were all inhabited by humanlike beings of superior accomplishments. The mid-1960s Mariner probe of Mars and lunar landings made those claims exceedingly difficult to maintain, despite Hinfelaar's heroic efforts to reconcile them to Adamski and keep the faith.[29] By the end of the decade NZSSRG had notably declined (it was disbanded in 1974); SATCU's fortunes were soaring.

This group published New Zealand's leading UFO periodical after the 1950s, *Satcu,* called *Xenolog* from 1973 to 1981, when it ceased publication. *Satcu-Xenolog* presented UFO news, articles, and reviews representing diverse responsible points of view. Bruce Cathie's theories, for example, received considerable discussion. Early issues contained anti-Adamski, proscientific astronomy material. During the late 1960s and early 1970s several other New Zealand UFO groups appeared, but most lasted only a few years.

One exception is the Tauranga UFO Investigation Group, headed over many years by Harvey Cooke. Founded as an Adamski Correspondence Group in 1957, it has since become intellectually much more diversified and has organized New Zealand UFO conventions in 1972 and 1975.[30] The Cosmic Centre, in Whangarei, run by Ron Birch, published *Kosmon News* since 1971. This interesting paper combines UFO and Spiritualistic perspectives freely, interpreting the UFOnauts essentially as spirit communicators.[31]

A somewhat similar publication, now defunct, was *Heralds of the New Age,* a periodical (and group) from 1956 until about 1980. Its issues contained a lively mix of UFO, Spiritualist, and Theosophical ideas, speaking of the space vessels as vehicles of the masters, who also spoke directly via intuition or through channels here below. This literature also contained predictions of imminent cataclysmic events on earth, which would be part of the birth pangs of the New Age.

The Heralds of the New Age group exercised an extraordinary international influence on the development of UFO religion as they sent out their messages from the saucer world. Gordon Melton, in the *Encyclopedia of American Religions,* observed, "Even though located in New Zealand, it was the single most influential group even in North America" in the 1950s. The Heralds formed a mail network of persons interested in its sort of occultist UFO studies.

Among those who joined that circle was Gloria Lee, a young American psychic supported by a group called the Cosmon Research Foundation. She was guided by a being from Jupiter known only as J.W. He produced numerous writings through her hand, including two books, that contained much esoteric and eschatological material of Theosophical tone. In 1962 Lee went to Washington with the plans of a spaceship she said had been given her by J.W., submitted them and a model to government officials, and secreted herself in a hotel room to await a response. None came, and she commenced a fast. After sixty-six days she died. But Lee became a martyr in UFO circles; within two months, the Heralds of the New Age began to produce messages channeled from her, including a book, *The Going and the Glory.*[32] Their influence, however, gradually declined like that of other contactee groups in the 1960s.

The tangled history of New Zealand UFO organizations can be sorted out into three periods, dominated by three groups, as follows:

1. Civilian Saucer Investigation (N.Z.), 1952–1959, was Harold Fulton's group, in correspondence with John Stuart's Flying Saucer Investigators, and publisher of *Flying Saucers* and *Space Probe*.

2. After the 1959 Adamski visit, there appeared the NZSSRG (1960–c. 1970), divided into North and South Island branches, under Henk Hinfelaar and the Dickesons, respectively. Both initially published newsletters only. A rift developed between the two branches, the North being pro-Adamski and the South Island strongly critical after his 1959 visit, endeavoring to move in a more scientific direction. This was also a peak period for the Heralds of the New Age.

3. New Zealand Scientific Approach to Cosmic Understanding, 1961–c. 1981, was essentially a continuation of the South Island group above under the Dickesons, which became the major group as the North Island body faded in the early 1970s, reportedly after Mariner and other space probes made Adamski's universe increasingly untenable. SATCU published *Xenolog*, 1973–1981, a magazine previously published as *Satcu*.

Also in the late 1970s a New Zealand branch of MUFON, a U.S. organization, was established. It was headed by Harold Fulton until his death in 1986, then by Murray Bott. Mr. Bott oversees the investigative activities of MUFON members in New Zealand and assists members and others in study of the UFO phenomenon.

Although organizations came and went, public interest, often stimulated far more by lecturers and the media than by small groups for the devotee, followed its own cycles. By those cycles 1978 certainly represented a UFO peak. Indeed, 1978 was described in one New Zealand magazine as "The Year of the Flying Saucer."[33] And that was before the climactic event at the very end of that year, the remarkable Kaikoura sightings. But the saucerian wave was swelling well before December, and the mythology was there before the pilots' nocturnal observations and the radar and the films.

In 1978 the best-selling writer Erich von Daniken lectured in New Zealand and was a featured speaker at the Seventh World Conference of the Ancient Astronauts Society held in Auckland in July. This Swiss author, best known for his *Chariots of the Gods,* is the major popularizer of the ancient-astronauts idea that extraterrestrials visited the earth millenia ago and are behind such antique wonders as the pyramids of Egypt and Saharan and Mayan art that, according to this authority, may depict beings in space gear. After acknowledging that most experts find his theories highly unconvincing, von Daniken startled a Wellington audience with the observation that if a spaceship landed in that city today and the city was destroyed five thousand years later, archaeologists would never find out about the alien callers. Only the mythologists, presumably folk like himself, could trace such things as a visit from outer space.[34]

UFO mythology was clearly at work in New Zealand as he spoke. The *Evening Post* for April 22 noted that the nonfiction best-seller in the country was Bruce Cathie's *Pulse of the Universe,* and the top paperback *Close Encounters of the Third Kind.* Turning to the movie page, *Star Wars* is prominent, along with such typical 1970s apocalyptic fantasy as *The Antichrist, The Light at the Edge of the World, A Clockwork Orange, Logan's Run,* and of course *Close Encounters.*

The Aetherius Society

It was also in the year of the saucer that the most notable, and most apocalyptic, of UFO religious groups, the Aetherius Society, was established in New Zealand. The founder of Aetherius is now know as His Eminence Sir George King, O.S.P., Ph.D., Th.D., D.D., D.Litt., Prince of Santorini, Count of Florina, Metropolitan Archbishop of the Aetherius Churches, etc. But in 1954 he was simply George King, a London cabdriver living in a tiny flat, though like his mother a student of occult lore. Born in 1919, King had reportedly been a serious practitioner of yoga since 1944. One day in May of 1954, as he was cleaning his flat, words from space spoke to him: "Prepare yourself, you are to become the Voice of Interplanetary Parliament." His yogic training standing him in good stead, King now prepared himself and by the next year acquired the first, and most fundamental, of his many titles. He was Primary Terrestrial Mental Channel for the Venusian Master named Aetherius, and later for others as well in the Hierarchy of the Solar System. King founded the Aetherius Society in England in 1956 and in Los Angeles, where he now lives, in 1960. Branches are located in Michigan, Australia, and New Zealand.

Aetherius teaching asserts that the other planets of the solar system are inhabited, paradisal worlds, millions of years ahead of earth—ideas he could have picked up in the early 1950s from George Adamski. These other worlds, as the latter also asserted, are led by spiritual masters. Those wise ones collectively make up the Interplanetary Parliament and are now, through the Aetherius Society and its Primary Channel, attempting to help earth catch up. Here the apocalyptic features come in. In a great event, earth was initiated on July 8, 1964. The process, however, is far from complete. Our home planet is under attack by cosmic dark forces, and on the other hand we can look forward to the coming of a great Master in a UFO.

Although it is not based on a specific UFO encounter, the spacecraft are a significant part of the Aetherius mystique. The religion is obviously grounded in the UFO enthusiasm of the early 1950s, and its literature contains frequent references to flying saucers. They are said to be envoys of Interplanetary Parliament, and the coming Master will arrive in one. Aetherians often talk about UFOs and use interest in the mysterious objects as drawing cards. The pictures of UFOs and accounts of spacemen in Aetherius writings are clearly based on Adamski's works.

Indeed, like the Adamski teachings, Aetherius can be thought of as apocalyptic Theosophy. Theosophical classics like *The Secret Doctrine* loom in the background; common theosophical ideas like karma, reincarnation, the etheric plane, and ancient occult wisdom are conspicuous; the planetary masters seem more than anything else updated versions of the Theosophical. But, significantly, the 1950s contactee literature and the Aetherius channelings convey—in the wake of the atomic bombs and amid the excitement of UFO sightings—an apocalyptic mood of imminent crisis and catastrophic change, accompanied by signs and wonders and superhuman saviors.

The main work of the Aetherius Society has been operations related to the initiation of earth and repelling cosmic evil forces, under the guidance of the hierarchy. These activities have characteristically sported military titles: Operation Starlight, Operation Bluewater, Operation Prayer Power. Described as intense spiritual pushes, they have consisted of charging mountains, ocean areas, or objects with psychic energy at strategic spots. The Aetherius Society's small but dedicated army and navy of the spirit has thereby carried the unknowing earth through crisis after crisis, by means of concentrated power focused in the right direction. Often these feats of unseen combat have involved heroic and adventurous ascents of major peaks, and forays far out to sea.

The society sponsors a number of other activities. It runs a health-food store and practices frequent spiritual healing, which is done by laying on of hands and assisting patients in "recharging" by visualizing their *cakras* as luminous and vibrant. The society also conducts regular Sunday religious services, with music, prayer, chanting, and instruction. Its small but attractive temples are well ornamented with the symbols of various religions and momentos, including photographs, of the founder and the great, much-remembered operations. Spiritual healing practices are also important in the services.

At the time of writing, the principal figure in the New Zealand Aetherius Society, with its some twenty members and its headquarters in Auckland, is Margaret Kilbey. She states that she first encountered Aetherius in 1978, when Richard Lawrence, European headquarters' secretary, came out from England to lecture about it. His lectures deeply moved her and led her to think that Aetherius put together much she had felt before but did not fully understand. She was led to establish the New Zealand temple, opened in 1982. She has found particularly important the Aetherius Society's taking a spiritual view of life in other parts of the universe. Extraterrestrials are not only there; they also try to help us, making the universe alive and a unity, she states.

In 1987 the society in New Zealand launched a campaign with an open phone line for people who had seen flying saucers. There were many, many responses, some very good, but often conveyed confidentially. Every two years the group makes a pilgrimage to Mt. Wakefield, near the base of Mt. Cook, for an outdoor prayer gathering. Wakefield is one of the nineteen crystalline-structure mountains that were charged by King and the Aetherius Society with special energy. (Margaret Kilbey wears a necklace made of stones from all nineteen.) Mt. Wakefield, therefore, is a holy spot for New Zealand Aetherians; many believers claim to have spotted UFOs during the society's pilgrimages there.[35]

Recent UFO Contacts

Other UFO contacts persist. In 1988 I received information by phone from a gentleman in northern New Zealand who told me he has a small circle that meets twice a month to receive messages from UFO entities. These are obtained by the not-unusual method of going around the circle, each person adding from his or her own inspiration a few more sentences of the message, which is carefully transcribed. Recently, he said, communications have been coming most frequently from a figure called Voltran, said to be a common voice in such assemblies. My informant said that Voltran came to him first early one morning when he was just waking up, a time of exceptional receptivity; the recipient immediately wrote down what his extraterrestrial mentor told him. The medium did not start receiving these messages until he had moved as an adult, to New Zealand, but even before he had been visited by very peculiar, vivid dreams and impressions; he had deliberately undertaken psychic development until the strange levels of awareness took the form of explicit communication from beyond earth. The content of these messages is characteristic. There is much cosmic philosophy, together with warnings of impending disaster if humankind does not change; we are at a point at which we must either move up to a higher spiritual level or face catastrophe. A valid perception, no doubt, of the human situation as we enter the twenty-first century, one for which the UFO enthusiasm of the twentieth seems both symptom and tonic.

The New Zealand UFO saga continues. In June 1988 a headline story in *N.Z. Truth* reported the belief of an Otago University senior lecturer that "a fleet of war-damaged spacecraft . . . may have exploded over Otago hundreds of years ago," causing the Tapanui crater. The same source proposed that New Zealand could build its own spacecraft and steal a march on the rest of the world. November 1988 brought the latest stellar international writer and lecturing UFO contactee to New Zealand in the form of Whitley Strieber, author of *Communion* and *Transformation.* In January 1989 a UFO over Wellington was widely reported in the press. That was followed by a hoax—which took in some people—on radio 89FM reporting a UFO had landed on Mt. Eden in Auckland. Several UFO channeling groups advertised in New Age venues. In April 1989 the press reported a new group for telepathic communication with UFO beings, Outer Space Connections, established by Daisy and Owen Kirkby of West Auckland; an advertisement that asked, "Are you interested in communication with alien beings or intelligence?" drew forty-seven people to the initial meeting.[36]

Perhaps the UFO appeal was best put in a letter from Phyllis Dickeson, widow of the late Fred Dickeson, long the editor of *Xenolog.* Speaking of their early involvement in the cause, she wrote: "Both Fred and I had been brought up in rigid religious beliefs of Church and its traditional limits, where we often wondered, but didn't always ask questions—we just accepted, and so it was that Life took on a whole new meaning—New horizons, a challenge, other inhabited worlds and Earth being visited by superior alien beings. We were elated. There were just so many questions and we wondered how we could help."[37]

4 The Ancient Wisdom and the New Age
Theosophy in New Zealand

Of all the new and unconventional spiritual movements in the English-speaking world in the last couple of centuries, none has had a more pervasive—if often indirect—influence than Theosophy. In New Zealand the Theosophical Society has been second to none in this league for membership, stability, and overall influence. Until after the Second World War Theosophy and Spiritualism were virtually alone as alternative faiths for the Pakeha population, and the lively new generation of alternatives spawned in the 1960s owes much of its success to Theosophy's pioneering role. It was the first voice in the country on behalf of drawing wisdom from the East as well as the West, karma and reincarnation, spiritual evolution and the role of masters.

Theosophy came in the wake of Spiritualism. Helena Blavatsky, on the quest that was to result in the formation of the Theosophical Society, came to the New World in 1873 because it was the homeland of the spirit faith, but the movement she and Henry Olcott inaugurated two years later was not entirely of the same stamp. Both, to be sure, saw themselves as new lights for a new spiritual era, both made much of commerce between this world and largely invisible spirits or masters, both were awake to progressive concerns and the unfolding liberal climate of the century in religion and society alike.

But the climate was not the same. Spiritualism was a movement largely of proletarian origins and constituency—the Fox sisters and Mrs. Harris-Roberts—even if it sometimes drew the fancy of journalists (like W. C. Nation, Chantry Harris, and Olcott) or aristocrats like those D. D. Home courted. Theosophy, on the other hand, attracted a solid core of middle-class business and professional people, together with a generous sprinkling of very well-placed supporters. Its general level of education and of savoir-faire was above that of the older faith.

This is manifest not only in Theosophy's ability to create enduring and prosperous institutions, physically evidenced in its monumental edifices in Auckland and Wellington, but also by the tenacity of many of its adherents, who constructed what for some decades amounted to nothing less than a Theosophical subculture in New Zealand.

Spiritualism, to be sure, had its indomitable W. C. Nations, Harris-Roberts, and Conan Doyles. But, compared to Theosophy, its birds of passage appear to have been in larger flocks and flightier. In no small part this is probably because of Spiritualism's greater dependence on the vagaries of immediate phenomena. Although Theosophists kept alive the lore of their founders' remarkable interactions with the Masters of the Wisdom, the focus was far more on books and the ideas in them. They read voraciously in such demanding works as *Isis Unveiled* and *The Secret Doctrine*. They devoted evening after evening to the lecture hall and the seminar room, whether or not one of the masters passed through to precipitate a letter or leave his turban on the table.

The intellectual and institutional orientation inevitably meant that Theosophy looked to sources other than Spiritualism, with its relative poverty in these areas. For ideas it drew from the whole nineteenth-century occult revival, including such writers well known to Blavatsky as Eliphas Lévi and Edward Bulwer-Lytton. (The latter's occult novels, such as *Zanoni*, had a discernible effect on the esoteric creativity of the Russian lady, and by a strange coincidence or karmic connection, when she and Olcott made their pilgrimage to India in 1880, the viceroy was none other than the novelist's son, the poet and Romantic imperialist Lord Lytton.)

For structure Theosophy found ready resources in the century's fascination with secret, initiatory degree lodges, Masonic and other, which characteristically laid claim to ancient confidential wisdom transmitted through its formulas to the worthy. Sometimes that assertion was not one taken very seriously, but Theosophical lodges really believed in their deposit of truth—and in their call to make it not secret but public. Nonetheless on various levels the lodge image has helped define Theosophy.

Edward Toronto Sturdy

Several of these themes came together in the first New Zealand lodge, founded in Wellington in 1888 by Edward Toronto Sturdy (1860–1957). Sturdy was rightly called by Olcott the father of Theosophy in New Zealand, despite the lack of immediate success in his efforts. His magazine lasted only four issues, and the Wellington Lodge was inactive by the end of 1889, though it was rechartered in 1894.

Sturdy's labors offer an interesting glimpse of the sort of persons and circumstances out of which colonial occultism emerged.

Sturdy came to New Zealand at age nineteen. He settled near Woodville, twenty miles from Palmerston North, in what was then virtually unsettled bush country. It was apparently in this idyllic setting that the first glimmerings of the mystical truth he was to find in Theosophy reached him. He later wrote: "It was the solitude and beauty of the mountains and forests among which I wandered so much, sometimes for weeks without seeing a human being, that helped to bring me from the ignorance of science to seek insight elsewhere. What I have, I owe largely to H. P. Blavatsky, to some extent to Anna Kingsford and Edward Maitland [English Theosophists], and perhaps, most of all, to the Vedanta and Buddhist teachings. . . ."[1]

There were also books in that solitude. In an important reminiscing letter dated October 28, 1945, and published in *Theosophy in New Zealand,* E. T. Sturdy mentions W. H. Terry, the Australian Spiritualist editor, saying, "I was a regular purchaser of books from him. Books that could be found nowhere else south of the Line." However, he goes on to say:

> But even in those early days the New Zealand bookshops carried lots of serious reading, people living thinly scattered being inclined to read standard books. E.g., I bought the two volumes of Schopenhauer's *The World as Will and Idea* in Napier. It is a book that I find has stopped many people upon their path, emphasised their agnosticism and checked their aspiration. Thomas Hardy was one of these, and his books are tinged with its influence upon him, which he did not deny. I was present at a discussion between Swami Vivekananda and Professor Deussen [a famous European scholar of the Upanishads], head of Kiel University, in which the former pointed out that blind will was a contradiction in terms, for before you can will—or desire—you must *know.*[2]

It was not the pessimistic German, however, but the *Bhagavad Gita,* that piqued Sturdy's theosophical interest. He wrote:

> I first heard of The Theosophical Society through a great friend, Edward Bold, who was inspector of telegraphs at Hawkes Bay in 1884. I communicated with Adyar, and I think my diploma of membership was dated 1885. . . . I had come upon a very old translation of the Bhagavad Gita made in the time of Warren Hastings [eighteenth century]. Bold and I used to study it together. In 1886 I determined to visit India, as Adyar could give me a footing there and bring me into touch with learned Hindus. I felt that in the 'Gita' there was teaching I had been seeking for long.[3]

E. T. Sturdy was indeed admitted to the society in 1885, and the following year traveled to India.[4] But when he arrived at Adyar in 1886, he found that Olcott was on a tour in Rajputana. He made his way there, caught up with the international president of the society, and traveled with him for a time. Sturdy then went on to England, where he saw much of Helena Blavatsky and her circle. Finally he returned to New Zealand by way of New York and San Francisco, in the course of his journey meeting W. Q. Judge and other prominent American Theosophists. He was thus well prepared to inaugurate work in the South Pacific colony. In this connection he wrote:

> Hitherto I had lived in Woodville, Hawkes Bay, and in that thinly populated bush where there were few indeed that could be approached with the great truths which H.P.B. had set before the world afresh. I went to Wellington and started a small symposium there. It had the sympathy of many of the leading thinkers there —Sir Harry Atkinson, Judge Richmond, Dr. MacGregor and others. . . . A small magazine was started, called *Hestia* (the goddess of the hearth fire, i.e., of domestic life), which I edited.[5]

Sturdy did indeed inaugurate a flurry of Theosophical activities in Wellington in 1888. His symposium was as distinguished as he indicates, and his magazine *Hestia,* later *The Monthly Review,* described on the title page as "A Magazine Devoted to the Teachings of the Ancient Sages and the Study of Philosophy and Science," was a remarkable effort in that lofty direction for a setting like New Zealand in 1888. But at the end of 1888 these endeavors were interrupted when Sturdy, for unexplained reasons, was suddenly "called Home" and departed for England, never to return to New Zealand. Back in England, he became an active part of Blavatsky's inner group until her death in 1891 but resigned from the society in 1894 to work independently.[6] As his correspondence shows, he in no way gave up enthusiasm for Theosophical ideas, though he seems to have felt the organization had become excessively sectarian in character.

Hestia

Four issues of Sturdy's magazine, *Hestia,* came out between June and September 1888, published by Edwards and Company, Printers and Publishers, Brandon Street, Wellington. The cover contained, in addition to the subtitle already cited, a quotation from Goethe:

> Arise, oh child, and bathe your earthly senses
> In yonder fountain of eternal light.

There was also a peculiar symbol: a sun surrounded by three concentric circles and a six-pointed star made up of two triangles. The premier issue begins with a note to the reader explaining the title "Hestia," "the sacred fire of the hearth" of the Greeks—"the fire which must be kept always burning. By this is signified the inner light or consciousness." Keepers of this flame, Sturdy continues, were such as "Christ, Buddha, Zoroaster, Plato, Pythagoras." Several lines of the *Bhagavad Gita* are quoted. Like those men, who often simply asked the great questions as much as answered them, *Hestia* seeks not to proselytize for any dogmatic system but rather to

> collate then, for those who, having no fixed belief, yet long to *know:* and who, involved in the continual rush of our nineteenth century life, have little time or opportunity to study those subjects which might bring them peace or satisfaction. Hence this magazine, will amongst some original writing, and scientific notes, have a large proportion of its pages devoted to abstracts from the works of those great ones, who have in all ages, in different parts of the world, been able to lift themselves above the turmoil of the external life, and from their exalted standpoints to see and to understand.

Hestia made good this fairly modest promise. The first issue contained a summary of scientific information about the cell, taken from "various writers on biology," the concluding paragraphs of Emerson's essay of "Heroism," "An Appeal for the Brute Creation, Attributed by Ovid to Pythagoras," which called for vegetarianism, a brief discussion of the Buddha's Four Noble Truths apparently by the editor, a similar piece on the Greek Mysteries, and a few paragraphs "In Memoriam" for Dr. Anna Kingsford, the distinguished British Theosophist and crusader on behalf of animal welfare whose death had just been reported. Subsequent issues follow a comparable format but are enlivened by controversial correspondence, especially on Spiritualism, and by a growing use of explicitly Theosophical materials.

Hestia was less than a rousing success. In November 1888 it was succeeded by *The Monthly Review.* The opening page of that periodical, again titled "To the Reader," minced no words in explaining what was going on. Sturdy writes:

> Six months ago a magazine was brought out in Wellington under the name of "Hestia." It was to be an organ for the interchange of ideas on all questions relating to religion, philosophy and science, and with a distinct intention of upholding the highest ethical standard. These motives were set forth in the first number, and also represented upon the cover. Owing, however, to certain misappre-

hensions—partly with reference to the name, which was disapproved by some, partly regarding certain symbols which appeared on the cover, misunderstood by others—many of those who evince a strong interest in philosophical and scientific subjects withheld their support and awaited further developments. The work of the magazine was hence thrown almost entirely upon the shoulders of the editor, and he having a distinct leaning towards mysticism and Eastern philosophy, tinged the magazine more and more with his personal bias. This was never contemplated at the beginning, and was a departure from the original lines. . . . [But] at length a committee representing many different schools came forward, making certain recommendations and offers of co-operation.

The result, *The Monthly Review,* was indeed a magazine of wider scope, mixing the Hestian program with articles on such topics as "Recollections of Corsica," "The Frozen Meat Trade," and "The Revolution in Brazil." But *The Monthly Review,* which first appeared on the eve of Sturdy's return to England, lasted only until December 1890.

The Wellington Lodge

The group Sturdy assembled in Wellington, and those who became members of the society in 1888 or, for the most part, in 1889 (fifteen or so persons) were an interesting assemblage. The first Wellington member to join (November 1888) was Edward Tregear, a man of many parts who was to become well known as a poet, Maori scholar, and architect of many of the 1890s social reforms. The next year Bessie Tregear, his wife, joined. 1889 also brought the membership of Sir Harry Atkinson, the prime minister, his wife, Anne Elizabeth (Richmond) Atkinson, and their son E. Tudor Atkinson.[7] An ecumenical note, much treasured by Theosophists, was provided by the adherence of the Jewish rabbi, M. van Staveren, and his wife, and the Maori *tohunga* Henry Matthew Stowell (Hare Hongi). In his 1945 letter, Sturdy recounts of those days:

> In 1886 I went to India and never lived much in Woodville on my return, but lived in a hut on the outskirts of Wellington. I edited Hestia there. After I was called Home it became Monthly Review. . . . Edward Bold was a great friend of mine. He died suddenly of ptomaine poison, through tinned salmon. He was a convinced spiritualist and his wife a medium. His home was at Hastings. . . . I knew everybody, the Premier Atkinson, Judge Richmond, and many others, and without vanity I may say they all listened to me, were nearly all broadminded, for these ideas from the East were World Ideas, fresh, not distorted, and nothing in them contradictory to the best in Christianity.[8]

HARRY ATKINSON

One suspects that the susceptibility of Harry Atkinson (1831–1892), the prime minister, to Theosophy was related to his very active Freemasonry (in contrast to lukewarm churchmanship), an involvement he shared with his governor, Lord Onslow, and with many colonial and imperial statesmen of their stamp. Masonry, with its paradigms of lodges, initiations, and the existence of ancient spiritual wisdom outside the Judeo-Christian revelation, offered an excellent preparation for Theosophy; for someone like Atkinson, the latter might have at first seemed little more than an advanced level of "speculative" Masonry.

At the same time, his biographer tells us that the prime minister was an eminent collector of fads both philosophical and political and a man of many curious interests and ideas, despite a rather distant public presence and a reputation for a gruff if not pugnacious manner. We learn also that, rather unusually for the time, as a child in England he was encouraged by his family to visit all the churches in his Cheshire neighborhood and choose his own; he selected the Anglican.[9] He was an advocate of temperance and women's votes and was said to have socialist leanings—all causes with which most Theosophists would have been sympathetic—though in Atkinson's case support for reform in principle was tempered by fiscal conservatism. Because Atkinson died in 1892, it is uncertain whether his interest in Theosophy would have survived the stage in which it might have been only one of his fads.

EDWARD TREGEAR

Perhaps a more interesting and convoluted case was Edward Tregear (1846–1931).[10] Reportedly he was deeply embittered with the conventional churches for personal reasons owing to their opposition to divorce. He is described as a freethinker and socialist. At the same time, the progressive idealism of the Theosophical Society must have appealed to the man who was a leading theoretician and apologist, and sometime secretary of labor, for the celebrated reformist cabinet of the 1890s. A probable connection with his Maori studies exists as well. Tregear's 1885 book, *The Aryan Maori,* had advanced the thesis that the Maori were of Aryan race, whose language and folklore proved them descended from a pastoral Indo-European people, but who had left India about four thousand years ago.[11] This work contributed to an emerging Maori myth, that this people were Caucasian, probably from India, heroic, intellectual, great navigators, and covert monotheists. The hypothesis would fit well with the Theosophical teaching that the widely dispersed Aryan or Fifth Root Race is currently dominant, having displaced the Atlantean, Lemurian, and earlier root races.

However, Tregear's later and better-regarded contributions to Maori scholarship, such as his most important, the 1891 *Maori-Polynesian Comparative Dictionary*, make less of the Aryan connection. (In his 1904 *The Maori Race*, Tregear grants the Maori are Polynesian, though he speculates that they may have come from or passed through India on their way to the South Seas.) There is also no evidence of his involvement in the Theosophical Society after the demise of the 1888–1889 Wellington Lodge. One suspects that his nascent Theosophy may have been snuffed out by the formidable Max Müller's disapproval of the movement; that world-renowned Orientalist and comparative linguist was clearly a hero to Tregear, who cited him with appreciation in his philological studies and who went so far as to dedicate his *Maori-Polynesian Comparative Dictionary* (1891) to the great comparative philologist.[12]

Nonetheless, Tregear's bout with Theosophy enjoyed a curious afterlife in a novel he published in 1895, *Hedged with Divinities*.[13] Like many other fantastic social novels of the 1890s, it combines expansive vision with cloisterish moral values. It moreover doubtless reflects Tregear's own pilgrimage through Theosophy, Maori studies, and social reform, for the tracks of these pursuits are evident. Thus, although clumsily written and of minimal literary value, *Hedged with Divinities* says something about both the man and the times.

The protagonist, Jack, betrothed to a lovely and high-principled young woman named Nelly, is in search of wisdom. In the course of this quest he meets in India an old Hindu sage who imparts to him learning of a distinctly Theosophical type and jargon. The pandit refers to masters, spiritual evolution, and the *devachan*, a Theosophical term for the heavenly after-death state. But this learning, though acknowledged, does not satisfy Jack's quest.

Jack continues his pilgrimage in Bali and the South Seas and then returns to New Zealand, where he is met by Maoris in the less exalted but still mystic atmosphere of the Humming House. He is wounded by a stingray and put to sleep for three years by an old priest. When he awakes and makes his way to Auckland, Jack is surprised to find that on a certain day during his long sleep all males in the world but he have died of some sudden plague. He is the sole man left, alone of all his sex in a world of women. In the city mobs of women, many ravishingly beautiful and passionately ardent, besiege him relentlessly. But the civic duty for the preservation of the human race, which might have impressed itself on some males under the circumstances, seems not to cross his brow. He has thoughts only for Nelly and for making the now-chaotic unisexual society into a smoothly running commonwealth. He busies himself with appointing committees and organizing work brigades until all tasks but one formerly wrought by males are now being well-performed by the other sex.

Jack is made king, but refrains from dealing with the progeny problem until he has found and consulted with Nelly, his betrothed, and until the all-female government has passed and presented to him for the royal assent a bill legalizing, for his sole benefit, polygamy. He signs only reluctantly, for he wants nothing more than to settle down monogamously with Nelly, but Jack now sees clearly what a man must do and is not one to evade responsibility. Nelly is outraged at first but comes around. Thus, finally, twenty wives are installed in a sort of hotel, each with a royal court of her own, and the next spring, to great rejoicing, the cries of baby boys (as well as girls) begin to be heard. Then, his obligations met, Jack plots with Nelly to leave all and sail off to a tiny island he knows of near Fiji, where they can "create a paradise."

This work has several motifs of interest both to the understanding of Theosophy and the larger themes of this book. First, it is one in a slim but significant series of stories—one thinks also of Samuel Butler's *Erewhon* and Aldous Huxley's *Ape and Essence*—that encapsulate the New Zealand myth. These scenarios postulate New Zealand as (a) the one place where a radical, utopian social experiment is most likely to succeed, (b) the last redoubt of humanity after some global catastrophe, or (c) both together. The myth is far from dead. New Zealand has its share of utopias, and the image of the whole country as a sort of utopia is still widespread abroad. Hardly a year passes, I am told, that a number of survivalists from overseas do not immigrate to New Zealand, in the expectation it will be the best place to ride out the nuclear or environmental apocalypse they foresee.

Tregear's work is clearly of type *c*. After the male holocaust, the thing to do is to get organized and create a well-oiled social machine, before such a disruptive force as sex can be allowed to rear its head, even when there is as desperate a need for its fruits as in this case. Before that need can be met, all must be made legal, and the forthcoming babies well planned for, in—one is tempted to say—an ideal Plunket Society sort of sterilized and socialized world. (Even so, an even better sort of paradise, just for Jack and Nelly, is envisioned elsewhere in the fulfillment of yet another and perhaps competing dream, that of the return to the primitive in the "island near Fiji.")

This novel, together with much of 1890s Theosophy and of 1890s culture generally, is given a dimension of depth by consideration of what Jill Roe, in her wonderful history of Theosophy in Australia, has called "Legends of the Nineties."[14] In its inner life that decade combined a fascination with lost civilizations and continents (Lemuria and Atlantis), with utopianism (Bellamy, Butler, and others), intense social idealism, women's rights, late Romantic aestheticism (Oscar Wilde and others), occultism (the Golden Dawn), and arts and crafts (Pre-

Raphaelitism to art nouveau). Many of these motifs were woven into the Theosophical fabric. In Australia particularly the theme of the lost continent of Lemuria was popular; this is understandable, because that forgotten land of the Third Root Race was held to have incorporated the island continent, and New Zealand as well. Not a few popular novels developed the theme, often discovering ominous or utopian survivors of the lost race in some obscure corner of the mysterious outback.[15] Theosophists in Australia and New Zealand also explored Lemuria—largely their creation as a place of spiritual significance[16]—to find there a usable past, and a primordial precursor of the new Sixth Root Race civilization some said was under preparation in the two young and forward-looking dominions.

The idealism of the 1890s about faithful love and duty to the world alike—so earnest in Tregear's awkward novel as to bring a smile to our jaded lips—must also be taken seriously if the decade and its manifestations are to be understood. The eminent Australian-born classicist Gilbert Murray and his wife of some seventy years, the former Lady Mary Howard, exemplified the spirit of the decade superbly in their 1890s courtship and marriage. Their austere, high-minded radicalism, cocooned by social propriety and Oxbridge ivy, could hardly be mistaken for the Romantic revolutionary style of an earlier era, or the post-Freudian conflation of sexual and social liberation of a later one.

A biography of Murray cites love letters from Lady Mary to him that contain real-life expression of sentiments that could well have been uttered by Tregear's Jack and Nelly: ". . . You will influence me every day as I grow to love and understand you better and better. Our love is not for ourselves alone but for humanity. . . . I love you as a believer would love her Christ. It seems too good to be true, the life that lies before us. . . . Oh my peerless Galahad, my maiden knight, I love you. . . . Let us help each other to make his or her life an intense flame of passionate, loving service, seeking truth and beauty and bearing them to those who do not know them."[17]

Continence as straitlaced as Jack's was embodied in the same set of chivalric ideals as true love and social service and embarked on with as much singleness of heart. The myth of the 1890s, like so many others, was shattered, for too many at Gallipoli or in Flanders' fields. But an elite of 1890s youth and some of their elders believed they were a new generation setting out, after self-preparation through moral discipline and fidelity to true love, to remake the world for the better, by advancing social reform and women's rights, art for art's sake, or the recovery of ancient wisdom—and for Theosophists these were all somehow one quest.

The Auckland Lodge

After the first Wellington Lodge's rise and demise, the next important Theosophical event was the founding of the Auckland Lodge in 1892. It included among its early members such important figures in subsequent New Zealand Theosophy as Mr. and Mrs. William Henry Draffin, Charles William Sanders, and Lilian Edger. Lilian Edger (1862–1941) was among the most remarkable of New Zealand Theosophists. The daughter of a well-known maverick liberal minister in Port Albert and Auckland, the Reverend Samuel Edger, she had a brilliant university career at Canterbury College, receiving scholarships in Latin, English, and mathematics, and was the second New Zealand woman to take a B.A. degree (her sister Kate Edger was the first) and the first to receive an M.A.[18] When she came to Auckland in 1886 after completing the university course, she opened a secondary school for girls in the old family house on Ponsonby Road, and had the upper story beautifully remodeled for the purpose.[19]

Although her fairly extensive books, lectures, and letters appear to reveal little of a genuinely personal nature about her interest in Theosophy, she joined the society in October 1891 in Auckland, was president of the Auckland lodge in 1896, and in 1896, when the New Zealand section was formed, she served as the first general secretary 1896–97. This tour of duty was cut short by an unexpected occurrence. The general secretary of the Australian section, J. C. Staples, died suddenly, and the fresh New Zealand section secretary went over to help with interim administration. There she met Henry Olcott, the president-founder, who had also come to Australia to assist in the time of need. They toured both Australia and New Zealand together, lecturing in all the lodges; those months, she wrote much later, "were amongst the happiest of my life. It is difficult, nay impossible, to put into words all that they meant to me. . . . We had not been together long when he decided that I should go to Adyar with him."[20] This she did.

The sixth and final volume of Henry Steel Olcott's *Old Diary Leaves,* covering 1896–1898, is full of Lilian Edger. There is little limning of her personality, no unforgettable word portraits such as he earlier in the series gave the inimitable Helena Blavatsky. But then as the project advances one senses the colonel wearying a bit and holding himself to bare chronicle. In any case, few subjects call as insistently for vivid writing as Blavatsky. One almost instinctively perceives in Lilian Edger instead a personality more serious and steady than dramatic or charismatic, the ideal second-generation leader or bureaucrat of a movement, coming in at the moment of what Max Weber would call the "routinization of charisma," and that is exactly what Lilian Edger was and did.

Yet, even the sober successor to the apostles can have his or her day, or night, and one is glad that Olcott chose to include this possibly quite telling incident on board ship to India in 1897:

> Among other amusements to relieve the tedium of the voyage there was a fancy dress ball on the evening of the 27th November which Miss Lilian Edger, M.A., etc., attended in the character of 'Night.' Her black dress besprinkled with stars and a crescent moon on her head, together with the excitement of the ball made her look very well from the human point of view if not from that of the university graduate. I confess that I was very pleased with her dissipation for it showed that there was the usual quota of human nature beneath the shell of collegiate enamel.[21]

Olcott does also speak finely of her lectures at Adyar and elsewhere, saying that, "as Miss Edger proceeded, her audience was drawn nearer to her and she seemed to communicate to them some of her own depth of earnestness when she strove to impress on their minds that, as religion was of the greatest moment to everyone, they should strive to make their religion purer and broader. . . . With a clear and well modulated voice and wonderfully sustained earnestness, she impressed her hearers with the sincerity of her convictions. . . . The thing that most moved and held the attention of her audiences was not her oratory, for in that she was not to be compared with Mrs. Besant [though as Olcott asks elsewhere, how many could be so compared?], but the tone of candor and unpretentious earnestness with which she elaborated her themes, and the commonsense way in which she showed how the ideas of Theosophy ought to enter into the lives and control the conduct of people. . . . She was more didactic than oratorical."[22]

Lilian Edger gave the Adyar convention lectures in 1897 and toured India, visiting most of the Indian lodges, with Olcott in 1898. In recollections written much later, she engagingly describes the memorable experiences of this tour, which often involved travel by primitive means in places where Europeans were seldom seen and their requirements poorly understood, but all was lightened by the forethought and good humor of "the Colonel."[23] Edger stayed in India to work for Theosophy in various capacities. She assisted Annie Besant at her new Central Hindu College in Benares, served as principal of a girls' school there 1913–1919, and was tutor to the sons of a maharaja 1919–1929; she finally retired to New Zealand in 1938. She wrote several books, including *Theosophy Applied* and *Elements of Theosophy*. At the time of her death in 1941, Miss Edger had been a Theosophist longer than anyone else in New Zealand.

Her niece Geraldine Hemus, also an active Theosophist, joined in

1898. Miss Hemus was an educator, as well as having been credentialed as a solicitor as early as 1906. She was among the founders of the Theosophical Vasanta School in Auckland. In 1938 she was elected president of the Auckland branch of the National Council of Women of New Zealand. Lilian Edger and Geraldine Hemus, further saints of the high-minded 1890s elite, were not alone as exemplars of a feminine lifepattern of which Theosophy was often the spiritual dimension in those days: they were brilliant, serious, articulate yet only moderately self-reflexive, educational and vocational pioneers, unmarried and career oriented in an era when genteel women generally had to choose between a professional career and marriage.

Edger was succeeded as secretary of the New Zealand section by Dr. C. W. Sanders, a homeopathic physician, who served 1897–1918. He in turn was succeeded by John Ross Thomson (1918–1925), and William Crawford (1925–1929). Both had come from Scotland. Thomson came to Theosophy through socialism, having been associated in England with such persons of the idealistic and sometimes spiritual wing of the movement as the Webbs, William Morris, and Edward Carpenter. Crawford, on the other hand, came to the ancient wisdom by way of Spiritualism. In them, two roots of Theosophy therefore met and united. They were staunch friends, living together for a time before Crawford's marriage in 1916 to Kathleen Hunt (sister of Emma Hunt, who became section general secretary in 1939). Both also became bishops of the Liberal Catholic Church. Also important were W. H. Draffin, headmaster of a public school in Auckland and first president of the lodge there, and his wife, a Theosophical lecturer; Olcott speaks of her as "having suddenly blossomed out as an eloquent platform speaker after having passed through a very severe illness."[24]

The 1890s also saw a series of distinguished outside speakers: Mrs. Cooper-Oakley in 1893, Annie Besant in 1894, Countess Wachtmeister in 1895, and Olcott in 1897. These prominent visitors were surely as important to nascent Theosophy as their equivalent had been to Spiritualism. But we note that of this list, the first three out of four were women; with Spiritualism, despite its great feminist importance, the opposite ratio generally obtained.

The Dunedin Lodge

The next branch of the Theosophical Society to be established in New Zealand, the Dunedin, was founded in 1893. A. Y. Atkinson has studied this organization in depth, and her praiseworthy scholarship enables us to use it as an important aperture into early Theosophy.[25] Although a less dazzling assembly than the group E. T. Sturdy was able to collect in Wellington five years earlier, the Dunedin Lodge is probably more typical of rank-and-file Theosophy down to the present and displayed in the 1890s a tenacity in belief contrasting markedly with the brilliant but ephemeral work in the capital city.

While never reaching more than some thirty-five members in that decade, the novel society generated much controversy in this predominantly Scots Presbyterian settlement that was also the seat of fierce debate over Spiritualism and Rationalism in the 1870s and 1880s. Atkinson has shown that the 1890s Theosophists were almost all British immigrants who had attained modest but respectable niches in society as chemists, teachers, clerks, or businessmen or were mates to the same. They sometimes recounted a strict religious upbringing in the old country. But in the course of the long progress to the antipodes that conditioning had for many fallen away; there was frequently a period of indifference or atheism.

At the same time, another characteristic of this group was that it contained voracious readers, one might say self-made intelligentsia. Atkinson rightly points out that the Victorian middle class, to which these Theosophists all essentially belonged, was literate, though not necessarily intellectual. But the Theosophists were worthy of being called intellectuals—that is, people to whom ideas and their passionate discussion were important—less by dint of advanced, university education, which none of them had, than as committed independent seekers. One gets a sense of outwardly diligent but inwardly lonely and searching persons far from their birthplaces, the sort who would rather spend an evening at home with a demanding book—as Theosophical literature certainly was—than in the pub. They were then ripe to seize at a system of thought that would interpret both the universe and their own often-solitary pilgrimage in it and that could offer an intellectual enthusiasm to take up the long southern evenings. Sometimes it seems purely by chance that a person came across a Theosophical tract or got one from another Theosophist, but, when this happened, the fortunate one latched onto what it taught with the characteristic single-mindedness of the Victorian convert.

The organizer of Dunedin Theosophy was Augustus William Maurais, a proofreader who began studying Theosophical literature in the late 1880s. Unknown to him, by 1890 a nearby couple, Robert Pairman, a ship's draughtsman, and his wife Susannah, were studying the same material. The Pairmans' story is of no small interest in understanding how such New Zealanders as these—folk of a different stamp from the Edgers and the Tregears—came to Theosophy.

Robert Pairman and Others

Pairman, born in Scotland to a family of strict and rigid religiosity, had like so many other restless and adventurous young men of his day left home early for the colonies, in the process throwing off the repressive piety of childhood. He gambled and drank his way to South Africa, Australia, and finally New Zealand. But there he settled down, married Susannah Stone, daughter of a prominent publisher and already a Theosophist. Soon that cause became central to both their lives. Once a week they invited friends and fellow students to join them for an evening's discussion of Theosophy. Mrs. Pairman's sister, Louisa Stone, a schoolteacher, was there, as were John Oddie (born in England to a Quaker family, an avid reader and homeopathic druggist) and Frank Allan, also a chemist. All later became members of the society.[26]

One day, while traveling on the train from Sawyers Bay to Dunedin, Maurais noted an elderly gentleman across from him reading a Theosophical magazine. Introducing himself, he learned that the stranger of similar interests was Grant Farquhar, a wealthy partner in a tannery factory at Sawyers Bay and an enthusiast of Theosophy, described as a very private man with a great love of reading. Farquhar in turn knew Mr. Stone, father of Louisa and father-in-law of Robert Pairman, and connections were made. Maurais then thought the time right to call a gathering of all these people with a view to forming a branch of the Theosophical Society in Otago. On December 20, 1892, eight people gathered in the shop of a prosperous Scottish-born draper named Thomas Ross, another enthusiast.

This meeting was less than satisfactory. Three of those present— including William Rough, whom we have met in connection with Spiritualism—considered themselves "advanced Spiritualists" and held that Theosophy had nothing further to offer them. The conference ended in disputation and some ill feeling between the two parties. But a second meeting in February 1893, excluded the Spiritualists and resulted in an application for a charter to the society signed by seven men: Maurais, Farquhar, Pairman, Allan, Oddie, Ross, and Robert Hawcridge. (The last, the head of an art school, was to soon become inactive, but the other six remained stalwarts of the Dunedin branch for years to come.) Farquhar was elected president and Maurais secretary. Membership grew to about eighteen the first year. Atkinson points out that, by all accounts, this small group was very close-knit, bound by friendships among their children as well as the adult members.[27]

That mutual support and coherence would soon be much needed, for hardly had it been formed than the young Society was virulently set on by opponents. In the spring 1893, a prominent local Presbyterian minister, the Reverend Rutherford Waddell, well known as a social activitist and literary figure, launched uncompromising attacks on

Theosophy from the pulpit. He drew particular attention to alleged "exposures" of Helena Blavatsky as a charlatan and worse and quoted Max Müller's famous denunciation, as well as the report by Richard Hodgson published by the Society for Psychical Research (SPR) concerning fraud in connection with her production of the Mahatma Letters. Further assaults on Theosophy dotted the pages of the *Christian Outlook,* a Dunedin publication edited by Waddell. This was a generally thoughtful periodical that, although basically of conservative Presbyterian perspective, was intelligently aware of the great religious issues of the day: Darwinism, "higher criticism," the church and social reform. The small coterie of Dunedin Theosophists did not receive these slings and arrows passively. A special meeting, held to deal with Waddell's campaign, resulted in writing to Olcott at Adyar for arguments and tracts to counter the clergyman and his party. Mail took many weeks in those days, however, and in the meantime the energetic Maurais, undertaking to write letters to local newspapers in response, generated a lively public debate on the new faith.

August Maurais

A few biographical facts about Maurais, reported by Atkinson, help put the debate in human perspective. Born in London in 1858, the son of a well-to-do bookseller, Augustus Maurais was privately educated and later apprenticed to the printing trade. But in 1875 he sailed for New Zealand, reportedly in search of the simple life and in reaction against the strict Anglican atmosphere of his home. He took a series of jobs in printing offices and in shipping and finally settled down to proofreading the *Evening Star* in Dunedin. He was married by then to a practical-minded woman who failed to share either her husband's enthusiasm for simple living or his custom of spending large amounts of money on books that only cluttered the house. But she tolerated his Theosophical beliefs and finally became herself a member of the society, though never a very active one. Nonetheless, the family's Theosophy made them unpopular in some quarters, and their children had to suffer abuse from a schoolmistress who chose to refer to their father as "the heathen over the hill." But his unusual faith notwithstanding, Maurais served fourteen years on the council of Ravensbourne borough and one term as mayor.

Liberal and idealistic, Maurais had been a freethinker from an early age. He vigorously supported the maritime strikers of 1890 with money as well as words. In this connection he had held the Reverend Waddell in high esteem for the latter's fellow labors on behalf of workers and their struggles. This made Maurais all the more hurt when Waddell turned against him on the issue of Theosophy.[28]

Responses to Theosophy

Theosophy got attention, then, and Theosophists responded with as good as they got. Disputed issues included the impersonal divinity of Theosophy (or Vedanta) versus the Christian personal God, Theosophists finding the latter capricious and vain, and Christians the Theosophical deity intolerably bleak and abstract. The topic of karma versus grace was often raised, Theosophists claiming karma was the only way the world's inequities could be justified; Christians saw its impersonal cause-and-effect empty of mercy or love. Finally, the authority of the Bible versus the other scriptures and revelations of the world was naturally a major bone of contention. In one argument, a Christian—like so many other apologists for his faith before and since—pointed to the terrible poverty of India, the land Theosophists claimed to find so spiritual. A week or so later, a Theosophical letter appeared in the same paper, asking what a Hindu, first settling foot in the dreadful slums of London's East End, would think of the way a supposedly Christian nation cared for its poor.

Another debate concerned the qualifications and reputations of Helena Blavatsky, Annie Besant, and other early Theosophical leaders. Here Christian writers, above all clergymen like Waddell—who opened the Dunedin imbroglio on this note—were capable of reaching veritable frenzies of satire and invective in retailing accounts of Blavatsky's chicanery, forging of missives from the masters, and exposure by the SPR, or of Besant's long career from unhappy wife of an Anglican parson, through free thought and close association with the notorious radical Charles Bradlaugh, to her last inanity, Theosophy.

In arguments like these, the Theosophists in Dunedin (as elsewhere) and their faultfinders never seemed quite to engage. The critics appeared to take for granted that such ad hominem (or rather, in these cases, *ad feminam*) arguments, once broadcast, would devastate Theosophy and turn its gullible proselytes back to their senses. Theosophists like Maurais responded, with disconcerting equilibrium, that, although some accounts of Theosophical scandal were doubtlessly biased, Theosophists did not claim their leaders were perfect. Some of the unappealing stories might in fact be based on truth. The important thing was the ideas those Theosophical giants taught—not their lives—and the important question whether or not those ideas were true. Judge Theosophy's books, not the persons who wrote them.[29]

One can hardly avoid detecting a strong note of classist and sexist feeling in much of the criticism, particularly when it comes from persons of high establishment educational and ecclesiastical status and when it is directed at women like Blavatsky and Besant, who, although obviously very intelligent and capable as well as spirited, could not have hoped in their day for similar pastorates or professorates. Yet these women were making a mark in the world, in some cases generating commitment and a level of spiritual conversation the churches could only envy. In the same light, one can understand the remarkable adherence of women like these, and status-inconsistent people of both sexes, to Theosophy, despite the scandals and the scorn.[30]

Indeed, the feeling may have cut even deeper. There is an account, interestingly in the *Christian Outlook,* of a Theosophical lecture in the Wairarapa by Countess Wachtmeister, the former intimate of Blavatsky, on her 1895 tour. During the question period she was harangued by an impassioned minister—the same had written hard-hitting, Bible-quoting tracts against both Spiritualism and Theosophy—until the discussion had to be terminated and the meeting apparently ended in an uproar. Shortly after, Wachtmeister put a letter in the local paper stating that she felt the clergyman was "an incarnation of one of the monks that tore the quivering flesh of Hypatia!"[31] (Hypatia, the brilliant fourth-century Alexandrian mathematician and Neoplatonist, was well known at the time, having been the subject of a popular novel by Charles Kingsley, who spared nothing to paint her a noble woman destroyed by Christian bigotry. Given Theosophy's Neoplatonist bent, it is more than understandable that a clerically abused modern Theosophical woman would see herself in Hypatia's role!)

A. Y. Atkinson nonetheless asks, quite properly, why Theosophy, which in this period never had more than three dozen adherents in the Dunedin area out of a population of many thousands, should have aroused such vehement Christian polemic. In an age of accelerating change and growing secularism, Theosophy was hardly the church's most serious foe. Atkinson's answer is, I think, perceptive and correct: "The Society was attacked largely because it seemed to give concrete form to undercurrents of fear and religious doubt prevalent in Dunedin."[32]

Theosophy, though miniscule, nonetheless represented an egregious and visible example of many things traditional Christianity now had to contend with in a age of doubt, Darwin, social change, and incipient globalism. Often these presences were amorphous yet threatening clouds, but in Theosophy they seemed personified in their most extreme shape, so it is little wonder that the society drew lightning. The 1890s were a time of increasing uncertainty in religion and of deepening polarization in churches between liberal and conservative wings. But on the issues at hand—evolution, the Bible, the claims of rival world religions—Theosophy, taking a more advanced position than even the most progressive churchmen, spoke of cosmic evolution in the most sweeping terms as embracing everything from atoms to consciousness, of the Bible as at best only a partial and distorted version of the ancient wisdom, of all religions—and especially some of those most despised by the orthodox, such as Gnosticism and Hinduism—as bearers of the occult light. On top of this, as we have seen, Theosophy challenged the Christian ecclesiastical establishment structurally, in the provision of lay and particularly female leadership.

One clergyman, rather than going into stern opposition, embraced the new claims, to the discomfiture of his colleagues. The Reverend S. J. Neil of Thames, the Presbyterian who was Spiritualistic and a great support to Jane Elizabeth Harris, joined the Theosophical Society in 1893 and wrote tracts for it. The *Otago Daily Times* showed no great alarm over this development, calling Theosophy only "a mild form of heresy" and inaccurately predicting that it would be "a very temporary craze" that could not last more than a year.[33] The Dunedin Theosophical Society circulated for signature a petition of support for Neil. He was nonetheless suspended by the Presbyterian church. The embattled minister then took up an independent liberal ministry in Auckland and was of much help to his new Theosophical friends.[34]

Theosophy at the Beginning of the Twentieth Century

During the first two decades of the twentieth century, Theosophy grew and prospered in New Zealand. Its periodical, *Theosophy in New Zealand,* founded in 1900, contains mostly upbeat and brief accounts of activities, schedules, and articles that were in large part reprints of talks by Theosophical luminaries like Besant and C. W. Leadbeater. One is considerably impressed by the sober and intellectually demanding standards of the articles and announced lectures presented in *Theosophy in New Zealand.* They are likely to deal exhaustively with the more recondite points of karma or cosmic evolution, or grapple with the spiritual meaning of art and the moral climate. Lecture titles at various lodges included, "Judicial Astrology," "One-Pointedness," "The Coming Race," and "Appollonius of Tyana."[35]

Indications appear of the particular way in which Theosophy was attuned to the high esteem that New Zealanders, and others in the world, held of the young country as a beacon light of progress and prosperity on the planet. New Zealand at the time was often considered to have the world's highest standard of living and its most advanced social legislation—as well as perhaps its highest per-capita number of Theosophists! A visitor, W. J. Colville, was quoted in *Theosophy in New Zealand* as saying, "I was in New Zealand as the 19th passed to the 20th century, and then I became convinced of what a very progressive country New Zealand really is." No spot on earth is more so, he added, and contrasted his impression with the view of some that New Zealand was "mediocre in all things." But, in a rather mysterious turn of phrase, he said that "the strength of a nation lies in its mediocrity, the mediocrity of all round strength. . . ."[36]

One source of strength, or supposed strength, very important to most New Zealanders in those days was their connection to the British Empire. But Theosophy, with its universalism and its vast temporal vistas in which nations, empires, races, and even worlds and galaxies rose and fell according to their immutable cycles, provided a subtle but often-telling aperture for criticism in the era of imperial illusions. A 1903 review in *Theosophy in New Zealand* of Annie Besant's lecture-pamphlet "Theosophy and Imperialism" is a case in point. The reviewer begins by saying: "There is no need to preach Imperialism to the New Zealander; he is in every fibre an Imperialist, having grasped the idea of Greater Britain, he scarce knows when or how, but grasping it strongly and vitally as becomes his race." No problem for him is entailed in "the larger patriotism of Kipling, the doctrine of 'The White Man's Burden. . . .' "

Then the Theosophical reviewer notes how Annie Besant quietly undercuts these bromides as absolute values by calling attention to the rise and fall of all races and empires, by pointing to empire's concomitant responsibilities, and by observing that Britons are almost universally ignorant of the traditions, religions, and philosophies of the East they claim called to rule. Here the reviewer and his "larger patriotism" seem a bit disconcerted. He grudgingly concedes, "It may appear that Annie Besant here and there has criticized the shortcomings of our race." But he recovers sufficiently to emphasize that she was speaking in England and—manifesting his own Theosophical awareness of Eastern philosophy—calls for a view of imperial responsibilities as having dharmic implications.[37]

Another development in these years was the establishment of the Vasanta Garden School on the grounds of headquarters, which instructed children from approximately five to eleven in accordance with the most advanced educational methods. There was no punishment or compulsory homework, but students were led to progress in accordance with quarterly work charts at their own pace. Unfortunately, this fine experiment ran into difficulties during the depression years and had to be terminated after World War II.[38]

Developments Abroad

Even as early New Zealand Theosophy was flourishing, new developments far away were shaping a colorful but agitated Theosophical future. In 1895, in a village north of the international headquarters of the society at Adyar, an infant named Jiddu Krishnamurti was born, and in 1909, after his father had moved his family to the headquarters estate, this child was "discovered" by Charles Webster Leadbeater, controversial and prominent Theosophical occultist, and declared by him to be the vehicle of the coming world teacher. A new stage of Theosophical history was launched.

C. W. LEADBEATER

In order to understand the tumultuous and traumatic effect of these events on New Zealand Theosophy in the early decades of the twentieth century, one must consider the character and career of C. W. Leadbeater and his protégé. Leadbeater (1854–1934),[39] after a few years as an Anglican curate, joined the Theosophical Society in 1883 and devoted the rest of his life to its cause. Those fifty-one years were often-troubled ones for the society, and not a few of the troubles swirled around Leadbeater. At the same time, those were also years of Theosophy's greatest relative strength in the world and of its greatest cultural influence, eminently in Australia, where Leadbeater long resided, and New Zealand. His books were among Theosophy's best-sellers—and still are—and his occult perceptions inspired many to Theosophical activism.

For Leadbeater was above all an occultist and visionary who codified —and some would say largely created—a Theosophical view of cosmos and history that went far beyond Blavatsky's oceanic works in its clear and precise detail. Leadbeater mapped the inner planes of human life, impaneled the inner government of the world with its hierarchy of masters and the rays on which they worked, and traced the evolution of the human race, its various root races and subraces, and numerous individuals including himself and other prominent Theosophists through many reincarnations on this and previous globes. Leadbeater was a close associate of Annie Besant (enemies called him her Svengali), and especially during her long years as international president (1907–1933) his place was assured and his interpretation of Theosophy established doctrine, reflected in many of her books as well.[40]

He was to need such highly placed protection, for Leadbeater suffered concerted attacks, centering not only on his "New Theosophy" but also on charges of improper relations with certain of the young men and boys he generally had around him under training. In 1906 he was forced to resign from the Theosophical Society on these grounds but was reinstated following Besant's election as president the next year. In 1909, the year of his official return to grace, he settled in Adyar in close proximity to Annie Besant, after years of residence variously in Adyar, Ceylon, and Europe, combined with extensive lecture tours.

In 1914 Leadbeater moved to Sydney, where he established himself as a quasi-independent Theosophical force. He took a quick interest in the occult meaning of his new homeland, and with it New Zealand. In 1915 he gave a series of four lectures on this topic in Sydney, lectures that were reprinted in a small book, *Australia and New Zealand: The Home of a New Sub-Race*. This work understandably became a favorite among Australian and New Zealand Theosophists. Knowing that the world was ready for a new subrace, precursors of the coming Sixth Root Race, Leadbeater now located signs of its appearance in the antipodes, as well as the already-determined West Coast of the United States. Indeed, Australia and New Zealand were now favored for this evolution, because of their isolation and their "glorious war dead," who would be reborn in their homelands at a distinctly high level. The new subrace would be characterized by intuition, leading to "wonderful mental development." The leaders of the two countries were called on to improve conditions of life, admittedly "still somewhat crude" in the young dominions, to create lands of beauty and splendour worthy of such noble beings; parents were forewarned to prepare themselves to raise children much in advance of themselves. Indeed, he already saw in Australia "children of a new type."

Even the indifference to religion characteristic now of Australia and New Zealand, compared to the continuing piety of the older subraces, was a sign, a token these peoples were preparing for something fresh. Psychic faculties, on the other hand, were on the increase as they prepared for a new kind of religion, one not dependent on priests and aligned with science. On another issue, although granting that some combining of subraces, as of the Celtic and Anglo-Saxon, was acceptable and even beneficial, Leadbeater held that races too far apart, especially root races, could not mix advantageously. He no doubt had in mind the aborigines, whom he claimed were mostly Lemurian, and he affirmed the "White Australia" policy as suitable to the new subrace's secure birth.[41]

In 1916 Leadbeater was consecrated to the episcopate of a new independent Catholic church, soon to be called the Liberal Catholic Church, and quickly became its dominant bishop. Closely aligned to Theosophical teaching and numbering many Theosophists among its members, the Liberal Catholic Church under Leadbeater's tutelage offered a liturgical expression, and channeling, of occult forces. (Like much else connected with Leadbeater, the church was intensely controversial; many Theosophists passionately embraced its cultic splendor; others vehemently denounced it as a return to "priestcraft," a betrayal of the advanced thought and critique of religion for which original Theosophy was supposed to stand.)

In 1922 the bishop moved into a large home and estate in Sydney called the Manor, which he shared with two or three families and the inevitable group of boys (much later girls, too) under his instruction. The same year, following complaints, Leadbeater was under intense investigation by the police regarding homosexuality (as he had been earlier in 1917). The irreverent Aussie press made much of the sensational charges in stories with such headlines as "Where Leadbeater Bishes" or "Leadbeater: A Swish Bish with the Boys."[42] (Krishnamurti and his brother, who had arrived in Sydney for a visit just in time to be thoroughly grilled by detectives concerning their knowledge of Leadbeater's sexual proclivities, were referred to in the same media as "dandy coloured coons."[43] When officials came to call, Leadbeater himself was invariably too ill to receive them.)

The investigators were unable to prove anything, and Leadbeater continued to teach, "bish," and pursue his clairvoyant studies. But the effect of the scandalous publicity had been severe. Australian Theosophy divided, several hundred members joining a lodge independent of Leadbeater; membership in the section fell from 2,309 to 1,823 between 1922 and 1923.[44] In New Zealand, where the storm across the Tasman could hardly have gone unnoticed, comparable effects were seen. According to census figures, Theosophy declined by eighteen percent between 1921 and 1926. The official Theosophical Society membership count also started to fall in 1922 from 1,299 to a low of 766 in 1940, after which it began to rise until it reached 1,671 in 1987. (However, it may be noted that, on a per-capita basis, 1922 was the high year. Then roughly one in a thousand New Zealanders were Theosophists; in the 1980s, because of population increase, it was about one in two thousand.)

JIDDU KRISHNAMURTI

The decade of the 1920s, unsettling though it may have been, is remembered as the great days by Theosophists, above all because of the excitement and expectancy created by the Krishnamurti adventure. In 1909 Leadbeater had discovered the slight and ill-nourished Indian boy Jiddu Krishnamurti, the son of a dedicated Theosophist and retired civil service employee. Leadbeater declared that this child was to become the Vehicle of the Lord Maitreya (the future Buddha, also identified with Christ), or world teacher, and must be trained for that purpose. To this end Leadbeater and Besant undertook his education, first at Adyar, finally in England and Ojai, California. In 1911 the Order of the Star in the East was formed to prepare for the coming; this organization spread excitement throughout the Theosophical world by means of its publications and conventions that tingled with anticipation. The order spawned a magazine, the *Herald of the Star,* a publishing house, Lotus Press, and a youth organization, the Servants of the Star.

Krishnamurti's father, Jiddu Naraniah, raising the issue of Leadbeater's sexual reputation as well as other matters, brought legal action in 1912 to gain custody of the boy and Nitya, Krishnamurti's brother, who accompanied him as a companion. Although lower courts gave rulings in the parent's favor, they were eventually set aside on technical grounds by the Privy Council in London, and the Vehicle remained under Theosophical control. Although the educational results were mixed—Krishnamurti was unsuccessful in gaining admission to a British university—the once-unpromising youth grew into a handsome and pleasing man, who satisfied his mentors with simple yet cogent talks and writings on spiritual matters. Leadbeater spoke knowingly of the high inner initiations he was receiving. The wise young sage showed every sign of being what he was prophesied to be.

The 1910s' and 1920s' extraordinary interest in Krishnamurti messianism seems to say something significant about those tumultuous times. Against a wildly erratic backdrop of progressivist optimism, the horror and despair of the Great War, and the 1920s' giddy mix of futurist dreams and anxious sense of the world's foundations shaking, Krishnamurti and his cause projected a tangible eschatological hope. Asian religion has often been presented in the West as a voice of the perennial philosophy or the ancient wisdom. Less frequently has the eschatological or apocalyptic thrust of its Avatar and Maitreya cults, often quite important in their homelands, had more than minor or nominal response, save as allegedly personified in a teacher like Meher Baba or Satya Sai Baba for their small bands of Western followers. But Krishnamurti, by now a man both Eastern and Western, was a Coming One who seemed to answer a widely felt need in the shell-shocked West. This world teacher was an archetype of the future as well as the past, of coming wisdom as well as ancient wisdom, of the reconciliation of all those progressive things the West knew but could not integrate into successful, harmonious living.

But in 1929 the star suddenly set. At a camp of the Order of the Star in Ommen, Netherlands, before an audience of some three thousand, including Mrs. Besant, Krishnamurti dramatically dissolved the Order of the Star, left Theosophy, and rejected for himself all organizations. In his speech he proclaimed:

> I maintain that truth is a pathless land, and you cannot approach it by any path whatsoever, by any religion, by any sect. That is my point of view, and I adhere to that absolutely and unconditionally. Truth, being limitless, unconditioned, unapproachable by any

path whatsoever, cannot be organised; nor should any organisation be formed to lead or coerce people along any particular path.

Henceforth, until his death in 1986, Krishnamurti pursued an independent vocation as a distinguished lecturer and teacher of nameless truth and "choiceless awareness."[45]

The end of the Theosophical Krishnamurti, the puncturing of trust in the Coming, at least in Theosophical terms, and the protégé's implicit rejection of the organization that had set its hopes on him, left the society in much disarray. It had to contend with these disappointments as best it could in the grimmer world of the 1930s. Beset by the Great Depression and a darkening world scene, and soon without the long-familiar figures of Annie Besant and C. W. Leadbeater, who died in 1933 and 1934, respectively, Theosophy in the 1930s and after was a smaller and soberer movement than before. Yet it did not go under, and in some ways became more stable and mature. Unplagued by further serious scandal and under competent leadership, Theosophy found a modest but secure place for itself in the world's spiritual ecology.

The Order of the Star in the East

In 1909, the year of Leadbeater's discovery of Krishnamurti, Reverend C. W. Scott-Moncrieff, an Anglican, was compelled by the bishop of Auckland to resign his position as warden of St. John's Theological College in Auckland and return to England after joining the Theosophical Society.[46]

The *N. Z. Free Lance* described the affair with characteristic vigor:

> The Anglican Communion in Auckland, which is presided over by that highly orthodox bishop, Dr. Neligan—who gave New Zealand such a bad name at Home for its alleged Godless schools—has just been treated to the spectacle of a "heresy hunt" . . . the national sport of the Presbyterians. . . . The particular heretic who was marked down for the hunt was the Rev. C. W. Scott-Moncrieff, who was imported from England less than two years ago to be Warden of St. John's Theological College, where pale young curates, with the Oxford bleat, are turned out year by year to the required church pattern.
>
> Mr. Scott-Moncrieff, being of an inquiring turn of mind, joined the Theosophical Society, in company with the vicar of an Auckland church. They thought they had as much freedom to join the T.S. as they would have to become Freemasons or Druids, seeing that it is not a dogmatic religious sect . . . But that is just where Mr. Scott-Moncrieff fell in. . . . The Governors of the College made things hot, and the parson has resigned.[47]

Little repentant, the ex-warden remained with Theosophy back home, and soon threw himself into the Star-in-the-East excitement. In 1911, just after the formation of that order, he read a paper, later published, to a group of London clergy titled, "The Coming Christ and the Order of the Star in the East."[48] In it he endorsed not only Theosophy but also its current enthusiasm for the imminent advent of a new Christ or world teacher.

Scott-Moncrieff made the program of the new messiah sound like no more than a natural extension of ultra-liberal Christianity. The Second Coming of Christ, he asserted, need not take the shape of the traditional Last Judgment; as at the first Advent, the expected one may arrive only in the simple guise of a teacher deeply attuned to the needs of the time. But now, through the order, the world can prepare itself better for His august mission. Christianity, the priest went on to say, may triumph in Him, but it will not do so as it is now but in a new form to which all world religions will contribute. East and West are no longer watertight because races and religions interact. There is a new universalism: the clergyman cited such international activities as the labor movement, the woman's movement, the Esperanto movement, "science itself," and groups like the Theosophical Society and Baha'i. The coming faith will, furthermore, be a "scientific religion" to which not only the natural sciences, but also such "sciences" as sociology, education, socialism, and eugenics will be reconciled. For all this the mighty vision of a new world teacher, to appear in the East, will be requisite.

In 1912 Scott-Moncrieff founded a Guild of the Mysteries of God and went on a world lecture tour with the Reverend Frank Waters Pigott, the Auckland vicar with whom he became a Theosophist in 1909. A later Theosophical source declares that Scott-Moncrieff "won many agnostics" with his "esoteric Christianity."[49] Pigott subsequently became a Liberal Catholic priest, and eventually presiding bishop of that church. C. W. Scott-Moncrieff himself apparently remained an Anglican, while, on the other hand, the son of the former warden of St. John's, George Irving Scott-Moncrieff, became a well-known writer on Scottish and Roman Catholic topics.

It might be worth noting that, even though back in England Scott-Moncrieff was able to retain his Church of England clerical status while pointing to the Star in the East,[50] his conflict with his church in New Zealand does demonstrate that Asian religion, however broadly and Theosophically read, can and often does serve to gauge the permissible limits of Christian liberalism. In those days, not a few Anglican clergymen were deeply involved in marginally Christian hermeticism of the Golden Dawn sort with apparent impunity, as some like Stainton Moses had been with Spiritualism. S. J. Neil, the Presbyterian Theosophical heretic, had previously been a regular at Spiritualist séances while a minister in Thames, but it apparently took his Theosophical affiliation to bring him before the bench. In both cases the Theosophical acknowledgment of light from the East as well as even the most esoteric Western sources, and of such characteristic doctrines as reincarnation, seem to have been the crushing straws.

The Order of the Star flourished in New Zealand until its dissolution in 1929. Its New Zealand head was D. W. M. Burn, one of the country's best-known poets and an avid Theosophist. David William M. Burn (1862–1951), an Otago schoolteacher, wrote verse, much of it on current events and originally published in the *Otago Daily Times,* more conventional than marked by individual vision or passion. During the First World War, he issued great amounts of standard patriotic odes, though there is also a poem on Annie Besant, dated October 1, 1916, which would have been during her presidency of the Indian Home Rule League and consequent severe difficulties with British authorities. Few of the verses are explicitly Theosophical, though some refer poetically to such motifs as spirituality and reincarnation.[51] Burn's personal life was, reportedly, a bit less predictable than his literary output; he commonly wore knickers and a skullcap and hiked extensively in the hills around St. Clair, where he lived—with his wife Alice and a daughter who also became an ardent Theosophist—almost as a recluse.[52]

Theosophy in New Zealand for November and December 1926 recounts the funeral of A. W. Maurais, the pioneer Theosophist in Dunedin, conducted by Burn. In the same issue, a news item describes Krishnamurti's appearance in Chicago at the American convention of the Theosophical Society, where he "completely disarmed his questioners" as he "parried questions with dexterity and spoke with an air of authority."[53] A bit later, in May and June 1929, on the eve of the young Indian's disconcerting announcement, there is news of Annie Besant's pressing for dominion status for India and an article by Burn, now in his capacity as president of the New Zealand and India League, on the importance of a liberated India to the empire and also to the plan of the masters. There is also a report of a lecture, again in Chicago, in which Krishnamurti was asked whether he was a member of the Theosophical Society. A pause—then the answer, "I am." And the further comment: "There is nothing wrong about it; there is nothing particularly right about it. It doesn't make a great deal of difference one way or the other."[54]

One who had read carefully such prior hints of Krishnamurti's mind should not have been overly surprised at his "Truth is a pathless land" speech and that was the position quickly taken by Theosophical apologists after the event. *Theosophy in New Zealand* for September and October 1929 opined that what he had said before 1929 had led up to the

Camp Ommen event, for those who had ears to hear—life, he had always insisted, is the teacher, and it does not matter to what one belongs. The present teaching of Krishnamurti sounds revolutionary, yet its truth is self-evident.[55]

In the November-December issue John Ross Thomson, general secretary of the Theosophical Society in New Zealand 1918–1925 and bishop of the Liberal Catholic Church, quoted in 1926 as saying he was confident the world teacher spoke through his chosen Vehicle, saw little reason to change this opinion dispite the challenge of changing appearances: Krishnamurti "is not very different from the youth I last saw in 1923, though he now combined the 'Man of Sorrows' with the boundless joy of eternal youth.[56] His exquisite charm of manner accompanies a gift of intuitive perception not equalled anywhere. Children run to caress him. . . . His message is revolutionary. He says 'Challenge belief,' but he means one's own belief, not the belief of one's fellows. . . ."[57] In May and June 1930, Thomson added, "The disturbance which has been caused by the teachings of Mr. Krishnamurti is the result of too much orthodoxy in ourselves,"[58] and further articles published in *Theosophy in New Zealand* by the prominent Theosophists C. Jinarajadasa, T. Tidswell, A. Besant, and C. W. Leadbeater echoed the same theme: Krishnamurti's actions were but a natural development of his status as a world teacher, meant to arrest us in any dogmatic complacency, Theosophical or otherwise, we may have, and thereby really confirm rather than discredit ordinary Theosophy and the hope Theosophists put in the teacher.[59]

Adjustment and Transition

Yet the abrupt end of the halcyon Theosophical 1920s, Order of the Star and all, was not so easily dealt with by many. An elderly Theosophical friend and informant, full of clear memories of those times, told me that before 1929 people looked up to their Theosophical leaders in "an adoring, uncritical way." There was, she added, a social hierarchy, perhaps unconscious, in New Zealand Theosophy. A leadership class, which included the higher Liberal Catholic clergy, was rich and well placed socially, but the Theosophical rank and file, though much less well-to-do, "adored" the leadership and did the work in a spirit of self-abnegation.

She remembers John Ross Thomson, who stood out with his silvery hair and sense of dignity, and a host of others, including herself and her family, for whom Theosophy in those days was a "whole world." The society offered not only its lectures and classes but also concerts and plays and youth groups like the Servants of the Star and Order of the

Round Table, Co-Masonry, the Liberal Catholic Church, and friendship networks and connections through which one got jobs. Moreover, in those "halcyon days" the Theosophical subuniverse of meaning took on an air of excitement and intense belief. My informant talked of how people "believed in these things so ardently." They classified themselves in terms of the seven rays, spoke of the masters as though they were "real as relatives," gossiped knowingly of visions and rites of passage. ("You know, she passed her Third Initiation last week"; "My boyfriend and I saw a Master walking on the beach the other night.") In their gorgeously robed organizations, youth acted out in dramatic pageants like the Krotona Ritual the yearned-for Coming and the new world it would bring. Young people like herself were *very* keen to become disciples to the awaited world teacher; it was rumored he would have twelve.

This whole universe of hopes and dreams and human connections, she recalls, is what Krishnamurti broke when he burst the bubble. "He was not just shattering beliefs, but also organizations, relationships, loyalties . . . saying they are not needed, he shattered lives, patterns . . . now ritual looked hollow and silly—people who had walked in a golden light now seemed small but pompous. . . ." It was, she emphasized, a "very, very real experience. . . ." She was "very let down."

Krishnamurti visited New Zealand to speak in 1934. As it happened, George Bernard Shaw was in New Zealand lecturing at the same time. These two quite different celebrities had in common one thing: they were both censored by New Zealand radio. Krishnamurti could not speak over it at all, and the epilogue of Shaw's *Androcles and the Lion* was not allowed to be broadcast in Christchurch. According to newspaper accounts at the time, the postmaster-general's department decided on the suitability of any particular subject or speaker for broadcast, and the decision in the case of Krishnamurti was probably made "by a Government radio inspector." "We do not propose to broadcast Krishnamurti," was the only comment made by the chairman of the Broadcasting Board, E. C. Hands.

Shaw generously remarked in Rotorua that the decision not to broadcast Krishnamurti was "far less excusable" than his own ban. "He is a religious teacher of the greatest distinction, who is listened to with profit and assent by members of all churches and sects, and the prohibition is an ignorant mistake." The great playwright went on:

> The excuse as to broadcasting being controversial is nonsense. Everything that comes over the wireless is controversial except the time signal and the weather report. For instance, 'Androcles and the Lion' is a violently controversial play, but it has been broadcast without any protest from an inspector. All my broadcasts are blazingly controversial, but they are quoted over the wireless and else-

where. Controversial means simply something that the government or an inspector does not agree with. But this does not apply
to the case of Mr. Krishnamurti. The authorities are evidently
ignorant of his standing, and his admirably catholic doctrine, and
class him just as an Indian heathen. When he becomes known in
New Zealand they will be sorry for it.

Although they never actually met in New Zealand, Shaw—who had
been a close friend of Annie Besant before she became a Theosophist—
had encountered Krishnamurti once or twice in London. He once went
so far as to call Krishnamurti "the most beautiful human being he ever
saw."[60] In New Zealand as well Krishnamurti, heathen or not, made an
impression. A reporter speaks of his "compelling eyes," his "great earnestness and obvious sincerity," and notes that "above everything else
he is dynamic." Questioned by reporters, the Indian said, "I do not
come under the auspices of any organisation. I was invited by some
friends, and I came. If I am not invited I stay where I am."
He explained he had dissolved the Order of the Star in the East
because it was becoming too much like what it was intended to transcend: it

> had become worldwide. It was tremendous. It had everything—
> land, property, buildings—and carried on its work as all other
> organisations do.
>   They say that religion helps people and brings them nearer to
> the truth. I say that in reality religions are a hindrance and are
> merely instruments of exploitation. They keep people apart and
> there are innumerable fights between the little pestiferous sects
> that are all over the world, each one trying to get the followers of
> the other. I saw that my own organisation was become the same as
> the others—that a new religion was being proclaimed which would
> be in the fight with all other religons striving for supremacy, and so
> I disbanded it and as far as possible gave the property back to the
> donors. . . . Organisations of this kind do not lead man to the
> truth—to God. Every person has to find it out for himself . . . I
> think I have a message to all the people of the world. I have some-
> thing to say. The whole of the social, economic, and religious
> sytem of the world is based on exploitation, and will continue to be
> as long as each individual does not trouble to find out for himself
> what are his needs both social and economic—not cravings, but
> real needs.

And to know this, Krishnamurti added, one must first of all be educated in a new way. When asked if his teachings were upsetting to orthodox Christians, he replied: "I hope so." For he would "eliminate both
nations and religions." It was announced he would give public

addresses and open-air talks. But there would be no radio chats to advance such startling proposals.[61]

Theosophy after Krishnamurti

New Zealand Theosophy, though chastened and declining in membership, persevered through the 1930s. My informant remarked that some Theosophists, in those depression years when economic and social problems became so acute, transferred allegiance from the Order of the Star to Social Credit. This may be somewhat borne out in an article in *The Theosophist* (Adyar), August 1933, "by a New Zealand F.T.S." (possibly Burn) titled, "Theosophists and World Economics: How It Strikes a Contemporary." This piece is sympathetic to the Social Credit movement of Major Douglas and says that in New Zealand as in Australia some lodges have formed circles to study it. However, in an appended note C. Jinarajadasa, editor and later international president, comments that he has read three books by Major Douglas "on the Social Credit Scheme" but has "not been thrilled with any realization that his solution is the one and only one which will lead the world to prosperity."[62]

The dream of a relation between Theosophy and social and economic reform on a practical, political level was given some degree of realization in the person of Henry Greathead Rex Mason, a Theosophist and minister of justice during the whole term of the first Labour government of 1935–1949, and again in 1957–1960. The vision of an alliance between Theosophy and Labour socialism had gone back at least as far as 1911, when Harry H. Banks, president of the Auckland branch of the Theosophical Society, wrote Michael Savage, then secretary of the (first) Labour Party, suggesting that, because the aims of Theosophy and socialism were in harmony and their general worldviews not incompatible, perhaps they could form a joint committee for combined action. Savage's reply was friendly but pointed out that such an arrangement was not possible under the party's constitution.[63]

Now, some twenty-four years later, Savage was prime minister and Mason attorney general and minister of justice. John Marshall, though a man from the other side of the aisle, wrote of him with respect: "Rex Mason . . . was undoubtedly an intellectual. He was also a vegetarian and a theosophist; a man of peace and sweet reason; a tall, gaunt, ungainly figure, striding through the corridors of power in uncongenial company. But they needed him for his knowledge of the law, and they respected him for his integrity. . . . It is perhaps going too far to say that he kept the Labour Party on a straight and narrow legal path, but their path was straighter and narrower than it might have been if he had not been there."[64] Mason's obituary in *The Dominion* adds that he "gave Labour an intellectualism and a dignity that helped them immensely."[65]

Mason did undoubtedly lend the entire Labour enterprise of that era a flavor of quality, integrity, and intellectual tone, and his name is associated with women's rights legislation. But his personal contribution seems best remembered in connection with certain causes, no doubt progressive but also no doubt of second-level importance, for which he crusaded mightily, especially daylight saving time and decimal currency. Both campaigns suggest a neat, logical, rather legalistic but well-meaning reformist mind in battle against the Anglo-Saxon's notorious attachment to quaint and irrational tradition. Perhaps the same temperament is reflected in the more substantive issue of Mason's treatment of conscientious objectors during the Second World War, which fell into his province as justice minister. We are told that his handling of COs in the highly charged wartime atmosphere was "correct but circumspect"; he did not respond to appeals by humanitarian or religious leaders on behalf of particular cases, but he did propose (not always successfully) to make the often harsh living conditions of those unpopular, detained pacifists more humane.[66]

Rex Mason's wife, Dulcia, was an important figure in the Theosophical Women's Association founded in 1940, serving as its first dominion secretary, under Emma Hunt as president. This organization presented as its first aim "To Exalt Womanhood," citing the Theosophical conceptions of "God in the dual aspects of Father-Mother" and the "World-Mother, who, as a mighty archangel, focuses the spiritual forces of the maternal nature of God." The many goddesses of humankind from Isis to Parvati to the Maori Papa-Tuanuku, are called to witness. Other purposes were "to encourage the development of a distinctive culture for New Zealand" and "to study dominion problems and their solution in the light of Theosophy."

In the 1940s and 1950s this organization manifested a striking sense of assertiveness. Newsletters indicate that it passed resolutions opposing capital punishment, took part in peace rallies, and issued long reports on the dangers of smoking. A March 1, 1948, address by Emma Hunt spoke of New Zealand as the "home of a new race." A new cycle is beginning within the present Fifth Root Race, leading to the next evolutionary development, and (in a coda that might not have occurred to Leadbeater) with it "a new type of woman is coming forward." In 1947 Miss Hunt looked forward to the time when Princess Elizabeth would be queen, which should herald an age of idealism and culture, and went on to say that "while she was in Huizen [a Theosophical center in Holland] she felt as never before something of Our Lady's influence; and she realized for a while the marvellous truth of the Indwelling Maternity of God."[67]

It is worth noting that in the mid-1940s Edmund Hillary, later the conqueror of Mt. Everest, was a member of the Theosophical Society, apparently through personal friendship with Brian Dunningham, of a leading Theosophical family. Later, in 1955, while Mr. Dunningham was serving his first term as general secretary of the New Zealand section, Sir Edmund, no longer a member but evidently a staunch friend, spoke to the Theosophical Society convention, relating that he climbed his first mountain in companionship with Brian Dunningham, speaking of his high regard for Geoffrey Hodson, and describing religious life in the Himalayas.[68]

Geoffrey Hodson in his own person brought a profoundly mystical dimension of Theosophical life to New Zealand. Hodson (1886–1983) settled in Auckland in 1940 and remained for the rest of his long life. A genuine Theosophical mystic and saint, he wrote some sixty books and booklets on Theosophical teaching and the esoteric interpretation of scripture but is best known for his clairvoyant explorations of hidden reality, presented in such gorgeously illustrated works as *The Kingdom of the Gods,* on the *devas* (nature gods) that Hodson, with his clairvoyant vision, saw animating the natural world.

Born in England of a rural landowning family, Hodson joined the Theosophical Society in 1912 after hearing Annie Besant speak. His second sight was already awakening; he saw the "golden blaze of light" of her aura fill the Manchester hall as she spoke.[69] He served as a tank officer in World War I, married, and after the war began the clairvoyant investigations for which he would become famous, including some in association with Arthur Conan Doyle. He worked in business and as a YMCA secretary but after 1925 labored full-time for Theosophy, as a wide-traveling lecturer, writer, and teacher at such centers as Adyar and The Manor in Sydney. He settled in Auckland in 1940 when, during the course of a New Zealand visit, his wife's health and wartime conditions intervened to disallow further world touring. During his forty-three years in New Zealand, Hodson continued to write and lecture. He served as the main speaker at the national convention of the New Zealand section in his ninetieth year. He was founder-president of the New Zealand Vegetarian Society. After the war, he resumed lecture trips to other parts of the world on a limited scale.

Geoffrey Hodson lived in a modest flat on the grounds of the Theosophical Society headquarters in Epsom, Auckland, and perhaps is best known to more than a generation of New Zealand Theosophists simply as an aging and deeply spiritual presence amid the society and all its works. Typical of Hodson's sort of vision is an article, "The Theosophical Society in New Zealand through the Eyes of a Visitor," he wrote for the 1946 jubilee edition of *Theosophy in New Zealand*. He speaks of each of the major lodges having its special esoteric keynote: Auckland is "Spiritual and Intuitional"; in Wellington "One always receives the impression of Active Power"; in Christchurch the major quality is "Devotion to the Cause," in Dunedin it is "Past Glory" and "Invincible Determination." Another perception: "Many New Zealand Theosophists are, in fact, ceremonialists. They display a natural power, through ritual and life, to portray that harmonious co-ordination of many differing personalities and activities which is a special faculty of the ritualist."[70]

Many stories are told of Hodson's quiet but remarkable works of spiritual guidance and healing. Although he wrote much, the most profoundly personal and revealing of his writings is *Light of the Sanctuary: The Occult Diary of Geoffrey Hodson,* containing autobiographical chapters and day-by-day accounts of his inner spiritual life, edited, annotated, and published posthumously by his second wife, Sandra.[71] Here we read of his frequent inner communication with the masters, his perceptions of supra-physical realities, and above all the rich, incisive wisdom of his mystical awareness. New Zealanders may not be fully aware that, for all the alleged secularity of their country, they may well have long harbored a man who—though such things are admittedly very difficult to judge—was worthy of compare with the greater seers and mystics of any land or time.

Among the last lines, penned in November 1982 when he was ninety-six, are these:

> Two great things exist: The Cosmos
> > That of which it is a manifestation.
> These can become experiences in consciousness—the true objective of yoga.
> Is there an aspect of THAT which is motionless? . . .
> One spirit exists in spite of myriad forms.
> The widest distances in space are here.[72]

Since Geoffrey Hodson's passing in 1983, New Zealand Theosophy has continued to rank among the most active national sections in the world, with frequent conferences, camps, and lodge meetings, some of which I was privileged to attend as guest and speaker in 1988. At one Theosophical conclave I had the honor of encountering Sarah McGhee of Gisborne, Maori healer, seer, and Theosophist, and a thinker able to present intriguing correlations of the two traditions. Perhaps she is a precursor of the coming century's Theosophy in a markedly multi-cultural New Zealand. A Theosophical community is being developed at Orewa on the Hibiscus Coast north of Auckland. In general one senses in Theosophy a once-rambunctious movement now settled into active but sedate middle age. Yet Theosophy remains the largest and best-organized voice for alternative spirituality in New Zealand, and there is future potential.

5 Magic in the Mind
Other Groups in the Theosophical and Esoteric Traditions

THE THEOSOPHICAL SOCIETY has not stood alone in serving the tradition of esoteric lore that it helped bring to a wide public in the late nineteenth century. The wisdom may have been ancient, but the society's format—charismatic and often female leadership, comprehensive books, controversial lectures, cross-cultural contacts and teaching, a lively international organization—was considered novel and in some circles regarded as highly provocative. Although some have been provoked to antagonism, others were provoked to support this cause, both within and outside of the traditional Theosophical Society. This chapter will look at the New Zealand representation of groups that are related to Theosophy but not identical to it. In some cases the relation is historical or personal, in others merely an ideological kinship. Four types of such groups can, in fact, be discerned:

First are what may be called allies of Theosophy. These groups, Co-Freemasonry and the Liberal Catholic Church, contain considerable overlapping membership with the Adyar Theosophical Society. Although they have been controversial within Theosophy, they are regarded by their adherents as positive supplements or parallel ritual expressions to Theosophical doctrine, in no way hinting at variants in it.

Second are the liberalizing children of the Theosophical movement, the Krishnamurti work and Anthroposophy, activities founded by one-time Theosophists who sought freedom from what they perceived as excessive supernaturalism, Orientalism, or institutionalism on the part of the traditional Theosophical Society.

Third comes what I term "new-revelation" Theosophy, groups founded on a belief in fresh communications outside the main Theosophical canon from masters the same as or similar to those who initiated and instructed Helena Blavatsky, C. W. Leadbeater, and others in the first and second generations of original Theosophy. The only such group highly active in New Zealand is the Arcane School, based on the teachings of "the Tibetan" through Alice Bailey, through the "I Am" activity and the Church Universal and Triumphant, substantial groups of this sort in the United States, have been represented there.

Fourth and last are what might be termed kindred groups. These two very different organizations, the Beeville community and the Builders of the Adytum (BOTA), have no major overlapping membership or direct historical links with Theosophy. They are put in this chapter partly for convenience, but the placement can be justified on the grounds of some historical interaction on the part of the first and ideological compatibility in the case of the second.

Allies of Theosophy
THE STORY OF CO-FREEMASONRY

We shall then turn first to the interesting story of Co-Freemasonry. Traditionally Freemasonry had been reserved strictly for men, and so it is in most lodges to this day. But in 1882 a French lodge initiated a woman, Maria Deraismes. Suspended from the Grand Lodge to which it belonged, this unconventional order sought a new affiliation, and in 1893 La Grande Loge Symbolique Écossaise de France was founded, admitting both men and women. The French connection is still acknowledged by the New Zealand Federation of International Co-Freemasonry, which flourishes the motto "Le Droit Humain" on its stationery. The first Englishwoman to enter was Miss Francesca Arundale, a Theosophist since 1881. She was aunt and adoptive mother of George S. Arundale, who became international president of the Theosophical Society after Annie Besant in 1934, as well as (in 1935) grand commander of the Eastern Federation of Co-Freemasonry. Miss Arundale helped found the first Co-Masonic Lodge in London in 1902, where it became popular with Theosophists. She introduced Besant to Co-Masonry the same year and pioneered its work in India the next.[1]

Among the early English Co-Masons was James Ingall Wedgwood, whom we shall also have occasion to meet in connection with Liberal Catholicism. Wedgwood (1883–1951), of the famous pottery family, as a youth was an Anglican of strongly Anglo-Catholic bent. He was studying both organ and theology (with a view to entering the priesthood) in York when, in 1904, he heard two lectures by Annie Besant that changed his orientation entirely. He renounced his Anglican vocation and joined the Theosophical Society. Wedgwood carried over from his past, however, an abiding love of ritual that shaped the character of his Theosophical career and was hardly less deeply to stamp the fortunes of

Theosophy in coming decades, through the immense influence he was to have on C. W. Leadbeater.

So it was that the former theological student, general secretary of the Theosophical Society in England from 1911 to 1913, was active in the Order of the Star of the East, a Co-Mason by 1910, from 1912 to 1914 prominent in the Temple of the Rosy Cross (a short-lived ritualist body with close Theosophical ties), and in 1913 was ordained priest in a tiny Old Catholic Church, a move that would soon lead to his becoming first primate of the Liberal Catholic Church. In the Masonic world, by 1911 Wedgwood had risen to the post of Very Illustrious Supreme Secretary 33 degree of the British Federation of International Co-Freemasonry, under Annie Besant in her capacity as Very Illustrious Most Puissant Grand Commander of the British Jurisdiction. Wedgwood was convinced that the ritualistic work now arising in Theosophy, which he was so active in promoting, was under the direction of the master the Count Saint Germain, lord of the Seventh Ray. That Ray, emphasizing ceremony, was emerging as part of the necessary preparation for the Coming of the world teacher. (In the second-generation Theosophy of Besant and Leadbeater, the concept of the Seven Rays was important. These were seven lines of spiritual force each under the direction of a particular master and emphasizing a particular virtue or spiritual emphasis, such as ritual under the seventh guided by Saint Germain. Persons might be aligned to one or another, and different historical periods fell under the domination of particular rays.)

In 1914–1915 Wedgwood traveled to India and Australia. On June 12, 1915, in Sydney, he initiated Leadbeater into Co-Masonry. At first the latter was hostile to the younger man and to the ritualism he was promulgating, perhaps out of jealousy of Wedgwood's sophistication and rising occult influence, but on meeting him the former curate was soon enough won over and indeed became no less a passionate partisan of ritual's esoteric importance. Leadbeater also found a place for himself in the new work, quickly rising to the highest Masonic rank and becoming Administrator General of the Universal Co-Masonic Order in Australia.

Wedgwood, on an around-the-world tour marking his first year as primate of the Liberal Catholic Church, brought Co-Freemasonry together with that church to New Zealand in late 1916. The founding lodge was established in Auckland January 27, 1917. Inevitably, the novel venture brought outrage from both traditional Masons and unimpressed Theosophists. But it took root and continues to live quietly in the four major New Zealand cities. International headquarters remain in France, and, although many Co-Masons are also Theosophists, no formal or mandatory link exists between the two organizations.[2]

THE LIBERAL CATHOLIC CHURCH

The early history of the other ally of Theosophy, the Liberal Catholic Church, parallels that of Co-Freemasonry in Australia and New Zealand. J. I. Wedgwood and C. W. Leadbeater attained very high status in both ritual organizations, and both fell afoul of similar charges and controversies. The negatives did not, however, fatally affect the long-term fortunes of the two groups. Furthermore, both lodge and church came to the two countries at the same time, in the luggage of Wedgwood's 1916 visit.

We may begin our history of the Liberal Catholic Church in 1913, when Wedgwood, sensing a renewal of his call to the priesthood, approached Arnold Harris Mathew, archbishop of the Old Catholic Church in Great Britain.[3] That prelate was sympathetic and, seeing no impediment in the postulant's Theosophy, ordained him priest on July 22, 1913. For a couple of years Wedgwood, laboring energetically in this vineyard, promoted ritual in Theosophical publications while encouraging fellow Theosophists to join his church. Before long the bishops, priests, and laity of the tiny denomination were predominantly Theosophical, apparently with Mathew's tacit approval.

Then, on August 6, 1915, the archbishop suddenly declared Theosophy heretical and ordered all his clergy to resign from the society. Mathew apparently had underestimated the extent of their commitment to Theosophy, for most instead withdrew into schism under Frederick S. Willoughby, a Theosophical bishop of the Old Catholic Church. (Mathew, left isolated, subsequently announced his submission to the Church of Rome.) Willoughby consecrated two other Theosophist priests, Bernard Gauntlett and Robert King, to the episcopate; the three then consecrated the personable and articulate Wedgwood on February 13, 1916 to become presiding bishop of the Old Catholic Church.

Leaving King in charge of the work in wartime England, Wedgwood lost no time in departing for Australia, where he conveyed to Leadbeater his enthusiasm for the new church as a vehicle for Theosophy and as preparation for the Coming. The former Anglican priest was by now highly susceptible to that contagion. On July 15, 1916 Wedgwood reordained his colleague *sub conditione,* and on July 22 consecrated him to the episcopate. They offered these efforts to the Lord Maitreya, the coming Buddha and world teacher, even as they sensed the church to be inspired by a "thought current" from the master, the Count Saint Germain. The two prelates then worked assiduously together to compile a Mass and other rites appropriate to a church of Theosophical doctrine but Catholic tradition, at the same time persuading Annie Besant to

share their ardor for these new-old liturgical channels for occult energies. The first public services using the new text were offered early in
1917. Leadbeater continued over a period of years to refine the liturgy
and to prepare revised or original hymns for its rites. The name Liberal
Catholic Church was adopted in 1918. "Old Catholic" no longer
seemed appropriate to a body viewed as very new in a positive sense,
being linked to current eschatological expectation.[4]

The essential Liberal Catholic doctrinal statement is C. W. Leadbeater's *The Science of the Sacraments*.[5] Here the bishop recounts the
results of his clairvoyant investigations into the hidden processes at
work in the Christian sacraments. These had commenced years before
at an ordinary Roman Catholic Mass in an obscure Sicilian church. In
that humble place Leadbeater's inner eye had been amazed to see powerful waves of prayerful feeling roll from the peasant congregation to the
altar, and splendid light descend from above onto priest and altar, irra-
diating the consecrated bread and wine as the rite reached its climax.
The occult side of the Mass, he pronounced, is the building of a psychic
temple on the inner planes by the combined words, gestures, and concentrated thoughts of the celebrant and the congregation. This invisible
sanctuary then funnels and focuses the transcendent energies that the
masters know and serve and culminates in the channeling of supreme
divine grace through the shining white lens of the consecrated Host.

The fundamental idea is of thought-forms. Leadbeater and Besant
wrote a book of that title, equipped with paintings illustrating what
Leadbeater saw clairvoyantly around persons in various mental conditions, from the rich vibrant colors of exalted mystical states to the dark
thunderous hues of desolation or rage.[6] Thought-forms, the two
Theosophists taught, can be modified by prayer, meditation, and above
all the manufacture of a spiritual cathedral by the words and gestures of
the most sublime rite of all, the Mass. The esoteric geometry limned by
this ritual concentrates and localizes immense power, energy that even
the cut of the vestments and the movements of sacerdotal hands manifest and manage. The clairvoyant bishop thus noted such details as that
the sacred incense is full of elves, delightful creatures who dance in its
aromatic clouds and help distribute its benedictions, and that angels
come to bathe in the light streaming from the Host.

Leadbeater, in *The Science of the Sacraments,* also discusses the inner
planes meaning of baptism, penance, and the other sacraments,
together with the esoteric significance of the Christian year and the
events in the life of Christ they commemorate. But the major focus is
the Eucharist. Rather ironically, in view of Liberal Catholicism's incep-
tion as a radically new liturgical departure tied to high eschatological
hopes, the enactment of this great Christian rite now has a rather dated,

period-piece air about it. Little touched by the epochal liturgical reno-
vations that swept through Roman Catholicism, and hardly less Anglicanism and other liturgically minded Western forms of Christianity, in
the wake of Vatican II, the Liberal Catholic Church in general continues to build its spiritual cathedrals by the blueprints of the old "western
rite" as Leadbeater read them; no new interpreter has yet arrived with
his visionary authority to provide fresh guidelines. Nor has the ordina-
tion of women, lately such a contentious issue within larger branches of
Catholic Christianity, yet come to the prematurely fossilized Liberal
Catholic Church.

The Liberal Catholic Masses I have attended in New Zealand and
elsewhere have always evoked, for me personally, bittersweet childhood
memories of old-style Anglo-Catholic Episcopalianism (Anglicanism), a
peculiar religion at once rigid and romantic, in which I was raised but
which is rarely encountered these days in that pre-1960s form. The Liberal Catholic altar, like those of that neo-medieval strain of Anglicanism, is against the back wall of the sanctuary rather than freestand-
ing and is ornamented with six candlesticks, missal stand, cross (though
not crucifix), and frontal. The only unusual item is a picture of Jesus
often placed directly over the cross on the altar, a distinctive Liberal
Catholic feature.

As the Mass begins, as of old, numerous clergy and acolytes in res-
plendent copes and chasubles and surplices, swinging censors that cloud
the church with the fragrant elvan incense, enter in procession. Moving
with the slowness of ancient ritual, they approach the altar chanting and
genuflecting. The words of the rite are in English and are generally
reminiscent of the Anglican or Roman Catholic missal, but with certain
variations in a Gnostic direction. The confession does not suggest that
"we are miserable sinners," but rather that "often we forget the glory of
our heritage and wander from the path which leads to righteousness."
Sacring bells chime as the priest genuflects and elevates the Host and
chalice at the consecration of the bread and wine. Then comes another
distinctive Liberal Catholic tradition: the singing of the hymn, "O
Come, All Ye Faithful," at each celebration after that climax of the rite.

The traditional Christian might, however, be most surprised at the
sermon. The visitor to a Liberal Catholic service may hear of an impersonal Absolute beyond God the Father, of masters and psychic phenomena, and of esoteric interpretations of Christianity in which the festivals
of the sacred calendar, or the parables and miracles of Jesus, and even
his birth, death, and resurrection, are depicted as signs and symbols of
occult realities far deeper than ordinary-time events.

In historical time, however, the Liberal Catholic Church suffered
vicissitudes no less than the Theosophical Society and closely related to

them. In 1922, the year of Leadbeater's close investigation by the Sydney police, James Wedgwood was forced to resign from the Liberal Catholic Church, as well as the Theosophical Society and Co-Masonry, because of his own alleged scandals involving homosexuality. He was succeeded in 1923 as presiding bishop of the Liberal Catholic Church by Leadbeater, who had by then outlasted his calvaries in connection with the same problem. Wedgwood, after an abortive attempt to gain a doctorate at the Sorbonne, at the same time reportedly living a wild Parisian life, returned to the church and other occult activities in 1924. But his mental condition thereafter grew increasingly unsteady, and the former prelate was pushed into semiretirement as Leadbeater remained primate of the Liberal Catholic Church for the rest of his life.

Liberal Catholicism in New Zealand, like Theosophy generally, experienced these trials only as distant thunder and lightning. Its own priests and bishops have generally been of sterling character, its bishops including respected general secretaries of the Theosophical Society and its priests such saintly men as Geoffrey Hodson. Thus in 1917 Bishop Wedgwood ordained to the priesthood two men who would hold both general secretarial and episcopal office, John Ross Thomson and William Crawford. Thomson served as Vicar General for New Zealand until, in 1924, he was consecrated Suffragan Bishop for New Zealand in Sydney by Leadbeater and two other bishops. He held this office until 1935, when Crawford was consecrated as Regionary Bishop (he was the first to hold this title) to succeed him. Crawford was followed as Regionary by H. H. Banks in 1962, S. G. Nicholls in 1971, and A. E. Lambden in 1980.

Parishes were established in the major New Zealand cities, though none have been large. Services were generally held on Theosophical Society premises, but, increasingly, a need was felt by Liberal Catholics for their own edifice. Planning began for the erection of the church of St. Francis in Auckland in 1944, and finally in 1964 the procathedral of that name was dedicated. In 1975 the Liberal Catholic Church became a member of the National Council of Churches in New Zealand, after lively discussion and some dissent in both the largely "mainline" council and the somewhat unconventional denomination of the appropriateness of this action. (An earlier application for membership by the Liberal Catholic Church in 1957 had been declined.)[7]

The New Zealand Liberal Catholic Church's golden age was certainly amid the intensity and expectancy of the 1920s, when it was new and tied to those hopes, and its silver age in the postwar decades when the St. Francis church project was underway. Now its membership appears to be aging and declining. But Liberal Catholicism—with several hundred adherents—remains stronger per capita in New Zealand than in virtually any other country, and may long remain a significant segment of the nation's religious life.

The Liberalizing Children of the Theosophical Movement

JIDDU KRISHNAMURTI

A prime example of the liberalizing children of the Theosophical movement is, of course, is Krishnamurti. Jiddu Krishnamurti was almost literally a child of Theosophy, having been raised and shaped by the movement, but who broke with its institutional and ideological expression in 1929 in order to live and teach a vision of truth as "a pathless land."[8]

His teaching, in brief, was that truth is found not in any intellectual content but in "choiceless awareness" of daily existence and mental activity. One constructs symbols and beliefs in the hope of securing the universe with them, but instead these ropes of the mind become toils from which it is difficult to escape. True freedom, therefore, is "freedom from the known," simple observation without past or future, simple doing without knowing. Through lectures and intimate, much-valued class meetings Krishnamurti communicated the experience behind these dicta to a growing audience. Much of this teaching was published in book form by the Theosophical Publishing House and through other outlets.

The Krishnamurti Foundation Trust, based in England, was established in 1968, as a successor to earlier organizations, to handle various aspects of his work. It is responsible for Krishnamurti work in all countries, including New Zealand, except the United States and Spanish-speaking Latin America, which are served by parallel foundations. The trust aids in distributing his books, tapes, films, records and videocassettes. Although a Krishnamurti denomination would be virtually a contradiction in terms, the foundations come as close to being such a holding corporation for the Krishnamurti legacy as can be, and since his death in 1986 they have set themselves up to preserve it for the ages.

As part of his world-ranging tours, Krishnamurti spoke in New Zealand before the Second World War in 1934 and again in 1939. (Postwar visits were planned but did not materialize.) The work of the Krishnamurti Foundation Trust in New Zealand was very much bound up with the life of Ray Falla (1923–1987), who served a number of years as its New Zealand agent. According to Elizabeth Falla, his widow, Ray served as a pilot during the war. Shot down over the Malay Peninsula and severely injured, he was a paraplegic for several years. Through strength of will as much as anything he managed to walk again. He was ordained into the Methodist ministry but left it after realizing that the doctrines and way of life demanded by that calling were increasingly incompatible with his own spiritual quest. The break with the church also marked the end of his first marriage.

In the 1950s Falla happened to hear of Krishnamurti and read his books with great interest. Still seeking a cause to which he could commit himself, he went to India, where for over five years he taught physics at the Krishnamurti school at Rajghat, and as it happened made the first recording of a Krishnamurti talk, because of his ability to operate then-novel equipment. Falla also reported mountaintop spiritual experiences in the course of extensive travels in the Himalayas. His diary has him say, after hearing Krishnamurti for the first time, "I was held like I have never been held before . . . not so much emotional as seeing one-self. . . ." Ten days later, after another talk: "Surely this day is a crisis in my life. . . ."

Falla took over the New Zealand work when the foundation was started in 1968. Yet he was always acutely conscious of the limitations of his abilities and his role. He continually studied Krishnamurti's teachings, but, according to his second wife, Elizabeth (whom he met in 1976), was often frustrated—as anyone would be—at his human incapacity always to live in accordance with them. He believed that Krishnamurti's way could not be taught in a proselytizing manner, and he likewise opposed interpretation and commentary. He felt his job was soley to provide information and to facilitate the circulation of films (later videos) and publications. When he was present at a showing, he would refuse to discuss the teachings but would freely give factual information, though he did greatly enjoy sharing his understanding of Krishnamurti with small groups of friends. According to Elizabeth, he showed great enthusiasm for life and in his last months often said, echoing early words of his guide, "There is no such thing as teacher and taught, only learning."[9]

After the death of Ray Falla, the Krishnamurti Foundation Trust set about arranging the establishment of a legally registered charitable trust in New Zealand, to be called the Krishnamurti Association in New Zealand; approval of this status was finally gained in 1990. Five of the trustees are New Zealand residents, the sixth is the trust itself, with which the association is legally affiliated. Its work continues as before—there is a newsletter, and a book and video library is maintained. The association has also been successful is organizing informal Krishnamurti study gatherings and in developing a list of local contacts throughout New Zealand, prepared to offer information, hold Krishnamurti video shows in their homes, and promote awareness of Krishnamurti's teachings in appropriate ways.[10]

ANTHROPOSOPHY

Anthroposophy, a second (and quite different) movement that can be seen as a liberalizing form of Theosophy, has had a marked influence in New Zealand. The Anthroposophical Society was founded in Germany by Rudolf Steiner (1861-1925) in 1913 and refounded in Switzerland 1923-1924. Steiner had been general secretary of the Theosophical Society in Germany 1902-1912 but broke with Theosophy in 1912 over what he considered the excesses toward which the society was moving under Besant and Leadbeater. He was particularly upset by the Krishnamurti enthusiasm and the Order of the Star of the East, which he had tried to prevent members of his German section from joining. (For a few years after 1906 he was also a member of the Ordo Templi Orientis [OTO].)

It was in any case likely that a mystical and occult mind as creative as Steiner's would sooner or later go its own way. Even as a Theosophist Steiner had shown considerable independence. Wishing primarily to explore the deeper traditions of his own part of the world, believing strongly in the importance of Christian and Rosicrucian esotericism and in the spiritual dimensions of Western science, he was more Western-oriented than many Theosophists. An authority on Goethe, philosopher of science, educator and linguist, his mind was brimming with esoteric ideas, and he was a born teacher who could make the most recondite concepts significant and exciting.

Fundamental to Steiner's doctrine was the description—in terms partly common to Theosophy—of four levels of human nature: the physical, etheric, astral, and ego. Each of these makes possible its own mode of knowing: the physical, sensory knowledge; the etheric, imaginative knowledge; the astral, inspirational knowledge; and the ego, intuitive or spiritual knowledge. In developmental terms the last came first; supported by his linguistic science, Steiner argued that the human physical body evolved from its spiritual nature rather than the other way around. Making use of all these levels of knowing, Steiner claimed ability to penetrate the spiritual nature of all entities and show how spiritual science could be applied for human good.

Rudolf Steiner gave over six thousand lectures that offered rich and specific insights into a remarkable range of endeavors on the basis of his imaginative, inspirational, and intuitive seeing. He described the inner etheric and other forces at work on both plant and human life and on this basis promulgated new methods of agriculture and medicine. He saw significance in color and music for health and human wholeness. He developed theories of education involving eurhythmics and a study of seven-year cycles of development; these are implemented by the well-regarded Waldorf or Steiner schools around the world. He also contributed to the theory of art, sculpture, and architecture; these ideas are embodied in the Goetheanum building, which headquarters the society in Dornach, Switzerland.

Steiner's teaching came to New Zealand as early as 1910, when Mrs. E. J. Richmond of Havelock North, of the family involved in early Theosophy, began reading his books with appreciation. Dr. Robert Felkin, who visited Havelock in 1912 and settled there permanently in 1916 and who was a great admirer of Steiner, employed some of his techniques in his medical practice. Havelock North, down to the present, has been a major center of Anthroposophy in New Zealand, Steiner's movement enjoying some overlapping membership with other activities in that extraordinary town, the Havelock Work and the Golden Dawn. After Mrs. Richmond's death in 1921, the Richmonds' daughter and son-in-law, Mr. and Mrs. Bernard Compton-Smith, continued to promote the Steiner work. Study circles emerged throughout the country, as far south as Invercargill, and in 1930 the Anthroposophical Society in New Zealand was formally established.

Although relatively few in numbers, "Anthropops" throughout the world have a most impressive capacity for organization and hard work on behalf of their cause. I have found Anthroposophists to be excellent people, but not entirely easy to meet with informally or at length because of their inevitably crowded schedules and numerous ongoing projects. It is not surprising, then, to find that New Zealand's few hundred Anthroposophists operate a teachers' college and several schools, including Queenswood in Hastings, a boarding and day school, the Hohepa Home School in Napier and a second home school, the Farndon Hohepa Home School on fifty acres of farmland near Clive, for children in need of special care. There is a new elementary school in Lower Hutt. The Prometheus Foundation in Napier engaged in community banking. The Bio-Dynamic Farming and Gardening Association, headquartered in Havelock North, promotes Steiner's agricultural methods, which among other things pioneered organic farming and the use of compost. Havelock North is also the New Zealand center of the Weleda Organization, a pharmacy that distributes remedies, largely herbal, prepared along Steinerian lines. It has its own attractive herb garden where many of the medicinals are grown.

On a Friday evening in 1988 I visited a local Anthroposophical meeting in Lower Hutt. Lower Hutt now has a Steiner school, constructed of cedar in a Steinerian architectural style, together with a center and reading room. My meeting, however, was held in a private home. Such discussions as the one I attended gather weekly, and this Friday about a dozen persons were present. The discussion was based on one of

Steiner's exceedingly numerous published lectures. It was one of those in which the sage of the Goetheanum, as was his wont, introduced notions likely to seem bizarre, even insane, to those unaccustomed to his spiritual acrobatics. On further reflection one may begin to get a perturbing sense of having inadvertantly glanced down a stunningly novel but not dismissible angle of vision, though one so off the ordinary coordinates of modern thought as to leave one stumbling, like Plato's escapee from the cave.

The topic was man as microcosm. Unlike most philosophers ruminating on this ancient concept, Steiner was not content to deal with generalities but insisted on highly specific correspondences between human and natural nature. The human head, then, is related to the bird. A bird's life is centered in its head, Steiner claimed, between eating, seeing, and song, and our thoughts correspond to the bird's plumage in their kaleidoscopes of color. The chest—lungs and heart—are related to the lion, whose life is centered on blood and breath and their balance. The stomach and digestion, with obvious rationale, is the realm of the cow. There are other correspondences, too: memories are butterflies, emerging from cocoons in the depths of the mind.

Many may regard these correlations as no more than poetic metaphors, appealing but of no scientific value. But Steiner was not so sure. He inhabited a middle ground all his own between poetry and science. His lectures explicated such notions as the foregoing much too fully for the fleeting conceits of the poet's art yet eluded also the supposed clinical objectivity of the laboratory. Perhaps his vision of the universe's web of almost unimaginably subtle connections had something in common with that of another great imaginationist who often rowed against the tides of his time, William Blake, who in "Auguries of Innocence" could write,

> The wild deer, wand'ring here & there,
> Keeps the Human Soul from Care . . .
> The Owl that calls upon the Night
> Speaks the Unbeliever's fright. . . .

Fundamental to Steiner's method was his linguistic awareness that metaphors are not merely poetic grace notes, but are thought itself; in the last analysis thought is seeing one thing as something else, and there are root metaphors behind which one cannot go, for as Steiner's disciple Owen Barfield put it, the abstractions by which one might want to do so are themselves but "decayed metaphors." To say that the human head and the bird have a special relation, with its feathers our intricate plumage of thought, may make no normative scientific sense whatsoever, however the case may be with the sciences of the etheric, astral, or spiritual planes Steiner professed also to have penetrated. On the other hand, I would guess that nobody really knows all the reasons why the countless entities of our universe have the shapes and colors they do or all the levels on which they are interdependent. Steiner maintained that we will never get all those reasons until we come to terms with the spiritual and inner-planes dimensions of evolution as well as the outer, and until we recognize metaphors—the seemingly adventitious "fit" of one entity with another—as ways of knowing, as well as of talking.

The Lower Hutt group of Anthroposophists was a well-educated, intellectual set, though not academic or scholarly in the narrow sense of the words. They were chiefly musicians and Steiner school teachers, it seemed; other Anthroposophical groups would certainly include a quota of artists and architects as well. They typically explain their interest in Steiner in terms of a concern for the harmony of one's inner and outer life, and of one's spirit and creative expression.

When I was in Havelock North, I dropped into the Weleda Pharmacy, named after an old Germanic goddess of healing, and was impressed by the wide array of gentle remedies and herbal toiletries. I surveyed natural, nonprescription aids for sleeplessness and headaches, oils for massage and bath, lotions for babies and bruises, elixirs for colds and coughs, and much more. Weleda was now also handling the Bach flower remedies. These botanical essences, dissolved in water, are used to counter fears, worries, and undesirable moods rather than physical ailments: Cherry plum combats uncontrolled, irrational thoughts; wild rose overcomes apathy and resignation. I walked in the lovely herb garden behind the pharmacy and sat in one of its bowers gazing at distant hills as I read some Anthroposophical literature. Although sometimes unconventional, I reflected, the Weleda and Bach recipes are like striking metaphors, like head and bird, now unexpectedly conjoining something in the human orbit with something in the world of roots, leaves and flowers.

At the pharmacy I met, by fortunate chance, a couple who were leaders in the Steinerian practice of bio-dynamic farming. Some ninety farms in New Zealand follow its principles, I was told, and they raise all New Zealand crops, including sheep and cattle for meat, wool, and dairy products. Bio-dynamics is basically organic farming that endeavors to progressively do away with chemical support systems in favor of astrological and homeopathic principles. Both of these principles are clearly further examples of the application of correspondences. Astrology presupposes intimate though invisible linkages between the stars above and the human and natural earth here below. Traditionally, it ties parts of the body, activities, and arenas of life to particular planets and signs of the zodiac. Bio-dynamic farming emphasizes the cycles of the moon and uses them—as have farmers for millennia—to schedule planting and harvesting.

Homeopathy is a medical system that relies on administration of very small doses of substances that, in a healthy person, would produce symptoms of the affliction being treated. It is based on the sound principle that many symptoms, such as fever, are not caused by the disease itself but by the body's efforts to fight the illness and destroy the alien bacteria. Homeopathy seeks to aid this effort. But it also holds that the effectiveness of such remedies is not related to strength and that in fact highly diluted prescriptions may be preferable, apparently because they better encourage the body's own natural struggle or attract benign bacteria to do the job. Homeopathy is not new; it received its modern formulation from Samuel Hahneman (1755–1843). It had some popularity in the nineteenth century and has received fresh attention from advocates of "alternative medicine" in the late twentieth century.

Bio-dynamics applies these homeopathic practices to agriculture, especially in the use of herbs to combat plant diseases and in fertilizer. I was informed, for example, that a cowhorn filled with cow dung that has been buried over a winter, then mixed with water and spread over one's fields, perhaps from a plane, will fertilize five thousand acres. The homeopathic use of very minute quantities of beneficial bacteria and nutritional substances, generated in the dung, magnetically attracts natural fertilizers. Once this process takes hold, my informant assured me, the results are dramatic. Anthroposophy, too, offers a radically original perspective on human life that, if it were to take hold, could bring vast changes in the workings of human life.

New-Revelation Theosophy

The term "new-revelation Theosophy" is a little misleading if it is taken to imply that these movements necessarily adhere to fundamentalist interpretations of their material, for the Arcane School at least also has liberalizing aspects. But it and the other new-revelation tradition, that of the I Am activity and its offshoots, nonetheless base their teaching on alleged new communications from masters identical with or similar to those with whom Helena Blavatsky and her associates were in touch several decades earlier.

THE ARCANE SCHOOL: ALICE BAILEY

The set of activities I am here labeling the Arcane School in fact goes under a rather bewildering set of names. In *Beliefs and Practices in New Zealand: A Directory,* they are headed "Goodwill," in reference to the Auckland Goodwill Unit of Service. But there is "another autonomous

Unit of Service," the Triangles Center, in Paikakeriki, which also operates a center and information service in Cuba Mall, Wellington. The tradition has been known more informally as the Full Moon Meditation Groups, because of their unifying tradition of practicing group meditation every full moon, and simply as the Alice Bailey Movement. Meditation Groups in Ojai, California, sponsors Meditation Groups for the New Age and Groups for Creative Meditation, terms that may also be used collectively for the tradition. But all these diverse activities are based on a set of books by Alice Bailey believed to have been inspired by a master known as The Tibetan. They are published by the Lucis Trust in New York and London. Their teachings are explicated in correspondence courses offered by the Arcane School, in New York, and by a rival center, also in New York, the School for Esoteric Studies. The Arcane School, which sponsors both the Triangles and World Goodwill, is the most important international connection in New Zealand for the Alice Bailey Movement, and for convenience I will refer to it by that name.[11]

Alice Bailey (née LaTrobe-Bateman, 1880–1949) was born to a well-to-do English family. A difficult and headstrong child, she became a fervent evangelical as a young woman, preaching hellfire sermons to British troops in India. Like Annie Besant, she was briefly and unhappily married to an Anglican clergyman. It was Alice's husband who brought her to the United States. After the emotional ordeal of that episode, she came to Theosophy. By the late 1910s she was working as manager of the vegetarian cafeteria at the Krotona Theosophical school in Hollywood, California; later she became editor of the society's magazine.

One afternoon in 1919 she was walking in the hills around the center. She felt she was being contacted by a master, the one she was to call the Tibetan, who wanted her to write for him. She began the long series of books, eventually published in uniform blue bindings, presenting his teaching. In a somewhat diffuse manner they offer a great amount of material: on the hierarchy of the masters, on methods of meditation, on astrology and the Seven Rays, and on the establishment of a New Group of World Servers. The defining teaching, though, is the emphasis on the Coming Reappearance of the Christ, or world teacher (in this Coming One the work of the Buddha and the Christ must fuse), and the importance of group meditation in preparing for the eschatological event by the setting up of spiritual currents conducive to it. This is done by repeating a prayer called the Great Invocation together with visualizing the funneling down to the power of the Hierarchy, as the grand company of benign earthly and cosmic masters, authors and directors of the great plan to which we must and shall return, is inevitably called. The Great Invocation goes like this:

From the point of Light within the Mind of God
Let light stream forth into the minds of men.
    Let LIGHT descend on Earth.

From the point of Love within the Heart of God
Let Love stream forth into the hearts of men.
    May CHRIST return to Earth.

From the centre where the Will of God is known
Let Purpose guide the little wills of men—
    The PURPOSE which the Masters know and serve.

From the centre which we call the race of men
Let the Plan of Love and Light work out
    And may it seal the door where evil dwells.

Let Light and Love and Power
Restore the Plan on Earth.

Conflict with officials of the Theosophical Society and her independent teaching led Alice and her fiancé Foster Bailey, who had been
national secretary of the society in America, to withdraw from it. In
1923 they established the Arcane School. World Goodwill was founded
in 1932 to mobilize spiritual energy for establishing right human relations, and dealing with world problems through education of public
opinion, together with giving support to individuals and groups. It has
no formal membership. The Triangles, founded in 1937, is intended to
link groups of three persons each who meditate daily to release positive
force into the world, thus creating a "network of light." During the
thirty years from her first contact with the master in 1919 to her death in
1949, Alice Bailey produced nineteen books of the Tibetan series as well
as other writings, including her uncompleted autobiography.[12] The
eschatological emphasis in the writing began to appear forcefully in the
1930s. Foster Bailey continued to direct the Arcane School work until
he died in 1977.

Although scattered individuals in New Zealand have long been
involved in the Alice Bailey work, it does not appear there was organized activity until 1976, when Janet and Steve Nation (she from Tas-
mania, he from Hawke Bay) started the Arcane School Triangles Center in Wellington by putting up a big poster in a shopping mall, inviting
interested persons to write. Only four responded at first, but those four
were enough, and the center opened. Soon it had a bookshop, lending
library, reading room, collection of New Age magazines, collection of
cassette tapes, and meditation room, all open for several hours daily.
The Nations went to London in 1978 to work for the Lucis Trust there,
but others have continued the Wellington activities, and another center
has opened in Auckland.

The spiritual life of the New Zealand Arcane School groups, like that of the Alice Bailey Movement everywhere, centers around group meditation at the full moon of every month, and the Three Linked Festivals held at the most important full moons of all, those of Aries, Taurus, and Gemini—roughly, the three months of (the northern hemisphere) spring. At those great holy festivals, groups from a wide area may combine to make it a particularly memorable occasion, with choral music, sacred dance, and distinguished speakers, as well as the solemn recitation of the Great Invocation and deep meditation uniting the spiritual energies of a goodly number of people.

The ordinary full-moon meditations of the other nine months, however, may be no less impressive as religious experience. The full-moon correlation should not, of course, be taken to imply any sort of gross lunarian superstition or moon worship, any more than does the Christian dating of Easter by the paschal full moon. It does, however, reflect the regard for a rather deep and philosophical astrology characteristic of the entire Theosophical tradition, and in particular a convention that the full moon especially opens the portals of communication between earthlings and the Hierarchy.

Although I have visited several full-moon meditations in the United States, the one in which I participated in Wellington, in the tiny meditation room of the Cuba Mall center, was definitely the deepest and most powerful of my experience. Perhaps it was the still crisp night, perhaps the close-knit group of very special people, certainly the leader's wisdom in talking little yet weaving a sense of common purpose, common direction, common energy, and common joy virtually without words. "Energy is Eternal Delight," said William Blake, and I felt something of that wondrous combination as I walked back home up the steep hills of Wellington after that hour of communion with the Hierarchy.

A couple of other new-revelation Theosophy movements deserve briefer mention because, although important in the United States, they seem to have taken much less hold in New Zealand. (Perhaps that is because they are less exportable. Unlike other forms of the Theosophical tradition, they have a rather right-wing political coloration, which puts a great deal of emphasis on the symbols of American patriotism and inculcates a special quasi-messianic role for America, though one by which all nations will ultimately be blessed.)

I Am Activity

While looking for a church named after some saint in the Auckland telephone directory, I serendipitously came across the Saint Germain Foundation. This I knew to be the sponsoring organization of the "I Am" Activity, an American movement with a remarkable history about which I had written an article.[13] The activity goes back to the troubled decade of the 1930s. Guy Ballard, the founder, claimed that in 1930, on the slopes of beautiful Mt. Shasta in northern California, he had encountered Saint Germain, one of the Theosophical masters and also, as we have seen, a special patron of Liberal Catholicism. This personage, in history an enigmatic occultist who ornamented the court of Louis XV and of whom many amazing stories were told, gave Ballard a wonderfully invigorating drink, assuring him it came from "Universal Supply . . . Omnipresent Life." The adept went on to instruct his new disciple in karma and reincarnation—including time-travel visits to ancient Peru, Africa, and elsewhere to scan his past lives.[14] In this and subsequent revelations Ballard also learned of the lives of the masters in their hidden retreats under the mountain fastnesses of the American West, of the occult past and future including the American destiny, of spiritual practices centering on chantlike "decrees," of the astounding claim that one can cheat death and ascend like Jesus or Saint Germain and the other Ascended Masters, and of the I AM presence, the "individualized God-presence," over each person from which one can draw strength. The "I Am" Activity has a unique atmosphere, with its extensive use of color and colorful titles for its masters, its temples characteristically decorated in the white-and-gold rococo of the Louis Quinze style together with American flags and paintings of masters and the founders, its harp and organ music, its leaders dressed in carefully tailored whites and pastels.

Under the leadership of Guy Ballard and his strong-willed wife Edna the movement based on these revelations grew with remarkable speed during the 1930s. By 1938, the year of its peak, followers numbered as many as a million or more, and the Ballards filled the largest auditoriums in the greatest cities of the nation with their dramatic presentations. Then, late in 1939, Guy Ballard suddenly died, leaving not a few believers wondering why this "Accredited Messenger" of the Ascended Masters had not himself ascended rather than dying in the normal manner.

On the heels of that tragedy came more trouble: a suit from the U.S. government against the leaders of the movement for mail fraud, alleging they had solicited donations using deceptive claims of healing power and special spiritual status. The Ballards, the government claimed, promoted a false religion for gain knowing it was false. Amid these disturbing charges and unwelcome publicity, "I Am" dwindled greatly. But finally, in 1944, the indictment for fraud against the "I Am" leadership was voided by the U.S. Supreme Court in a landmark religious liberty decision, on the grounds that it could only be justified if the faith of the Ballards in the masters could be proved false. The high court declared that the truth or falsity of religious faith is beyond the power of the law to determine, and religious advocates cannot be forced to prove its veridicality. As Justice Douglas asserted in the decision, "Men may believe what they cannot prove. They may not be put to the proof of their religious doctrines or beliefs." (Justice Jackson, in concurring, proposed further that the sincerity or insincerity of religious belief is also beyond the province of the law, but this doctrine has not yet been tested.)

In the postwar world, though it never relived the high days of the 1930s, "I Am" recovered some ground to become a modest but apparently enduring part of the American religious scene. Its adherents have some three hundred temples and a beautifully designed and landscaped headquarters in suburban Chicago and mount an impressive pageant at Mt. Shasta every summer.

When I called the number of the Saint Germain Foundation in Auckland, I received only a recorded message in typically mellifluous "I Am" tones greeting me and telling me where I could write for further information. I found no evidence of any visible "I Am" center or group in New Zealand.

THE CHURCH UNIVERSAL AND TRIUMPHANT

The Church Universal and Triumphant (CUT), yet another New-revelation devolution of Theosophy, is focused on messages from masters channeled through Elizabeth Claire Prophet. Clearly influenced by "I Am," it shares with it many of the same masters, including Saint Germain, the same conservative attitudes, and somewhat similar "decree" practices. Also like "I Am," it has experienced dizzyingly precipitous cycles of rise and fall. In the 1970s and 1980s the movement was highly visible if controversial, its ads and books everywhere, its headquarters on a series of campuses. But in the late 1980s, after setbacks from lawsuits and defections, Prophet and the CUT's hard core of adherents retired to form a commune in rural Montana, where they proclaimed imminent apocalypse while encountering tension with the natives over land purchases and trouble with the law for alleged stockpiling of weapons.

The CUT appears in *Beliefs and Practices in New Zealand: A Directory* under an older title, Summit Lighthouse. But a letter sent to that Glenfield, Auckland, address was returned, and I could find no evidence that this movement was active in New Zealand at the time of my research.

Kindred Groups

BEEVILLE

The curious Beeville community was located at Orini, seventy-five miles south of Auckland, between Taupiri and Morrinsville. It centered around two brothers, Ray and Dan Hansen, and several women. Beeville was a self-sufficient agricultural colony that derived its cash income chiefly from the production of high-quality honey—hence the name. Its inhabitants were also pacifists, vegetarians, advocates of complete individual freedom including sexual freedom, and reportedly sought to eliminate any sense of personal possessiveness not only in material goods but also in domestic relationships.

In the 1940s and 1950s, Beeville received a fair amount of media attention, both because of its members' wartime objection to war and their unusual marital arrangements. Headlines like "N.Z's Strangest Community: 'Beeville' Has Peculiar Views on Family Life" (*N.Z. Truth,* August 18, 1959) appeared frequently.

Theosophical connections emerge early in the Beeville story. The original Hansens had immigrated from Denmark in the 1880s. Ray, born about 1910, joined the Hamilton branch of the Theosophical Society at eighteen, a course followed by the rest of six Hansen brothers, and they were all active for a number of years. (However, only Ray and, later, Dan were involved in Beeville.) Ray also became a poet, which brought him in touch with the Theosophical poet D. W. M. Burn. Through Theosophical contacts he apparently also became very active in the Social Credit movement in the early 1930s. He vigorously campaigned in the press on its behalf, and at one time even carried a Social Credit placard on his truck.

Through Theosophical connections Ray met the woman he married, Olive. In 1937 a second woman, Anne Sanders, joined the household. According to Ray's account as given to the press, Anne had certain personal problems that led Olive and him to offer her a home:

> It was either a question of asking Anne to leave or finding some way of living harmoniously together. Both he and Olive shied away from asking Anne to leave. . . . Olive, Ray says, was prepared to live as a trio if Ray accepted the responsibility for taking this step. Without her co-operation no move could have been made, he says. It was at their joint invitation that Anne shared, and still shares, their intimate life. This was made possible, Ray maintains, because of the completeness of his own and Olive's relationship and not because of any dissatisfaction.[15]

In the end, Olive had ten children by Ray, who also had four with Anne. In 1955, Olive and Anne, then both fifty-one, were described as "charming and intelligent women."[16]

By the 1950s, the community was large and flourishing: there was the original trio; Dan, Ray's brother, paralyzed from the waist down by an accident and unable to have children, whose wife Edith was therefore impregnated on his behalf by one of Ray's sons; all the dozen and a half or so offspring and, as time went on, their spouses and children; and several nonfamily members who from time to time joined the community. The last generation, and the children, however, showed less stability in attachment to Beeville than did Ray's generation, not seldom coming and going, wavering between the bond they felt to the unusual ménage and its values, and youth's natural desire to leave home and find one's own way in the world.

The Hansens and all other long-standing members of Beeville were conscientious objectors to military service. Some of them suffered imprisonment during the war for their objection to force or coercion in any form. Dan had, in fact, met Edith in 1945, when he was conveying friends and relatives to visit inmates of detention camps; Edith's brother was in one of the camps at the time. The objection to force was, however, sorely tried after the war when, in 1948, a former prisoner of war arrived to take advantage of Beeville's hospitality and lack of definite leadership—decisions were made by consensus. The stranger was a sun worshipper, nudist, argumentative nonpacifist, and financial finagler of strong and ingratiating personality who proved to be extremely divisive —and so gave a bad public impression—over the two years of his stay. Although the community had difficulty finding agreement on what to do about him, he finally left just ahead of a newspaper investigation of Beeville and its accounts.

The spiritual focus of Beeville early shifted from standard Theosophy to Krishnamurti. According to a 1959 article, "Most 'Beeville' members are serious students of the teachings of Jeddu Krishnamurti, the Indian philosopher, protege of the late Annie Besant and C. W. Leadbeater. . . . 'Beeville' people pursue what they term 'truth in daily living.' They hold with Krishnamurti's statement that if truth is individual, eternal, unique, then organisation born of time can only imprison and distort that truth, which is of eternity."[17] Krishnamurti does not, however, appear to have impeded Beeville's relations with the Theosophical Society. An article from *The Young Theosophist* of November 1957 enthusiastically describes a visit to Beeville, as it relates that the Beeville "children's friendly smiles greeted us from all sides" and speaks of the healthy vegetarian food, from carrot juice to soya bean flour. Of living arrangements we are told:

> Twenty-three people live on the farm and the smaller section, enjoying communal life because they believe that this is the right way to live in order to develop initiative and co-operation in the individual. They do not aim to separate themselves from society, but rather to integrate with it.
>
> There are no rules and no programme and they face difficulties

as they arise. Each individual strives to pull his or her weight for the sake of the community. There are not any wages, all cheques being made out to the community account from which two members are authorised to draw. Thus each member needs only to ask for money to meet his or her requirements. Decisions involving large amounts of money require the unaminous consent of the members, but this seldom causes difficulty.

Much later, in 1970, a letter from Ray and Olive Hansen discussed their showing of Krishnamurti films—and, it turned out, also answering eager questions about Beeville!—at the Theosophical community in Orewa and the Theosophical Society convention. Relations appeared to be good.[18] There are hints about this time of a Beeville interest in Scientology also, but it seems to have been brief.

I have not ascertained just what the fate of Beeville was. The Turnbull Library collection of Beeville clippings and papers, themselves for the most part running no later than around 1970, were donated by Ray Hansen in 1984 and 1985. He, presumably in retirement, then had a Whangamata address. Letters to that address were not answered. But no natural decline, from age or the tides of human affairs, can eclipse the freedom of spirit that once was Beeville.

THE BUILDERS OF THE ADYTUM

One of the most impressive of alternative spirituality temples in New Zealand is the home of the Builders of the Adytum (BOTA) in Lower Hutt. The name "Adytum," from Greek for the inner sanctuary or "holy of holies" of a temple, ought to suggest that, like the Golden Dawn, this group is in the tradition of the Western Mystery Teaching, as its devotees like to call it, the tradition of Neoplatonism and Gnosticism, of the kabbalah and tarot cards, of angelic chants and banishing rituals. All this—except the last, for the BOTA does no ritual magic—is indeed the case. The visitor to this externally simple but attractive white structure will be greeted, on entering, with large brilliantly illuminated reproductions of the greater trumps of the tarot cards—the magician, the priestess, the hermit, the hanged man, all those stunning archetypes of human experience—around the walls.

At the front, where one might expect an altar, there is, between the white and black pillars of Solomon, a large and beautiful representation of the kabbalistic tree, that bright chain of *sephiroth* or supernal divine attributes linking the infinite deeps of God with the world and the depths of human experience. It is the heart of Jewish mysticism, but also much drawn on by Christian and other Western seekers after profound theosophic wisdom. The endless shifting play of the strands in its "tapestry of light" on each other and their reflections amid the weavings of human life, together with the kabbalist's reading of the Hebrew scriptures on several profound numerological, allegorical and spiritual planes, offer the thinker much food. Here, in a house built by the BOTA, in a setting independent of conventional Judaism and Christianity alike, this transcendental arbor stands alone in its own glory.

The founder of the BOTA was Paul Foster Case (1884–1954), an American musician. As a youth, as an amateur magician interested in playing cards, he met a Theosophist who introduced him to the tarot deck. Fascinated, he began collecting literature on the cards and in time wrote a book about their meaning. He also heard an inner voice that he identified as one of the Masters of the Wisdom. Through this guidance, around 1910 he joined the Thoth Hermes Temple, New York branch of the Order of the Golden Dawn. He eventually became Praemonstrator General, or head of the Hermetic Order in America, after the sudden death of the previous incumbent. But then, again under the guidance of his master, Case left the Golden Dawn. That order was by then in an international state of disruption, and in New York there was, according to some reports, also dissension over Case's youth and the allegation that his publications on the tarot revealed order secrets.[19] In 1929 Case formed a very small organization consisting mostly of personal pupils, the School of Ageless Wisdom, in Massachusetts. In 1933 he moved to Los Angeles and there established the BOTA in 1938.

According to Mr. William Chesterman, leader of the New Zealand BOTA, the Golden Dawn failed in large part because it became "lost in psychism," more concerned with magic and psychical powers than real wisdom or spiritual growth. But its initiates, he granted, were important as pioneers of much of the Western Mystery Teaching again made public. The BOTA endeavors to present that wisdom in its pure form, using the kabbalistic tree and the tarot cards as teaching devices. It employs ritual and chants both as further pedagogic experiences and to raise the force for inner development latent in them, for the concept of the universe as a great ritual that we can join for empowerment is important to the BOTA. But the BOTA eschew all emphasis on psychic phenomena, evocational magic, or use of sorcery to achieve personal goals.

No act of Paul Foster Case's esoteric career was more important for the future of his work than, in 1943, his taking an energetic young woman named Ann Davies (1912–1975) as a student. Before that, by her own account, she had been through atheism, agnosticism, Buddhist mysticism, and yoga. But on meeting Case there was an "immediate recognition" that this was her spiritual guide. Of New York Jewish background, survivor of a very difficult childhood, she was a dark-haired, vivacious, outspoken woman who clearly found her life in the BOTA and made it a spiritual presence in Los Angeles and internationally. After Paul Foster Case's death in 1954, Davies succeeded him as prolocutor general of the order, serving until her own death in 1975. Undoubtedly she had more charisma if less scholarship than Case. Under her, the BOTA advertised widely, developed extensively circulated correspondence courses, and established centers in other U.S. cities and in various parts of the world, including New Zealand.

I well remember visiting Sunday morning services at the flagship BOTA temple in Los Angeles during Ann Davies' tenure. Although she walked with a limp, her entry in a spectacular gown, her flashing, engaging eyes greeting her congregation, was an unforgettable moment. As she then stood by her robed and chanting choir, amidst the splendid tarot cards, between the pillars of Solomon and before the kabbalistic tree, she seemed indeed a priestess in the midst of her temple, as mighty as any of old. I could not help loving her and fearing her more than a little.

The BOTA literature published back then described Ann Davies' mystical experiences in some detail, and made much of the remarkable healing of a tumor in her dog Tzaddi by the power of prayer. Despite the intricate and sometimes rather abstract worldview of the Western Mystery Teaching, her sermons were anything but pedantic. They were, as I recall them, full of anecdotes, digressions, and warm affirmative sequences almost more reminiscent of positive-thinking preaching than occultism. The sermon was cushioned by ritual and communal work—chanting, singing, raising hands, even swinging lamps. After the dramatic entry of prolocutor and choir, the choir responded to a series of declarations. Following announcements and the sermon came prayers, scripture, music, and silent meditation, all rather Gnostic in tone but phrased in such as way as not to be offensive to the average liberal Christian. The service ended with healing decrees for the sick in mind or body somewhat typical in style of New Thought churches, though enriched by Ann Davies' occult imagination.

In an interview, Ann Davies explained to me the importance of ritual. The world itself is the ritual of God, she said, down to the atoms and electrons. All life is ritual; without it one would have no evolution because there would be no reorganization. Consciousness in everything is the Creator, but that cosmic consciousness works through ritual. She affirmed reincarnation.[20]

Ann Davies visited New Zealand to lecture in 1963. By all accounts the aureate pond of New Zealand occultism was greatly roiled by the imposing guest. The still-lingering Havelock North Golden Dawn was divided over its response to this woman's lively, populist presentation of a version of the venerable tradition it represented. Some were put off, some thought she was precisely the revitalization they needed. Theosophists and Anthroposophists were also agitated, though to a lesser degree. In any event, she left behind enough BOTA enthusiasts to constitute a branch, and perhaps unwittingly she probably hastened the decline of the Golden Dawn. The New Zealand group was initially led by Alastair Wallace, a long-time member of the Havelock North Temple of the Golden Dawn and the man who had initially made contact with Ann Davies and arranged her 1963 visit.

William Chesterman has led the New Zealand chapter of the BOTA since Wallace's death in 1969. Chesterman came to the work through a close relationship with the famous architect James Walter Chapman-Taylor (1878–1958), a man of long-standing and deep interest in occultism. (He was closely associated with Theosophy and Anthroposophy and built the Havelock North temple of the Golden Dawn, Whare Ra.) Chesterman, a man of considerable business experience and acumen, was called to Los Angeles after Ann Davies' death in 1975 to set the affairs of the movement in order. Following this reconstruction, the New Zealand order has become one of the most important venues of the Western Mystery Teaching tradition in the Southern Hemisphere.

6 The Wizards of Havelock North
The Golden Dawn under the Southern Cross

NO STORY from the annals of alternative spirituality in New Zealand is more remarkable than the tale of the Hermetic Order of the Golden Dawn, that celebrated phenomenon of 1890s London, in its second and greater incarnation in Havelock North. There it possessed a finer temple, more members, and greater ritual finesse than the British model and moreover lasted longer than the decade or so (in its original form) given that faction-ridden body. The Hawke Bay order was founded in 1912 by Dr. Robert Felkin, a colorful former member of the London group, and continued its occult rites until 1978.

Although there are tiny revivals of the Golden Dawn tradition in several parts of the world, including Wellington, the Havelock North group was the last major expression of the Hermetic Order, and perhaps the only one possessing undisputed direct continuity with the original. It was also probably the best twentieth-century expression of serious wizardry in the Golden Dawn's 1890s tradition. Such is the view of not a few cognoscenti of modern magic. As one contemporary American magician reportedly put it, "If you want to hear Elizabethan English, you go to Appalachia; if you want to see what the original Golden Dawn was like, you go to New Zealand."[1]

The Havelock North Golden Dawn was the convergence of two lines of development on opposite sides of the globe: the Hermetic Order in Victorian London, and the Havelock Work, as it was called, in Edwardian New Zealand. The former prepared the tradition; the latter, the people who were to embrace it.

The History of the Golden Dawn

That order was the culminating expression of the nineteenth-century occult revival. This revival in turn represented a marriage of the Romantic spirit and earlier esoteric traditions such as those embodied in Swedenborgianism and Freemasonry. Spiritualism and especially its more recondite successor, Theosophy, were precursors of the Golden Dawn's vivid fin-de-siècle manifestation of that revival; the new lodge brought together the Spiritualist's sense of direct contact with the otherworld, the Theosophist's knowledge of inner planes and forces, the Mason's antiquarianism and graded initiations, and the romantic era's love of theatrical rites. Its chief intellectual source was the French former seminarian and occultist Alphonse-Louis Constant (1810–1875), who wrote under the name Eliphas Lévi.

Lévi promulgated three fundamental principles of magic, which the Golden Dawn sought to put into practice: *(a)* that the material universe is only a part, and by no means the most important part, of total reality —beside it are other planes and other modes of consciousness, which must be taken into account by one who would have full knowledge and full power in this multiversal reality (very important among them is the "astral light," a cosmic fluid capable of being molded by will into visible forms); *(b)* that human willpower is a real force—when properly trained and concentrated it can achieve *anything,* including supernatural-seeming results; and *(c)* that microcosm and macrocosm mesh together— in other words, the human being is a miniature of the universe; there are correspondences between great and small, the cosmic and the terrestrial or human; causes set in motion on one level can have effects on another.

The Golden Dawn added to Lévi's three a fourth "law," the power of magical imagination. By mentally imagining or visualizing a desired reality, one can concentrate one's will on it, molding its form in astral light and finally in the plainest physical reality. Put all these together, and one can see how magical operations in the Golden Dawn tradition might work. Suppose one wished, for example, to evoke a divine spirit such as Aphrodite or Hermes or, if one preferred operating only within the Judeo-Christian tradition, a corresponding angelic being, and to develop the gifts of love or communication associated with that entity. The occultist would first assume that spirit or angel's existence in this multileveled spirit-matter universe. Then the adept would prepare by surrounding himself or herself with the colors, numbers, and substances associated with it and select a propitious hour, such as the rising of the planets Venus or Mercury. He or she would then finally evoke the entity by employing the proper chants and rituals, buttressing them by fervently shaping in the imagination the form and personality of the desired god or angel and intensely concentrating the will on its appearance.[2]

THE SOCIETAS ROSICRUCIANA IN ANGLIA

The immediate backdrop of the Golden Dawn was a group devoted to the study of esoteric lore called the Societas Rosicruciana in Anglia, founded in 1866 and open only to Master Masons. In 1887 a member of this society, William Wynn Westcott (1848–1925), a London coroner with a deep interest in occultism, came into the possession of certain reputedly antique eighteenth-century documents in cipher. He allegedly received them from the Reverend A. F. A. Woodford, who died in December of the same year. Woodford was an elderly clergyman and Masonic writer. By one account he had inherited the mysterious texts from a mid-century student of magic, Frederick Hockley (1808–1885); another more romantic version had the learned parson discover them pressed between the leaves of an old volume in an occult bookshop.

Westcott managed to decode the documents. He found they contained five mystical quasi-Masonic rituals, information on esoteric grades, and the address of one Fraulein Sprengel, a Rosicrucian adept in Germany. Corresponding with her, Westcott received further information together with authorization to form a British branch of her German order "Die Goldene Dammerung," (the Golden Dawn). Westcott then called together two colleagues in the Societas Rosicruciana, Samuel Liddell Mathers (1854–1918) and the society's supreme magus, Dr. William Robert Woodman (1828–1891). On February 12, 1888 these three signed themselves founding chiefs of the Isis-Urania Temple, the London headquarters of the Hermetic Order of the Golden Dawn.

The story of Woodford's mysterious manuscripts is now generally thought to represent a deliberately created legend. The documents give every indication of being 1880s constructions based on recent Masonic and occult sources. They were no doubt composed by Westcott, or possibly by him, Woodford, and others, but they described the German order in such a way as to lend the new foundation that aura of mystery, antiquity, and participation in an occult apostolic succession so much desired by esoteric lodges. Fraulein Sprengel was undoubtedly no less a fabrication than her order.[3]

Nonetheless, the old priest's puzzling papers struck the opening chords of a modern mythic concerto with profound resonance, for the new order quickly attained remarkable success, probably far more than the three chiefs had anticipated. A compact but influential public was there, it seemed, which knowingly or not was ready for a comprehensive magical order. It would be one that pulled together all the bits and pieces in the century's spiritual underground storehouses and made of them a coherent, progressive system, wherein, if one really worked, one could attain mastery of that strange world. Within a year the Golden Dawn had three temples and sixty-one members. At this point, in 1890, word was conveniently received from Germany of Fraulein Sprengel's death, leaving the chiefs entirely in charge of the English work.

In 1891 Woodman died, putting the leadership in the hands of the volatile Mathers as imperator and the quiet, kindly Westcott as praemonstrator—an uneasy alliance, as time was to tell. But the effort continued to flourish. By 1892 membership reached 150, despite the serious and strenuous work that the order's training entailed.[4]

Some members were to achieve prominence. Among them pride of place must go to William Butler Yeats, who entered as early as March 7, 1890, taking as his magical name "Demon est Deus Inversus." Yeats was a very serious adherent of the Golden Dawn, who had a part in writing its rituals and strove desperately to be a conciliator in its increasingly bitter internal wars. Critics rightly opine that the esoteric order's magical openings to other planes and inner worlds had a major role in shaping the master poet's rich and complex imagination. Others of some fame who shared the Golden Dawn experience were the writers of occult fiction Arthur Machen and Algernon Blackwood, the wife of Oscar Wilde, and Florence Farr, a celebrated actress who was a close companion of G. B. Shaw.

Increasingly, effective headship of the order passed into the hands of S. L. Mathers. This unusual and ambitious person was an authority on military history and ancient magical texts and ruled his sect with an autocratic will. But chronic penury dogged him, and he depended on various patrons for support. His wife, Moina, was the sister of the philosopher Henri Bergson, but that apparently was not sufficient vicarious fame, for Mathers took as a second surname MacGregor in a spurious claim to distinguished Jacobean ancestry, and even liked to call himself the duc de Glenstrae. S. L. MacGregor Mathers, as he came to be known, was not content with the Golden Dawn's original "outer" pedagogical degrees, and by 1892 had created a second "inner" order of adepts, the R.R. et A.C. (Ordo Rosae Rubeae et Aureae Crucis). Its initiates were supposed to be prepared to practice real magic, at least on the level of such arts as astral projection and exorcism. A third, still-higher order comprised those "secret chiefs" who were the true heads of this and all other authentic Rosicrucian orders. Mathers perfected the hierarchy in a degree table that was used in the New Zealand lodge as well.

GOLDEN DAWN DEGREE TABLE

Grade	Numerical Symbol
First order:	
Neophyte	$0 = 0$
Zelator	$1 = 10$
Theoricus	$2 = 9$
Practicus	$3 = 8$
Philosophus	$4 = 7$
Second order:	
Zelator adeptus minor	$5 = 6$
Theoricus adeptus minor	$5 = 6$
Adeptus major	$6 = 5$
Adeptus exemptus	$7 = 4$
Third order (the secret chiefs):	
Magister templi	$8 = 3$
Magus	$9 = 2$
Ipsissimus	$10 = 1$

The Golden Dawn, however, failed to function with the smooth polish those sonorous titles suggest. By 1896 friction within the second order had reached a point that called for the intervention of the chief, Mathers, from his Parisian home, but his pontifications were sufficiently bizarre to raise questions about his mental stability and did little to alleviate matters. Mathers then expelled the well-to-do Annie Horniman, who had been the first initiate of the second order. Her disgrace came in no small part, it was whispered, because she had refused to continue funding Mathers and his wife. Almost all the remainder of the R.R. et A.C. petitioned for her reinstatement but to no avail. Then, amidst these and other troubles, Westcott, the most balanced of the Golden Dawn's leaders, resigned all esoteric titles in 1897 under pressure from the home office, which governed his position as coroner and came to disapprove of such eccentricities.

As though to replace the mild Westcott in spades, in November 1898 the order acquired a new member of quite different temperament, Frater Perdurabo, otherwise known as Aleister Crowley. This magician, who was soon to claim for himself the supreme title *ipsissimus* and to attain a journalistic reputation as "the wickedest man in the world," thoroughly disrupted the dovecotes of the Golden Dawn. By January 1900 he had cajoled Mathers into admitting him into the second order. That was just before the same imperator, with whom Crowley was then in league, had thrown the *adepti* into an uproar through a letter to

Florence Farr. In that epistle Mathers warned the actress against West-cott, whom he now accused of forging, or causing to be forged, the Sprengel letters on which the Golden Dawn was founded.

The second order demanded proof from Mathers, ensconced in Paris. Instead, the imperator sent the then-loyal Crowley back to London to seize the the the R.R. et A.C.'s property in the name of his chief's legitimacy. On April 19 Crowley, sharing for the moment his spiritual sovereign's Scottish Romanticism, arrived in full Highland regalia, with a white cross on his breast, to repossess the order's halls at 36 Blythe Road. The rebels had, however, changed the locks and the mission was unsuccessful. Soon after, Crowley suddenly decamped for New York. In the meantime, the great majority of the second order proceeded to depose both Crowley and his erstwhile master, Mathers. Yeats was made imperator of the Isis-Urania Temple.

The troubles of the order were, however, far from over. In 1901 the Golden Dawn was acutely embarrassed by the highly publicized trial for sexual offences of a Mr. Theo Horos (Frank Jackson) and his wife. This pair of spiritual swindlers had established a bogus version of the Golden Dawn, using certain authentic rituals they had somehow obtained, among their other occult-degree and diploma-mill frauds. Worse, these operations were fronts for sexual as well as pecuniary exploitations. Mr. Horos was sentenced to fifteen years penal servitude for the rape of a young woman entrusted to him for spiritual instruction, and Mrs. Horos, a.k.a. Swami Viva Ananda, to seven years as an accomplice. The sensational trial brought the legitimate order much very unpleasant publicity in the popular press. Authentic initiates were, to be sure, spared the odium of criminality. But before the hordes of investigative reporters were done the adepts of the Golden Dawn had been made to look like gullible fools, their rites held up before a snickering public as ridiculous mummery. Not a few once-serious magicians resigned and slunk away.[5]

Those left found their vision of the Golden Dawn's future hopelessly divided. By 1902 there were three successor groups, the Independent and Rectified Rite of the Hermetic Order of the Golden Dawn under the Christian mystic A. E. Waite (who retained control of the Isis-Urania Temple until it was closed in 1914), the Alpha et Omega sect of Mathers loyalists, and a group primarily interested in the magical dimension of the Golden Dawn called the Stella Matutina, under the leadership of the rapidly rising occultist Dr. Felkin, who was to visit Havelock North, New Zealand, in 1912, bringing with him the Golden Dawn, and settle there in 1916.[6]

Robert Felkin and the Stella Matutina

Robert William Felkin was born in Nottingham in 1853, the son of a Nonconformist lace manufacturer. After school he worked for a time in Germany, commencing a lifetime of special relations with that country, and acquiring fluency in the German language. But Felkin had other dreams. A childhood meeting with David Livingstone, the great African doctor and explorer, had led him to contemplate a career as a medical missionary. He began medical studies in Edinburgh about 1876 and, though not yet a licensed physician, left to join a mission in Uganda in 1878. The same year he joined the Church of England, attracted by its liturgical and sacramental richness; for the rest of his life he was to remain, by his own lights, a faithful churchman as well as an occultist. He spent two adventurous years in Africa, becoming personal physician to a king who had earlier tried to kill him and gaining expertise in tropical medicine, about which he was to publish several articles in medical journals.[7] (He also wrote *Uganda and the Egyptian Soudan* [1882]; *Egypt Present and to Come* [1885]; *Uganda* [1886], and other African works.) But his own deteriorating health caused him to return to Edinburgh to complete his academic program, which he did in 1884. Felkin subsequently returned to Germany for further study, acquiring an M.D. from Marburg in 1885. He had married his first wife, Mary, in 1882; a baby girl, Ethelwyn, was born the following year.

After Marburg, Felkin worked as a doctor in Edinburgh. Both spiritual seekers, he and Mary joined the Theosophical Society in 1886, but finding it inadequate to their yearning for powerful ritual experience, entered the Amoun-Ra Temple of the Golden Dawn in Edinburgh March 12, 1894. Subsequently, after a period of rest following a breakdown from strain and overwork, he transferred his practice to London in 1896. He and Mary entered the second order the same year.

The fullest account of Felkin's life is a curious document called "A Wayfaring Man," written by his second wife, Harriot, and published in installments in 1936–1938 in *The Lantern,* an attractive magazine of esoterica and inspiration she edited and produced in Hastings (New Zealand) between 1936 and 1949. "A Wayfaring Man" represents an unusual genre: the story of a man's life by his widow (Felkin died in 1926) cast in fictionalized form. The widow herself is ostensibly the storyteller, but in as much as half the book—especially those parts before Felkin met Harriot—the subject himself becomes narrator as he recounts his reminiscences to her at length. The names are largely changed, and undoubtedly conversations and incidents now decades in the past are inexactly rendered, though it is likely that Harriot drew on diaries and memoranda in her possession as well as fickle memory.

Moreover, as in the best of marriages, there were probably facets of this life of which even the spouse was unaware, or did not understand aright. Nonetheless, there seems no reason to question that this unusual work of just over two hundred pages fairly represents Felkin, at least as Harriot perceived him.

She makes no attempt to conceal—though she does endeavor to understand—the less flattering features of her husband's life. She reveals his long struggle, not always successful, with alcoholism. But the widow attributes its commencement to a prescription unwisely given him by another doctor during his Edinburgh period, to take a "stiff dose of whiskey and quinine" whenever he felt a bout of the recurrent malaria he had picked up in Africa coming on. The persistence of his habit was also partly attributable to his first wife, according to Harriot. For all her virtues as a beautiful and spiritual person who shared both Felkin's esoteric quest and his worthy practical labors on behalf of child welfare, she was often too unwordly to plan adequate meals on time, leaving him to come home from his medical calls cold and wet and unprovided for. The temptation of a liquid pick-me-up in such a case was irresistible.

The second wife acknowledges that the first was lovely, with "her shining golden hair, her clear grey eyes, her slender erect figure." But Harriot cannot resist making one thing clear. When her text reaches the point of Mary's death in 1903, the successor insists that Felkin, although "stunned" and described as weeping at his partner's grave, "was not in love" with the deceased mate, though they had been "close friends" since "they were children and during twenty years of married life."

It should be added that at his moment of personal crisis after Mary's death Robert Felkin took pains to reinforce the very real commitment he had to Anglican Christianity as well as to occultism. In his anguish of soul the fresh widower made a retreat at the monastery of the Mirfield fathers, the Community of the Resurrection, an Anglican religious order, and gave serious thought to becoming a lay brother in that fellowship. It may be noted that several of the Mirfield fathers, like a remarkable number of Church of England priests of that time, showed definite interest in Rosicrucian or Golden Dawn styles of interpreting the Christian mysteries and regarded Robert Felkin, though a layman, as an eminent figure in that tradition. One priest Felkin met at Mirfield, Father Fitzgerald, was later to play a crucial role in his invitation to New Zealand.

One thing that both Felkin's wives shared was enthusiastic sympathy for his interest in spirituality and the occult. In the beginning years of the young doctor's practice in Edinburgh, he and Mary joined a small group of friends interested in discussing the Bible. It was apparently an open-minded circle, for soon they had gone on to conversations on other scriptures, such as the *Tao te ching* and the *Bhagavad Gita*. Two or three members of the set, in fact, were Theosophists, and it was presumably through this influence that Robert and Mary entered the society and were led toward their eventual commitment to the Golden Dawn in 1894.

By all accounts, including that of "A Wayfaring Man," Felkin's first half-dozen years or so in the Hermetic Order were fairly inconspicuous. Next, according to that text, came a time when the Golden Dawn "had gone into abeyance for nearly two years"—no doubt the period of the crises of 1900–1901. But then: "An intimation now reached me that it was to be reconstituted, and that I was appointed as one of the Leaders. At first I was not a little dismayed at this proposal. I felt myself quite inadequate to the task thus thrust upon me, but I was given no choice. . . ."

Undoubtedly we have reference here to his taking up the leadership of the Stella Matutina, though it is not clear when that name was first used. Interestingly, according to Harriot, Felkin's initial concern on being presented this new responsibility was that his daughter by his first marriage, Ethelwyn, and his prospective second wife (who incidentally was fewer than ten years older than that daughter—they were to become lifelong companions) should be admitted to the work. Ethelwyn at first demurred, being at the time a very devout Christian. (But Harriot was apparently an occult "natural"; she quotes her husband as saying to her, "you took to the whole system of training as though you were entering upon your proper heritage.")

Robert Felkin himself, however, may have been less modest about undertaking the responsibilities of high occult office than his widow intimates. Ellic Howe, in his history of the Golden Dawn, indicates that Felkin also had highly esoteric reasons for assuming the leadership he then took up. From around this time, the doctor came increasingly under the influence of direct contact with supernatural teachers and chiefs of the order. In response to the extensive reforms undertaken by the Golden Dawn, including abandoning that now much-maligned name, J. W. Brodie-Innes, a leading figure in the Edinburgh temple, wrote in a letter of April 11, 1902: "This thing was rushed by a clique. I took no part in it and don't accept it now. Has F[inem] R[espice—Dr. Felkin] got any direction from the ☉ [Sun] Masters—of course that might modify my point of view considerably."[8]

FELKIN'S OTHERWORLDLY CONFIDANTS

The mysterious sun masters, adepts on the astral plane with whom Felkin was apparently in special communication, were thus in demand for guidance by some other members of the now-divided fraternity, and this obviously put Felkin in a position of prominence. Nor were they his only otherworldly confidants. Around 1908 Felkin contacted an "Arab Teacher" called Ara Ben Shemesh, from a Near Eastern "Temple in the Desert" inhabited by "Sons of Fire." This adept had been given special permission to get in touch with Western students of wisdom and help them.

His advent seems to be described in "A Wayfaring Man," though he is here named only as "the Chaldean." Felkin had been talking in his consulting room with Arthur, presumably A. E. Waite, for the guest is denominated as a "man profoundly learned in the mysteries," but who "had his own group of students; but for a good many years we had worked together until his jealousy forced a quarrel upon us." That can only allude to the split between Felkin's Stella Matutina and Waite's more Christian-mystical Independent and Rectified Rite after the crisis. But as the two occultists conversed, no doubt a little warily, Felkin began to perceive "a shadowy presence." He called for Harriot, whose psychic vision was well tested. Coming in, she said she saw "a tall man in Eastern dress, kuftan, galabieh, and turban. He has a smooth olive face, and large dark eyes." Felkin asked Harriot to inquire why he had come, and the visitor replied, apparently through her in some mental manner, that he was in search of "someone who would work with him towards the union of Eastern and Western teaching." He reassured them, in answer to a further question, that he "believed in the Lord Jesus Christ," and thereupon the pair agreed to collaborate with him from that time on. He led them to "certain Centres which we might call Power Stations," among them "a Hall of Memory, and there we could see scenes from the past unrolled before us, very much like a cinematograph, with this difference that we could actually enter and take part in them."

Yet another mystic teacher was a Sri Parananda, who was first encountered by Felkin in the baths at Bad Pyrmont in Germany, a favorite spa of his. "I was," he avowed, "lying in the delicious hot water and watching the steam rising, in the pleasantly dreamy state that these baths induce, when I saw the head and shoulders of a man forming in the steam. . . . by degrees I made out a dark Eastern face with a beard and large black eyes. The man was wearing a peculiar conical cap, not a turban, and the steam appeared to be forming the outline of flowing robes." On gaining voice, the coinhabitant of his bath informed Felkin that "one month from today I will meet you in London. Go to the lounge of the Carlton Hotel and wait for me." At that more conventional rendezvous, Felkin did indeed again meet the Hindu gentleman —now clean shaven—who had first introduced himself in such an unusual manner. He had valuable conversations with Parananda over a period of years on many topics, from vegetarianism (which Felkin, unlike the Hindu, never fully accepted) to Florence Farr's conclusion of her varied career as headmistress of a school in Ceylon.

FELKIN AND THE ROSICRUCIANS

Felkin was also very eager to contact the Rosicrucian order in Germany that was allegedly the fountainhead, through the mysterious Fraulein Sprengel, of the Golden Dawn. He seems to have harbored no doubts of the existence of those magicians, nor of their exceedingly high occult status and power. But the Englishman realized that for this very reason the continental guild would be under very deep cover and likely to regard even the head of the premier esoteric order in the British Isles as no more than a novice, with dubious right of access to its sanctuaries. Yet Felkin, persisting in the quest, traveled to Germany in 1906, 1910, and 1914.[9] He turned up a couple of women named Sprengel, one or two esoteric groups he thought at least related to the potent but ultra-secret lodge he was seeking, and a meeting with Rudolf Steiner, founder of Anthroposophy. Felkin felt sure Steiner was an extremely high initiate, virtually godlike in fact, but one who chose to present himself to the world as no more than a popular philosopher, a teacher honored in certain groups dabbling on the fringes of true esotericism.

The head of the Stella Matutina and Harriot, while seeking out Rosicrucians in Germany in 1914, found themselves in an enemy nation with Britain's declaration of war against the Reich that August 4. Perhaps Felkin's unworldliness caused him to ignore the screaming headlines that sent many others scurrying to the frontiers that fateful summer, or perhaps, as "A Wayfaring Man" hints, the Chaldean had predicted the cataclysm but posted him on an occult mission that required his presence in Germany precisely at that terrible moment.

In any case, they were in a difficult spot. Shopkeepers turned cold and refused to take their British money. They were possessed by a lively fear, driven home by the fate of others around them, of being interrogated or even shot as spies. As late as August 14, 1914, Ethelwyn sent a circular letter to members of the second order to say that Dr. and Mrs. Felkin would be "unable to communicate with us until after the war is over," and it was signed by one of her occult names, "Maria Poimandres," called "Chief in Charge."[10] But with the help of German Masons the Felkins finally made their way back to England through neutral Holland.

Later Felkin apologists have claimed that he brought with him information of interest to British intelligence. Nonetheless, when he subsequently offered himself for national service, the army took no advantage of his special acquaintance with the opponent. Dr. Felkin was instead

given a less glamorous, but no doubt important, assignment as inspector of sanitary facilities for troops in the London area. At the same time
he continued his work as head of the Stella Matutina. A document of
November 11, 1915 indicates this order had then eighty-three outer-
order members (forty-three men and forty women), and forty in the second order. In July 1916 Felkin founded three new temples, one in Bristol and two new foundations in London, one for former members of
Waite's temple, one restricted to members of the Societas Rosicruciana
in Anglia. However, his English Stella Matutina, like the Golden Dawn
before it, was riddled with jealousies and dissensions. For the most part
it did not long survive his permanent removal to New Zealand in 1916.

The Havelock Work

Preparations for the Golden Dawn in New Zealand focus on the
intriguing cultural milieu known as the Havelock Work, and its noteworthy literary vehicle, *The Forerunner*, which ran (with one interrup-
tion) from May 1909 until terminated by war in 1914.[11] Havelock
North, a small but prosperous village of no more than a thousand souls,
was then (as later) home to many of the elite of the Hawke Bay region.
In those expansive and now-distant Edwardian days, this community
became for a few shining years the Vatican of a peculiar but locally powerful cultural wave, albeit one set in a remote colony of a far-flung
empire. The Havelock North sensibility paid homage simultaneously to
Pre-Raphaelite Romanticism and "Merry England" idealization of the
homeland's rural past, to craftsman architecture and the new century's
optimistic expectation that a bright new age was dawning, to liberal
Anglicanism and the decade's vogue for an Evelyn Underhill style of
interest in mysticism. It gave voice to forcefully expressed social concerns, while nourishing an inward but growing intimation that the
Havelock set's spiritual journey might eventuate in the discovery of a
surprising array of occult meanings behind the world's surfaces.

Much of this, to be sure, reflected widely distributed turn-of-the-century themes. As the world stood Janus-like at that juncture, the Mauve
Decade's aesthete epigoni of Romanticism looked backward to the Age
of Chivalry and the Ancient Mystery Schools with one eye, while keeping a sharp lookout for the brave new world of the twentieth century
with the other. It was a paradoxical but nonetheless attractive mood,
providing—for those able to afford it—a graceful combination of elegant living and advanced thinking. And, I would venture, it was done
as well in Havelock North, New Zealand, as anywhere.[12]

Seldom were these diverse motifs more smoothly intertwined than in
the pages of *The Forerunner* or its spiritual implications so well explored

as in that magazine's congenial symposium, and nowhere did it produce such a remarkable spiritual result as the New Zealand resurrection of the Golden Dawn. For all this, if anything can be singled out beyond chance or occult destiny, credit must no doubt go to the unusual homogeneity and isolation of a New Zealand village of upper-class settlers—one a few years behind the fads of London or New York, perhaps, but all the more ready to take them very seriously when they come and to make of them a way of life in the fullest sense of the words.

REGINALD GARDINER

John von Dadelszen is no doubt correct in saying that the Havelock Work truly began in 1907.[13] In that year Reginald Gardiner and Ruth, his wife, came to live in Havelock. (The village did not become Havelock North until 1910.) Reginald Gardiner had been born in 1872 in New South Wales, where his father was an Anglican clergyman. After losing both parents in childhood, he was raised by relatives in England until coming to New Zealand with his stepmother and sister when he was thirteen. Ruth Scott, the woman he married, was Canadian, and Gardiner lived in her country 1900–1907. In the latter year the couple returned to New Zealand, settling in Havelock, where his brother, the Reverend Allen F. Gardiner—also a major participant in the Havelock Work—was Anglican vicar.

Reginald Gardner initially established an import business in Hastings, but in 1910 became first chairman of directors of the company that published the *Hawke's Bay Tribune* (later merged with the *Herald*), a position he held until his death in 1959. Reginald and Ruth Gardiner built a home, Stadacona, in what is now Keirunga park. Here *The Forerunner* was first produced on a hand press, and many of the earliest productions of the Havelock Work discussed and executed. Although a few years later Stadacona was sold, and the work moved to a room in the village, thanks to the generosity of the subsequent owner, George Nelson, Stadacona (renamed "Keirunga") has become the community and cultural center of Havelock North, an honor this fine home richly deserves.

John von Dadelszen tells us that in 1908 a meeting of more than one hundred people was held in Frimley, near Hastings, to discuss cultural affairs, with Reginald Gardiner as one of the main speakers. This meeting led to the commencement of the work. The 1908 opening sessions were little more than readings from Shakespeare and Dickens in a bare church schoolroom, with only a half dozen to a dozen present. But out of this came Wednesday-night entertainments employing "all the local talent," and social afternoons as well. Next arrived carving classes, drama classes, flower and fruit shows, arts and crafts exhibitions, chil-

dren learning Morris dance, and the famous festivals. In 1911 these cultural endeavors climaxed in the Old English Village Fete, opening in a
wonderful procession of over a hundred men, women, and children
dressed in medieval costume and carrying banners. Thereafter its
Morris and folk dances, its refreshment stands and crafts shops, its
tourneys and playlets, were all presided over by King Arthur and his
court.

The next year, 1912, still greater efforts brought forth the Shakespearean Pageant. This splendid occasion began with a great procession
led by two heralds and two pursuivants, followed by none other than
Queen Elizabeth I attended by her court, then the bard himself and a
group of players. During the afternoon the visitor could choose between
teas and games, sixteenth-century songs and dances, a musical program
of sixteen items provided by the Hastings Town Band, and a production
of *Much Ado about Nothing* by the girls of Woodford House. The evening
brought scenes from *Twelfth Night* and *The Merchant of Venice,* more concerts and Shakespearean games, and on the weekend a ball in Shakespearean costume.

Behind all the fun was a solemn purpose, if *The Forerunner* is to be
believed: the festivity "aimed at cultivating a feeling for what was beautiful and true," for "behind the outward manifestation of things lay the
ideal" and "it is by the 'power of harmony and the deep power of joy
that we see into the life of things' "—a mantic statement that could well
be said to represent the ideal behind the Golden Dawn's outward mani-
festion at its best.

The first issue of *The Forerunner* (May 1, 1909)—the words are perhaps Reginald Gardiner's—thus set the tone by declaring, "We all seek
expression for the ideals that well up from time to time from the deeps of
our eternal self." So this magazine would endeavor to draw together
persons who lived for the same ideals. In color-splashed and probably
Theosophically inspired language, the periodical's editorial artist proclaimed that, "As each proves true to his own special Ray, he will speed
for his Birth-star in the vast horizon, and revolving in the fire-mist of his
own special hue, will unite with the others and form a vortex of glowing
whiteness which will be a Beaconlight to attract the seekers after love
and truth and beauty."

This expresses, albeit in rather flowery bouquets of words, the clean
and clear ideals of Edwardian, pre–World War I liberalism: unfettered
self-expression, the sense that a new age swept free of Victorian fusti-
ness was in the air, and the reborn Platonism of the symbolists in art
and letters who concretized spiritual ideals in distinct but subjective
images—like those of the Golden Dawn magicians—to make all the
riper their realization. For in further words that could be of esoteric, rit-

ual significance and point toward *The Forerunner*'s impending occult ful-fillment: "Remember that the words and deeds of a man today are the materializations of the ideals and aspirations of the real man years back." Finally, as the editorialist put it succinctly, "Let our aim be Unity in Diversity."

Typical 1909 articles included entries on St. Francis, on the welfare of fishermen, and on protection of birds hunted for their plumage. A piece on the "Gift of the Spirit among Quakers" joined one that went so far as to ask, "Is the Bible in Its Final Form?" Put these together, and there appears a most characteristic combination of social concern, very liberal religion, and idealization of high saintly spirituality. Add to them others on science and religion, which do not hesitate to mention the Society for Psychical Research and eminent parapsychological scientists like Sir William Crookes and Sir Oliver Lodge, and toss in still more on the beloved arts and crafts of the English village; then a more complete picture, a stunning combination of reformist zeal and High Tory moods, emerges.

Another consideration: the theological and scriptural liberalism in religion, with its compensating admiration of the saintly and mystical, by no means implied an advanced Protestantism. An article of Febru-ary 10, 1910 on sacraments, although acknowledging that "sturdy, wholesome Protestantism" has swept away abuses of ritualism, high-lighted "a growing interest among church people as to the true value and inner significance of ritual," which the author (known only as "Stu-dent") held to culminate in the concept and practice of a "Word of Power."

That was only an adumbration, however, of the celebrations of ritual to appear after the first advent of the Felkins in 1912. An article, "Con-cerning Ceremonial" (July 1913), by C.-T. (Chapman-Taylor, the nationally famous architect and participant in several esoteric societies) informs us that ceremonial is the way of the earth, of nature and the sea-sons; ceremonial in the church reaches the soul through the senses, being a language that even those who do not "know" can read. In the same issue, "Symbols and Symbolism" by H. F. (Harriot Felkin), observes that a good symbol must (*a*) have an essential correspondence to that which it symbolizes and (*b*) must be reduced to the barest sim-plicity attainable. But the examples the writer produces would scarcely be obvious to anyone not immersed in the kabbalistic or occult tradi-tions: the pentagram or star as symbol of the "just man," Adam Kad-mon; the hexagram for God and humanity; the tree for life.

Yet, as the Felkins would have wished, the movement stayed within the Christian faith as its principals understood it, and they were appar-ently for the most part devout Anglican churchgoers. Several writers quote Stopford Brooke to the effect that "Christianity is the most romantic of all religions."[14] An article by the Reverend Edgar Wood, "The Hidden Treasure" (June 1914) indulges in a quite esoteric interpretation of the "mystic Christ." In the same fateful year, an ongoing published correspondence between a pseudononymous "Miss Butler" and "Richard Wickstead" combines a tepid and implied romance with fervent discussion of Bergson, Ruysbroeck, Law, Augustine, and the like. An attractive March 1910 piece by Ruth Gardiner, "The Daily Sacraments," spoke of morning, noon, and evening as "beads on a daily rosary," each with its own divine glory, especially reflected in children as they are at that hour.

Other concerns arise as well. Also in 1910 Emma Richmond, of the family mentioned in connection with Theosophy, wrote on prison reform.[15] Other writers in *The Forerunner* include such prominent local names as Margaret Chambers (wife of Mason Chambers), H. C. Chambers, Reginald and Ruth Gardiner, the Reverend A. F. Gardiner (Anglican vicar and brother of Reginald), Harold Large, Thomas Tanner, S. W. and Katherine Fitzherbert, Miss M. M. McLean (sister of Mrs. Mason Chambers), Bertha V. Goring, Miss E. T. Hamilton, and W. J. Rush. Writers from further afield included Sir Robert and Lady Stout, and the prominent scholar of Maori history and culture, Elsdon Best.

Harold Large requires special mention. Von Dadelszen, although perhaps not concurring in the judgment, remarks that "Reginald Gardiner, with a modesty which was typical of him, gave most of the credit for organising the Havelock Work" to Large. S. W. Grant portrays Large as "something of an eccentric who, when walking about the village, carried with him a quarterstaff that he used for the purpose of jumping fences and gates, rather than proceeding in the conventional way."[16] Be this as it may, it seems that he and Reginald Gardiner were old friends who met again soon after the latter's return to New Zealand in 1907. At this point Large had recently left the Theosophical Society and taken confirmation in the Anglican church. According to von Dadelszen, "His reason for forsaking Theosophy was that he considered the eastern methods of training were unsuitable for western people. Furthermore he was convinced that some form of esoteric training must also exist in the West, and he was determined to find it, for it was inconceivable that Christianity, of all the great world religions, should be the only one lacking in this respect."

This was to become the fundamental conviction of the Havelock group, the presupposition that underlay their exoteric and esoteric labors alike. They were all dedicated Christians and churchmen. At the same time, they were convinced that the church had somehow lost esoteric teachings that Jesus had bequeathed his disciples, the mysteries of the kingdom of God the Son of Man had said were given them to know, while to the others they were imparted only in parables, "that seeing they might not see, and hearing they might not understand" (Luke 8:10). The Havelock seekers were determined to make themselves worthy of those secrets promised the Christian elite and were willing to undergo whatever rigorous training and awesome initiations were needed to reach that sublime end.

The quest that would eventuate in the Golden Dawn's improbable implantation in tiny Havelock North was thus already mounted in its future initiates' hearts. First, however, it would find expression in more conventional piety. Harold Large stayed in Havelock only two years before returning to London. Yet during those months he not only imbued Reginald and Ruth Gardiner with enthusiasm for that quest but also spent time each day with them in prayer and meditation. That group of three was soon joined by Miss M. M. McLean and Reginald's unmarried sister, Miss Rose Gardiner. Miss McLean, a highly educated Scotswoman, had aspirations similar to Large's and had earlier met people in Britain with comparable interests. Among them was Father Fitzgerald, the Anglican priest of the Community of the Resurrection or Mirfield fathers, the same whom Robert Felkin met on his retreat at Mirfield after his first wife's death.

Von Dadelszen records the following: "From notes made by Reginald Gardiner in 1951 it is quite clear that he viewed what was generally known as the Havelock Work as an outward expression of this more personal quest, for he refers to the Havelock Work as a cultural society, 'built around this silent power station.' " Some may wish to contend that the unusually healthy quality of the Havelock Work's cultural renaissance in those years stemmed from its grounding, unlike much modernism, in disciplined spirituality. In any case, even after Large returned to the homeland, the unseen work of the prayer and meditation group continued. Indeed, as it grew in numbers, and came to be called the Society of the Southern Cross, simple forms of ritual began to be introduced into its practice—rites that were to exfoliate until they became the full-flowered esoteric liturgies of the Golden Dawn!

FATHER FITZGERALD

The next stage in the curious tale of how that came about happened in 1910. In that year the Mirfield fathers sent a mission of help to preach and conduct retreats in various New Zealand parishes. One of the visiting priests was Father Fitzgerald whom Felkin and Miss McLean had, at different times, encountered. Miss McLean arranged for Fitzgerald to meet members of the Havelock prayer group—roughly identical with the core group organizing the Havelock Work—at

Bishopscourt in Napier. There, in the residence of the diocesan, the British priest agreed to serve, albeit at long range, as a sort of spiritual director of the Havelock group. The promise was fulfilled through exchanges of letters pointing them in the direction of a Christian mysteries approach to their corporate spiritual life.

But after a time Father Fitzgerald told them a level had been reached at which, if further progress were to be made, personal instruction would be necessary. He recommended a Dr. Robert Felkin as the ideal person for this task. Within a week of receiving that letter, Reginald Gardiner, thanks to the generosity of John and Mason Chambers, cabled three hundred pounds to pay passage for Felkin and his wife and daughter to come to New Zealand for three months.[17] Felkin was at first reluctant to accept the call because of his medical practice, but on the other hand, according to "A Wayfaring Man," he felt "it would be a terrible pity to let such an opportunity as this slip. We would be pioneers in a new world with virgin soil to work with." Westcott helped by giving Felkin introductions to several Masonic groups in Australia. As a thirty-two-degree Mason (though he had become a Freemason only in 1907), Felkin was one of the highest thus far to visit New Zealand. He was also appointed an inspector for the Societas Rosicruciana in Anglia, the Golden Dawn's parent body, though he does not seem to have functioned in this capacity.

If the words put into Robert Felkin's mouth in "A Wayfaring Man" are to be given credence, the Felkins' initial experience of New Zealand was a mixture of warmth and kindly amusement. The Wellington welcome "made us feel at home immediately," and the city "looked an odd ramshackle place to us, with its dingy houses, but the harbour and the circling hills were beautiful." Then:

> The railway journey that followed seemed to us rather in the nature of a joke. The leisurely rate compared with our express trains at Home, with frequent cups of tea brought to us; the stop for midday dinner while the whole trainload of passengers filed into a big barn of a dining room, bolted their dinner, drank scalding cups of tea, and filed solemnly back to the train, each one paying at a little ticket booth at the door as they passed. Later on we became accustomed to this procedure, but the first time it struck us as comical. It also seemed to me a pretty direct route to dyspepsia for we were only allowed 25 minutes to consume a three course meal plus the inevitable tea. I should think New Zealand must use more tea per head of this small population than any other country in the world. . . .

Eventually they arrived at their destination, Awatea, apparently a cipher for Havelock North. "Thus began a busy, happy, and most amusing experience which lasted for three months." Culture shock remained. "Coming fresh from England it seemed very odd to us when people dropped in and volunteered to do all kinds of jobs for us. One man used to come and clean all the knives and boots, another attended to the oil lamps as there was neither gas nor electricity. People were continually calling with offerings of cakes and scones, or baskets of fruit and flowers. . . . We duly admired the tree ferns, and the cabbage palms reminded us of the dom palms in Egypt. But the native bush seemed to us dark and sombre after the lovely English woods."

As for the business at hand, apparently it went well. "Father O'Connell [Fitzgerald] had paved the way, but these people were hungry for the teaching we had come to give them. Our time was so short, and there was so much they desired to learn. Several of them showed very marked aptitude for what is commonly termed 'psychic' development, that is to say, they had that peculiar power of seeing, hearing, or feeling with the inner sense that exists independently from the external sense organs." Judging from "A Wayfaring Man," this psychic development would appear to be the main fruit of Felkin's 1912 labors in New Zealand, but von Dadelszen reports that during that brief stay one room of the small house in which the visitors resided had to serve as a temple, and twelve members were admitted to the order. Moreover, he says,

> they were advanced through the grades, much more quickly than was usual, to a stage where it was hoped they would be able to continue with the work and instruct others, with only such assistance as could be given by mail. In the meantime Mason Chambers and his wife had generously given the land on which was built the house designed by Chapman-Taylor and known as 'Whare Ra.' It was to become the headquarters of the Order in New Zealand, and the first part of the building was consecrated before the Felkins returned to England.[18]

Documentary evidence is cited by Ellic Howe to confirm that Felkin then founded the Smaragdum Thalasses (Emerald Seas) Lodge of the Stella Matutina; although undated he does not doubt the rescript is from the 1912 visit. (R. A. Gilbert opines that the name was given by Felkin's astral mentor, Ara Ben Shemesh.)[19] In a private collection of Golden Dawn documents Howe found a contemporary warrant for the Havelock temple, which reads:

> The G.H. Chief Frater Aur Mem Mearab [Dr. Felkin] 8 = 3 and the V.H. Soror Maim Chioth [Mrs. Felkin], members of the R.R. et A.C. under the Obedience of the Rites of Germany and Great Britain, and the V.H. Soror Maria Poimandres [Ethelwyn] 6 = 5

permit three V.H. Fratres
Piscator Hominum 5 = 6
Kiora 5 = 6
Lux e Tenebris 5 = 6
to form and rule both the Inner and Outer Orders of the R.R. et
A.C. and the Stella Matutina in Australasia.

For the Outer Order the Smaragdum Thalasses Temple of the
Stella Matutina in the Outer.

Havelock North, Hawkes Bay, New Zealand [no date][20]

"A Wayfaring Man" informs us that "Suzanna" (Ethelwyn) stayed
for a couple of months after her father and stepmother returned to England, and that "she thoroughly enjoyed her two months of solitary
authority. As long as we were there she kept very much in the background, always eager to help but never putting herself forward. Once
we were away she was forced to take the lead and it did her a world of
good." (The daughter was, nonetheless, destined to remain at home,
unmarried and to all appearances a self-effacing subordinate in the
household and order until her stepmother's death in 1959, after which
she once again enjoyed "solitary authority" for three scant years until
her own death in 1962. Von Dadelszen states that she was "very
devoted to her stepmother and faithfully served to the last the Hermetic
Order, which had been so much part of her life.")

"A Wayfaring Man" also informs us that before the two older Felkins
left for home they visited Taupo and the thermal districts. To Felkin's
occult eye, this extraordinary region of hot springs and boiling mud was

> full of the very queerest elementals I have ever seen. Both of us are
> fairly familiar with the inhabitants of earth, air, fire, and water, we
> have talked to dryads, and watched fairies at their play, and at
> work too, for no nature spirit is idle, but these fantastic creatures
> filled us both with amazement. The old legends of dragons and
> griffons must have had their origin in some such place; reptiles
> with wings and birdlike heads, birds that were partly frog or lizard,
> monstrous parodies of human form with misshapen limbs and
> heads, weird and horrible yet fascinating creatures, too alien for us
> to describe. We seem to have gone back to the primordial slime
> whence life and form first emerged.

FELKIN IN NEW ZEALAND

Thus was set in motion the course of events that led to the
Felkins' permanent removal to New Zealand in 1916,[21] in the midst of
war, when their lightly passengered ship made its long monotonous
voyage with lights doused.[22] According to "A Wayfaring Man," they
were met in Auckland by "Kingsland Horton," obviously Reginald

Gardiner, who traveled with them to Havelock. Robert Felkin is here made to remark,

> As we sat in the train hour after hour I studied the man who had exercised so great an influence over our lives. . . . At that time King was in the prime of life, but he had knocked about the world and experienced a good deal of hardship as a youngster, and these things take their toll. He was a tall dark man, while his wife was small and fair. She was very psychic, and he had a profound admiration and respect for her gifts. I foresaw that it might be exceedingly difficult for them to accept the strict discipline involved in our training; it is far easier as a rule to train an entire novice than one who had developed a natural gift along a different line. . . . As it turned out King and Mercy [Ruth] passed this exacting test and proved themselves to be true disciples, loyal and affectionate throughout the ensuing years.

Felkin was the first medical doctor resident in Havelock North, except for one or two temporary practicioners in the nineteenth century, and this role naturally give him an immediate position of community prominence. S. W. Grant, in his history of Havelock North, notes that after the terrible influenza epidemic of 1918 had abated by mid-December of that year, with no deaths occurring in the city itself, the town board expressed its thanks to Dr. Felkin, who had been head of a committee set up to combat the disease.[23] Seeing him in this role leads one to appreciate that Felkin, clearly a man of many parts, was by no means always the unworldly being indited by Golden Dawn historians.

Yet his practice, like his beliefs and his life, was not without its controversial aspects. Grant himself, though no student of the esoteric, was well aware of the doctor's other lives. He notes that Felkin "became something of a character in the Village, an aura of mystery clinging about him," and was interested in "theosophical and philosophical ideas." Grant cites his subject's strong belief in the importance of ritual, both within the Anglican church of which he was a staunch communicant and otherwise, stating that Felkin "carried this belief to the extent of observing the arrival of the solstices and the equinoxes by ritualistic ceremonies at 'Whare Ra,' " which may reflect the extent of public knowledge of what went on in the physician's mysterious temple, of which those who knew did not speak. "Naturally," Grant continues, "the Village being a place where gossip was, and is rife, dark rumours circulated about secret meetings held underground at the Felkin residence, titillating the imaginations of the good, credulous people of Havelock."[24]

(It must be recalled that it was also the good—and credulous?—folk of Havelock and surrounding area who were involved in the enigmatic doings of that whispered-about house. Not a few of the order's most stalwart members were also among the town's most prominent citizens, though secrecy was such that initiates would make no open acknowledgment of their occult fellowship outside the temple. As an outsider from far away visiting Havelock, I was told in 1988 that the subject of the order was still a touchy one to raise, so deeply were neighbors and families divided over it. One story I heard was that once a newcomer to Havelock, picking up disturbing rumors of dark and mystical goings-on, went to the town board to request an investigation. He was cordially promised it would be done, and several weeks later the petitioner was reassured to hear the matter had been looked into and there was nothing to worry about. What he did not know was that four of the five members of the board were themselves also members of the mysterious order that had given rise to the gossip.)[25]

Dr. Felkin's medical practice included a belief in the healing powers of color, techniques apparently borrowed from Rudolf Steiner of Anthroposophy, whom as we have seen Felkin greatly admired. Grant says that patients were given color treatment in a basement room especially designed for that purpose.[26] Whether this refers to the vividly hued lodge room is not clear, but it is unquestionably true that the doctor embraced unorthodox therapies, some reportedly inspired by Steiner and Anthroposophy. Among the Havelock rumors I have heard is that the lives of certain Felkinite schoolchildren were made miserable by their having to wear stockings of mixed and unusual colors, which naturally invited ridicule on the part of more conventional mates.

Patrick Zalewski, a New Zealander and Golden Dawn occultist, who personally knew people involved in Felkin's order, tells us that during the ten years Felkin lived at Whare Ra, he "ran the temple like a military operation." Classes were held on week nights for outer-order participants in which instruction in esoteric philosophy and ritual was imparted. On weekends classes for inner-order members enhanced their more advanced knowledge through work on ritual, meditation, and Enochian pronunciation. (The Enochian "keys," or calls, are evocational chants derived from the Elizabethan magus John Dee; believed by some to be very powerful if said correctly, they have a conspicuous though sometimes mysterious and controversial place in modern occultism.) By 1926, the year of Felkin's death, the inner order alone had more than one hundred members and was, according to Zalewski, collectively a very wealthy and locally powerful group, naming on its secret roles many of the most important persons in the Havelock North and Hastings area. Outer-order members numbered more than two hundred at the peak.

This level of success in recruiting presumably hardheaded graziers and businessmen and their kin, followed by getting them in class week after week to meditate and chant the names of angels, certainly suggests that Felkin was a man of considerable authority and ability as well as metaphysical vision.[27] By all accounts he was a perfectionist who demanded much of his students and often got it. Zalewski is undoubtedly correct in questioning those occult historians who, generally writing from the London perspective and in total ignorance of the New Zealand phase of his career,[28] portray Felkin as little more than a dreamer given to delusional visions and quixotic quests, as in his search for the true Rosicrucians in Germany.[29] Whether this was ever entirely the case, or whether his character underwent a remarkable sea change with the 1916 move, is perhaps an open question. But there is no doubt that, after arriving in Havelock North as (for the first time in his personal Golden Dawn history) the occultist undisputably in charge, he came into his own and proved equal to a challenging task.[30]

Zalewski states that Golden Dawn rituals were actually far more strictly performed at Whare Ra than they were in England even before the 1900 crisis. Further, he observes, the Havelock ceremonies, though at first done under the aegis of the Stella Matutina Order, were in fact not the modified Stella Matutina rites Felkin composed for his Stella Matutina temples in England, but the original Golden Dawn rituals, now virtually for the first time done as they were really meant to be enacted. Zalewski says that in fact many of the ritual papers and lecture texts used in Havelock North merely had "Golden Dawn" crossed out and "Stella Matutina" written in.[31] (In 1933 the New Zealand order broke with the remnant of the Stella Matutina in England, becoming what it in effect was, simply the Golden Dawn. But, despite difficulties with the Amoun Temple in London, under the direction of the increasingly unstable Christiana Stoddart, Havelock maintained good relations with the Hermes Temple in Bristol, the order's last British stronghold.[32] A certain number of people emigrated from Bristol under this influence to study under the Felkins and live in New Zealand, and others came to visit.)

There is reason to think that Felkin's extraordinary contacts moderated subsequent to the New Zealand move. Early in September 1918 Ara Ben Shemesh reportedly told Felkin "that after six weeks we were to call him no more as his work for us was done then, and he asked us to tell all who had been to his meetings in London *not* to call him again." Yet on September 22, 1918 Felkin wrote Miss Stoddart in London of psychic attack in New Zealand: "I do not know what happened to me on the higher planes, but I have been away from here most of the time. All is fog. At the Equinox I had at one time, when the outer door was opened and shut, a big fight to keep out some awful presence. I did it, but since I have had a bad headache and queer visions and both nights was far away and could bring nothing back at all."[33]

Whare Ra

Something should be said of Havelock's magical-mystical house. Whare Ra (House of the Sun), the Chapman-Taylor edifice and one of the first residences made of reinforced concrete in New Zealand, was waiting for the Felkins. It had a huge temple area in the basement of some fifteen hundred square feet. But the house was unfurnished, and the three occultists had to stay with various members of the group for some six weeks until their furniture arrived, an arrangement that no doubt strengthened their hosts' relationship to the order. Later Robert Felkin added an annex to the house that he used as a consulting room for his medical practice. The mysteries of Whare Ra, once home to the Smaragdum Thalasses Temple of the Stella Matutina offspring of the Golden Dawn, are now open. When I visited Havelock North in 1988, I found the sturdy old edifice, with its craftsman adzed-timber beams and inglenooks, in the possession of a pleasant young couple becoming seriously interested in their lovely home's extraordinary story. (A previous owner after the winding up of the order, I have been told, was a Roman Catholic family who found much going on in the place to make them uneasy until it was exorcised, but the commonsensical present inhabitants have reported nothing unusual.)

The home's most exceptional feature, of course, is the basement temple. Here one can still go down turning cement staircases from the neophyte's waiting room into the subterranean hall of rites and symbols. Descending, I imagined myself to be a nervous and excited blindfolded postulant approaching his or her unforgettable first encounter with the mysteries. The novice would be wearing an ankle-length black robe. Eyes would be covered, and a cord triple-coiled round the waist. The rope's free end was in the hands of a guide, also robed, but with a majestic white cloak over his somber gown and a red cross on his left breast. In the mentor's free hand would be a regal red and gold scepter and around his neck a large cruciform emblem.

As the trembling, sightless seeker entered the hall, she or he would be greeted by billows of incense and the words: "Child of earth, why seekest thou to enter our sacred hall? Why seekest thou admission to our order?" The guide would answer for him: "My soul wanders in darkness and seeks the light of the hidden knowledge, and I believe that in this order knowledge of that light may be obtained." The entrant would then be led forward before a cubical altar, on which lay a red cross and a white triangle. Here the postulant would kneel, and swear an oath to keep the secrets of the order, including the names of its members. The admittant would then vow to persevere and not to debase mystical knowledge.

He or she was then led around the temple and was purified at various stations with sprinklings and censings. An invocation to "the Lord of the Universe" was pronounced. Finally the postulant heard the words: "Child of earth, long hast thou dwelt in darkness, quit the night and seek the day!" At this the blindfold was removed. The amazed novice now found himself or herself facing the cubical altar. Standing by him or her were three robed magicians, two of them holding scepters, the other a sword. On the altar before him or her stood, in addition to the triangle and cross, offerings of bread, salt, wine, a lamp and a bowl of rose petals. On either side of the altar were two pillars, one white and one black. Three high priests, in yellow, blue, and scarlet, sat watching from a dais near the altar.

Moving into this now-bare and silent great hall, the visitor of today sees niches where sigils of gods and angels may once have reposed, and from which torches cast their dim light on such now almost-forgotten proceedings as this initiation. One can see where the cubical altar once stood and where the pillars still rise. To the front, most interesting of all, is a wall with concealed doors on either side, from which vestured hierophants might advance with slow and solemn pace at a well-timed moment, as the order commenced another ritual evocation of supernormal realities or prepared to bring another novice into its mystic kingdom. And between the doors still lies something even more intriguing, a hexagonal chamber, the vault.

Here those undergoing intiation into the second order would spend an entire solitary night lost to the outer world, dwelling in some subheaven of esoteric symbols. The inside walls and ceilings of this room are still covered with kabbalistic diagrams, and targetlike sets of concentric circles said to serve as sights for astral projection. Perceiving its wonders with no help but that of a flashlight, I became dizzy in spirit after only a few minutes in this strange place. I can well imagine that one who, on top of an evening of secret ceremonial, spent a night here with such companions as the golden eye of Horus and the Tetragrammaton, and no clear way out save via the astral plane, would emerge the next day mightily transfigured.[34]

Ellic Howe has published an excerpt from a manuscript account, probably by Felkin, of W. B. Yeats' 6 = 5 degree initiation October 16, 1914 in a Stella Matutina ritual Felkin had written. It remarkably evokes the strange inner weather raised by the order's rites. At one point, the postulant is required to lie in the Pastos, a highly ornamented coffin, within the vault, while a series of thirty-six bells were rung:

"At the thirteenth Bell he is faint; at the Fourteenth he is very cold; at the sixteenth he again emerges into a further higher plane; at the Seventeenth he is like a transparent rainbow. The Colours of the Planets play upon him. Then they merge into brilliant Light and for the rest of the Bells he shone with it. The rising from the Tomb and the Sprinkling appear to involve a very great and serious effort on the part of both Postulant and Officers. . . ."[35]

At the same time, Felkin's devoutly Anglican aspect should not be overlooked, though sometimes it merged with the esoteric. Thus on Januaruy 9, 1915 his occult guide, Ara Ben Shemesh, told the Felkins that a special group for healing should be formed.[36] This group was formed, and the fraternity eventually became the Guild of St. Rafael, now a respected and theologically quite conventional society within the Anglican church devoted to the healing ministry. Felkin spoke to church groups frequently, generally on behalf of the guild and a staunchly orthodox albeit highly sacramental and ritual-centered vision of Anglican Christianity.[37] As a churchman he had much in common with his frater Reginald Gardiner, for many years an Anglican lay reader and synodsman.

After Robert Felkin's death in 1926, at the age of seventy-three, a change in the leadership of the order was required. The tradition, going back to the Golden Dawn in 1890s London, was that the order should have three chiefs. During his lifetime Felkin was senior chief; his wife and daughter occupied the other positions. In 1926 Harriot became senior chief, Reginald Gardiner joining Ethelwyn to complete the complement.[38]

Harriot Felkin was now ready to begin her own notable career of spiritual influence in New Zealand. She was afflicted by near-total deafness and chronic ill health. But she was a person, as von Dadelszen put it, "of indomitable spirit and unusually wide interests." Although she maintained the order and her role in it as leader to her life's end, probably she was more ecumenical—if that is the right word—in her spiritual sympathies than her husband. She was a great correspondent and sent letters of opinion and support to persons of many persuasions around the world, exempting neither religious nor political figures. Between 1936 and 1949 she published her magazine, *The Lantern* (monthly until July 1944, thereafter bimonthly), which in some ways revived the tradition of *The Forerunner*, though it was more modest in scope and, apart from a leader generally by Gardiner, almost entirely written by one person, Harriot Felkin herself. *The Lantern* was the vehicle for "A Wayfaring Man," but the author also composed serial stories on biblical topics including "Jesus and His Friends," "Joseph of Arimathea," and "Paul the Apostle." Articles likewise appeared on such subjects as "The Church and the Sacraments," "Living Rhythmically," and "Civilisation and History," as well as poetry and epigrams.

THE TAUHARA TRUST

Harriot Felkin was greatly interested in gardening, especially different methods of organic horticulture. This interest brought her in contact with Charles McDowell, an Australian Anthroposophist, who had an especial concern for Steiner's bio-dynamic system. As she came to share ideas with McDowell, Harriot found that she also held with him a vision of a new spiritual center to be built in the Southern Hemisphere. Determined to make the vision reality, in October 1938 she found a tract of nearly sixty acres of land in Taupo to be used as its site. It was purchased in the name of three trustees, John von Dadelszen, Ethelwyn Felkin, and Reginald Gardiner. This was the beginning of the Tauhara Trust, a further fruit of the Golden Dawn–Havelock legacy, one intended as a place for "the study and practice of Spiritual Wisdom in all its aspects; a centre designed to link together all men and women of goodwill, irrespective of their particular beliefs or methods of working."[39]

On January 7, 1939, with McDowell present, the site was dedicated and declared a *zoekaiphos* (a place of life and light). Harriot spoke of the new work as growing out of the work at Havelock North but now cast, she seemed to imply, in a more universalist vesture. Not long after she wrote, "Preconceived ideas must not be allowed to constrict growth; the old must indeed act as a foundation, but when the foundation is laid then it must be built upon, and though the foundations do, to some extent, indicate the plan of a house, they must never be regarded as the house itself."[40]

But the war years then intervened, and the project was suspended. After the return of peace Tauhara grew, though there were problems owing to rising rates and expenses. Part of the land had to be sold off piecemeal to meet obligations. Then in 1970 the Taupo borough council sought to acquire the most valuable part of the holding for a reservoir. In 1971 the trustees sold what was left of the original property and purchased the present beautiful estate commanding a spectacular view above Acacia Bay. This land has subsequently been developed with attractive buildings, admirably fulfilling the original purpose of providing meeting and conference sites for spiritual groups of all sorts, most characteristically those with a meditation, Eastern, New Age, and increasingly deep-ecology flavor. Thus has the latest of several improbable developments in the Golden Dawn saga been built on the order's firmest foundation, its sense of the interrelatedness of all fragments of the cosmos, to provide a meeting place for minds of many bents and a center for the care of the earth.

Reginald Gardiner died at the beginning of 1959, Harriot Felkin at the end of the same year, both at the advanced age of eighty-six. Although Ethelwyn Felkin continued to live at Whare Ra and to serve as leader of the order for the three years left her, the original generation of the Havelock Work and the Golden Dawn in New Zealand was now clearly becoming history. Harriot's 1939 vision had not been amiss; the new postwar population taking her generation's place generally lacked the patience, the studiousness, and the sense of the importance of ritual and tradition that had informed the earlier Havelock. Its spiritual requirements were obviously better attended to by the free-flowing discussions and "happenings" of Tauhara than by the robed rites of Whare Ra. As the former prospered, the latter declined. Numbers, enthusiasm, and energy perceptibly fell, until in 1978, von Dadelszen tells us, "the chiefs of that day reluctantly came to the conclusion that its particular method of working was no longer appropriate to the times and that it had served its purpose."[41]

THE ORDER OF THE TABLE ROUND

One interesting cousin of the Golden Dawn remains alive in Havelock North: the Order of the Table Round. According to its own literature, this order was intended as "a School of Christian Chivalry" in parallelism to the Golden Dawn's role as "a School of Christian Spiritual Wisdom."[42] Reportedly, it was established by Felkin in 1912 along with the more famous order, and Reginald Gardiner served as its grandmaster for some years after Felkin's death.[43] Felkin, in turn, is said to have received transmission of the order from his close associate in esoteric work in England, Neville Meakin, who himself died in October 1912. Meakin was, by all accounts, not the most balanced of individuals, and his claim that the Order of the Table Round has been alive since the days of King Arthur, having been then revived from an original founding by Joseph of Arimathea, and that he was its thirty-seventh grandmaster by virtue of secret descent from the House of Tudor, seems improbable and totally unproved. This leaves its actual genesis slightly mysterious, though it certainly fits the turn-of-the-century cult of chivalry and the gentleman, which spawned hundreds of lodges and youth groups with such leitmotivs.[44]

But the Havelock Order of the Table Round is a particularly harmless and attractive example of the type, one that stands out by emphasizing linkages between chivalry, the Arthurian mythos, and the occult. Indeed, in the early years only members of Whare Ra who had reached the inner order were asked to join the Order of the Table Round. At first the two orders shared the Whare Ra facilities, but tensions developed and eventually the order moved to a small house on the woodsy outskirts of Havelock North. This attractive oblong building, still in use, features a round table on which the twelve knights of the ancient king's court are identified with the twelve signs of the zodiac. It is not far from the home of the late Jack Taylor (d. 1986), a prominent figure in the endgame of the Havelock North Golden Dawn and also in the Order of the Table Round. He was, moreover, a man of local reputation as a mystic and healer.

Near the order's edifice is a small shrine where people repaired to pray and meditate after receiving therapy from Taylor, who, almost like Felkin before him, did color and other psychic remedies. Some still find their way to the little shrine, and at least at the time of my visit in 1988, this half-hidden fane was still maintained by someone, though Taylor's house had been sold. Its altar held a Christian cross and, like a counterweight from the esoteric tradition, symbols of the traditional four elements: salt, roses, water, and a candle. That obscure cross and those few but still-fresh rose petals seem a fitting momento with which to conclude the strange story of Havelock North's Rosicrucian adventure.

7 Cults and the Commonwealth
Concluding Reflections

I was initially attracted to the study of alternative spirituality in New Zealand through an article by Roy Wallis in the *Journal for the Scientific Study of Religion*, which argued that British settler societies, particularly New Zealand, lead among comparable first-world societies in receptivity to new religious movements.[1] Wallis' article is basically a response to the theory of Rodney Stark and William S. Bainbridge in their *The Future of Religion*.[2] One body of data Stark and Bainbridge employ suggests that new religions appear disproportionately in settings where traditional religion is weak and that Europe therefore is markedly more receptive to them than is the United States. Wallis finds that claim wanting. Through reanalysis of the data, and the addition of new material, he demonstrates that, although cult activity may increase with declining church attendance, it is also particularly high in Anglo-Saxon, Protestant-dominated, immigrant-based societies, despite continuing high rates of church attendance as in the United States.[3]

Both Stark and Bainbridge and Wallis seem to me at this point to rely excessively on a small number of recent groups—the Hare Krishnas, Scientology, the Unification Church, the Children of God—and on sometimes questionable statistics provided by these groups themselves. A fuller picture can, I think, be obtained by referring to long-standing alternative spirituality groups such as Spiritualism and Theosophy, the central foci of this study. These traditions not only enable appreciation of a society's historical, ingrained, as well as current, patterns of "cult receptivity," but also are more likely than newly emergent groups to present meaningful statistics, whether their own or census figures. The main purpose of this book is to provide that historical dimension in the case of New Zealand. The working through of this task has, I believe, only enhanced Wallis' point that largely Protestant British immigrant societies manifest particularly high rates of cult activity, as well as Stark and Bainbridge's that this activity correlates with low conventional church attendance. New Zealand may well, in fact, be a prime exemplar of all corners of this argument because it has comparatively low church attendance—estimates run from eleven to sixteen percent of the population in an average week, compared to forty percent in the United States, twenty percent for Australia and ten percent for Britain—has comparatively strong alternative spirituality, and is a British settler society par excellence.

The relative strength of New Zealand alternative spirituality can be sampled by means of a few figures. The Theosophical Society is now a venerable institution that, beyond doubt, produces honest and compatible figures throughout the world. At the time of writing, it reported about seventeen hundred members in New Zealand and about five thousand in the United States. Given that New Zealand's population is only one-eightieth that of the latter country, this means more than twenty-five times as many Theosophists per capita in New Zealand than in the United States, the nation of Theosophy's founding. (More per capita, in fact, than in any other country in the world with the possible exception of Iceland, which in some ways oddly parallels its Southern Hemisphere island counterpart.)

Results on the same scale can be derived for other such old standbys of alternative spirituality as the Liberal Catholic church, Anthroposophy, and probably—though figures are much less reliable—Spiritualism. The same can be said for the new generation of Eastern spiritual paths brought in by the 1960s, and even for the later New Age vogue, which took on well in New Zealand. Despite the image that many foreigners and Kiwis alike have of New Zealand as a blandly conformist if socially progressive society, it is one that nonetheless has responded with some enthusiasm to spiritual experimentation. I cannot say that I have come up with final answers to the question of why this is so. Final answers are no doubt never really possible in a matter as irreducibly subjective as spiritual choices. But I do hope to offer a few insights.

Unconventional Spirituality:
The United States versus New Zealand

Both the United States and New Zealand are fundamentally settler societies, with institutions originally shaped by British colonizing and governing. But an American sense of national identity and destiny —perhaps even divinely ordained destiny—was wrought by a long war of independence. By the time New Zealand emerged in the mid-nineteenth century as a coherent settler entity, the mother country had profited from the American experience, and at the same time was charged with great imperial responsibilities around the world. It pushed those remote but loyal islands toward national self-government under the crown at a good pace, sometimes (though not always) faster than they wished themselves. At the same time, the New Zealand population, unlike that of the United States, has remained predominately British in national origin.

Yet, like her sisters in the "white" commonwealth, Canada and Australia, New Zealand, with the queen on its coins and local fauna from its strange ecosystem on its stamps, has suffered a certain confusion about exactly what it is. New Zealand's crisis of identity is now exacerbated by a fast-growing Pacific Island population. Like Canada and Australia, New Zealand never experienced myth-making, destiny-confirming, nation-creating war or revolution comparable to those of the United States, Latin America, or the twentieth-century ex-colonial nations. Like Canada and Australia, New Zealand enjoys a basically good life, with a high level of living by world standards, but sometimes wonders whether it is a backwater to the onrushing river of history.

Some fear New Zealand has now little sense of important mission and has lost the prestige of being in the social vanguard it once felt, when the labor and welfare reforms of the 1890s Ballance and Seddon governments, or of the 1930s Savage administration, were the admiration of the liberal world. (The strong support most New Zealanders gave the country's 1980s defiance of U.S. nuclear policy, when it refused admission to New Zealand ports of American warships that might be carrying nuclear arms, was certainly related to a feeling that through this gesture of independence something of the former stature might be recovered.)

Lately the American discussion of civil religion has reached New Zealand. Religion scholars have devoted some effort to trying to figure out whether New Zealand has a civil religion or not.[4] If it does, it should be quite different in character from the American; as in so many cases, the United States is more profoundly different from seemingly similar states in the area of religion, civil or otherwise, than in any other.

The three commonwealth countries just named, together with the United States and the United Kingdom itself, do have, ultimately, a common British-based spiritual and social foundation. All five nations share the complex heritage of what has been called religious "monopoly-pluralism." In all the notion of a state church—whether loved, hated, or ignored, whether current or a distant memory—hovers somewhere in the collective mind. This side of the British spiritual mind carries the idea that one religion can and perhaps ought to have a unique *general* responsibility for the spiritual welfare of a national community and, secondly, that, in an almost mystical sense, a nation can and perhaps ought to be a spiritual as well as a pragmatic, temporal entity. The British monarchy, especially as defined in the deeply religious coronation rite, articulates that side of those nations' spiritual lives. Something of the same feeling lies behind the notion of civil religion, with its implication that, if no one church can any longer meaningfully manage the national role, it should be supplemented by some sort of supra-denominational national spiritual identity and purpose.

THE DENOMINATIONAL SOCIETY

At the same time, all five of these nations have been dealt the pluralism side of the equation in generous portions. They all share the heritage of the fissiparous, often cantakerous sectarianism that has also characterized British religion since the Middle Ages. Sometimes—especially in the case of the United States—this sectarianism was a major incentive for the overseas immigration that created the "outer four." At least since the advent of toleration in the British world after 1688, each of the five countries has been, or has has come into being as, a denominational society in essential respects, and except for Britain itself de jure as well as de facto. Even the system's pragmatic but hardly rational plurality of state churches—of Scotland and of England, and de facto in colonial America, Congregational, Catholic, and Quaker as well as Presbyterian and Anglican—reinforced the denominational idea.

A denomination is basically a particular institutional and sociological organization within a larger religious tradition. Although acknowledging the spiritual authority of that tradition, including (to varying extents) its scriptures, creeds, and ways of worship, it admits to no structural authority over itself, though it may in practice and even in theory grant that other denominations are parallel entities within the same great tradition. At the same time, the denomination links a number of local religious bodies under its governance and provides a recognized religious identity—Lutheran, Baptist, and so on. In effect denominations minister mostly to the needs of their members, apart from missionary endeavors, without a state church's sense of plenary responsibility to the nation as a whole. Except for dependent mission churches, denominations, lacking the international magisterium of the Roman Catholic church, are generally organized along national lines.

In essentially monopolistic religious societies, such as Spain or Yemen, minority movements can be described in church or sect terms, with all that implies in terms of withdrawal, alienation, and intensity on the part of the sectarians. But a denominational society is characterized instead by the presence of several long-standing religious groups of broadly comparable size, effectiveness and prestige operating in the same territory. In those countries, even Roman Catholics, Jews, and Eastern Orthodox Christians have had little choice but to operate in practice as denominations and to observe the unspoken rules of a denominational society.

Although there may be sectarian and cultist outsiders to the denominational cartel who do feel some alienation and even persecution, accepted denominations recognize that collectively they are the church in a denominational society. Although they can aspire to nothing more than parity with others, in immigrant societies like those of the Americas and Australasia, it is no small thing for a denomination made up of latecomers to be able to attain recognized equality with one that arrived with the First Ships. Even groups once thought exceedingly sectarian, such as Swedenborgians and Mormons, can and have won more or less equal acceptance as small and unusual but proper denominations through many years of playing by the rules.[5]

All five countries have become world-class examples—I would say the world's best examples—of relatively smoothly functioning denominational societies. Further, the pluralistic model they demonstrate, and the capacity for tolerance they have perforce developed, have made them relatively accessible to new religious movements seeking, one might say, their own slice of the multidenominational pie. The entry of such groups has not always been easy, for denominational societies can be quite sharp about what constitutes a legitimate, accepted denomination and what does not. Yet, in the end, their pluralistic and tolerance virtues have tended to prevail, and persevering newcomers have found a niche and eventual accreditation as part of the pattern. But differences also obtain between the religious ecologies of these countries.

RATIONALISM AND ROMANTICISM

One deep-level difference between the United States and New Zealand is that the European settler community in America was well in place in the eighteenth century. The basic institutions, including the attitudes that go with them, had and to a remarkable degree still have the rational, individualistic, Lockean, Jeffersonian stamp of that era. New Zealand, deriving instead from the mid-Victorian world, was more influenced by Romanticism in several forms, from secular utopianism of the Wakefield and Owenite colonization schemes to the staunchly Anglican settlement at Christchurch, all tempered as we have seen by evangelical missionary and philanthropic concern for the natives, and by the populist reformism of the 1890s. (In this respect New Zealand is more like the West Coast of the United States, notably California, which did not receive substantial "Anglo" settlement until about the same time as New Zealand, and which—especially in the late

nineteenth and early twentieth century—was notoriously open to utopianism, reformism, and spiritual experimentation, although relatively
lower than other parts of the country in conventional church attendance.)[6]

THE ROLE OF RELIGION

The role of religion in the two settlements was no less different.
Both America and New Zealand share the background sect-formation
proclivity of English Protestantism going back at least to the seven-
teenth-century revolution, with its plethora of Puritans, Baptists,
Quakers, Seekers, Levellers, and Fifth-Monarchy Men as well as hard-
core Anglicans and Roman Catholics. But New Zealand's immigration
was less grounded in the pressures of that era than the American. Several of the Atlantic colonies were established explicitly by freedom-seek-
ing sectarians in the spiritually supercharged atmosphere of the English
civil war era. No such godly compulsion brought most settlers out to the
the South Pacific.

Religion may have come in the luggage of some immigrants to Victorian New Zealand, but few came for explicitly religious reasons, a situation vastly different from the myth, at least, of pilgrim-founded
America. Church is attended in New Zealand today by some eleven to
sixteen percent of the population on an average Sunday, compared to
forty percent in the United States—the latter country still amazingly
divergent from the first-world norm in religious matters.[7] The church
historian Hugh Jackson has estimated that in late-nineteenth-century
New Zealand attendance was at around twenty-five percent, only half
that of the England and Scotland from which most settlers came, presumably already putting the island colony well on the road to secularization.[8] (I have, in fact, heard New Zealanders describe their country,
whether in pride or sorrow, as the most secular in the world—but that
may be only half the story.)[9]

Why this low religious participation from the colony's earliest days?
First, despite the high level of bourgeois church attendance in nineteenth-century Britain, New Zealand was settled when the working
class from which many colonists derived was already beginning to be
alienated from church, if indeed it ever had much hold on them.[10] Second, religious institutions were slow to make adequate provision in New
Zealand for churches, especially in the hinterland. Third and most
important, immigrants tended to come to New Zealand as single individuals or at best as families, rather than as substantial ethnic groups
for whom church (or temple or synagogue) was an important center of
identity and support in a strange land. Despite the only half-successful
Christchurch experiment, New Zealand really has had nothing on a

nation-shaping scale comparable to the icon of the pilgrim fathers and
the Puritan heritage in America, whereby a settlement justified and
interpreted religiously was held up as a paradigm of the whole society.
(If anything has played that role in New Zealand, it would, significantly, be rather secular utopian visions of the Owenite sort.)

Nor has New Zealand known the large ethnic and nationality groups
—eastern and southern European, African, Jewish, German, Dutch,
Scandinavian—so much a part of the fabric of American life, who more
often than not came in groups and settled in clusters, in a land to them
far stranger in ways and language than what confronted the average settler arriving in New Zealand. For those American immigrants or
bondsmen, religion was a crucial psychic link to something familiar,
and religious institutions became vital centers of community and support. Their understandable religious loyalty has done much to maintain
the high American level of religious participation. Most New Zealand
settlers were instead of British origin, and for them this new Britain in
the antipodes was not sufficiently different to create tensions calling for
American-style ethnoreligious solidarity.

Anglicans and Scots Presbyterians built their churches, but apart
from some individual cases displayed no more than perfunctory piety,
there being little in New Zealand to compare with the revivalism and
circuit-riding evangelicalism of the American frontier, or the burgeoning immigrant-based Lutheran or Catholic churches of the farmlands
and great cities.[11] The pioneer norm was more the isolated, hard-drink-
ing, and less than devout male immigrant who drifted under pressure of
London or countryside poverty, or middle-class oppressiveness, out to
the sheep stations or quaysides of nineteenth-century New Zealand.[12]
In this regard, as we have suggested, New Zealand was more like the
nineteenth-century American West with its miner, logger, and cowboy
cultures than other aspects of American society. The West significantly
has the lowest church attendance in America and reputedly the greatest
interest in Eastern and alternative spirituality.

Cases appear of immigrants to New Zealand who claimed to have
been raised in a strict religious environment at home and then found
that it somehow fell away in the course of a long and often-adventurous
progress to a new life Down Under. Thereafter some of these pioneers
discovered themselves open to new light from Spiritualism or Theosophy. Something comparable also happened to many traditional American Methodists and Baptists who made the long trek across the deserts
to magnets of renewed life, and of the esoteric, like San Francisco and
Los Angeles.

However, most Americans have also shared a sense that religion,
though it may take a thousand forms, remains an important aspect of

American identity. This has to do with the half-mythicized para-digmatic role of the religious-motivated first settlers, and the even more mythic religiosity of the 1776 founding fathers, and is perpetuated in a pervasive notion that being religious and frequenting a place of worship is quintessentially American. It matters less what that temple is so long as it is not perceived as wholly beyond the ever-expanding pale. (At one time mainstream British-derived Protestantism—Episcopalianism, Presbyterianism, Congregationalism, etc.—clearly constituted the in-ner circle. Then the famous Protestant-Catholic-Jew formula emerged around the end of the Second World War. In the 1970s evangelical Prot-estants, long looked down on as country cousins by the mainstream, made a bid for social, and political, equal status. Recently the first Bud-dhist has been commissioned a military chaplain, a sure sign of chang-ing religious frontiers in the United States.)

However, New Zealand's lightly attended churches do not appear to be regarded in quite the same way. Although they have surely had a part in New Zealand history, they are neither widely considered para-digmatic of the whole colonizing enterprise nor thought to have much to do with being a Kiwi as such. To be sure, during the highly British-ori-ented dominion period, for the first two or three generations of immi-grants, many churches epitomized both local colonizing struggles and links with home and were greatly valued. Yet religion hardly defines a New Zealander in the way Islam does an Arab or even Presbyterianism a Scot. Although this is a very subjective assessment, I would venture to say that—compared to the American church mystique—churches in New Zealand are almost sensed to be slightly alien, institutions come in from elsewhere and more deeply connected with the history and culture of other times and places than of the young Pacific nation. (A percep-tion like this had a positive role in the view of certain Theosophists, inspired by C. W. Leadbeater, that Australia and New Zealand were the breeding ground of a new root race with a new spirituality.) Churches are all right for people who like that sort of thing, many New Zealanders might say, but inessential to the cohesion of the nation as such.

One observer has argued that the strongest focus of New Zealand civil religion has been not the conventional churches, nor the queen whose image and superscription grace the currency, nor even rugby, but Anzac Day and its rites—and has noted that curiously the monuments found in virtually every town to the tragically large number of New Zealanders killed in the two world wars tend to be not Christian but pagan in style, not crosses but Egyptian obelisks or Roman arches, as though these were more suitable to fallen warriors.[13] In the lack of a founding war or revolution, the First World War, the war of the Anzac heroes, in which New Zealand chivalrously proved its loyalty to king and empire by sustaining losses grotesquely disproportionate to its small population or (in hindsight) necessary geopolitical investment in the outcome, had to serve as surrogate.

But as living memory of that titanic conflict, and even of the second, closer-to-home one, fades with time, so has intense, quasi-religious involvement in Anzac Day. Yet despite—or because of—the absence of a national religion or even much civil religion, and despite the colorless mediocrity that New Zealanders (and others) often imagine as characteristic of the society, a remarkable response to alternative spirituality has obtained.

New Zealand's Response to New Religions

The response started with Spiritualism as early as the 1860s. Spiritualism was important in New Zealand, as in Britain and the United States, not only for its own sake but also because it paved the way for Theosophy and later new religions. Spiritualism provided a direct model for the sort of communication with unseen masters claimed by Blavatsky of Theosophy and other magi. Together with its precursors Swedenborgianism and mesmerism, Theosophy did much to shake multitudes loose from conventional pieties in favor of a faith better aligned with both the forward wave of progress and the inner landscape of consciousness. These claims would be made by Theosophy and other emergent creeds.

More explicitly, apart from the obvious appeal of immediate contact with those beyond the veil, nineteenth-century Spiritualism offered several timely and often-reiterated themes. It professed to be the most democratic of religions, because mediumship was in principle accessible to anyone regardless of education, status in ecclesiastical hierarchies, or, most significantly, sex. Spiritualism presented women, like Jane Harris, a virtually unique opportunity to make religious, social, and even political statements—even if they were formally attributed to spirit mentors—and to exercise spiritual leadership. This was the case in New Zealand Spiritualism, and Theosophy as well. In New Zealand as elsewhere, the highly charged issue of women and religion appears as a covert but unmistakable subtext in most of the controversies provoked by new religions.

Given the nineteenth-century prestige attached in forward-looking circles to the concepts of science and progress, the claim of Spiritualism to be the most scientific of religions, because it was based on empirical evidence rather than the dogma and authority of the past, was much discussed—and disputed. So was Theosophy's imposing claim to be a modern synthesis of science and religion and likewise its vision of a coming new age and new race. Spiritualism (like Theosophy) was also commonly associated with social reform, and indeed in some places, as in the rhetoric of Jane Harris, was a proletarian movement with a radical as well as utopian edge.[14]

Not a few of these Spiritualist and Theosophical themes enjoy a sometimes-hidden but real congruity with important features of New Zealand society, whether on the level of practice or ideals. We must therefore look at certain of those features relevant to the understanding of new religious movements. In doing so, we may detect reasons why, despite the alleged conformist nature of New Zealand society, some strikingly unconventional religions have gained a foothold in it. Certain of those features go in directions other than conformity and may be subtly at odds with the king-and-empire values of the era of the two world wars, but for those very reasons deserve to be isolated.

Secularism

New Zealand is and has long been an exceptionally secular society by most criteria. What does this mean? Secularism, whether explicitly or by strong implication, argues a belief that religion is an inadequate, and in fact false, response to human needs. First, the secularist platform assumes that human problems are most effectively solved through scientific technology or social planning. It assumes, too, that science—and, some would say, its societal correlate, social engineering—possesses an inherent capacity for self-improvement—hence the idea of progress. Given half a chance, the technology and social organization of the next generation is better than the present. The nineteenth century, still unchastened by the horrors of the twentieth, produced quite a few believers in inevitable progress who were in no way prepared to let religious obscurantism stand in its way. Understandably, that century's immigrant communities were especially susceptible to science and progress, above all social engineering, because they offered especially advantageous settings where bold new experiments could be ventured. The 1890s in New Zealand offer an excellent example, and again, science and progress had been major themes of the Spiritualist and Theosophical vision.

Erik Olssen, in a interesting article on the Plunket Society, founded (originally as the Royal New Zealand Society for the Health of Women and Children) around the turn of the century to promote infant and child welfare, observes how much its implicit ideology embraces several sides of the New Zealand mind.[15] First, the society serves those who see the country as an embryonic utopia, at the forefront of the employment of advanced technocratic and scientific thought for human betterment, essentially secular so far as serious matters are concerned. Its sterile layettes and nursing schedules reflected the latest scientific knowledge, and assumed them to be final.

At the same time, the Plunket approach also tacitly reaffirmed traditional family and sexual roles and conformist values (New Zealand babies ideally were all to be raised in the same progressive way) and mandated in effect that mothers and fathers have the self-discipline to accept regimens inculcated by the society's faceless committees— benign socialism, the planned society guided, like Plato's republic, by wise guardians, now beginning where it ought to begin, in the crib. Starting with nursing by the clock and rigorous toilet training, self-discipline was expected of those favored babies as they grew up, because their lives (and deaths, in event of war) were not for their sake alone but also for that of the (white) race and the empire. Soon enough this healthy, self-controlled style of life was continued in diet, exercise, and sport. We noted that these ideals seem articulated in a curious 1890s novel by Edward Tregear, sometime Theosophist and spokesman for the reform government of that decade.

Olssen contended that the austere, secular-progressive ideal of the Plunket Society suffered much undercutting from Hollywood movies with their glamorizing of indulgent life-styles and sexuality dedicated to other ends than motherhood and healthy babies. It has also, needless to say, been challenged by the rival ideals of Freudian and humanistic psychology (e.g., at Centrepoint, a commune north of Auckland based on principles of the latter school).

In Tregear's utopia, uncontrolled sexuality was the root enemy of a planned paradise and must be managed to create an ideal Plunket sort of world. (Yet even there, as we have seen, the two principal lovers have a rival private scheme, to flee utopia and make another "sort of paradise" on an island near Fiji—this dream suggesting less socialism than a steamy movie poster from the golden age of Hollywood.) But it must be acknowledged that the success of the Plunket mentality in New Zealand helps interpret the success of movements like Theosophy, with their serious futurism and their inculcation of healthy self-discipline.

No less important to secularism and the new religions alike was anticlericalism. As part of the secular ideology, and as reflected in the writings of someone like Helena Blavatsky, or in much Masonic discourse, it could become a passionate and very explicit harping on all the evils perpetrated by priestcraft throughout the ages. Spiritualism in the 1870s and 1880s formed an alliance, at least in the minds of some, with Rationalism to attack clerical bigotry and to further progress. But there was also a soft kind of anticlericalism less concerned with verbal assault on the churches and their professional ministries than with quiet do-it-yourself spirituality and lay leadership.

Freemasonry is a good example, even though in the English-speaking world it was, while anti-Catholic, not anticlerical as such and numbered some clergymen of the respectable Protestant churches among its initiates. Yet, more than some (though not all) Masons perhaps wished to concede, its extra-ecclesiastical myths and rituals, with their occult roots and its lay hierarchy, virtually created an alternative church, and an important one. The role of Masonic contacts, visitations, and friendship networks in building and cementing the British imperial establishment of the nineteenth century is not to be underestimated. Although only in passing in this book, Masonry forged links within New Zealand governing circles and linked them in turn to the right sort of confreres in London and elsewhere throughout the far-flung world then beneath the Union Jack. More to the point, Masonry is important as precedent, model, and ideological preparation for both Theosophy and the Golden Dawn. Yet for our groups, lay leadership generally meant something else not granted by most Masons, the further equality of men and women in that leadership. This issue even led to Theosophical involvement in Co-Masonry, an order of the Masonic type that did allow full ritual and governing equality for both sexes.

Here is another side of secularism in New Zealand, its meaning for the role of religious institutions themselves, and therefore for the place of unconventional religions in the spiritual landscape. An insightful article by W. J. Stuart, "Secularization and Sectarianism: The Struggle for a Religious Future for New Zealand," holds that secularization is the single most important factor creating the future of religion in New Zealand.[16] Citing census and poll figures, Stuart maintains that the average New Zealander has little interest in organized religion in any case, and churches have much competition in a country devoted to sports, travel, and free weekends.

But this situation, Stuart holds, does not necessarily mean New Zealanders in the future will become even less religious than the present low level of activity would suggest. Although they may not be easily quantifiable, certain contrary straws are in the wind. Among the Maori and Pacific Island populations, a growing desire to preserve a distinctive religiocultural identity, either through recovering Polynesian spirituality or through Christian church life within a homogeneous ethnic community, may revitalize some religious institutions. (The same sort of immigrant and African-American community religiosity has done much to maintain the United States' high level of religious life.) Second, Stuart notes that many New Zealanders undoubtedly handle religious needs in their own way, often without joining a religious group. Sometimes the choice will be a therapy group with its secular equivalents to ritual, priesthood, and guru, or it may be entirely individual. Do-it-yourself-ism undoubtedly works more to the advantage than disadvantage of alternative spirituality groups, because many of them provide useful resources for various kinds of individually customized therapy and religion. They often do not hesitate to seek casual or part-time participants as well as highly committed ones, which is why they advertise lectures and meditation classes widely.

The more New Zealanders want religion but not *organized* religion, the more alternative groups—which may actually have their own tight but small-scale organizations yet do not look like establishments—are apt to do well. This tendency has in fact long been there, helping to account for the nineteenth-century vogue for Spiritualism as much as for the late-twentieth-century New Age style of independent spirituality. The pioneer legacy of the pragmatic "I'd rather do it myself in my own way" mentality remains a very important part of New Zealand character, in religion as much as in anything else.

Third and most important, Stuart observes that secularization inevitably entails religious pluralism. As Stark and Bainbridge also noted, the lack of a strong religious center can catalyze the proliferation of alternative movements, mostly small, but cumulatively a significant phenomena. Stuart points to the growth, indicated in the census and other sources, of both fundamentalist and pentecostal Christian sects, and of quasi- and non-Christian groups, particularly in ethnic minority populations. He predicts, however, that, "while the number of such groups will continue to increase, the number of people who affiliate themselves with these groups will either remain constant or decline," apparently due to the counterpull of sheer secularism. "For instance, if Buddhism continues to increase, its increase will probably be due to an increase of Buddhist people settling in the country, i.e., refugees from South-east Asia."[17]

Here, however, it may not necessarily be a matter of either . . . or. Certainly New Zealand's Buddhist population has increased markedly since the Vietnam War era because of immigration, but I have also observed a surprising number of non-Asian faces at Buddhist centers. The Buddhist upsurge may connect both with immigration and with Stuart's second point, that New Zealanders handle religion in their own ways, owing to the ease with which Western Buddhism can present itself as culturally independent, concerned only with spiritual therapy, growth, and meditation—however much that may be at odds with what *ethnic* Buddhists seek in dharma centers, precisely their cultural roots.

In any case, paradoxically or not, New Zealand's secularism is of a piece with its receptivity to new religious movements, and for that reason is now simply a continuation of a pattern that began with the first settlers. As Roy Wallis put the case succinctly, "In a society where virtually every aspect of culture is imported or a recent innovation, less stigma generally attaches to adopting any particular innovation or import, than in a traditional, or a culturally homogeneous society. Cultural pluralism encourages the acceptance of further additions to the range of available beliefs and life-styles as at least potentially legitimate."[18]

New Zealand meets this criterion particularly well, perhaps better than any comparable society. Here are some reasons: (a) virtually every aspect of Pakeha culture is an import or a recent innovation, generally since 1840; (b) settlers came from what was in practice a denominational society, which therefore offered a model of pluralism—a pattern carried out in early missionary work in New Zealand; (c) settlement was at its height in the mid- to late nineteenth century, when alternatives to traditional religion like Spiritualism and Theosophy were in the air, as were the utopian visions which frequently joined forces with them.

In summary of this material, then, let us look at some features of nineteenth-century British (or western United States) settler societies especially relevant to new religious movements. Eleven come to mind:

1. Many immigrants came as isolated individuals, primarily male, or at best as nuclear families, who generally felt less social pressure for religious participation than at home.

2. Religious needs were less well provided for than in the sending societies; churches were fewer, and clergymen not always of the best caliber or prepared to adapt to colonial conditions.[19]

3. Immigrants were often from classes already quasi-alienated from religion or were footloose, adventurous sorts of persons without deep inner commitments, but were perhaps open to new spiritual forms.

4. Often immigrants experienced a sea change suggesting that they, and the world, could be different from how they had known it.

5. At the same time, immigrants tend toward a pragmatic mentality; with so much to be done, the bent is toward that which works; in religion, this can mean religions like Spiritualism that emphasize immediate empirical phenomena may be favored.

6. Yet immigrants also have a capacity for utopian dreams that promise to justify all the hardships they have undergone in making a new home in a new land; they value concepts, like modernity and progress, that are congruous with those dreams. In religion, they may reject forms that seem to be dependent merely on the authority of the past, in favor of those able to legitimate a commitment to progress, the best of the modern world, and building the kingdom of heaven on earth.

7. The equality of women, and democracy generally, has been important in some pioneer societies. Even where, as in the Puritan Massachusetts Bay Colony, gender or unqualified democratic egalitarianism was not initially realized, the settler experience clearly contained the germ

of later developments in those directions. It is no mere coincidence that women first received the vote in Wyoming, certain Australian states, and New Zealand. Gender egalitarianism can apply to spiritual matters, too, by creating pressure in favor of religions valuing lay and female leadership no less than professional male. Ultimately equality in religious language and symbol, an objective toward which Theosophy took brave steps, may be sought as well.

8. On another level, the frequent isolation of pioneer life, the immigrant's break with the past and with supportive contexts, means that, much more than before, settlers far from home must take responsibility for their own subjectivity; how one feels, what one experiences within, will be less conditioned by traditional influences; one must handle all this oneself, or run grave risks of anomie or inner chaos.

9. At the same time, the romantic mood with its exaltation of feeling and experience over reason, its talk of love reaching beyond the grave, its belief in the human ability always to transcend prior limits, together with its dreams of the distant and the past, of wisdom hidden and primordial, set a climate conducive to Spiritualism, Theosophy, the occult, and the East.

10. However much they sometimes wished to deny it, the settler societies of both the American West and New Zealand were far from Europe and relatively close to Asia. Sooner or later, trade and immigration were to make Asia, including its spiritual traditions, a visible presence, and so a present option.

11. Also present were indigenous religions, Maori or Native American. They presented a challenge of comprehension to settler society, often—despite times of hatred and bloody conflict—with mixed and interesting results. Early Spiritualism in North America and New Zealand alike had some limited interaction in both conceptual and personal respects with native shamanism (e.g., the importance of Indian guides in the séance room, the Maori recognition of kinship to Spiritualism in the Nation narrative). A Maori *tohunga* (shaman-priest) was among the first Theosophists in New Zealand, and in both New Zealand and the U.S. sympathetic interest in indigenous spirituality is evident in Theosophical and Spiritualist literature over many decades.

General Characteristics
of Alternative Spiritual Movements

Despite a sometimes amazing surface diversity, alternative spiritual movements tend actually to have quite a bit in common, both in ideology and structure. In part, that is because the present examples in the English-speaking world have some common roots and interlocking histories. But history is not a sufficient explanation; new religions in other places, such as India or Japan, can also share these features. Many, in fact, appear to be simply what is requisite in a novel faith seeking to challenge an established religious pattern.

WACH'S THREE FORMS OF RELIGIOUS EXPRESSION

This discussion is based on the three forms of religious expression developed by the sociologist of religion Joachim Wach.[20] These three are the *theoretical*, essentially the religion's verbal expression in narrative, creed, and concept; the *practical*, the religion's practices, whether public worship or private devotion; and the *sociological*, its forms of leadership and organization. (New religions of the sort discussed in this book are "metaphysical" or Eastern strands within Western culture that are largely independent of the mainstream, not sectarian Jewish or Christian movements like Hasidism or Pentecostalism.)

Theoretical.—Far more than the personal theism of conventional Judaism or Christianity, alternative spirituality tends to see the divine in impersonal monistic terms, as an all-pervasive consciousness or ground of existence that takes many forms. The individual soul is an outcropping, so to speak, of that universal spirit and so has a separate origin and destiny from the physical body—a view that obviously justifies Spiritualist mediumship and Theosophical reincarnation. The physical body is only more indirectly the creation of spirit, being the product of karma or a lower emanation.

As though to compensate for the transcendent impersonality of ultimate reality, alternate spiritual worldviews tend thickly to populate what might be called the middle range between the human and the supreme—as does the popular piety of many religions with their saints and local gods. Here in this middle ground are the souls on the other side of life of Spiritualism, the space brothers of UFO cults, the masters of Theosophy, the avatars, buddhas, bodhisattvas of Eastern religions in the West.

The goal of the spiritual life is generally not understood to be salvation in the ordinary Christian sense so much as a form of self-realization or self-understanding, attained through mystic or ecstatic experience as well as learning, which makes real the truth about the soul, its origin and destiny, and relation to ultimate Godhead.

Practical.—The practical expression of new religious movements varies considerably, from older groups such as the Spiritualist and New Thought churches with basically a Protestant Christian format, to groups that simply center on chanting or meditation public and private. The former set can be seen as wishing to maintain symbols of continuity with the environing religion and as stressing that the new, perhaps exotic, faith does not represent a *total* break with it but only the addition of a new teaching or practice.

The latter, those that do not look like ordinary Sunday morning, appeals to people sufficiently alienated from the society's traditional religion to wish instead symbols suggesting something quite different. Or, they want to see the new teaching as only supplemental and so as requiring no more than a concise presentation of its doctrine and practice, not a full service. In any case, different presentation indicates the new is discontinuous in style as well as content from the old. Instead of a standard service with the usual hymns and offering and sermon, it may be a *satsang* or "dharma talk," a séance or class, in the evening, with casually dressed devotees sitting on the floor or in yogic postures, and a whiff of incense in the air. Liturgical development need not be the only path. Spiritualism moved from informal, almost-spontaneous circles, generally in the evening, to Sunday-morning church services of a Protestant type.

Either way, though, the practical expression of alternative spirituality usually centers around a single practice or activity, a single simple sure key to the power and realization the religion offers, whether it is mediumship, positive thinking, ceremonial magic, meditation, yoga, chanting, or Theosophical study. This practice may be lifted out of the vast storehouse of occult and Eastern techniques, but it alone is the main practical focus.

The reasons for the single focus—typical of new and reformed religions generally—are obvious. An alternative religion, without the social supports—family, ethnic, community—of the dominant faith, must offer an experience of sufficient self-validating intensity to counterbalance their natural pull, and compensate for the cost many will feel, in giving up or commingling the faith of their fathers, for a perhaps-unpopular minority religion.

The new faith, therefore, cannot merely present general truths. It must center on a practice that can be counted on to give some people prompt and tangible results, in the form of peace of mind, prayers answered, a new sense of power and purpose. In sum, alternative spiritual practices have structural as well as content messages. They align and demarcate the group; they buttress and justify the adherent's participation in it.

Sociological. —Much the same sort of messages accompany the group's sociology. First, the new religion, above all in its first generation, is likely to be centered on charismatic leadership. It may, as in Spiritualism, find a number of charismatic mediums or lecturers, like Peebles, Hardinge, Conan Doyle, or Harris-Roberts, or in its UFO aspect Adamski. Or, as in Theosophy, there appear a few like Blavatsky and

Besant. In some Eastern imports the novel spirituality may be centered on one person who is the founder, the communicator of a special revelation or initiation, the authoritative teacher of the group's special practice, and the heir of a unique spiritual lineage in this world or the worlds of spirit. In any case the charismatic leader gathers a band of disciples; for them he or she is above all a personal center of spiritual life, more important as a person than as the promulgator of any particular doctrine or practice.

The new group of teacher and disciples is relatively small but intense; again, it must compensate as a surrogate family or community for the natural attractions of former bonds. It is not seldom in tension with the surrounding religion and society. All that may generate pressure toward internal conformity and evoke symbols of separatism from the outside, for example, in dress, diet, or occupation, such as the vegetarianism of some Spiritualists and Theosophists.

CHANGE AND DEVELOPMENT

New religious movements, however, are continually in a process of change and development. Of particular importance is the transition from the first generation, that of the founder or founders, to the second, when his (or her, or their) charisma must be passed to a successor generation. Inevitably this means that it must be routinized, packaged in rites or standardized teaching rather than as the spontaneous and continuous flow of grace of the first formless years. An institutional structure, with officers and programs, is needed, and so (even more than before) are regular meetings or services. Only by such means can a new religion avoid the fate of the many that have not survived their first generation and make itself a force felt down the ages.

It is worth noting that the New Zealand movements presented here came to that country only during or after the routinization of charisma had been effected to some extent; the first generation of Spiritualism, Theosophy, and the Golden Dawn was begotten elsewhere, though these groups came soon enough for some of the often-hard routinization process and its effects to be clearly visible. Spiritualism did advance from circles to churches while in New Zealand, the long-lingering storms surrounding Theosophy's move to the post-Blavatsky generation of Besant and Leadbeater certainly darkened New Zealand's Theosophical skyline, and the Golden Dawn came to the antipodes in the wake of its premature generational crisis.

Finally, it should be observed that movements like these, far more than conventional churches, have both intense and diffuse followings. They may have an inner circle of highly committed, even communal, adherents. But they probably also have a wide invisible congregation of persons who merely read the literature, perhaps attend an occasional mediumship demonstration, class or lecture, do the chant or the meditation, all the while perhaps also attending another church for family reasons, or even appearing to the world as quite secular.

This diffuse influence means that census or membership figures do not tell the whole story of an alternative religion's effect. Although most persons at an average Anglican or Presbyterian service are Anglicans or Presbyterians, it is a safe bet that the majority at the average Spiritualist meeting are not formally or exclusively Spiritualists. Even wider is the circle of those who have merely read a book from the tradition, one of the White Eagle or Silver Birch volumes, for example, or knew someone who did and talked about it, and who nonetheless picked up an idea that made a personal difference. These are, in other words, not only religions with alternative ideas or practices but faiths with alternative ways of spreading their influence. They do not always contend altar against altar on Sunday morning against the mainstream churches; they may also spread like underground streams finding various channels of opportunity, perhaps even seeping into the basements of those same churches. The institutional strength of the religions considered in this book, then, does not tell the whole narrative of their power in the life of New Zealand or any other society. In an image used before, against the mighty institutional churches, they are like the amoeba to the whale, smaller and weaker yet in a real sense far more immortal.

Appendix 1
Autobiographical Writings
of Jane Elizabeth Harris-Roberts

JANE ELIZABETH HARRIS-ROBERTS "The Mater" of
New Zealand Spiritualism, left two accounts of her life, each of about
three pages. One was published in the periodical *Aquarius* (October 21,
1939); the other is a handwritten document of about the same time now
in the possession of Mr. J. W. Graham of Auckland. They are thus
both from shortly before her death at age ninety in 1942. There is much
overlap but each contains some distinctive material as well. I therefore
endeavor to present a coherent picture of Jane Elizabeth Harris' life by
combining selected material from both sources. The *Aquarius* material is
labeled A, the manuscript MS.

A: Very simple indeed was the method of my "calling" into the spiritual
movement. As a girl, I was brought up in the Church of England. In 1873 I
married Mr. Harris, a lover of nature, of gardens more than churches. A
noble yeoman was he; an ardent student of social questions; his favourite
teachers were Stainton Moses, Professor Denton and Andrew Jackson
Davis. But he came to church with me, for he was broad-minded. I was just
20, he 12 years older; and his thoughts went far beyond my narrow understanding. He had a friend, Mr. H—, who was investigating spiritual science. He subscribed to "Banner of Light," "Progressive Thinker," and the
"Harbinger," [well-known Spiritualist periodicals] and kindly lent them to
my husband, who eagerly devoured their teaching.

Mr. H— and the Rev. L. J. Neil, of the Presbyterian Church, attended
a circle, to which they invited Mr. Harris. Excellent trance addresses and
clairvoyance were given. Mr. Neil's sermons were instructive, his interpretation of the Scriptures quite devoid of fear, terror of death or the after-
wards. [This clergyman, actually Samuel James Neil, was minister of
Thames Presbyterian church 1877–1894, when he was suspended for holding Theosophical views.] It was the gospel of spirit communion by inspiration.

I was very troubled about the circle. The Indian guide sometimes used my husband, and I was frightened. I would not read the "Harbinger," but very carefully placed it on a high shelf!

MS: Beloved! I have much sympathy for those who are conscientiously striving to "prove all things," because it was very difficult for me to accept the teachings of Spiritualism; and I was extremely nervous in those early days of phenomenal manifestations. My husband was a very practical person; cautious, thorough in his investigations, and was privileged in attending a circle of well balanced minds in sincere desire to receive the truth, and have actual knowledge of "survival" after so called death.

I was afraid when tables turned, and tappings were heard; I was afraid when the pencil wrote of its own accord, and adhered to the table during all the tipping and rocking. I was afraid when the Indian guides chattered, and my entranced husband was not himself at all.

The "Harbinger" and "Banner of Light" gave strange, wonderful messages from the other side which caused me much anxiety. My own hand was used to write on various subjects; in the silence of the night I would hear voices, uttering beautiful thoughts in prose or poetry.

But I was afraid of being "controlled" by invisible entities, or of being deceived by untruthful messages; so I decided not to read any more spiritualistic literature, or listen to the unseen speaker. I placed the "Harbinger" on a high book shelf, and tried to forget what I had read.

A: A traveller came to our home, selling draperies. He also was a student, and Mr. Harris enjoyed his conversation, after which they sat at our table, which was heavy. They placed their hands upon it; it rocked to and fro. Mr. Harris laid a lead pencil on it, and the pencil never moved. It seemed fastened to the table. I sat near, watching. The table rose up in the air, touching the ceiling, came down again, quietly. I sat still, frightened, and presently the table rocked towards me, and I lost consciousness. . . . I was entranced. The control spoke to Mr. Harris, told him I was to be a messenger, and work for the cause. When I came to myself, Mr. Harris told me, and I could not believe it. I thought it was hypnotism!

However, to please him, we sat in a circle in our own home. There were seven of us, my husband's friends and Mrs. Neil, with two lady friends also. Again I was entranced, and still afraid.

One day there was a high wind, and the little pile of newspapers was blown down upon the floor. The "Harbinger" flew open at the supplement, which was "A Little Pilgrim in the Unseen," by Mrs. Oliphant. Almost afraid, I read the story, and found how beautiful was the life "over there," where is no death, no sorrow. I gained courage, and read with avidity books, journals, writings, prncipally books borrowed from the Manse library, to which Mrs. Neil gave me free access. I had many talks with her, and other friends.

I began to gather faith, but was still afraid of phenomena. For instance, one day I was troubled because I could not get my work done; baby was fretful, would not rest. I had to leave things undone. Mr. Harris came in from his garden and, smiling, took up a straw broom, with which he commenced to sweep. Presently he left hold of the broom, and it still went on sweeping, though no hand was guiding it. I caught up the baby and ran outside.

I did not like circles, trance and clairvoyance. I tried to persuade Mr. Harris to "leave it alone," but he could not. He was very magnetic, could relieve pain with his hand, and soothe a crying child. One day a silent, invisible presence came to our home. I had not seen death, but now my lovely little son of four months was sick, and very soon he passed in spite of all human aid.

It is written, "A little child shall lead them." Our clergyman came to me. He was white with age, very "reverend." The tears stole down his face and he expressed his sorrow that we had allowed our little child to die unbaptised. Oh! the pain of it; the thought of it! He was not "a child of God, an inheritor of the Kingdom of Heaven." Mr. Harris was angry and refused to believe that baby boy was not in Heaven. Gravely he bade the clergyman leave us; and then came a neighbour, a beloved soul, a member of the Rev. Mr. Neil's church. She tried to comfort me, and sent her son to the Manse to ask Mr. Neil to take the burial service.

He came, and poured the balm of Gilead into our hearts. He told us to trust in the Divine Master, who had said: "Suffer the children to come unto Me." He took the service, but there was no fear, no sorrow. He said, "There is no death." He quoted Swedenborg's "Children in Heaven." He spoke of their unfoldment in that painless life, and bade us realise that our child would be our "angel messenger." It almost seemed that life here could not be perfect except we had "hostages in Heaven."

Years passed. I received inspirational writing which, being sent to the "Harbinger," opened the way for undreamed of future work.

MS: One day a severe draught blew the papers down from the shelf, and the Christmas supplement to the Harbinger lay wide open on the floor. It presented the beautiful story of life on the other side by Mrs. Oliphant, entitled " A Little Pilgrim in the Unseen." Fascinated by the name, I read it through, and sensed its wondrous truth, the comfort of reunion with loved ones, continual progress, increasing happiness, joyous peace.

I joined the next circle that met and was soon entranced. The friends told me I gave a joyous address on the words, "Seek ye the truth, and the truth shall set you free!"

When I awoke, I found my husband rejoicing over this sudden change; and after that we sat eagerly and various spirit friends spoke through my organism. So passed two years, when very suddenly my husband was called to the higher life, and we were bereft of our protector. A little family of five and their very incapable mother, who had "no head for business at all"!

During those two years I had sent many "writings in prose and poetry" to the "Harbinger," and was known as "Jenny Wren." Mr. Terry, the editor, kindly accepted, and approved the "guides" who wrote them; so when he, as President of the Victorian Association of Spiritualists, perceived a vacancy in the position of "speaker," he wrote me an invitation to come to Melbourne, and accept an engagement for the platform. This it appeared almost impossible for me to accept; I had spoken for a few gatherings of progressive thinkers, from time to time; but did not feel qualified to become more prominent. I was not financially able to meet the demand either; for I must take the family with me, and my income was but small. However it is *true,* I have proved it many times, that marvellous promise, "He will give his angels charge concerning thee, to guide thee in *all* thy ways." Unknown to me, the various New Zealand journals for which "Jenny Wren" [Mrs. Harris' pen name] scribbled, hearing of our bereavement, had started a fund at the office of one of the "weeklies," to assist in some way; so kindly bridging the difficulty of "fare to Australia."

So the way was made plain. In a few weeks we were on board the S.S. Tarawera bound for Sydney. Such kind references had been given me, that I felt I should obtain work, and had already prepared a ms for a Sydney journal.

A: In 1887 Mr. Harris passed suddenly to the higher life, leaving me with six children. The youngest was six weeks old, and he was spared for one sweet year. Then scarlet fever came. All the children recovered except little Denton, whom I called the angel child because he was so beautiful. If I tell you that, as he lay in my arms, he waved one wee hand and said, "Ta-ta! Mamma," could you believe it?

It was hard to see him pass, but I knew he was only lent and that in some way he and I would work together between the two worlds.

Then I felt I must leave my peaceful country home and go where I was asked by Mr. Terry and told to go by the angel friends . . . to Melbourne. My experience as a psychic demonstrator had been limited to my own home, and on three occasions I had read papers before audiences. But I took the five children and went, as "Jenny Wren," with references from New Zealand journals, to Australia. In Sydney I took rooms, visited editors, received orders for a serial and articles from three papers. I was well received by a committee of spiritualists, who asked me to accept an engagement for three months and then go to Melbourne. My first Sunday in West's academy was successful and was well reported.

MS: I should be a stranger in a strange land. I knew no one in Sydney; but I was told by the unseen, write to a Mr. Munro, President of the Sydney Society of Spiritualists, and offer my services for those Sundays prior to the Melbourne engagement. This I did, and we were met at the boat by Mr. Munro and the secretary. For a few days we were the guests of Mrs. Munro, whose gracious kindness I shall never forget. (They have both "risen," to the reward of all their labour.)

The first Sunday in West's academy, Castlereagh St., was a record one. When I saw the large audience I was very nervous; but most graciously the guide entranced me, so that I knew no more until the service ended. I awoke to the soft music of the organ, and presently the singing of the choir.

During the week we held seances, received visits from various supporters of the cause, and found suitable rooms for our short stay in Sydney.

Such kindness was extended to me, such sympathy for the "new medium," who certainly was sustained by invisible agencies; or she would not have consented to appear before such advanced students, and devoted workers; to whom she must have seemed an infant in comparison.

A: Now, just as my earlier writing had helped me to secure engagements on Australian platforms, so, as soon as my name was published in advertisements for spiritualist services, formerly kind editors turned me down and would not accept my work.

This important source of income was lost to me, and there were the children to be provided for. I asked for help from the beyond, and simply enough it was shown to me that they knew and cared. I had given an address on vegetarian cookery at an exhibition on women's work in Sydney, and Lady C— [Lady Carrington, wife of Lord Carrington, governor of New South Wales], the patron, was much pleased with it. To the noble lady was born a daughter, little Lady Judith, and much was made of the fact that the baby was Australian-born. Several "welcomes" in prose and poetry were published, and one signed "Jenny Wren" attracted her Excellency's attention. There came a messenger to my room with a kind invitation to visit her Excellency. I went.

Gently the kind lady strove to persuade me to "keep very quiet" about "this spiritualism," which was not popular, and to depend on literary work which, she thought, would soon increase. She made mention of a possible position as a private secretary or librarian and other favours that could be extended. In fact, there need be no more anxiety about my children's daily bread if I would give up psychic work. What should I do?

Some unseen helper came to my aid and gave me words to reply to this offer. So I parted from her Excellency. Weeks passed, bringing anxiety about rent and food. At last I decided I would follow many other mothers and take my bag to the charitable aid depot for supplies.

As I walked across the park I met a man who gaped at me as though trying to bring something to memory. He raised his hat, inquiring if he had the pleasure of meeting "Jenny Wren," for if so he had a message to deliver. He asked if I remembered reading a paper on vegetarian cookery at the women's exhibition, adding that Lady C— had written to the board asking them to give me an engagement for a series of lectures on home science. Then he drew an envelope from his breast pocket, saying, "If you can give the first talk on Thursday evening, I may as well hand you the payment now."

In the envelope was a cheque for two guineas. Such a dinner the children had! How they enjoyed the pudding and asked who had sent it. I explained to the elder ones, so that their thoughts would turn to the unseen who were mindful of our needs.

A few days later I received an invitation to a seance to be held by a Mrs.

Mellon, a materialising medium from England. After we had sat for a time in semi-darkness, floating lights appeared. Then the cabinet was opened to show Mrs. Mellon sitting with closed eyes, entranced. There were presented to our view several friends of the sitters who were recognised. Then with delight, I recognised the figure of my husband. He came to my side and spoke gently to me, telling me not to doubt or fear and that I should be guided every step of the way.

One more incident will bear out the assurances given me from the other side. One day two men called at my rooms. One was a publisher; the other an ardent student of spiritualism, in whose garden, in bright moonlight, Mrs. Mellon had given a seance, many forms materialising and walking about the garden. The publisher asked me to gather up the poems I had from time to time written for the "Harbinger" so that his friend might arrange their publication in book form. So we were helped in many ways.

MS: I had a very happy time in Sydney with the little church started in Reichardt by Mr. Nettledon [?]. He bought the property, on which was a five room house and at the end of the section, a building that had been a tannery. This was taken down, renovated and placed beside the house. It was then furnished with chairs, a piano was loaned, and a hall opened for services. [Then follows a sentence that seems garbled.] By then chairs, [?], platform and all were arranged, and many happy meetings were held there in the "hall of love."

We had a lyceum there, circles were held weekly for development, and socials were given for the building fund. We were a happy little company; and all was harmony and peace.

A: Later I was called to Melbourne, where I met Mr. Terry, president of the spiritualist organisation; Mr. Stanford; Major Cavalier Smith, a noted Egyptologist; and many mediums, among whom were the veteran Milner Stephen, the healer; Mr. Evans, the independent slate-writer, and his gifted wife, a materialising medium, with whom we had wonderful manifestations of psychic power. I also met Mrs. Morris, who was medium for the Sun Angel Order. She taught me, and I was admitted into their service. I listened to wonderful teachers through these sensitives.

I had sorrow, too: sorrow which I do not think I could have borne without the help of the risen ones. My eldest son, Willie, aged 16, was engaged in a carriage factory and met with an accident at his work, which resulted in blood poisoning. He received both medical and psychic aid, but naught could avail. His work was to be done in another world. Then I realised what our faith was worth at such a time.

I was clairvoyant and clairaudient the night Willie passed. I heard his father's voice and saw my son carried by his father to the land where is no sorrow. So were they, too, united to work together. Since then another son, the last of my four, has joined them.

Some time later I saw wonderful phenomena through the mediumship of Mr. Bailie, whose guide produced apports [objects apported in by spiritual means] such as living birds, seaweed and rock from the ocean, and articles from an Eastern Temple. I knew a gifted Dunedin man, a Mr. Rough, who could carry red embers from the fire in his hand, and who, in trance, could give marvellous messages and treatments. I have had prophetic readings from mediums who knew nothing of me or my work, which have proved wonderfully correct. I have received writings that have brought help and comfort. I have been entranced, like the "man of whom Paul knew," and have had glimpses of spirit life so beautiful that it was with reluctance that I returned to the body.

MS: And now to Melbourne!

Welcomed by Mr. Terry and his daughter to their lovely home at Caulfield, until such time as should find a suitable lodging in or near the city. We had the privilege of meeting Mr. & Mrs. Fred Evans, from America, the well known independent slate writing medium, and his gifted wife who was a medium for materialisation. Such wonderful sittings, when my husband wrote on the locked slates, in his own hand writing, messages of cheer and loving care for us. Happy days in Melbourne.

Wonderful friends, marvellous mediums from England and America, among whom were Mrs. Mellon, Mr. Cooley, Mr. Colville, Dr. Peebles, Mr. Spriggs [?], Mr. Milner Stephens, Mrs. Morrison and others. These were among the pleasures of that ten years. There was also sorrow, for I had my eldest son, Willy, with me at Mr. Terry's home. He worked in a carriage factory, there was an accident, a bruise, blood poisoning and a sudden passing; although surrounded by helpers; he was met by his father and two brothers; I know he is very happy, and will try to help us whenever he can. (Five years ago, his younger brother passed on at the age of 53; so now the four brothers are with their father.)

At last, on account of uncertain health, I came back to New Zealand. A pleasant surprise awaited me, for I had heard that Spiritualism was dead, or forgotten now. However the large audience that filled the Opera House on our first night showed at least an active interest in our mission and we were able to meet all expenses. Three months there [Auckland], then we were asked to form and start a society, which we easily did, from the audience, willing friends came forward, now the "Society for Spiritual Progress" was formed, under Mr. Resnor [?] the first President. Joyously we opened the first service in the Oddfellows' Hall Pitt St.—"all set"—organist included, choir of young voices, helpers on committee, and lots of good will. I was told by the guides to go through N.Z. to start churches where possible, to form circles, and "lift up the spiritual banner." In due time came a good brother to take the Auckland platform and start a Lyceum. Then I was called by Mr. MacLean—Wellington—where we had a happy year, and presently good brother MacLean, who was a member of the House, got the bill he had formulated through, and we could have our own churches, and be registered. Then I was sent to Christchurch, and formed life long friendships there with noble souls who had studied Truth, and were eager for services. Mr. McCloud Cross [?] followed on, provided loyal service for the rest of his earthly life, in the work of healing and teaching. He too is "risen." Then a visit to Dunedin, very happy time, met some grand pioneer workers, among whom was Mr. Rough, now risen. Visiting New Plymouth, we started a church there, which was carried on by the devoted service of Mrs. Butler, until she also passed on.

Then to Nelson, where we started a church in the old Atheneum, which contained the Oddfellows Hall, willing helpers came around, and many sensitives developed. Now they have a church of their own, and many workers, among whom stands my dear sister as Pastor and leader. We also visited Gisborne, Wanganui, where many happy meetings were held, especially by Mr. Roberts also risen.

Good Mr. and Mrs. Newton have risen to the higher life, but their work is lovingly remembered, the little hall still used for lectures or circles—all welcome. As I look down the years, I remember the love and sympathy of the people, their earnest devoted effort has not been in vain.

Many souls have been helped and comforted. Auckland once more is "home," and the beloved churches throughout N.Z. have my love and my blessing, now in the twilight of my days. I can only send thoughts to them and all who work for them. God bless them. Peace, power, and progress be theirs in His Name whom we serve.

                                                                Mater

Appendix 2
The 1960s and After

T<small>HE GREAT</small> tradition of alternative spirituality in New Zealand centers on the Spiritualist and Theosophical lineages. Their disciples have kept watch and ward over its sacred flame longer than anyone else and have helped others as well as themselves by legitimating the notion of the spiritual alternative. But, although those older movements, deeply rooted in the passions and opportunities of the nineteenth century, have borne the heat and burden of the day, they have understandably become a little tired and have settled into well-worn grooves over the decades. Newcomers to the quest have rediscovered their original fire and have used it to ignite the oil of other lamps from East and West.

Virtually all alternative spirituality groups in New Zealand outside the Spiritualist, Theosophical, and Golden Dawn traditions are effectively products of the 1960s worldwide spiritual revolution. One way or another, they are reflections of the searchlight that generation cast about as it looked for new ways of being, body and soul, in the world. If not directly offspring of the celebrated 1960s counterculture, they were precursors of it, responses to its quest and its chaos, or followers in its wake. The 1960s' decade is the great watershed. What went before was essentially in the Victorian style of alternative spirituality, heavy on reading, lectures, and at best bookish antiquarian magic together with Crowley-type bad-boy rebellion. The 1960s were something else: alternative spirituality thoroughly mixed up with popular music, street theater, the drug experience and its surrogates, communalism, Eastern gurus coming west by the planeload, and the famous generation gap.

Although the earlier seekers were interested in the ideas of the East or the occult, they were often more than a little frightened of really dropping out or going native. They continually reassured themselves by establishing symbols of continuity with liberal Protestantism or Catholicism or, at the most, Freemasonry, and by cultivating gurus who were either ordinarily invisible, like the Theosophical or Rosicrucian, or well tamed like Krishnamurti.

For all that, those really into the 1960s scene could not have cared less. They wanted symbols of discontinuity rather than continuity. Their chantings or meditations were in incense-heavy basements or storefront centers rather than public lecture halls, and at any time of day other than eleven o'clock on Sunday morning. Their beads and bells and paisley shirts were hardly what the establishment wore to church. Most important of all, what they sought was not a classroom-type discourse on karma, or the spirit of a son killed at Mons, or even a rite resurrected from some British Museum *grimoire,* but the spiritual equivalent of tripping and a pilgrimage to Katmandu. They wanted experience, hands-on religion, and they were more than willing to dispense with head trips in favor of embracing total practice and total life-style. If they took up yoga or Zen they wanted the food, the dress, the sounds and postures of India or Japan, not merely the ideas. They wanted sacramentals they could see and touch, smell and wear—mandalas, crystals, joss sticks, and medallions—as well as consciousness-expanding notions to think about.

In New Zealand the flavor of the 1960s counterculture is well distilled in the magazine *Mushroom,* although it does not seem to have been published until about 1970. (The first issue has no date.) It was primarily focused on alternative living: communes, back-to-nature life-styles, organic farming. But *Mushroom* number 16 (January 1979) was devoted to spiritual themes, with features on astrology, Maori spirituality, meditation, Mahikari (a Japanese new religion), and a directory of spiritual resources in New Zealand.

Types of 1960s Alternative Spiritual Groups

As a preliminary, here are some types of alternative spiritual groups the 1960s epoch generated, or greatly enhanced: First, there is what, for want of a better term, may be called occult or Western (including Islamic) initiatory groups, groups that present experiences designed to facilitate spiritual growth and awareness on the basis of some special knowledge of inner reality that they hold. The knowledge, for them, is not couched in the language of the East, but in the terminology of Western esotericism, like that of the Golden Dawn, or is drawn from modern science and psychology, or is largely of their own making. These would include Aleister Crowley's Ordo Templi Orientis (OTO), the Guardians, the Emissaries, Subud, and groups in the tradition of

G. I. Gurdjieff, in which tradition I would place the Gnostic Society, the School of Philosophy, and Emin.

Then come groups of Eastern religious background. These include those of Indian origin, such as various yoga schools, the Brahma Kumari, Ananda Marga, Transcendental Meditation, and the Satya Sai Baba and Da Free John movements; Buddhist groups like the Zen Center, Friends of the Western Buddhist Order, Vipassana, Theravada, and Tibetan Buddhist centers; and, in a separate category, Baha'i.

A miscellaneous category would include the Unification Church (Moonies), an unconventionally Christian group of Korean extraction; the quasi-spiritual Centrepoint community,[1] very much based in 1960s humanistic psychology; British Israel; and a couple of groups in the New Thought or "independent" Christian Science tradition, the School of Radiant Living and Infinite Way.[2]

Finally, there is a growing number of groups in the neopagan and women's spirituality families. Often centered on worship of the goddess representing earth and cosmos, and identifying with the Wicca or traditional "white" witchcraft lineage, these groups reflect feminist, ecological, and primordialist concerns. They are certainly connected with a worldwide neopagan movement, which has been especially strong in Britain, the United States, and Australia. At the time of my research in New Zealand, however, this movement was still in the process of emerging in that country. It consisted mostly of informal or at least undocumented groups and was inaccessible within the parameters of the research schedule and capabilities I had. This was somewhat disappointing because I have had very fruitful contacts with comparable neopagans and their kin in the United States. But I will offer a few reflections on New Zealand paganism and witchcraft.

Here is one interesting possibility: In the United States, the European-based modern pagan movement, once eager to recover the traditional craft (witchcraft) or authentic ancient Egyptian, Greek, Celtic, or Germanic religion, has—as it has gained confidence—steadily become increasingly eclectic, wanting not only to reclaim the past but also to create, or allow to emerge, new forms in the pagan style appropriate to today's life. At the same time, pagans have forged links with a parallel movement, the discovery of Native American spirituality as a resource by persons of European descent. These people have profitably undertaken the vision quest, endured the sweat-lodge experience, and explored the shaman's paths between the worlds. Perhaps the twenty-first century will bring a distinctly New Zealand style of modern paganism, in which the Kiwi love of nature and its powers, the sacred space of sport, and the utopian New Zealand myth, blend powerfully with themes from Maori spirituality to create something new.

Pre-1960 Sources

Some of the groups cited above have sources much earlier than the 1960s and indeed may have had strong organizations elsewhere though only coming to New Zealand around that tumultuous decade. One example is the Gurdjieff movement, well known to New Zealanders through its relation to Katherine Mansfield in the 1920s but not apparently an organized presence in the land of her birth until the late 1950s.

GEORGE I. GURDJIEFF

Born in Russian Armenia, George I. Gurdjieff (1872?–1949) was of mixed Greek, Armenian, and Russian parentage. Like his countrywoman Helena Blavatsky, he wandered much in central Asia during the earlier years of his life, combining adventure (and, according to some reports, political intrigue on behalf of the czarist government) with spiritual seeking. The details of his travels are less than clear, and his own account, *Meetings with Remarkable Men,* mingles autobiography and allegory with a free hand.[3] But down whatever trails he had walked to obtain it, when Gurdjieff appeared in Moscow during World War I and on the eve of the subsequent revolution, he had a well-developed spiritual system in hand and was ready to impart it. By all accounts the system, the man with his unforgettably piercing black eyes, and the unfathomable and traumatic disciplines through which he taught it, were inseparable. Above and beyond all else, the Gurdjieff experience was Gurdjieff, for those privileged to follow the master during his lifetime.

The system is based on the idea that most human beings are asleep. We are machines, operating by habit and a complex series of laws that Gurdjieff enumerated. It is possible, though, for one to become a higher man by mastering oneself and altering certain of the laws in one's own case. The key to this process is deep self-awareness and what Gurdjieff called self-remembering, together with exercises requiring attention and firm self-control.

Gurdjieff left Russia with a small band of disciples following the revolution. After several vicissitudes they ended up at a chateau, the Prieuré, near Fontainebleu, France, in 1922. Here his most famous work was carried out, and here Katherine Mansfield died in 1923. Like her, many of those who stayed at the Prieuré for varying lengths of time were writers and intellectuals; the remarkable experience of life with Gurdjieff has been described by several hands.[4]

The heart of everyone's account is the magus's magnetic and enigmatic personality, the hard manual labor he demanded of them, the abrupt starting and stopping of projects, the austerity alternating with abundance and insults with warmth. All this was clearly intended to shake students out of habit and force them to know themselves in unaccustomed situations or relationships. Gurdjieff was no less famous for the sacred dances, apparently based on Sufi models, that he taught and that his troupes performed in Europe and America. But for all his authoritarianism, this master differed from some in his insistence that students stay with him only for a limited time; when that time was up, he would send them off, sometimes forcibly. The upshot was that before long Gurdjieff groups, under disciples of the seer but otherwise largely independent, sprang up around the world. They would study his works and strive to inculcate his methods, some in one way and some in another, one perhaps by harmonious dance and another in rigorous self-awareness techniques.

P. D. Ouspensky

Russian mathematician, philosopher, and sometime disciple of Gurdjieff, P. D. Ouspensky's (1878–1947) vivid account of the master in *In Search of the Miraculous* (1947) and substantial metaphysical tomes, such as *Tertium Organum* (1912; English translation, 1922) and *A New Model of the Universe* (1934), attracted considerable attention on publication. Like Gurdjieff, he left Russia at the time of the revolution, landing finally in England as Gurdjieff did in France. A careful, systematic thinker and lecturer in contrast to Gurdjieff's irascible charisma, Ouspensky put many of the latter's key ideas into polished form, though relations between the two men were not always smooth. But despite this, and despite the difficulty of some of Ouspensky's mystical-mathematical metaphysics for all but the most devoted student, many groups in this tradition include both names in their canon and owe something to both the freewheeling magus of the Prieuré and the professorial, pince-nezed visionary of the London lecture hall.

Neil Dougan

In the 1950s, a New Zealand builder and spiritual seeker, Neil Dougan (1918–1987), chanced to hear about Gurdjieff and became interested in his way. He joined a Gurdjieff study group in Auckland. Later, in the 1960s, Dougan formed his own group under the direction, from England, of the Gurdjieffian C. S. Nott. By 1968 Dougan was in Afghanistan exploring Sufism, the Islamic mystical teaching that is the probable background of much of Gurdjieff's work. That quest culminated in Dougan's formally becoming Muslim, under the tutelage of an Afghan *shaikh* who was his spiritual guide. (As testimony to his new faith, he took the additional name Abdullah.) Back in New Zealand in 1969, Dougan founded a Sufi study group separate from the Gurdjieff group.

In 1974 Dougan went on another spiritual journey, including a forty-day fast he undertook while traveling through India and Afghanistan. This audacious but, in his view, spiritually successful ordeal is re-counted in his fascinating book, *40 Days*.[5] After its completion, he undertook the *hajj*, the Muslim pilgrimage to Mecca. Aspects of this experience, however—the greedy commercialism of the locals, the legalistic wranglings of Islamic theologians, the unpleasant animal sac-rifices—were highly disconcerting to Dougan and his New Zealand companions. The disillusionment is well expressed in the following long sentence, which expresses also a return to Gurdjieffian criteria of judg-ment:

> It was only towards the end of the actual Hajj that I began to realise that what Allah was doing was forcing us to face the conclu-sive fact that Islam was just another religion captured by the Law of Seven [a Gurdjieffian hypothesis of historical-spiritual cycles]; that the Ka'aba and the Prophet's Tomb and even the Shatan stones had become objects of ritual worship; and that the only lively reform movement in Islam—represented by the Tabliah Jumat fellowship—not only ignored the possibility of an inner spir-itual teaching in the Koran, but actively campaigned against the very idea that there might be, with a rigid literalism which might have done justice to a society of jurists.[6]

Thereafter Dougan made no pretence of being an observant Muslim in any conventional sense, though he continued to hold its mystical wing in high regard and to keep such facets of Islam as seemed helpful to him, such as the fast of Ramadan. He also fasted every Monday and got up to see the sunrise every day. The quest, however, moved in still another new direction. Before long Dougan and his group of some fifty companions of the search were studying Gnostic texts and calling them-selves the Gnostic Society. But now the emphasis seems less on norma-tive Gnosticism, or Islam, than on a general pantheistic mysticism of self-awakening, and on Dougan's own precepts.

It seems clear that, for the companions, the real attraction was not to any specific doctrine but to Neil Dougan himself as combined mentor and seeker. He is described as having been on one level a hearty, pipe-smoking, middle-class, ordinary-seeming New Zealander.

Here is his story: His father had been a sociable but improvident rail-road man. Neil dropped out of the University of Auckland after one year, never to return, when World War II broke out. He joined the army, saw action in North Africa and Greece, and was wounded. After the war his life was at first energetic but chaotic; there were several jobs and house building on the side, a marriage that ended in divorce, and a spiritual emptiness that clearly preyed on him. (Until about eighteen he had been an Anglican altar boy, but he then took up rationalistic agnosticism, much to the distress of his mother.) He read books from Havelock Ellis' *Psychology of Sex* to Paul Brunton's *The Hidden Teaching beyond Yoga*. In this condition he met a Jew who told him of Ouspensky and Gurdjieff. Intrigued, he made contact with an Auckland Gurdjieff group and spent some five years with it, leaving about 1960 to start his own after conflicts with the leader of that group. He contacted C. S. Nott in England for Gurdjieffian guidance, as we have seen, and also around this time met Rose, who would become his second wife and companion in his spiritual work.

In 1988 I attended a regular meeting of Wellington followers of Dougan. Some twenty men and women were crowded into the pleasant suburban home, including Neil's widow Rose, down from Auckland for the occasion. (In Auckland there is a larger group of some two hundred Douganites, many of them living as a sort of informal community in Dougan's Birkdale neighborhood; the society is now headed by Rose.) As it happened, the meeting I visited was during the Muslim fast of Ramadan, which these people, like Neil, still kept. They took neither food nor drink between sunrise and sunset, though I saw no sign of the daily prayers facing Mecca, nor any other orthodox Muslim practice.

The evening began with a sharing of Ramadan experiences. That fast had clearly contributed much to a Gurdjieffian sort of intimate self-awareness for these ordinary mothers and fathers, office workers, and business people. Voices rose to say that Ramadan had made one get up a little earlier to eat before dawn, that it made one more aware of the self and its dependence on the satisfaction of physical needs, of how a special spiritual practice as radical as not eating or drinking all day long affects one's temperament and one's relation to family and coworkers. I was quite impressed by so many New Zealanders, no doubt alienated like most from churchly Christianity, undertaking such a rigorous a practice borrowed from another faith. I could hardly imagine a like group so eclectic yet so obviously serious in my own country. The meeting then proceeded to a discussion of writings of Dougan, read and analyzed with care and openness line by line.[7] The evening ended (after sundown) with tea and refreshments.

Western Movements

The School of Philosophy

Another movement that seems to be broadly in the Gurdjieff-Ouspensky lineage is simply called the School of Philosophy. It is found in now-separate Auckland and Wellington centers. The Wellington edifice, a monumental building on Aro Street that once belonged to the Salvation Army, is the most imposing structure possessed by any group in this book; it looks as though it should be a court of justice or a particularly select preparatory school. In a sense it is, for it inculcates the laws of life and is a preparation for better living in which one can "realise his own potential and . . . understand his own nature" by dealing with the "simple and fundamental questions of life. What is its purpose? Why was I brought into being?"[8]

The School of Philosophy has roots in the School of Economic Science, founded in London some years ago by Leon McLaren. This institution, not to be confused with the famous London School of Economics, was designed originally to promote the theories of the eminent single-tax advocate, Henry George. However, according to information given me at the Wellington School of Philosophy, the school soon came to realize that something was missing, that issues of economic justice and the best use of of natural resources can hardly be resolved without recourse to a wider philsophical perspective. Before one could know what justice and the good life truly are, one would need to grasp the deeper truths about human nature and natural law. At around this point those monetary mystics somehow discovered the views and practices of Gurdjieff and Ouspensky and seem to have found in them what was needed. Indeed, by the 1970s the School of Economic Science apparently had little to do with interest rates or the price of gold but was described as "an esoteric school based on Ouspensky's and Gurdjieff's teachings."[9]

The School of Philosophy commenced articulating these teachings in New Zealand about 1960. The basic curriculum is a series of twelve weekly lectures, beginning February, May, and December, at a cost to the attender of thirty-five dollars. Beginning with the queries, "What is philosophy? What is its practical use?" they proceed to such considerations as "the condition and refinement of the human instrument" and "the worlds within man" together with "the use of attention in speaking and listening." A Gurdjieffian cast is lent by the tripartite division of human nature into intellect, emotion, and moving parts and in the emphasis on awareness. Exercises and practices are employed, in line with that tradition, to "verify" the theories inculcated and to give the student experience in knowing oneself and truly "being present." However, other techniques both Eastern and Western, such as meditation, are also used. More advanced courses are available for those who complete the introductory series of twelve classes. The Wellington and Auckland schools, now independent of each other as they both are of the London school, have been relatively successful; at the time of my visit the Wellington school reported a continuing population of around eighty enrollees and supporters.

THE EMIN FOUNDATION

Another interesting group that, in my view, has Gurdjieffian background, is the Emin Foundation. Emin first publically appeared in England in 1972, the fruit of many years of private study and research by a Mr. Raymond Armin into the "understanding and experience that is vital to the progression of human life." His four published works are *Dear Dragon, Gemrod, Frownstrong,* and *Cobwebs and Tears.* These intriguingly titled volumes refer to no other book or teaching, though spokesmen acknowledge some debt to Gurdjieff and Steiner.

Their instruction proposes that humankind is embarked on a millions-of-years-long development toward ultimate perfection but is now in danger of falling away from the plan entirely toward egotism and then self-destruction. Only through self-knowledge and reorientation toward our true nature can we get back on track. The Emin (the word means "faithful one" in Arabic) offers a diversity of complementary ways for one to so rectify oneself; one leader offers the encouraging observation that, constricted and habit bound though we may seem to be, "It is our aim to make people aware of other ways in which they exist. One has only to go beyond the self and its limitations. Once we are free of our conditioning we learn very fast."[10] This learning relies little on books, much on hands-on techniques ranging from astrology and tarot to drama and dance to psychic experimentation, reinforced by lecture and discussion.

In 1988 I spent a fascinating though long evening with the Emin in Auckland. The group gathered in a splendid, almost palatial, old mansion. The forty-some people present included both inquirers and active members; they were predominantly young, attractive, successful-looking men and women whose talk buzzed with references to dormant faculties like astral traveling and numerological significations.

The first exercises were designed to develop awareness of the aura, one of the many aspects of human nature more than half forgotten in our race toward shallow egoistic satisfaction, but a necessary part of our ultimate perfection, and so something of which we must recover cognizance. We first "warmed up" with practices like "patty cake," done faster and faster until the hands tingled, and then "Simon says" until the brain whirled. Next, members stood several feet away from a partner, then moved in slowly toward the other, palms extended. It was expected one would begin to feel the aura of the other at about three feet away; there would be a very soft rubbery barrier in the air, a change of temperature, a tingling sensation, all very subtle but real to those rightly attuned.

Then the teacher held out objects like flowers and gemstones over the extended left hand of a student; one was expected to sense a faint magnetic or rolling feeling from the invisible forces channeled by those power centers. All this explained why, we were told, traditional societies with a sense of the sacred like the Maori use ritual gestures, or why Christians clasp their hands in prayer—these acts circulate or transmit the spiritual, auric energies we were now experimentally handling.

Then we visitors stood in the center of a large room while four dancers moved around us to balance our energies and auras with stroking gestures impressively like the passes of the old-time mesmerists. It was said that heavy emotion can rupture or distort one's aura and require it to undergo healing. Then, properly healed, we withdrew and the quartet performed steps and gestures no doubt of esoteric purport, ranging from gentle fluttering motions to militant marches. This was followed by tea.

Tea was succeeded by lecture and discussion. The young, nice-looking speaker had a gentle but definitely you-have-the-questions-we-have-the-answers tone to his presentation and responses; he reminded me of certain too-youthful, plausible, and quite orthodox clergymen I have known, including myself many years ago.

He diagrammed a person's life as like a circle, with several spokes coming from the center: one's family, job, hobbies, and the like. But in the very center is the aspect of the profound, the mysterious. Awareness of this disturbingly deep inward core can cause people to look for answers before they even rightly formulate the questions. This "profound and mysterious" is that with which the Emin has to do. It is the basis of religion, but the Emin—a touchstone of sanity in a mad world —approaches it through many venues: healing, comparative religion, astrology, theater, dance, tarot, the aura, ancient Egyptian lore, and much else—all spokes that can be ridden back in to the center.

Some teachings I heard about in the Emin ambience seemed a bit more recondite: the shape of one's hat can affect one's energy; bells and incense can clear a room of psychic static; after death one can reincarnate, survive as an astral body, or "feed the moon" (a Gurdjieffian notion), which is becoming another world. Much is made of anagrams: Genesis comes from "Genes of Isis," which has to do with a belief that gods married the daughters of men and then tried genetically to remove the traces of their misdeed.

It will perhaps be clear that I retired after my evening with the Emin with strong but confused, conflicting feelings, and no doubt some things I did not correctly understand. But Emin was growing, and perhaps is destined more powerfully than any other movement to transmit something of the active, experimental and experiential Gurdjieffian style of esotericism to a younger generation.

SUBUD

An interesting link between Gurdjieffism and another spiritual style is the group called Subud. It was founded by an Indonesian called Muhammad Subuh (1901–1987), or Bapak (father), and clearly has connections with the highly mystical, Sufi forms of Islam so powerful in his homeland. In 1925, and again decisively in 1933, Bapak received authoritative inner illuminations that released tremendous energy and that he came to believe he was called to transmit to others. The movement spread quietly in Indonesia until after the Second World War, when certain Westerners discovered it and its simple power.

The basic Subud experience is in what is called the *latihan*.[11] In it, initiated or "opened" members enter a room—separate rooms for men and women—and simply release themselves to the power of God for a period of an hour. The result is frequently seemingly wild and uncontrolled shouts, cries, moans, jumping, dancing, and other motor activity. Prayer and healing is often said to take place.

When Subud first came to England in 1957, it received considerable publicity and drew particularly wide support among followers of Gurdjieff. The process is vividly described in books by Anthony Bright-Paul and the leading Gurdjieffian John G. Bennett.[12] This was justified by reported prophecies Gurdjieff had made late in his life of a coming prophet from the area of Indonesia who would open the "higher emotional centers." One also has a sense that the simple emotional release and free-form spirituality proffered by Subud, so much in contrast to the intricate intellectualism and high levels of inner control demanded by Gurdjieff and Ouspensky, had their own appeal to disciples of the Russian masters. At the time of writing, Subud had three centers in New Zealand holding the *latihan* twice weekly, in Auckland, Wellington, and Christchurch.

Although I did not have opportunity to visit a *latihan* in New Zealand, I have done so in Los Angeles. I sat in a chair outside the curtained entryway to the men's *latihan*. Visitors and postulants are expected to participate in this way, and also to have met with "helpers," or Subud counsellors, for a period of about three months before being permitted in the room. At that time, their desire to enter Subud being judged serious, they are "opened" in a very simple manner: a helper reads some words from Bapak to the candidate and then goes with him into the *latihan* room, and says something like, "Now close your eyes and begin."

The sound of the *latihan* is unforgettable, the sound of total spiritual expression. There are the cries of the jungle, the cries of the nursery, the laboring lamentations of profound prayer, and deep, utterly strange and moving wordless hymnlike chants. One detects the thumps of jumping and hopping, and the softer rustles of individual or, as the spirit takes them, collective dancelike motions. As participants come out, they are likely to be bathed in sweat but radiant and at peace.

The Society of Guardians

A very interesting group in the Western esoteric, though not Gurdjieffian, tradition is the Society of Guardians. As I entered the modest-seeming house which is its center, the Sanctuary of the Angels on the lower slopes of Mt. Eden in Auckland, I was overwhelmed by a sense of entering some realm of reality other than the ordinary. There to greet me, in the small library, was the senior guardian, Michael Freedman (Michael Tyne-Corbold), rotund, bearded, smiling, in brown monkish robes and cowl, surrounded by heavy magical tomes and volumes of kabbalistic lore. The walls were bedecked with charts of the *sephiroth* and astrological sigils. The slippery nature of reality, well known to the magician as to the mystic, was on the senior guardian's lips as we talked. I was told that "reality is important, what is not so important is any explanation of reality" and that "to some extent we are discovering the universe, to some extent creating it."

The senior guardian related something of the traditional history of this group of "technical mystics," as it describes itself, with its extraordinary custodianship of reality. Reportedly it originated in a group of twelfth-century Christians in southern France who were interested in the Jewish kabbalah. In 1282, disguised as Franciscans (hence the brown robe), they rescued the celebrated kabbalistic rabbi Abraham Abulafia from prison and subsequently studied on more advanced levels with him. They formed a small order—the maximum was twenty-two members—which, drawing mostly from within the same families, continued down to the twentieth century in German and British branches. In the 1930s the German order was destroyed by the Nazis, and the English senior guardian, Freedman Burford, decided to immigrate to Australia with a handful of followers to avoid the coming Holocaust. In time the transplanted guardians all died, and no new members joined save one Australian, the present senior guardian, who received that title a week before Freedman Burford's passing. He took the traditional guardian name, Freedman. After he and his wife—now abbess of the Guardians—moved to New Zealand in 1970, where he worked as a psychologist, he was for a time the only surviving guardian. But he has since then built a flourishing work in the Guardian tradition in Auckland.

Ritual and astrology are important to the Society of Guardians, for they see the universe a vortex of great tides and cycles that these arts adequately mirror. There are rites—"Mithraist in a very broad sense" —offered in conjunction with the solar and lunar cycles. The Mass of the Holy Archangels is held Saturdays after sunset vespers to mark the beginning of a new week, and there are seasonal festivals. The ritual room was most impressive, with its large pentagram, its gemstones and symbols of the traditional elements, and the rites I gather no less so, involving dancing and offerings of bread, salt, honey, wine, and incense as libations to Mother Earth, and elements redolent of the Christian Mass, and the recited words of Jesus and the Buddha.

Meditation is also important.[13] In 1978 Michael Freedman received quite a bit of publicity when he offered a free meditation course that, he said, he and his associates' scientific research at the University of Auckland showed produced results as beneficial as those for which the Transcendental Meditation movement charged as much as twenty-five hundred dollars. "Mystical 'mumbo jumbo' wasn't needed to learn to relax," he said.[14] He still teaches meditation on a donation-only basis.

THE EMISSARIES OF DIVINE LIGHT

Another small but interesting group—this one international— are the Emissaries of Divine Light. The Emissaries were established by an American, Lloyd Arthur Meeker, in 1932, but have received major impetus through the support of an English aristocrat, Lord Martin Cecil. Headquarters are at the Sunrise Ranch in Colorado, with approximately two hundred residents; it is the model for some twelve residential communities around the world; there are also about 160 meeting locations. Basic teaching is that humans were created to manifest the image and likeness of God—that is, to enact the divine design. We allow evil influences, such as jealousy and fear, to block its expression, but because manifestation is a constant process, healing, and putting negatives behind one, is always a possibility. The Emissaries emphasize community life because true manifestation of the divine in the human entails cooperative ventures, but the communalism is far from authoritarian or even highly religious in a conventional sense. The purpose is expressed more in a spiritual attitude toward everyday work and human relations than in services, which are likely to be simply lectures, forums, or meditations without highly dogmatic content.

The New Zealand Emissaries have a regular group of about fifteen followers plus other friends and drop-ins. They maintain a house in Birkhead, Auckland. At the time of writing, six persons lived there— five adults (including one married couple) and a child. Spiritual growth is their major concern, I was told in a telephone interview. On Wednesday evenings the Emissaries sponsor a free-discussion public meeting in which topics as varied as "How to Put on an Event," "Male Experience," and "Universal Law" have been considered. On Sunday mornings there is a "Radiation Service." An "attunement time" is set aside every evening.

THE LECTORIUM ROSICRUCIANUM

A small but interesting activity is the Lectorium Rosicrucianum, or International School of the Golden Rosycross, with a New Zealand center in Auckland and international headquarters in the Netherlands. It appears to be primarily a study group. The Lectorium's esoteric Christianity seems to represent a more thoroughgoing reconstruction of the profound cosmic dualism of the Manichaeans, radical Gnostics, or medieval Cathars—to all of whom these Rosicrucians explicitly link themselves—than any other modern group of which I am aware. They believe there are "two absolutely unrelated creations or nature orders, one being of God, the other that in which we are at present existing as human beings." The latter order, not part of the original divine plan, came about as the product of an ancient catastrophe and has left us totally estranged from God and our original true human nature. Yet we cannot leave this fallen world even by death— heaven, hell, purgatory, whatever we call the other place, is still "merely circumstances within the same degenerate nature order." The only way in which true liberation, restoration back to the other order, may be attained is instead through transfiguration, exemplified by the transfiguration and resurrection of Jesus Christ. The Lectorium Rosicrucianum's instruction points the way to transfiguration through transmutation of the personality and the self, by working with the last remnants of the true divine still encapsulated in the human being.[15]

THE ORDO TEMPLI ORIENTIS

Still another rare experience is offered by the Ordo Templi Orientis (OTO), the mysterious and celebrated occult order refounded by the notorious Aleister Crowley. I had lunch at the University of Auckland one day with a pleasant young man, then a student there, known in religion as Frater Ameth, master of the Kantheros Oasis—the New Zealand branch—of the order. All his letters to me had opened with a standard epigram: " 'Do what thou wilt shall be the whole of the Law.' Greetings and Salutations on All Points of the Triangle. Peace, Honour, Truth; Respect to the Order."

Although claiming continuity with the medieval Knights Templar and founded under the present name in Germany around the turn of the century, the OTO was essentially taken over by Aleister Crowley

who gave the order its present shape.[16] Crowley—poet, magician, liber-
tine, humbug, drug addict, surprisingly profound when he wanted to be
as a philosopher of "magick" (his spelling, to distinguish the real thing
from stage illusionism) and the occult—has been mentioned in connection with Golden Dawn. Crowley's magick combined the Golden
Dawn, yoga, sexual magic (from Tantrism and the OTO), and the Law
of Thelema: "Do what thou wilt shall be the whole of the Law." He
contended, on the basis of revelation he had received in Cairo from a
spirit called Aiwass, that a new Aeon of Horus was dawning in which
this law would be the fundamental principal, and a new religion would
prosper called, inevitably, Crowleyanity. But if the values Crowley
really took to heart are anywhere enshrined, it is surely in the OTO. Its
basic text is Crowley's *Liber al vel legis* (The book of the law), and no
passage is more often quoted than the Thelemic Law, "Do what thou
wilt. . . ."

Like much Crowleyana, that sacred text can be parsed from several
perspectives. Crowley was no puritan, and the line could be taken simply to permit unfeigned hedonism. Yet Crowley insisted that doing what
one wills is actually a high and demanding ideal. It requires the utmost
self-discipline, and the painstaking mastery of magick—for magick is at
root the mobilized power that enables one to accomplish one's inner-
most will. It is this power that the OTO apprentice is prepared to know
and use.

Progression in magick follows a scale of ten grades or degrees, in turn
based on the Hindu *chakras*. The names of the degrees, however, reflect
the world of Western esotericism refracted through Crowley's vivid
poetic imagination: one moves from Minerval 0, I, II, and III up
through VIII (Perfect Pontiff of the Illuminati), IX (Initiate of the
Sanctuary of the Gnosis), and X (Rex Summus Sanctissimus [Supreme
and Most Holy King]). Grades I–III (Frater Ameth was on III at the
time of our conversation) involve study of the *Book of the Law,* undertaking a technique like yoga, astral work, learning the "lesser banishing
ritual," keeping a magickal diary, and self-awareness practices—all fundamental skills that would help anyone cope with oneself and our mysterious universe and that would stand the perfect pontiff or holy king in
good stead. At least a year must pass between initation from one grade
to another. Those rites of passage are order ceremonies, but the other
practices are mostly done alone. In addition, the OTO adept does invo-
cations often—to Horus, Osiris, Apollo, and the like.[17]

Although there had reportedly been earlier versions of the OTO
abroad, such as that associated with the enigmatic Vyvyan Deacon in
Australia and possibly New Zealand (who by some accounts brought
the original German, pre-Crowleyite OTO to the two southern domin-

ions as early as 1908), the order in its present semipublic form commenced in the latter country in the early 1980s. A New Zealand woman
lived at the Grand Lodge in the United States and then returned in
1982 to perform the first initiations. The New Zealand group has about
twelve members.[18]

Groups of Eastern Background

These have proliferated mightily in the 1960s and since, and no
attempt to describe them all in detail will be attempted here. The Massey University directory, *Beliefs and Practices in New Zealand,* provides
adequate summaries, and some of these groups, such as the Hare
Krishnas and Baha'i have been dealt with in many other studies, even if
not always explicitly in the New Zealand context. Here I can only give a
sampling in the form of a few groups I was able to visit during my six
months in New Zealand.

Of these, one of the most interesting and attractive is the Brahma
Kumaris, a new Hindu religious movement now found around the
world. I myself first encountered it on the Maidan in Calcutta, India,
where one bright morning during a visit there I went out to find this
vast park unexpectedly ornamented with several large brilliantly col-
ored tents. Out of curiosity I approached, to discover they were the display of a religious group, the Brahma Kumaris. The exhibits within
were no less vivid. Parading around the walls were multihued charts of
human spiritual evolution, the subtle spiritual components of our consciousness and anatomy, and above all demonstrations that the human
soul is ultimately a dimensionless point of pure light, whose original
habitat is a supreme realm of golden red light, also the realm of the
supreme soul, God. Radiating out of this central source—named as the
deity Shiva—were portrayed numerous blessings, oceans of love, peace,
bliss, and knowledge; the transcendence of birth and death, true harmony and health. To realize all this, one should practice raja yoga, the
method of meditation (not really *hatha* or physical yoga) by which one
can link one's own soul with the supreme soul. For, I was assured, I *am*
my soul, not my physical body, though the health of the body depends
on the health of the mind, which in turn depends on whether the soul is
stabilized in its original state and in right relationship to the ultimate in
the world of reddish gold.

Of no less interest to me was the fact that the assuring was being done
by white-robed women. For, though founded by a man believed to have
been an incarnation of God, the Brahma Kumaris are virtually unique
as a religous movement ministering to both men and women, but
administered entirely by women. The founder was Dada Lekh Raj (Sri

Prajapita Brahma [d. 1969]), a jeweler in India who in the 1930s had a series of spiritual experiences, culminating in 1936 when he believed God entered him, saying "I am the Blissful Self, I am Shiva, I am Shiva, I am the Knowledgeable Self, I am Shiva, I am Shiva, I am the luminous Self, I am Shiva." Shortly after, he gave up business to devote himself entirely to the religious mission to which he believed this experi-ence had been a call, in 1937 founding the Brahma Kumaris World Spiritual University to give instruction in raja yoga. Its instructors, the Brahma Kumaris, are all single women or mothers who have received fourteen years of training. Pitashriji, as the founder is often called, believed, under divine guidance, that women should do this work in order to bring forth the maternal love of the Shakti, the consort of Shiva who as the great goddess takes many forms, but above all is the divine mother. The group is vegetarian and emphasizes purity and celibacy. Its world headquarters are at Mt. Abu, in Rajasthan, India.

Its New Zealand headquarters are on Mt. Eden, in Auckland, though there are also centers in Northcote, Auckland; in Petone outside Wellington; and in Christchurch. The Wellington work is, I have been told, largely patronized by the ethnic Indian community, but the Auck-land activity is mostly European; both centers commenced in 1981. When I visited the Mt. Eden Raja Yoga Centre, a modest but ample house on a busy corner, I found it had three residents, with eight attending the morning classes, and many other supporters. As in all Brahma Kumaris centers, raja yoga instruction was the main activity. The house had the quiet, peaceful and spotlessly clean ambience of any well-run convent.

I had a most interesting conversation with a young man, deeply involved with the movement, who was in the house. He pointed out to me that New Zealand has no real religious tradition of its own, unlike England or India, and that a younger generation of Pakehas is rejecting the imported churches. But at the same time, he said, other souls on other quests are beginning to fill the country's streets, perhaps because of the lack of established competition. New Zealand is a young nation, but it is attracting ancient Hindus who are taking birth here in a West-ern body, and other "old souls" from the world's troubled past seeking a fresh venue for their latest life—a novel twist on the New Zealand myth. Thus the small and seemingly fairly homogeneous island nation is, actually, a carnival of diverse spirits—which perhaps explains the remarkable assortment of religious paths I found.

But if many of these souls find their way to the Brahma Kumaris, any tensions created by this pluralism ought to be resolved peacefully—as, if these teachers have their way, will the greater tensions of the world at large. According to Sister Jayanti, a senior *yogini* in the movement who lectured in New Zealand in 1985, raja yoga meditation is the key not only to personal happiness but also to world peace. "It is not weapons that are the cause of war," she said. "The cause of war is in the human mind. We can restore some sort of humanity in human minds by removing stress and fear through the power of silence."[19]

ANANDA MARGA

Ananda Marga (Path of Bliss) is a movement which seeks to combine inner spiritual liberation with social reform. Founded in India in 1955 by Sri Sri Anandamurti (P. R. Sarkar [b. 1921]), it has attracted no small amount of controversy.

Its ostensible ethics and goals, based on the Yoga Sutras of Patanjali, seem unexceptionable enough. They include *ahimsa* (harmlessness), *satya* (benevolence in thought, word, and deed), not depriving others of what is rightly theirs, simplicity, and purity of life, mental equilibrium, working to alleviate the suffering of others, and the like. Its social program is based on "Progressive Utilisation Theory" (Prout), which is said to blend spiritual and social liberation, and is described as progressive socialism. Its principles include a guaranteed provision of essentials of life, food, housing, clothing, medical care, and education; equitable distribution of wealth; a decentralized economy, with cooperative worker-owned and controlled industries; full employment with lessened working hours; economic independence for women; and the social, cultural, and scientific fields kept free of political or business pressures.[20] To provide models of such an ideal society, Ananda Marga has established cooperative communities. In India a Proutist bloc party ran candidates for office in 1967 and 1969, in opposition to both the Communists and the ruling government party. Perhaps it was that political presumption which put Ananda Marga too much in the limelight.

In 1971 Sarkar was accused by a former member of conspiring to murder certain ex-followers. He was arrested and jailed to await trial, his imprisonment lasting through the national emergency declared by Indira Gandhi in 1975; under those conditions, Ananda Marga was one of the organizations banned nationally by the prime minister. In the meantime, Ananda Margis were involved in a number of antigovernment incidents, some allegedly violent, protesting their leader's incarceration. Sarkar was finally brought to trial and convicted in 1976, but under the conditions of the emergency, which meant among other liabilities that he was not allowed to call any witnesses on his behalf. Subsequently, in 1978, he was retried and found not guilty. But, although reported incidents linked to the movement have decreased markedly since then, its reputation has not been entirely cleared.

Ananda Marga came to New Zealand in 1974, and its troubles in

India had repercussions in this country. In July 1977 the New Zealand government deported Erik Fossum (Arun Brahmacarii), a Norwegian who was the movement's New Zealand leader and meditation teacher. A newspaper account speaks for itself:

> When a slight wispy-bearded Norwegian in the unlikely orange garb of an Indian holy man flew out of New Zealand for New Caledonia one day last week still vowing that he would return, officials in the Indian High Commission in Wellington heaved a collective sigh of relief.
>
> They were seeing what they hoped was the end of a long campaign they had waged to get rid of overseas-trained leaders of what they regard as a dangerous terrorist movement. Now, at last, it seemed, they were getting through to the New Zealand Government.[21]

The article speaks further of the Indian High Commission's active lobbying of the minister of immigration and other parliamentarians, and even reports that when the Indian High commissioner made his introductory call on Prime Minister Muldoon a year ago, the tiny sect was a major topic of conversation. To be sure, in 1975 there were incidents in New Zealand as well as India involving Ananda Margis. Two Margis were asked to leave the country, and four others were jailed, on charges ranging from conspiracy to blow up the Indian High Commission to kidnapping and burglary. The movement responded that the perpetrators of these alleged offences were acting on their own to draw attention to Sarkar's imprisonment, and had no official backing from the sect. Margis used nonviolent means, too, from banners to hunger strikes, to protest their leader's persecution.

Although affirming that "there can be no doubt that the jailed Ananda Marga followers were responsible for violence in the celebrated 1975 incidents," *The Dominion*, in a 1977 series of articles on the sect, was able to find little more than unproved allegations behind most other charges. In the end the paper viewed this group as generally a "relatively harmless nuisance" like a number of other "fringe" religions, unworthy of the hysteria it had apparently generated in some circles. The feature on Ananda Marga cited a letter to *The Dominion* by Wellington poet Denis Glover calling it no more than "another of those potty little religious sects." The article noted also that the Ananda Margis in turn accused the police of excessive harassment and "some minor denials of civil rights in police stations." The conclusion: "If Ananda Marga is a threat it is a well-covered one. If it is not it has proved a very expensive nuisance for New Zealand."[22]

The *Dominion* articles then proceeded to give quite a good summary of Ananda Marga teaching and practice. The practices include initiation by an *acarya* (authorized spiritual director), *kirtan* (spiritual singing, chanting, and dancing), and above all meditation. *Dharmacakra* (*kirtan* and meditation done collectively) is especially powerful, as one would expect in a group so oriented toward human cooperative endeavors: "As the dancer becomes lost in the chant feelings of separateness and ego are said to be replaced by feelings of intense happiness and inner peace."

Ananda Marga, headquartered on Sandringham Road in Auckland, continues to work quietly in New Zealand to promote its principles and practices.

BHAGWAN SHREE RAJNEESH

Hardly less controversial has been the movement of Bhagwan Shree Rajneesh, the late Indian guru noted for his sexual freedom doctrines and his collection of Rolls Royces. Rajneesh (1931–1990), a former philosophy professor, established an ashram at Poona, in India. In the 1970s it acquired worldwide fame for its doctrine that *sanyas,* the ancient Hindu concept of renunciation, did not necessarily mean asceticism but simply conscious living and so could entail deliberately jumping into the depths of sensual, physical experiences as well as their rejection. For some people, this guru said, guilt-free sexual and other carnal experience may be more spiritually salutary than denial of the flesh. Needless to say, the unusual ashram drew streams of pilgrims from West as well as East, ranging from jaded veterans of the 1960s counterculture to erstwhile celibate priests and nuns.

In 1981, partly because of impending investigations by the Indian government, Rajneesh and many of his followers transferred to America. Land was purchased in Oregon, where a model community, Rajneeshpuram, was established, and where Rajneesh—now practicing public silence—housed the scores of Rolls presented him by wealthy devotees. Friction with neighbors and with state and local governments, however, plagued the project, and factionalism within Rajneeshpuram was no less abrasive. Utopia came to an abrupt end in 1985, when several top officials of the community were arrested on various charges, and others (or the same ones) defected after being accused by Rajneesh of serious offences, including attempted murder.

Then Rajneesh was himself charged with multiple violations of U.S immigration law. After a mysterious disappearance, exuberantly reported in the press, he was apprehended in Charlotte, North Carolina, and deported. Attempts to revive the work in Uruguay, Greece, and other countries brought visa denials, further deportations and little success. Loyal devotees have attempted to keep in touch, but it seems unlikely, after Rajneesh's death in 1990, that the movement can expect much future, despite some claims by loyalists to the contrary. The 1985 Massey University directory reported a Rajneesh center on Symonds Street in Auckland, but when I went to the address in 1988, I found no sign of it.

THE INTERNATIONAL SOCIETY FOR KRISHNA CONSCIOUSNESS

The Hare Krishnas, of the International Society for Krishna Consciousness, are another Hindu-based group in the West that has not avoided controversy. The society was founded in 1966 by A. C. Bhaktivedanta Swami Prabhupada, who had brought Krishna devotion in the pure bhakti tradition to the United States a year earlier. So far as is possible, its devotees endeavor to live a community life and give over their time and energies to the work of Krishna. There have been New Zealand temples at Riverhead, Auckland, Wellington, and Christchurch.

THE JOHANNINE DAIST COMMUNION

The Johannine Daist Communion, earlier the Free Primitive Church of Divine Communion and later the Free Daist Communion, is best known in New Zealand for its highly visible Laughing Man Institute and Dawn Horse Bookshop on High Street in Auckland. It was founded by Franklin Jones (b. 1939), a one-time Lutheran seminarian in America and student of Swami Muktananda in India. He has, like his work, marked spiritual progress with changes of name, having been Babba Free John, Da Free John, Da Love-Ananda, and Da Kalki. His basic teaching is the Way of Radical Understanding, which involves moving to Transcendental Consciousness through a series of seven steps. These include the experience of sexuality and of the pursuit of money and material rewards, but only to show their futility in the end.

Nonetheless, Free John has been accused of attachment to those goods. In 1985 a group of defectors from his movement, including a New Zealand woman, publicly accused the guru of extortion, degradation and false imprisonment of cult members, physical and sexual exploitation of them, and of living in luxury at the expense of followers. Lawsuits followed, which have led Free John to leave the United States for refuge in Fiji, where he allegedly lives in seclusion and luxury, surrounded by nine wives and indulging in "drinking binges . . . and gluttonous feasts." New Zealand and other leaders of the Free Daist Communion deny the charges—and the wives—attributing them to disgruntled ex-members.[23]

THE SAI BABA MOVEMENT

Satya Sai Baba (b. 1926) is perhaps the most famous of all holy men in India today, certainly for the miracles he is reported to perform continually. Although he has never traveled outside of India, apart from one trip to East Africa, his reputation has brought him a coterie of followers in many countries of the world, including New Zealand. Devotees gather to sing hymns and chants in his honor, talk about his teachings and mighty works, and organize trips to his now-vast ashrams in South India.

Unfortunately, the Sai Baba movement in New Zealand has been touched by scandal, although through no wrongdoing on the part of the guru or the movement's New Zealand leadership. In the later 1970s, Amrit Lal (Andy) Narain, a New Zealander of Indian descent, performed spiritual healings for substantial fees, particularly in the Maori community. He claimed to do so in the name of and through the power of Sai Baba, whose pictures were prominently displayed at his healing sessions. But at Christmas in 1981, while Narain was at Sai Baba's ashram in India, the guru forcefully announced that "only he, and he alone, could perform healing works in his name, and no one had ever been or ever would be delegated to do such things; there was no need for such delegation."[24] Since then the New Zealand and international Sai Baba organizations have frequently repeated that statement in their publications.

Although it has nothing to do with Sai Baba, it may be noted that three years later the same Amrit Narain was convicted of kidnapping and unlawful detention and imprisonment, in connection with a spiritual commune he had established in Greytown.[25]

YOGA SCHOOLS

Several yoga schools exist in New Zealand. The Divine Life Yoga Society is based on the teachings of Swami Sivananda (1887–1963), the spiritual grandparent of much of modern yoga instruction in the West, as in India. Its simplified instruction in yoga as a physical practice combined with a healthy, spiritual way of living for people in all walks of life began in New Zealand as early as 1936 as the Balmoral Physical Culture and Yoga School, though the present ashram was not established in Henderson, Auckland, until 1969.

Another important modern yoga teacher is B. K. S. Iyengar, represented by the New Zealand School of Yoga. The New Zealand branch of the International Yoga Teachers Association brings together some independent instructors in the art. Siddha yoga, taught by the controversial Swami Muktananada until his death in 1982 and subsequently by successors, emphasizes spiritual awakening through the grace of a Siddha guru. The Self-Realization Fellowship emphasizes a spiritual way of life and a simple practice known as *kriya* yoga taught by Swami Yogananda (1893–1952), one of the pioneer Indian missionaries to the West.

Transcendental Meditation, as taught by Maharishi Mahesh Yogi, is the simple practice of stilling the mind, through the use of a mantra given at one's initiation. This movement has had a remarkable career since its association in the 1960s with the Beatles. In New Zealand, as in most countries, one can find Transcendental Meditation teachers and centers.

VEDANTA SOCIETIES AND THE RAMAKRISHNA MISSION

Before leaving groups of Hindu background, a word might be said about modern Hinduism in the tradition of Vedanta Societies and the Ramakrishna Mission. The latter is a teaching and service monastic order established after the death of the great modern Hindu saint Ramakrishna by several of his disciples. Among them, the dynamic Swami Vivekananda was particularly interested in bringing Hinduism to the West in a form it could appreciate. After making a forceful impression as Hinduism's representative at the World's Parliament of Religions in Chicago in 1893, he returned to Europe and America in the late 1890s to lecture and establish fledgling groups, commonly called Vedanta Societies, of occidentals interested in pursuing this path. In the United States and several European countries, they represent the first institutional establishment of intellectual Hinduism, in the form of its dominant philosophical tradition, nondualist (Advaita) Vedanta. Though never large, over the years this movement has attracted a quota of creative thinkers, such as the novelists Aldous Huxley and Christopher Isherwood, and has made Vedanta an intellectual and spiritual presence in the West.

Although I have not been able to discover any trace of an institutional presence of the Vedanta Society in New Zealand, a correspondence involving it has turned up in the papers of a New Zealand woman who can certainly be considered a creative thinker and intellectual, as well as activist (a combination dear to the heart of Swami Vivekananda), Blanche Edith Baughan (1870–1958). This remarkable woman, born in England, was one of the first woman graduates of the University of London, taking honors in Greek, while also walking the streets as a suffragette. She moved to New Zealand in 1900, where she wrote poetry, became active in prison reform, and served as New Zealand secretary of the Howard League (involved in penal reform) in 1928. At the same time, she corresponded on spiritual matters with swamis of the Ramakrishna Mission in San Francisco and India, and with the great Indian writer Rabindranath Tagore. The last offered her some wise words: "I wish I could point out a way where a way is needed. We go into vague and very often worthless generalities when we advise others—because we cannot enter into the intricacies of a life not our own. . . . Let our love find out its true course through some daily service which refuses to accept any profit for itself. . . ."[26]

Whether from this or another source, such sentiments, combined with commitment to the spiritual quest, were clearly at the core of Blanche Baughan's long and useful life. An editorial in *The Akaroa Mail* (she lived in Akaroa, Canterbury) at the time of her death declared, "She had an intensely religious outlook, far beyond sectarianism, and she admitted it was from this centre she found the courage to do the unpopular work she had to do for so long of her own great and sure choosing."[27]

THE SANT MAT

An interesting collection of Indian movements belong to what is often called the Sant Mat, or saintly teachings, group. These derive generally from the Punjab, where the boundaries, one might say, of Sikhism, Hinduism, and mystical Islam meet. Sant Mat movements are characterized by an emphasis, as in early Sikhism, on the importance of a lineage of living gurus; by a cosmology of the gnostic type with increasingly rarefied spiritual planes above earth, and a focus on sacred sound as the essential of initiation and meditation. They generally inculcate a vegetarian diet and austere way of life. The largest is no doubt Radha Soami, found in New Zealand as in many countries of the world, with both Indian and occidental adherents. Kirpal Ruhani Satsang represents a similar teaching and is essentially the result of a succession dispute over the Radha Soami guruship.[28]

ECKANKAR AND DIVINE LIGHT

Eckankar, called the ancient science of soul travel, was founded by an American, Paul Twitchell, apparently on the basis of documents in the Sant Mat school. Finally, also of Sant Mat background, there is (or was) the Divine Light Mission of Guru Maharaj Ji, the celebrated teenage guru of the early 1970s whose meteoric career collapsed into scandal and debt after the failure of a much-publicized convention in the Houston Astrodome in 1973. But Maharaj Ji, now billed simply as a Humanitarian Leader rather than as Lord of the Universe, still visits New Zealand from time to time and meets with friends and followers, though there is no formal organization.

Groups of Islamic Background
INTERNATIONAL SUFI MOVEMENT

Apart from Subud, a few other new religions in New Zealand have an ultimate origin in Islamic culture areas. The International Sufi

Movement presents the teachings of Hazrat Inayat Khan (1882–1927). This activity offers Sufism worldwide essentially as an independent spiritual force, based on universal monotheism realized through knowing the divine within, by means of breathing and chanting exercises derived from Sufism.

BAHA'I

The best-known religion of this background is certainly Baha'i, based on the teachings of the Persian prophet Baha'u'llah (1817–1892); it emphasizes the oneness of God, the oneness of the prophets of God in all religions, and world unity. Baha'i is known for simple worship and dedicated work on behalf of global harmony. Baha'is rightly stress that their faith is an independent religion, not simply a sect of Islam or anything else. It has long-standing roots in New Zealand; in 1913 Margaret Stevenson invited interested friends to her home in Parnell to study the Baha'i faith; the number of believers grew, and the first Spiritual Assembly was founded in Auckland in 1926.

Movements of Buddhist Background

THERAVADA BUDDHISM

Buddhism has also made its way to post-1960s New Zealand, in both Theravada and Mahayana forms—and with both European and Asian adherents. One of my most pleasant memories of New Zealand is of a visit to the new Theravada Buddhist monastic center in Stokes Valley, just north of Wellington. This monastery is a branch of the remarkable Chithurst Forest Monastery in West Sussex, England, which has brought scores of Westerners into the Samgha. The three monks and one novice in Stokes Valley were all Occidentals, though thus far the religious life has attracted no New Zealanders. (The head monk is a Canadian of Latvian origin, the others a Swiss and an Italian, the novice English.) Yet the Buddhist laity who visit and support it are almost entirely of Southeast Asian (Sri Lankan, Burmese, Thai, Cambodian, and Lao) immigrant background. Here one can witness the extraordinary spectacle of European monks in saffron robes quietly receiving from Asians—the monastics as representatives of the religion, of course, not personally—the profound reverences and offerings of food and clothing that are customary in Theravada lands.

Surely few settings in the world could more induce one to the contemplative life than the Stokes Valley paradise of these few monks. I was delighted with the clean rustic temple blending into the hillside above the sparkling, rushing stream, where the religious odor of incense met the fragrance of wood and rain, and the soft hum of sutra chanting before the great bronze Buddha harmonized with the wind and the whir of insects. Scattered up the hill were the small hermitages of individual monks, where they live their peaceful and austere lives, practicing four hours of meditation daily, interspersed with manual labor, study, and worship in the temple.

In Wellington itself I attended a couple of meditation classes at the busy center run by the Friends of the Western Buddhist Order. This somewhat oddly named organization represents another quite-successful Western Buddhist movement out of England. It has been concerned with overcoming traditional divisions of Buddhism considered less than relevant to the western seeker—Theravada versus Mahayana, laity versus monks—and so presents a modern, eclectic but effective Buddhism based on the simple verities of the Four Noble Truths and the Eightfold Path, and fundamental meditation techniques.

At the same time, the lively color that is so much a part of the Buddhist world was not forgotten. The teachers, whether technically monks or not, wore bright robes, and the art of Buddhism, from deeply glowing gold images of the enlightened one to the enigmatic, symbol-laden *tanka* paintings of Tibet, bedecked the walls and altar. The instructors gave out plain, no-nonsense Buddhism of almost homiletic simplicity, and I was surprised at the number—in the scores—of Wellingtonians who came to hear that their lives are made lives of quiet despair by the masks they wear and the frustrations they bear, that this suffering is caused by false identities and attachments of the mind, and that these mental parasites can be left behind by cutting through the ego to reality in meditation. Then the assembly tried some simple Buddhist forms of meditation, and afterward, seated in a circle with a teacher, each person told what had happened, or not happened, and where he or she was at on the path.

VIPASSANA MEDITATION

A related tradition is that of Vipassana meditation. Vipassana, the meditation of analysis (i.e., of understanding where thoughts come from and where they go and that life is actually in continual flux, unsatisfactory as ordinarily lived, and without an ego center), is the heart of Theravada practice. But it can also be practiced, many would say, on its own without the trappings of conventional south Asian Buddhism. To teach its independent use is the mission of S. N. Goenka and his students, who offer popular ten-day Vipassana retreats throughout the world. The Vipassana Meditation Centre in New Zealand sponsors these courses.

There are other Buddhist paths, too—or, if one wishes, pathless paths, for as the mighty Heart and Lotus sutras remind us, the path vanishes when the goal is reached, and one realizes one was really there all the time. One searches for enlightenment like a man desperately searching the world, over mountains and seas, jungles and deserts, for a lost jewel, having forgotten it was in his pocket all the time.

ZEN BUDDHISM

This is particularly the attitude of Zen Buddhism, which emphasizes the jewellike intrinsic Buddha nature that everyone has and that can be realized in quiet sitting, or even more in the ordinary events of everyday life, but of course the deep, total naturalness of such a realization requires rigorous pruning away of the contrivances and self-delusions that clutter most of our lives. That is what *zazen* (Zen sitting) just being alone with one's mind and nothing else is for. The *roshi* (Zen master) with his challenges and riddles and reassurances, can also help one cut back to reality. The Zen experience is available in New Zealand. But as a recent issue of *Manawa,* the newsletter of the Zen Society, put it:

> We must work to establish genuine Kiwi Zen (something which is likely to take two or three hundred years at least), but we must also be aware of Kiwi failings—such as the "She'll be right" attitude engendered by our relatively easy-going lives, an attitude which meshes with "buji Zen"—the fatal error assuming to ourselves that since we are all intrinsically Buddhas, there is nothing to strive for. When Dogen talks of the importance of "seeking nothing" he is talking to monks in a highly disciplined monastic setting. Although we are not ordained people, there is still a real need in our distraction-filled and increasingly acquisitive and violent society to establish Buddhist communities.

Current Zen work in New Zealand began in 1973 with the visit of Joshu Sasaki, a Japanese Zen master long resident at the Cimarron Zen Center in Los Angeles. He has frequently returned to conduct *sesshins* (intensively Zen training sessions) in New Zealand. One New Zealand student of Sasaki-roshi, Michael Radford, has become a prominent Zen teacher both in his homeland and at the Cimarron Center. Radford has told me of initial opposition from neighbors and the community to his emergent Zen center in Auckland, but, as time has passed and times have changed, antagonism has turned to respect. Although small, the Zen Society of New Zealand (formed as such in 1983 to replace looser affiliations) is well established, and has *zendos* (meditation halls) in Glen Eden, Mt. Eden, and Wellington as well as regional contacts.

Vajrayana Buddhism

The Vajrayana (Tantric or Esoteric) Buddhism of Tibet has very different means, though ultimately the same end, as Theravada or Zen: the realization of one's original nature, prior to the accretions welded on by ignorance and craving. In Theravada they are dissolved by analysis of what they are; in Zen faced down with fierce samurai courage; in Vajrayana pried loose through skillful technical manipulations of words, images, and even the passions themselves.

The Vajrayana adept will identifies with a buddha, who is one with his or her own true nature, through chanting mantras proper to that figure, visualizing it in all the symbolic richness and detail with which it is portrayed in the *tankas,* and undergoes long and arduous initiations. These may, in the crazy-wisdom tradition, mandate doing things contrary to one's superficial nature, arousing strong anger, fear, or desire, which a canny scientist of the soul can finesse into purification and even into breaking out of all one's previous boundaries. Such a savant is the Vajrayana lama or guru supposed to be, and nothing is more important to that tradition than the tight bonds linking master and disciple. Thus Vajrayana movements are always founded on the lineage of a great teacher, and the lives of serious practitioners center around successive initiations or power impartations bestowed by the current incumbent. There are two Tibetan Buddhist centers in New Zealand: the Dorje Chang Institute, and the Karma Kagyu Trust. Each has a resident lama representing important lineages. Karma Kagryu has built the first Tibetan-style stupa in the Southern Hemisphere.

Other Western Groups: New Thought

Turning to the West again, we shall mention two groups representing the New Thought and what may be called reformed Christian Science traditions, Radiant Living and the Infinite Way. New Thought, the tradition obviously behind Radiant Living, is a late-nineteenth-century movement emphasizing the power of thought and affirmation to attain health, happiness and success; it has produced a number of religious movements, such as Unity, Divine Science, and Religious Science, and perhaps even more important, is at the heart of such widespread extra-denominational teachings as positive thinking.

Radiant Living

Radiant Living was founded by Herbert Sutcliffe (1886–1971) and is centered at the Peloha Homestead in Havelock North, a health resort described as the international headquarters of the Sutcliffe

School. According to his obituary in the *New Zealand Herald Tribune* (October 28, 1971), Sutcliffe was born in England but immigrated to Australia where he lectured on physical and spiritual health and became president of the Australian Health Society (1925–1930) and editor of *Radiant Health*. He traveled widely in 1931–1941, establishing schools in the United States, Canada, New Zealand (first in Canterbury in 1938), and elsewhere. He settled in New Zealand in 1941 and purchased the Havelock property in 1942. The present periodical of the center, *Radiant Living,* presents a mix of advice on diet and health, inspirational pieces of a liberal Christian cast, and quotes from such sources as White Eagle, Paramahansa Yogananda, the New Thought writer Emmet Fox, and Herbert Sutcliffe himself, in paragraphs with such highly New Thought titles as "Abundant Supply," "Divine Understanding," and "Divine Supply." The last heading sums up all New Thought extremely well as Sutcliffe writes:

> Material life and matter cannot exist without a cause. A search reveals that all causes are invisible, beyond the lower or slower expressions of matter. Therein is the source of supply. You have your contact with divine Supply within yourself. By training the mind you can release the cause of your desire, for it belongs to your I AM, the invisible Self and God Power within. . . . Be thankful that the supply of your needs can be contacted by your own spiritual desire and your imagination, your faith and persistence. Seek Divine Supply.[29]

The Christian Science movement has always insisted that it differs from New Thought on an important point. Its reading of a passage like the above would be that the New Thought writer is under the impression health and all good things are the result of effort aimed at training and concentrating the power of mind to produce quasi-magical results, a process Christian Science disparages as mesmerism. Instead, Christian Scientists would say, the point is that God is and has always been spirit, infinite and perfect, hence matter has no room to possess even the relative existence that could make its enhancement or healing the object of the New Thought mind cure. Mary Baker Eddy, the discoverer of Christian Science, insisted on letting go of mortal mind with its belief in matter and its ills, and called for realization of the divine perfection already here.

The Infinite Way

No one has taught this radical principle more firmly, or winningly, than Joel Goldsmith (1892–1964), an American who worked for many years as a Christian Science practicioner but who withdrew from the institutional church in 1946 to pursue an independent career as a spiritual lecturer and teacher of radical monism in the Christian Science style. He emphasized God as the one mind, the one consciousness of which we are all a part, before which the many is only a secondary appearance; to establish awareness of the one is to tap into the source of healing and supply. Goldsmith did not wish to establish an organization, and during his lifetime had only an informal circle of students. After his death, however, a modest organization has issued a newsletter and continued to make his tapes and books available. Meetings are held from time to time at which the tapes are played. Goldsmith lectured in New Zealand and has followers there; a center in Auckland continues the Infinite Way work, as it is called, after the title of his most popular book.[30]

Other Movements
The Church of Scientology

The controversial Church of Scientology, founded by L. Ron Hubbard (1911–1986), is also based on a view that the inner human essence is radically distinct from the physical shell, though with quite different practical consequences. The Church of Scientology was established in America in 1954 as an outgrowth of the enthusiasm generated by L. Ron Hubbard's 1950 book, *Dianetics*. Scientology spread forcefully to a number of countries, especially the English-speaking commonwealth. In developed Scientological teaching, the individual is actually a Thetan, a spiritual entity trapped in matter, energy, space, and time (MEST), a fate explained in various mythological ways. In this state we suffer and lose effectiveness because of engrams, conditioned responses the result of traumalike experiences in this or previous lives. Scientological counseling, or "processing," can help one clean out the engrams, "go clear," become "at cause" in one's own life, and finally become an "Operating Thetan."

Controversy has arisen around Scientology's fees and financial practices, its alleged harrassment of dissidents, its alleged misleading claims, its alleged improper psychiatric procedures, and its numerous legal actions. Of the last, the church has won some and lost some, but in the process has aided several nations in defining more closely than before freedom of religion and freedom of information and has advanced the cause of public access to government documents. A 1965 ban on Scientology by the Australian government led to a lengthy legal battle, resolved in the church's favor in 1983 by the Australian high court. That landmark decision defined religious freedom for the first time in Australia.[31]

THE UNIFICATION CHURCH

Known more formally as the Holy Spirit Association for the Unification of World Christianity and less formally as the Moonies, the Unification Church has also attracted controversy because of its business activities, its militant anticommunism, its alleged authoritarianism and brainwashing of converts, and its unconventional version of Christianity. (In regard to its unconventionality, it is the first—but will probably not be the last—of the many spiritualistic and messianic versions of Christianity that have sprung up in recently missionized territories, conjoining the new faith with native charisma and practices, to reinvade the sending countries forcefully.) Founded in 1954 by a Korean, the Reverend Sun Myung Moon, it inculcates an ideal society based on the home and right relationships, propounds that Jesus' mission to establish such a world was only imperfectly accomplished, and hints that Moon may be the messianic vehicle for the rectification of God's work. It has established centers worldwide, including work in New Zealand, which have particularly drawn young people who have become intensely involved in the movement, often living communally and entering into marriages arranged by the Moon.[32]

THE BRITISH-ISRAEL WORLD FEDERATION

Another group often accused of right-wing ideological sympathies is the venerable British-Israel World Federation, whose basic belief is that the British peoples are the actual descendents of the biblical Israelites and heirs of God's promises to them. Founded in England in the late nineteenth century, this movement prospered in Britain, the United States, and the commonwealth until the 1940s, when it began to decline, until by the 1980s membership was small and aging. While I was in New Zealand in 1988 the national organization and the Wellington branch were disincorporated, but a bookstore, with an independent relation to international headquarters in England, remained on Queen Street in Auckland. When I visited it, I noted a selection of British-Israel tracts together with a large selection of international extreme rightist, anticommunist materials of the John Birch Society type. But British-Israel people to whom I talked were unfailingly courteous and mild mannered, stressing that their doctrines were not racist but simply pointed to the special mission and destiny—with attendant trials—laid upon persons of British descent.

WICCA AND NEOPAGANISM

By the 1980s witchcraft and neopaganism had reached New Zealand. A product, in its present form, of the 1950s and 1960s, these closely related movements, unlike some, only continued to grow after the latter tumultuous decade. As we have seen, neopaganism refers essentially to the revival of religions long thought dead, especially those of pre-Christian Europe, such as the cults of the ancient Egyptians, Greeks, Celts, or Norsemen. Their modern adherents often combine a Romantic love of the past with a keen artistic sense, sometimes mounting rituals of exquisite beauty and evocativeness. In addition, pagans affirm the spiritual meaning of polytheism, seeing the sacred as pluralistic rather than monolithic, nuanced and different in each glade, grove, and human mood whether of love or war. They contrast the ecological sensitivity of paganism with the alleged dominationism of the dominant religions, holding that the old religion's polytheistic holism gives humanity a proper ecospiritual niche in nature while offering no comfort to our dreams of dominion over our ancient mother. Many pagan rites are profoundly geared to the seasons and presences of the natural world. The new worshippers of the old gods also emphasize paganism's sensitivity to the equal spiritual power of men and women. They reverence god and goddess together and consecrate both priests and priestesses.

Modern witchcraft, or Wicca as it is often called, makes much the same claims in a more eclectic way. Witches are more likely than neopagans to create new rituals in the pagan mode, and relate them to current problems. However, in general the movement seems to be going in this direction, and the distinction is blurring. (A third tradition often related, both sociologically and ideologically, to these is ceremonial magic; I am not familiar with any New Zealand expression of it other than the OTO.) Although neopaganism has been represented in New Zealand by the Ireland-based Fellowship of Isis, most activity seems to be in the Wicca tradition, especially as it is closely related to the women's spirituality movement.[33]

Neopaganism and Wicca in the Euro-American-Australasian world has benefited from three concurrent developments: The first is feminism, especially feminist spirituality, which has led some women to yearn for sacred names and roles coequal with those of men—goddesses and priestesses, and rites affirming female physical and emotional experiences.[34] The second is the environmentalist movement, with which the nature emphasis of paganism has resonated well. The third is the rediscovery of primordial and indigenous religious ways—Native American, African, Maori, pre-Christian European—with their shamanism, herbal healings, vision quests, and initiations, as viable paths for others as well. In England and America, the pagan and Wiccan movements appear to be answering to a surprisingly widespread spiritual need, and by all indications are progressing well in Australia and gaining ground in New Zealand.[35]

SATANISM

At this point Satanism must also be mentioned. Witches, pagans, and ceremonial magicians very properly bridle at the common insinuation they are Satanists. They point out, first, that they do nothing licentious or cruel to human or beast in their worship, such as Satanists are alleged to do, being instead gentle, ecological people who are lovers of nature and nature's gods and goddesses. Second, they correctly indicate that they are simply adherents of the old religion, the faith of pre-Christian Europe and have no stock in the later religion of Christ; to honor Satan, the great rebel against the Judeo-Christian God, implies accepting in some sense the whole theological system of which he is a part.

Apparently there are Satanists in New Zealand. I have heard rumors of a Satanist church in Eastbourne, and a motorcycle gang, Satan's Slaves, was in the news in 1988. The 1986 census reported 186 self-professed Satanists (165 males and 21 females), a category unreported in previous censuses. Although some of these responses may have been frivolous, it could well be the case that in 1986, for the first time, there were scores of New Zealanders, mostly male, who seriously thought of themselves as worshippers of he whom the dominant faith considers the antagonist of God and of all that is good. I was able to learn nothing about these people. But they must not be confused with those who are merely followers of what they account the old religion revived.

THE NEW AGE

By the late 1980s the New Age had hit New Zealand in the form of bookstores, tapes, crystals, acupuncture, holistic healing, and articles in the press on the new vogue.[36] Perhaps one should say new old, for the artifacts of the New Age track back not only to antiquity, but more directly just to the 1960s—and the New Age people by and large give the impression of being 1960s people, now well into middle age and looking for reaccess to the wonders of their youth. But now under new terms: being putatively well established in families and careers, not to mention susceptible to the lassitude of noonday and the skepticism born of a little experience, they are much less likely than they once were to drop out, to commit themselves entirely to a guru or a gospel, to trip out to Katmandu or the antipodes of the mind.

On the other hand, they are now affluent enough to be able to put down cash in spiritual salesrooms, and self-assured enough to want to put together their own redemption kits, with gemstones, tapes, teachers, doctrines now from this tradition, now from another. The New Age seems to represent a virtually unprecedented level of spiritual independence and commercialism together. People get fragments of Tibet or

Chaldea in an enlightenment emporium and practice it on their own at home, apart from any living priest or temple, with a confidence both wonderful and appalling, with an attitude less of credence than of, Let's check it out, and I'll take from it what I can use.

☆   ☆   ☆   ☆

What does it all mean? Examining some common themes of these 1960s and after groups, we find, first. that even more than the older spiritual communities, they focus on a charismatic leader, a Gurdjieff or Rajneesh, who is himself their true center. Certain worldview concepts seem generally to be taken for granted—reincarnation, an entity capable of spiritual growth—but the real focus is the person not the creed. The ponderous books of old-fashioned Theosophy, like the scattered and shifting charisma of Spiritualism, is no longer where it's at.

Second, the recent movements put compensatory emphasis on practice, usually on a single simple sure technique, a chant or method of meditation, or the varied but simple psychic evocations of the Emin and the OTO, inculcated by the charismatic teacher and forceful enough to bring rapid and appreciable results in the meeting of needs or the changing of consciousness.

Third, one gets a strong sense of sexuality as a powerful problem or presence in these newer groups, whether in its affirmation as in Rajneeshism, or in the heavy sexual symbolic overtones of something like the OTO's Western tantra, or in its conspicuous renunciation, as in the Brahma Kumaris.

Thus far most of the new groups seem more ephemeral than Spiritualism or Theosophy. The mid-twentieth century has produced far fewer of the diehard lifetime converts who gave passion to the debates and built the lasting spiritual instititions of the Victorian era. All in all, our age—especially in New Zealand—has seen religion less as something to argue about or throw oneself into for the long haul than as something to taste and sample, capable at its best of producing a series of "good experiences." The series may in practice be valued above finding the single one that lasts from here to eternity. The will, or any sense of the need, to create chartered, enduring alternative spiritual institutions, or to stick with only one over the long pilgrimage of a lifetime, has faltered.

Notes

Chapter 1: From Nineveh to New Zealand

1. John Rockey, "An Australasian Utopist," *New Zealand Journal of History* 15, no. 2 (October 1981): 157–178. "Owenite" refers to his following of Robert Owen (1771–1858), the celebrated Welsh manufacturer, reformer, and utopian theorist who became a Spiritualist late in his life.

2. Thus in 1869 W. T. L. Travers could write, delicately but with no mistaking the point, "If by the intrusion of the vigorous races of Europe, smiling farms and busy marts are to take the place of the rough clearing and hut of the savage, and millions of a populous country, with the arts and letters, the matured policy, and the ennobling impulses of a free people, are to replace the few thousands of the scattered tribes now living in an apparently aimless and unprogressive state, even the most sensitive philanthropist may learn to look with resignation, if not with complacency, on the extinction of a people which, in the past had accomplished so imperfectly every object of man's being." W. T. L. Travers, "On the Change Effected in the Natural Features of a New Country by the Introduction of Civilized Races," *Transactions and Proceedings of the New Zealand Institute* 2 (1869): 312–313. Cited in Alfred W. Crosby, *Ecological Imperialism: The Biological Expansion of Europe, 900–1900* (Cambridge: Cambridge University Press, 1986), pp. 267–268. Travers may have had in mind words written ten years before by Charles Kingsley, that paladin of Christian Socialism and mid-Victorian reformism as well as of robust patriotism, who put the matter succinctly: "The human species have a right to demand . . . that each people should either develop the capabilities of their own country, or make room for those who will develop them" (*Miscellanies* 2 (1859): 21–22).

3. For further discussion, see Miles Fairburn, *The Ideal Society and Its Enemies: The Foundations of Modern New Zealand Society 1850–1900* (Auckland: Auckland University Press, 1989).

4. See Peter J. Lineham, "Freethinkers in Nineteenth-Century New Zealand," *New Zealand Journal of History* 19, no. 1 (April 1985): 61–81.

5. For New Zealand Masonic history, see F. G. Northern, *History of the Grand Lodge of Antient, Free and Accepted Masons of New Zealand 1890–1970*

(published by P. J. Oliver on behalf of the Grand Lodge of New Zealand, Gisborne: Te Rau Press, 1971). For the nineteenth-century social role of Masonic and similar organizations, with special emphasis on their role of providing rites of passage and bonding for males in a highly gender-divided society, see a very interesting study by Mark C. Carnes, *Secret Ritual and Manhood in Victorian America* (New Haven, Conn.: Yale University Press, 1989). Although focused on the United States, I imagine Carnes' observations are generally valid for New Zealand and elsewhere, though I suspect the political role of Freemasonry was more secure in New Zealand than in America, where the lodge, though potent as a bastion of the Anglo-Protestant establishment, was also always controversial, countered at one point politically by an anti-Masonic party and continually opposed by the powerful Roman Catholic church and certain conservative Protestant denominations. See also Lynn Dumenil, *Freemasonry and American Culture, 1880–1939* (Princeton, N.J.: Princeton University Press, 1984).

6. Brother R. Ward, *Druidism Past and Present* (Auckland: Geddis and Blomfield, 1902). The account in the Centennial Banquet brochure, May 8, 1976, of the Druid's Friendly Society of Canterbury, puts the origin of modern Druidism differently than Ward, tracing it to a "gathering of gentlemen" at the Kings Arm Tavern in London in 1771, when a certain Henry Hurle proposed regular meetings under the "title of Druids" to "promote good fellowship, hilarity and brotherly love," in emulation of the ancient Druids who "sought to ameliorate the conditions of mankind."

7. *New Zealand Branch, Manchester Unity Independent Order of Oddfellows, Official Handbook 1907–1908* (Psalmerston North: Watson and Eyre, 1907). Lillas F. A. Benzoni, *A Century of Oddfellowship* (Dunedin: Pageant, 1962).

8. W. H. Oliver, "Social Welfare: Social Justice or Social Efficiency?" in D. A. Hamer, ed., *New Zealand Social History: Papers from the Turnbull Conference on New Zealand Social History, 1978* (Wellington: Turnbull Library, 1978).

9. See Robert Ellwood, "Religion and the Discovery of History," in *The History and Future of Faith* (New York: Crossroad, 1989).

10. Eliza M. Butler, *The Myth of the Magus* (New York: Macmillan, 1948).

11. Frances Yates, *The Occult Philosophy in the Elizabethan Age* (London: Routledge and Kegan Paul, 1979).

12. Frances Yates, *The Rosicrucian Enlightenment* (London: Routledge and Kegan Paul, 1972).

13. For a fascinating discussion, see Colleen McDannell and Bernhard Lang, *Heaven: A History* (New Haven, Conn.: Yale University Press, 1988), especially chap. 7, "Swedenborg and the Emergence of a Modern Heaven."

14. Signe Taksvig, *Emanuel Swedenborg, Scientist and Mystic* (New Haven, Conn.: Yale University Press, 1948).

15. For Mesmer's life, see Vincent Buranelli, *The Wizard from Vienna* (New York: Coward, McCann, and Geoghegan, 1975).

16. H. P. Blavatsky, *Isis Unveiled* (Wheaton, Ill.: Theosophical Publishing, 1972; facsimile of 1st ed., New York: Bouton, 1877) 1:129.

17. Andrew Jackson Davis, *The Principles of Nature, Her Divine Revelations, and a Voice to Mankind, by and through Andrew Jackson Davis, the "Poughkeepsie Seer" and "Clairvoyant"* (New York: Lyon and Fishbough, 1847).

18. See Andrew Jackson Davis, *The Magic Staff: An Autobiography* (New York: Brown, 1857); and William Fishbough's introduction to his *The Principles of Nature*.

19. The thought of the visionary French social theorist Charles Fourier (1772–1837) was popular in the progressive circles amid which early Spiritualism was at home; Fourier also promulgated a mystical eschatology no less congenial to the Spiritualist style. His agriculture-based communes, or phalanxes, in which labor was rotated and wealth distributed equitably, inspired some forty such communes, mostly short-lived, in the United States around the 1840s and 1850s; the most famous was Brook Farm in Massachusetts (1841–1846), an experiment that attracted several leading Transcendentalists.

20. There is, surprisingly and unfortunately, no good scholarly book on the Fox sisters to recommend, though the movement they sparked was certainly significant, and their subsequent lives as mediums beset by controversy, marital troubles, and alcoholism holds much tragic but human interest. But see Ernest Isaacs, "The Fox Sisters and American Spiritualism," in Howard Kerr and Charles L. Crow, eds., *The Occult in America: New Historical Perspectives* (Urbana and Chicago: University of Illinois Press, 1883), pp. 79–110. For a readable summary of the early years of Spiritualism, see Slater Brown, *The Heyday of Spiritualism* (New York: Hawthorne, 1970). A major primary source, by an author who was later to play an important part in the story of Spiritualism in New Zealand, is Emma Hardinge, *Modern American Spiritualism: A Twenty Years' Record of the Communion between Earth and the World of Spirits* (New York: Hardinge, 1870).

21. The relation of mid-century Spiritualism to the age's optimistic views of science and progress, in which the new faith was itself the highest example of both on the spiritual plane and the guarantor of their values in the world, is exuberantly expressed in an 1856 article by Henry Steel Olcott, later a founder and first president of the Theosophical Society but then a fervent Spiritualist:

> Progression! Progression is the eternal law of our existence; from lowest to highest, from bad to good, from small to great, its ceaseless, silent and irresistible march bears us on, upward, onward, to something more perfect, more Divine!
>
> Nations dying to give birth to more intellectual nations; governments and just laws succeeding to barbarism and misrule; houses replacing huts; steam and electricity supplanting the paddle canoe and the foot messenger; and more glorious far, the spirit being more rapidly developed, and sooner fitted for its immortal home. . . .
>
> [Spiritualism] cultivates the sentiment of love, both to God and to man; it fosters a true manhood; it makes demonstrably certain the fact of immortality; it extinguishes all forms of tyrannical governments, and thus is most democratic in its tendencies; it reconciles opposing factions, uniting North and South in common interests and a common destiny; it sweeps away all *false* religious organizations, retaining only what it true. . . .

"The Spiritualist's Faith," *Spiritual Telegraph* 4, no. 51 (April 19, 1856): 201.

22. Although sometimes speculative and somewhat weak on intellectual background, see Marion Meade, *Madame Blavatsky: The Woman behind the Myth*

(New York: Putnam, 1980). A new substantial biography is Sylvia Cranston, *Helena P. Blavatsky* (New York: Putnam, 1993). For primary sources see Mary K. Neff, *Personal Memoirs of H. P. Blavatsky* (1937; reprint Wheaton, Ill.: Theosophical Publishing, 1967).

23. Henry Steel Olcott, *Old Diary Leaves: America 1874-1878*, 1st series (Adyar, Madras, India: Theosophical Publishing, 1895), pp. 17-18.

24. For a history of Theosophy, chiefly in America, see Bruce F. Campbell, *Ancient Wisdom Revived: A History of the Theosophical Movement* (Berkeley and Los Angeles: University of California Press, 1980). See also Robert S. Ellwood, "The American Theosophical Synthesis," in Kerr and Crow, *The Occult in America,* pp. 111-134. A major primary source is the six volumes of Olcott's *Old Diary Leaves* (Adyar, Madras, India: Theosophical Publishing, various dates).

25. He was editor of the Allahabad *Pioneer,* an important Anglo-Indian paper. Sinnett was dismissed from it in 1883 because of his Theosophical sympathies, a year after Rudyard Kipling took up editorial duties at the sister *Lahore Civil and Military Gazette.*

Chapter 2: Unbroken Circles

1. The 1986 New Zealand census yielded 2,679 self-professed adherents of the Spiritualist church, up from 2,403 in 1981 and only 1,725 in 1976. Allowing for the large number of nonmembers who regularly attend Spiritualist services, and the fact that Spiritualism may be particularly well represented in the "other" and "object" categories, this faith can very conservatively be estimated to express the major spiritual focus of at least one in a thousand New Zealand-rs. But in the United States—although certainly there is a great deal of cryptospiritualism in all sorts of things from New Age channeling to Hispanic movements like Santería—the 1988 membership figure for the old-line National Spiritualist Association of Churches is only 5,558, which, even if it were tripled or quadrupled to account for the many independent Spiritualist churches and nonmember attenders, would come to only one in ten thousand out of a population of 240 million.

2. This prelate, after being consecrated in England for the southern see, arrived in January 1869 but was disapproved by the first synod of his new diocese on the grounds that he was a ritualist and eventually returned home.

3. The controversy is suggested by a pamphlet by "a spiritualist" in the Robert Stout collection in the library of Victoria University, Wellington, dated January 11, 1870, and titled "Spiritualism, to the Reverend the Synod of the Presbyterian Church of Otago and Southland." The anonymous author presents his vigorous defence of his faith "because some of your number are enquiring after the subject of Spiritualism," and (if we take him at his word) goes so far as to offer a one-thousand-guinea wager that Spiritualism is true.

4. This periodical lasted until 1956, when it became the *Psychic Science News-Magazine.* New Zealand Spiritualists contributed to the *Harbinger* and received much of their working information on Spiritualist affairs from it.

5. On James Smith's lecture tour, see *Otago Daily Times* April–May 1872 *passim.* For published lectures see James Smith, "Spiritualism; or the Magnetic Teaching, Its Method and Its Objects; Being Three Lectures, Delivered in

Dunedin, April 28, May 5, and May 12, 1872," *Dunedin Daily Times*. (In the Stout Collection, Victoria University). For his life see *Australian Dictionary of Biography: 1851–1890* 6:146.

6. Actually James M. Peebles (1822–1922) was no more than fifty at the time, only halfway through a life of nearly a hundred years. (In 1884 he confidently published, amid his Spiritualist and travel books, *How to Live a Century and Grow Old Gracefully* and in 1912, as though to keep tabs on his own progress in this respect, *Ninety Years Young and Healthy: How and Why.*)

The 1873 journey was recorded in Peebles' *Around the World* (Boston: Colby and Rich, 1875). The New Zealand chapter disappointingly says very little about the Spiritualists with whom he interacted in that country, though there is much rather pedestrian description of scenery, climate, and economy, together with characteristically opinionated views on sundry matters. An encounter with Christchurch Anglicanism seems to have provoked a discourse on the Christian Eucharist as cannibalism, and with the indigenous peoples on the Maoris as Spiritualists. He does, however, provide an account of the John Logan affair in Dunedin.

On January 1, 1897, Peebles arrived in Auckland for a second visit to New Zealand, described in a 1898 account eventually collected in his *Five Journeys around the World; or Travels in the Pacific Islands, New Zealand, Australia, Ceylon, India, Egypt and Other Oriental Countries* (Los Angeles: Peebles, 1910). Unfortunately, this account of New Zealand adds little to the 1875 one and indeed borrows generously from it, including barely rewritten versions of the cannibalism and Maori Spiritualism material—save that in the later book one senses a man who, now in his seventies, has become even more cantankerously set in his views than when a mere fifty. (It was on the 1897 trip that Peebles visited Henry Steel Olcott of Theosophy in Ceylon. Olcott rather aptly dubbed him a "combative sage" and once took a wicked delight in setting his fellow American astride on an elephant without warning him of the perils of that mode of transportation for the unprepared; the Theosophist thought that it might do the Spiritualist good "if his pride should have a fall." Olcott, *Old Diary Leaves* (Adyar, Madras, India: Theosophical Publishing, 1935, 1975), 6:182, 189.

Interestingly enough, Peebles, now Dr. Peebles, has emerged as a major spirit guide and cult figure in contemporary American Spiritualism. Several important mediums communicate out of trance his gruffly spoken but often pertinent advice to their clients, though for some reason this American-born (if Scottish-descended) divine sometimes turns into a Scottish doctor and acquires a Scots accent. But, although séance-room trails are often murky, and there is evidence of a spiritual Dr. Peebles even before the death of the historical figure, it seems beyond doubt that the name of this current mentor from the other side is now derived from the opinionated Victorian who became a patriarch of his faith. See, e.g., Don and Linda Pendleton, *To Dance with Angels: An Amazing Journey to the Heart with the Phenomenal Thomas Jacobson and the Grand Spirit, "Dr. Peebles"* (New York: Kensington, 1990).

7. *Otago Daily News,* February 3, 1873.

8. Alfred Deakin, later prime minister of Australia and architect of Federation, was an enthusiastic Spiritualist as a young man, becoming president of the Victorian Association of Progressive Spiritualists, the leading Australian organ-

ization, in 1878. Because most of the world-traveling Spiritualist lecturers combined their visit to New Zealand with an Australian tour, Deakin was familiar with them. His remarks make it clear that these visits were a necessary but mixed blessing. Highly touted Spiritualist lecturers from abroad were the main source of publicity and income for local groups, but the wandering stars who presented them, Deakin indicates, were hard to manage and likely to sow squabbles over the mantles and the receipts in their wake. Peebles left dissension and a schism in Melbourne behind him. Alfred Deakin, *Autobiographical Notes* (unpublished material in the care of Prof. J. A. La Nauze, University of Melbourne), p. 44, cited in F. B. Smith, "Spiritualism in Victoria in the Nineteenth Century," *Journal of Religious History* (Sydney) 3, no. 3 (June 1965): 252–253. For this period in Australian Spiritualism, see also A. J. Gabay, "The Séance in the Melbourne of the 1870s: Experience and Meanings," *Journal of Religious History* 13 (1984): 192–212.

9. J. O. Barrett, *The Spiritual Pilgrim: A Biography of James M. Peebles* (Boston: Colby and Rich, 1878), p. 37.

10. For Britain, see Logie Barrow, *Independent Spirits: Spiritualism and English Plebeians, 1850–1910* (London and New York: Routledge and Kegan Paul, 1986). For the United States, with special reference to feminism, see Ann Braude, *Radical Spirits: Spiritualism and Women's Rights in Nineteenth-Century America* (Boston: Beacon, 1989).

11. Perhaps rightly so—Barrett, Peebles' biographer, does not even mention the Cincinnati school but states only that Dunn's medical training was by spirit teachers and that he was "Dr. E. C. Dunn" by virtue of his being "duly diplomatized in the medical school of the spirit-world." Barrett, *The Spiritual Pilgrim*, p. 70.

12. *Otago Daily Times,* Jan. 29, 1873.

13. Ibid., March 21, 1873.

14. Ibid., March 6, 1873. Peebles, *Around the World,* pp. 102–103, gives a brief account of the Logan trial, including the wording of the summons from the session clerk to the accused.

15. *Dunedin Echo,* March 8, 1873.

16. Emma Hardinge-Britten, *Nineteenth Century Miracles* (New York: Lovell, 1884), p. 270.

17. Deakin, *Autobiographical Notes,* pp. 433–444, cited in Smith, "Spiritualism," pp. 253–254. For a short biography of Hardinge-Britten, see the new introduction by E. J. Dingwall to Hardinge's 1870 work on American Spiritualism, *Modern American Spiritualism.* New Hyde Park, NY: University Books, 1970, pp. ix–xviii.

18. Hardinge-Britten, *Miracles,* p. 271. For Green's assault see M. W. Green, "Mrs. Hardinge-Britten in the Crucible, Being a Lecture Delivered . . . in Dunedin . . . July 9, 1879, in Reply to 'Spiritualism Vindicated, and Clerical Slanders Refuted' " (pamphlet; Dunedin: Clark, 1879); and Green's "The Devil's Sword Blunted; or Spiritualism Examined and Condemned," (pamphlet; Dunedin: Clark, 1879). Both pamphlets are in the Stout Collection, Victoria University.

19. Hardinge-Britten, *Miracles,* p. 274.

20. *The Communicator*, winter 1987.

21. Moncure Conway, *My Journey to the Wise Men of the East* (London: Constable, 1906), p. 87.

22. *Freethought Review (Wanganui)*, July 1, 1885. On free thought and Rationalism, see Peter J. Lineham, "Freethinkers in Nineteenth-Century New Zealand," *New Zealand Journal of History* 19, no. 1 (April 1885): 61–81. The relatively brief vogue for free thought in the late 1870s and early 1880s closely followed similar developments in England that owed much to the widely publicized elections to parliament and trial for promoting an obscene book (on birth control) of the radical, atheistic Charles Bradlaugh, whose close associate in those days was Annie Besant—the same who later, in Theosophical guise, would lecture to full houses in New Zealand.

23. "Our Legacy," *The Communicator* (a Spiritualist periodical) (Winter 1987). Rationalist sources also say the Free Thought Association collapsed over disputes on Spiritualism, but in 1890, not in 1893. See, e.g., Gordon Stein, *Freethought in the United Kingdom and the Commonwealth: A Descriptive Bibliography* (New York: Greenwood, 1981), p. 124.

24. J. Chantry Harris (1830–1895), described as "a freethinker and a Spiritualist," was born in Bath, England, and made his adventurous way to New Zealand as a sailor, becoming proprietor of the *New Zealand Times* and *New Zealand Mail* (Wellington) in 1880. He sold the papers in 1890. After the transfer of ownership, the tone of the paper toward Spiritualism, already climbing down from its 1884 high, distinctly changed. Harris' wife was president of the Society for the Prevention of Cruelty to Animals.

25. W. C. Nation, *The Unseen World*, 3d ed. (Levin, N.Z.: private publication, 1920), p. 63 ff. In this interesting book Nation recapitulates the original Wairarapa material and adds other Spiritualist incidents and discourses.

26. The Maori land courts met to determine and record customary owners of Maori tribal land prior to its sale. The Maori interest in ancestors is characteristic; they kept lists called *whakapapa* of their forebears.

27. The Rev. Theophilius Le Menant des Chesnais, S.M., *A Lecture on Spiritic and Magic Manifestations in the Nineteenth Century* (Wellington: Edwards and Green, 1884).

28. William McLean, *Spiritualism Vindicated and Clerical Slanders Unmasked* (Wellington: New Zealand Times Office, 1887). Dowie came to the United States in 1888, where in 1900 he founded the Christian Catholic Church with its theocratic community in Zion, Illinois. There scriptural literalism was to reach the extent of flat-earth belief. On Dowie's visit to New Zealand, see James E. Worsfold, *A History of the Charismatic Movements in New Zealand* (Bradford: Julian Literature Trust, 1974), pp. 86–87.

29. *New Zealand Mail*, June 13, 1884.

30. McLean, *Spiritualism Vindicated*, advertisement at end.

31. *New Zealand Mail, passim*. James and Priscilla Hackett were also active in Australia and were exposed by T. Shackleton Henry in *Spookland: A Record of Research* (Sydney: Maclardy, 1894).

32. Through visiting lecturers, *The Harbinger of Light*, and experience of visitors like Mrs. Harris, Australian Spiritualism, always centered in Victoria, was

clearly a major resource of the religion in New Zealand. This relation is witnessed to in an unusual way by Katherine Bates, a Spiritualist writer who sailed for Australia and New Zealand "shortly after the Jubilee of 1887" and in her memoirs tells of seeing a ghost at a sheep station near Dunedin on New Year's 1888. The apparition was later found to have been projected to her by a circle in Melbourne! E. Katherine Bates, *Seen and Unseen* (London: Greening, 1907), p. 49. Later, on p. 64, she refers to a "Dunedin Circle or Metaphysical Club."

33. "Jenny Wren," *Woman's Work and Destiny* (paper read before the Thames Mutual Improvement Association; pamphlet; Thames: *Evening Star* office, 1884).

34. "Jenny Wren," *Leaves of Love* (Sydney: Jerrems, 1890). Lady Carrington is, of course, the "Lady C——" of the autobiography. Wife of Lord Carrington, then the popular governor of New South Wales, she was active in charity work, especially for distressed women.

35. *Lectures Given by Mrs. T. Harris at the Opera House, Wellington* (pamphlet; Thames: *Thames Star* Office, 1897).

36. On Bailey, see H. J. Irwin, "Charles Bailey: A Biographical Study of the Australian Apport Medium," *Journal of the Society for Psychical Research* (London) 54, no. 807 (April 1987): 97–118. Irwin (p. 107) confirms that Bailey visited New Zealand in 1909, where, in Wellington, he was challenged by a stage magician, who claimed he could reproduce Bailey's performance by legerdemain. But the outcome of this confrontation is unclear. Houdini, that great bane of mediums, asserted in his *A Magician among the Spirits* (1924) that the conjurer effectively demolished Bailey's pretensions, but a Spiritualist, M. C. Benson, writing in *The Harbinger of Light* in 1935, claimed that the skeptical magician withdrew when he learned how stringent the controls for the test would be.

37. Deacon, who later in life spelled his first name "Vyvyan," is a rather enigmatic figure, very active in Australian Spiritualism in the 1920s. Leaf describes his Melbourne séances with appreciation, and in 1929 he received great publicity by suing the Melbourne *Truth* for libel over an article accusing him of fraud in his mediumship; he won and was awarded a record sum in damages, although the paper was defended by none other than the rising legal star Robert Menzies. Deacon, making much of a family connection with the poet Robert Browning, claimed to be the custodian of certain esoteric Browning family lore. That claim was expounded, though with little supporting evidence, in a book by Deacon's daughter Vivienne Browning, *My Browning Family Album* (London: Springwood, 1979). According to his own words in "The Medium Who Thrashed a Newspaper! A Relative of Robert Browning: The Story of His Life, as Told to the Editor," *The International Psychic Gazette* 29, no. 208, January 1931, he lived in New Zealand between two years and three years, apparently about 1920–1922 (he is also dubiously said to have organized Doyle's tour), "doing public and private mediumistic work," though I have found no other confirmation of this activity. But to this day Deacon is rumored in New Zealand esoteric circles to have used Spiritualism, though he was very proficient in it, as a front for introducing "harder" occult groups such as the Ordo Templi Orien-

tis (OTO) to the island nation. Although the OTO, which included esoteric sexual practices in its repertoire, was to become associated with the notorious Aleister Crowley, Deacon reportedly introduced it to Australia in its pre-Crowley, German form. He is rumored also to have secretively planted it in New Zealand during his 1920 tour or stay. For Deacon's involvement in the OTO in Sydney, see Neville Drury and Gregory Tillett, *Other Temples, Other Gods: The Occult in Australia* (Sydney: Methuen Australia, 1980), pp. 28–29, and Browning, *My Browning Family Album, passim.* See also Gregory Tillett, *The Elder Brother: A Biography of Charles Webster Leadbeater* (London: Routledge and Kegan Paul, 1982), pp. 284–285, for a discussion of connections in Sydney between Deacon and the noted Theosophist Leadbeater, possibly involving the OTO and training in sexual magic.

38. William Rough is the author of a book, *Forty Years' Experiences of Occult Research* (Pahiatua: Pahiatua Herald, n.d. [c. 1920]), which affords an interesting look at the development of a New Zealand Spiritualist in this period. Born in Scotland about 1854, Rough came to New Zealand as a youth in 1870, where he married in 1874, and became interested in Spiritualism in 1882, attending séances and, according to his account, obtaining remarkable proofs. He himself received a high teacher, the Sage, who had lived in Atlantis over sixteen thousand years ago. About 1886 Rough helped form an association of Spiritualists in Dunedin, which gained over sixty members in two weeks. He became a vegetarian and gave up tobacco and liquor, after which he commenced to receive "an Oriental Band called The Sun Angel Order of Light, organised in the Fifth Heaven as invisible workers upon the earth plane, and to influence mortals to assist them in their hours of slumber." (No doubt this was the same Sun Angel Order with which Mrs. Harris had been brought in touch in Australia.) In 1891, Rough states, these high guides foretold the Great War of 1914. The volume ends with much discussion of prophecy, healing, the practice of "sublime meditation," and the "Elder Brotherhood," together with several spirit sermons, including one of a universalist cast by John Wesley. Unfortunately for the reputation of the author's guides, prophecies for world events after the book's putative date of 1920 go very much awry, but the work remains an intriguing chronicle of a spiritual life.

39. Clive Chapman, *The Blue Room: Being the Absorbing Story of the Development of Voice-to-Voice Communication in BROAD LIGHT with Souls Who Have Passed into the GREAT BEYOND* (Auckland: Whitcombe and Tombs, 1927) (an account, with a journalist "G. A. W.," of Miss Judd's mediumship).

40. Thomas J. McBride, *Glimpses into Spirit Life* (Christchurch: Whitcombe and Tombs, 1927).

41. Based on J. W. Graham, "A Brief Resume of the Developmental History of Spiritualism in New Zealand," *New Zealand Psychic Gazette* 103 (July 1988): 12–13. For the 1981 statutes, see "Spiritualist Mediums & the Law," *The New Zealand Psychic Gazette* 30 (January 1982): 1, 11. See also the not entirely reliable history in Harold S. Sell, *A Guide to Modern Spiritualism* (Auckland: Spiritualist Church of New Zealand, n.d. [c. 1975]), pp. 16–17. The 1981 New Zealand Act actually follows the 1951 British Fraudulent Mediums Act,

which replaced the 1735 Witchcraft Act, closely in effect if not in wording. For the British 1951 action see Doreen Valiente, *The Rebirth of Witchcraft* (London: Hale, 1989), pp. 9–11.

42. Unidentified newspaper article in *Alexander Hogg Scrapbook* 17, p. 65, in the Turnbull Library. In regard to Arthur Conan Doyle's patriotism, it may be noted that his knighthood was not bestowed for his creation of the Sherlock Holmes stories or other fictional endeavors, but for his journalistic support of the British cause in the South African War.

43. Arthur Conan Doyle, *The Wanderings of a Spiritualist* (London: Hodder and Stoughton, 1921; reprint: Berkeley, Calif: Ronin, 1988).

44. Arthur Conan Doyle, "An Epoch-Making Event—Fairies Photographed," *Strand* (Christmas 1920); *The Coming of the Fairies* (London: Hodder and Stoughton, 1922; reprint, New York: Weiser, 1972). See also Edward L. Gardner, *Fairies: The Cottingley Photographs and their Sequel* (London: Theosophical Publishing, 1945, 1966). This book by Doyle's Theosophical collaborator in the fairy photo investigation contains further accounts of modern fairy sightings by correspondents from around the world, including New Zealand. (The original Cottingley pictures have, however, been thoroughly discredited, including admission in old age by the two percipients of their fabrication—though the women also insisted to the end of their lives that they really did see real fairies in the Yorkshire dales around Cottingley, and this inspired the doctored pictures. See Joe Cooper, *The Case of the Cottingley Fairies* [London: Hale, 1990].)

45. Arthur Conan Doyle, *The New Revelation* (London: Hodder and Stoughton, 1918). This work contains some autobiographical information, including the *Lusitania* incident (p. 52). The Leckie incident is from an introduction by Colin Wilson to the 1988 reprint edition of A. C. Doyle, *The Wanderings of a Spiritualist,* and other sources. Doyle apparently mentioned it in his Wellington address, as the summary in *The Dominion,* December 13, 1920 suggests. But Doyle was chary of citing any particular experience as triggering a "conversion" to Spiritualism. His own and secondary accounts of supposedly significant events like these vary in weight and detail. He does, however, acknowledge that the war greatly deepened his beliefs, especially in the religious side of Spiritualism, which he now saw as of far greater importance than the scientific side. Spiritualism was "not merely the study of a force outside the rules of science, but . . . really something tremendous, a breaking down of the walls betwen two worlds, a direct undeniable message from beyond, a call of hope and guidance to the human race at the time of its deepest affliction" (*The New Revelation,* p. 49).

46. For further discussion of Doyle's Spiritualism in relation to his life, personality, and literary work see Sherman Yellen, "Sir Arthur Conan Doyle: Sherlock Holmes in Spiritland," *International Journal of Parapsychology* 7, no. 1 (Winter 1965): 33–63; and Kelvin Jones, *Conan Doyle and the Spirits* (Wellingborough, England: Aquarian, 1989).

47. Horace Leaf, *Under the Southern Cross* (London: Palmer, 1923).

48. A much later account of his investigations into comparative Spiritualism is James Aubrey Moyle, *Reality* (Wellington: Reed, n.d. [c. 1960]).

49. Harold S. Sell, *A Guide to Modern Spiritualism*, p. 17.

50. See J. M. Henderson, *Ratana: The Man, the Church, the Political Movement,* 2d ed. (Wellington: Reed, 1972).

51. A. C. Doyle, *The Edge of the Unknown* (London: Murray, 1930), pp. 147–149. Reference is to "Lord Northcliffe in New Zealand," *Harbinger of Light,* July 1, 1927.

52. *Harbinger of Light,* Sept. 1, 1930.

53. Ibid.

54. It must be noted, however, that Violet May Cottrell left a thick file of publications and papers, both Spiritualist and non-Spiritualist, with the Alexander Turnbull Library; these materials, together with copies of the 1930s newspaper articles, and her and her husband's obituaries, kindly supplied by the Napier Public Library, form the principal basis of this discussion.

55. Three folders of materials from the Psychic Research Society of Wellington are held by the Alexander Turnbull Library.

56. On Mary Dreaver, see Barry Gustafson, *From the Cradle to the Grave: A Biography of Michael Joseph Savage* (Auckland: Reed Methuen, 1986), p. 280.

57. For an interview with Beatrice Swaby, see Garth Carpenter, "Spiritualism, With Liberty of Interpretation," *Thursday,* September 3, 1970, p. 30 ff.

58. Rosemary Vincent, "Mary Lets the Spirits Guide Her," *New Zealand Times,* April 11, 1984.

59. "Radio Psychic Switched Off," *The Dominion,* September 24, 1983. See also Mary Fry's autobiography, *New Zealand's Radio Clairvoyant: Mary Fry's Own Story* (Wellington: Grantham, 1987), which concludes with her side of the radio controversy.

Chapter 3: Powers of the Air

1. J. Gordon Melton, *The Encyclopedia of American Religions* (Wilmington, N.C.: McGrath, 1987) 2:114–115.

2. *The Book of Gwineva* (Tapu: Culdian Movement of Mahara, 1981).

3. "An Introduction to the Culdian Trust" (leaflet), p. 5 (Tapu: Culdian Movement of Manara, n.d.).

4. Thames, which the reader may recall was Elizabeth Jane Harris' original New Zealand home, was a center of gold mining in the 1870s but has been something of a ghost town since then.

5. *Oahspe* (London: Kosmon, 1975). For a helpful interpretation, see J. Nelson Jones, *Thaumat-Oahspe* (Melbourne: Stephens, 1912). This book was originally a series of articles the *Harbinger of Light,* indicating continuity between mainstream Spiritualism and the "Teaching Spiritualism" of books like *Oahspe.*

6. *Urantia Book* (Chicago: Urantia, 1955).

7. For a summary of the history and teaching of the White Eagle Lodge, see Ingrid Lind, *The White Eagle Inheritance* (Wellingborough, Northamptonshire: Turnstone, 1984), See also the numerous works of the White Eagle Publishing Trust.

8. C. G. Jung, *Flying Saucers: A Modern Myth of Things Seen in the Sky* (New York: Harcourt Brace, 1959), and later paper editions.

9. Jacques Vallee, *Passport to Magonia: From Folklore to Flying Saucers* (Chicago: Regnery, 1969). See also Thomas E. Bullard, "Folkloric Dimensions of

the UFO Phenomenon," *Journal of UFO Studies,* New Series, vol. 3 (1991), pp. 1–57.

10. Daniel Cohen, *The Great Airship Mystery* (New York: Dodd, Mead, 1981). See also David M. Jacobs, *The UFO Controversy in America* (Bloomington: Indiana University Press, 1975).

11. Tony Brunt, "The New Zealand UFO Wave of 1909," *Xenolog* 100 (November 1975), and *Xenolog* 101 (December 1975). See also the account in Mervyn Dykes, *Strangers in Our Skies: UFOs Over New Zealand* (Taita, Lower Hutt: INL Print, 1982).

12. Quentin Fogarty, *Let's Hope They're Friendly!* (North Ryde, NSW: Angus and Robertson, 1983). Despite the flippant title, this is a sober account, with photographs, of the episode, including reports of interchanges between the observers and skeptics such as Phillip Klass. Bill Startup with Neil Illingworth, *The Kaikoura UFOs* (London and Auckland: Hodder and Stoughton, 1980), is an account by the pilot of the television crew's plane and contains analysis of the photographs.

Other science-oriented books on UFOs in New Zealand include Dykes, *Strangers in Our Skies,* and Michael Hervey, *UFOs over the Southern Hemisphere* (London: Hale, 1975), dealing with phenomena over Australia, New Guinea, and New Zealand. Neither puts much stress on spiritual aspects of the enigma.

13. Gray Barker, *They Knew Too Much about Flying Saucers* (New York: University Books, 1956; London: Laurie, 1958).

14. Ibid., p. 216.

15. Ibid., pp. 243–244.

16. "Was It Sorcery You Saw, Sir, or a Saucer?" *N.Z. Truth,* September 2, 1958, p. 22.

17. *Flying Saucers* 4, no. 4 (2d quarter 1957), p. 19.

18. John Stuart, *UFO Warning* (Clarksburg, W.V.: Saucerian, 1963).

19. George Adamski and Desmond Leslie, *Flying Saucers Have Landed* (New York: British Book Centre, 1953; London: Laurie, 1953). George Adamski, *Inside the Space Ships* (New York: Abelard-Schuman, 1955).

20. A transcript of one of the tapes has responses like the following on religion:

Q. Do the people of the other planets worship the same God as we do on earth?

A. Well they don't call it God as we do any more than they call the planets Venus, Mars and so forth as we do. They name their planets by orbits, only, which is the logical thing to do because that would be universal, and so it is true with their word for the name of God, instead of using the word God they say Supreme Being of the Universe or Supreme Intelligence of the Universe which is even broader than the word God.

Q. Do they have a Sabbath day that they observe?

A. A Sabbath day to them is every day because every day is a holy day of the Supreme Being and perpetuated by the Supreme Intelligence of the Universe. And that being holy they consider all things holy." "75 Questions and Answers. Asked Geo. Adamski by the New Zealand 'Adamski Flying Saucer Group' in Timaru. Taken from Tape Recording Made on 16th June 1955" (Mimeographed) Timaru: Adamski Flying Saucer Group, 1955, p. 5.

21. This paragraph follows Henry Quast, "A History of the UFO Movement in New Zeland," *Xenolog* 100 (September–October 1975), pp. 5–9.

22. See articles on Adamski in J. Gordon Melton, *Biographical Dictionary of American Cult and Sect Leaders* (New York and London: Garland, 1986), pp. 2–4; Ronald D. Story, *The Encyclopedia of UFOs* (Garden City, N.Y.: Doubleday, 1980), pp. 2–4; and, for the best critical account to date, with extensive bibliography, see Jerome Clark, *The Emergence of a Phenomenon: UFOs from the Beginning through 1959*, vol. 2 of *The UFO Encyclopedia* (Detroit, Mich.: Omnigraphics, 1992), pp. 1–12. For a more sympathetic treatment, see Lou Zinsstag and Timothy Good, *George Adamski: The Untold Story* (Beckenham, Kent: Ceti, 1983). See also Lou Zinsstag, *UFO . . . George Adamski: Their Man on Earth* (Tucson, Ariz.: UFO Photo Archives, 1990). This book, written prior to Zinsstag's collaboration with Good but published later, contains much material also incorporated into their joint work, together with other material, including reproductions of Adamskian photos, publications, and correspondence.

23. George Adamski, *Pioneers of Space: A Trip to the Moon, Mars and Venus* (Los Angeles: Leonard-Freefield, 1949). Discussed in Zinsstag and Good, *George Adamski: The Untold Story*, pp. 188–194.

24. Thus his Civilian Saucer Investigation (CSI) journal, *Flying Saucers* 5, no. 1 (3d quarter 1957), p. 21, reproduced a 1953 letter to the editor of a London publication by Adamski's coauthor, Desmond Leslie. Needless to say, Leslie is supportive of Adamski's integrity and his story. The introductory note says, "CSI headquarters neither encourages nor discourages belief in such-like claims. However, in view of the evidence of this nature, no one can afford to completely reject it nor is it wise to go completely overboard with it."

25. *Evening Post* (Wellington), January 23, 1959, p. 14.

26. Ibid., January 31, 1959, pp. 7, 16.

27. Ibid., February 2, 1959, p. 7.

28. George Adamski, *Flying Saucers Farewell* (New York and London: Abelard-Schuman, 1961), pp. 121–133.

29. However, it should be noted that, according to Zinsstag and Good, *George Adamski: The Untold Story*, pp. 70–71, 80, 85, 91, and Zinsstag, *UFO . . . George Adamski*, pp. 78–80, Henk Hinfelaar was much concerned about a perceived shift in Adamski's message and reported experiences about 1962 from contact to "spiritualism." Thereafter Adamski's writings and lectures contained a very high quota of material on witchcraft, telepathy, trance communications from the space entities, and reports of his virtually out-of-the-body travels to other planets. This change, which these writers, like Hinfelaar, deplore, seem to divide his postcontact career into two parts: (1) 1952–1962, centered on physical intereaction from benign space beings, and (2) 1962 until his death in 1965, in which Spiritualism came to the fore and nearly destroyed the contactee's important work. Zinsstag and Good suggest that the change could have been due to contact with, or intrusion by, another more sinister band of space entities, and there are hints in Adamski's own words of this happening. Insofar as the shift is real, other possible interpretations might be these: it was a means by which Adamski sought consciously or unconsciously to deal with an increasingly untenable scientific position (despite defences like Hinfelaar's of Adamskian "science"); as a sign that our hypothesis about the close relation of Spirit-

ualism and religious UFOism is on track, and this development is therefore a natural and predictable evolution of Adamski from charismatic contactee to medium, using trance or magical means of perpetuating the experience; and as (like John Stuart's experience) an early manifestation of a generational move away from the wise, anthropomorphic space brothers of the 1950s to the rather more ominous and enigmatic slit-mouthed medical examiners of later contact accounts. In any case, it is significant that Zinsstag and Good give the New Zealander Hinfelaar more attention than anyone else as an alarmed observer of the shift, which came to be basic to their own ambivalent interpretation of Adamski.

30. In a personal letter of May 26, 1988, Harvey Cooke told me that over the years the Tauranga group has come to a deepening understanding of the spiritual meaning of their UFO experience. The UFO idea, and reading books of the Adamski sort, from the beginning somehow helped them to fully realize that there is intelligence and purpose behind the universe, and that we can draw on cosmic mind to handle problems here and now. One gets a feeling that, in some sense, the UFOs and space beings are but triggers of trancendence that have enabled people to break through to what, in the end, was more important, this kind of spiritual awareness. But most of the Adamski-era spirituality and contactee groups have by now faded. The Tauranga group is one that, thus far, has not.

31. Quast, "A History of the UFO Movement in New Zealand," p. 8.

32. J. Gordon Melton, *The Encyclopedia of American Religions,* 3d ed. (Detroit: Gale Research Inc., 1989) pp. 122–123.

33. Terry Bell, "Year of the Flying Saucer," *N.Z. Woman's Weekly,* May 8, 1978, pp. 34–35. This short but interesting article includes reference to a mellowing of public opinion on the reality of UFOs, and says that people now talk openly even of the "Men in Black," who represent a "delinquent element" among spacemen. It also mentions mediums who receive space messages.

34. "Outer Space Visitors Are Recorded," *Wellington Evening Post,* April 27, 1978.

35. Karen Nimmo, "Aliens . . . 'They're Here to Help,' " *N.Z. Woman's Weekly,* February 29, 1988, pp. 52–53. On the Aetherius Society, see also, inter alia, in Melton, *Encyclopedia of American Religions;* and Story, *Encyclopedia of UFOs;* and the numerous publications of the Society.

36. "Aliens chat up couple!" *Sunday News,* April 16, 1989, p. 13; "Telepathic contact with aliens," *Western Leader,* April 3, 1989, p. 1.

37. Personal correspondence, June 11, 1988.

Chapter 4: The Ancient Wisdom and the New Age

1. Letter dated March 30, 1940, from E. T. Sturdy to the New Zealand section of the Theosophical Society, published in *Theosophy in New Zealand,* n.s., 1, no. 5 (August–September 1940), p. 20.

2. *Theosophy in New Zealand,* special jubilee no., 7, 2 (April–June 1946), p. 59.

3. Letter from E. T. Sturdy dated October 24, 1939, to Emma Hunt, published in *Theosophy in New Zealand,* n.s., 1, no. 3 (April–May 1940), p. 17.

Cited also in Mary K. Neff, *How Theosophy Came to Australia and New Zealand* (Melbourne: Australia Section Theosophical Society, 1943), pp. 43–44.

4. It should be pointed out that, although E. T. Sturdy formed the first Theosophical group in New Zealand, he was not the first New Zealand member of the society. The honor of being the first belongs to Augustine Les Edgar King. He applied for membership while in London in 1879, was sponsored by the prominent English Theosophists Charles C. Massey and Alex Ayton, and held a diploma dated April 3 of that year, less than four years after the founding of the society. He was not only the first New Zealand member but also the first from the Southern Hemisphere and only the 192d on the lists of the society as a whole. In 1883 three more members joined by mail: Thomas George De Remzy of Dunedin, and Charlotte and James Cox of Auckland. Of James Cox, Olcott wrote, "He had such a reputation as a psychometrist, principally by way of distinguishing disease, that he made a good living by practising the profession, constantly going between Auckland and Sydney to see his patients." A few others, including the John Sinclair and Francis Crossley Fulton mentioned in the charter, joined in 1884 and 1885 ahead of Sturdy's October 1885 diploma; Sturdy was chronologically the ninth New Zealand member. Emma Hunt, "Golden Jubilee of the New Zealand Section of The Theosophical Society 1896–1946," *Theosophy in New Zealand* 7, no. 2:34.

5. Letter to Emma Hunt, *Theosophy in New Zealand,* n.s., 1, no. 3:17. In the ellipsis Sturdy declares that he did not use the name Theosophy or form a branch of the society in connection with this group, but this claim must be the result of a lapse of memory because the Wellington Lodge's charter is dated November 1888, and moreover Neff, *How Theosophy Came,* p. 44, cites an item from Terry's *The Harbinger of Light* for July 1889 headed "New Zealand Theosophical Society" and stating:

> A Charter having been recently granted to Messrs. E. T. Sturdy, J. Sinclair and F. Fulton to form a Branch of The Theosophical Society, several meetings of members have taken place with satisfactory results, and a Branch is now established with headquarters in Wellington, Mr. Sturdy being elected President for the ensuing year, also to act as Secretary pro tem., Mr. Sinclair being elected Treasurer. All communications are to be addressed to the above gentlemen at Box 383, Wellington. The Branch numbers about 15 members, resident in Wellington, besides those resident in other parts of the colony. Meetings are to be held every second Tuesday evening at which papers will be read and discussions take place on subjects of interest to Theosophists.

The explanation may be that, because Sturdy left New Zealand in December 1888, the charter did not actually reach the new branch until after his departure and hence the formal establishment of Theosophy in Wellington was not well remembered by him. Most of its members, moreover, did not formally join the society until 1889.

6. For the Inner Group and Sturdy's role in it, see H. J. Spierenburg. *The Inner Group Teachings of H. P. Blavatsky to her Personal Pupils (1890–91).* (San Diego, Ca: Point Loma Publications, 1983).

7. On the much intermarried and interrelated Atkinson and Richmond clans, see Fairburn, *The Ideal Society and Its Enemies,* p. 162.

8. *Theosophy in New Zealand* 7, no. 2:59.

9. Judith Bassett, *Sir Harry Atkinson* (Auckland: University of Auckland Press, with Oxford University Press, 1975), pp. 2, 170.

10. On Tregear, see K. R. Howe, *Singer in a Songless Land: The Life of Edward Tregear* (Auckland: University of Auckland Press, 1991).

11. Edward Tregear, *The Aryan Maori* (Wellington: Didsbury, 1885).

12. See Max Muller, *Theosophy or Psychological Religion* (London and New York: Longman, Green, 1893. At the end of the preface to this work, his 1892 Gifford Lectures, Muller explained why the word "Theosophy" was added to the title: "It seemed to me that this venerable name, so well known among early Christian thinkers, as expressing the highest conception of God within the reach of the human mind, has of late been so greatly misappropriated that it was high time to restore it to its proper function. It should be known once for all one may call oneself a Theosophist, without being suspected of believing in spirit-rappings, table-turnings, or any other occult science or black art" (p. xvi). Although the confusion of Theosophy with séance-room phenomena amounts to a caricature of the movement, there is no doubt where Muller stood.

13. Edward Tregear, *Hedged with Divinities* (Wellington: Coupland Harding, 1895).

14. Jill Roe, *Beyond Belief: Theosophy in Australia 1879–1939* (Kensington: New South Wales University Press, 1986), chap. 3, "Legends of the Nineties," pp. 64–107.

15. See J. J. Healy, "The Lemurian Nineties," *Australian Literary Studies* 8, no. 3 (1978). Healy points out that, although the term "Lemuria" had been coined in the 1850s by C. L. Sclater to refer to a prehistoric continent stretching from Madagascar to Malaya, postulated to account for the distribution of the lemur, it became associated through the writings of Blavatsky and others with Atlantis as a lost continent and the site of a lost civilization. The primordial quality of the Australian bush helped foster such fancies, and in the 1890s a spate of adventure stories in the Rider Haggard style appeared, set in Australia, based on the Lemurian connection, full of mysterious ruins and hidden outposts of the past.

16. Mrs. Campbell Praed, previously mentioned as a Spiritualist lecturer, was also much influenced by Theosophy. She wrote: "But before Atlantis was, old books say that the world had shaped itself into a great and different land which was Lemuria. And of Lemuria the largest part which remains is Australia." This is seen, she adds, in the nature of this ancient land, "like no other." Mrs. Campbell Praed, *My Australian Girlhood* (London: Unwin, 1902), p. 10.

17. Francis West, *Gilbert Murray: A Life* (London and Canberra: Croom Helm, 1984), pp. 30–34.

18. Samuel Edger (1823–1882), born in Sussex, was originally a Baptist minister but came to oppose denominationalism. He arrived in Albertland, New Zealand, with a group of settlers in 1861 in the hope of putting his convictions into practice by establishing a nonsectarian ministry among them. In 1866 he moved to Auckland, where he preached for many years in Parnell Hall and other places, practicing an independent ministry of liberal bent. His sermons were reputedly very scholarly, too much so for some. His social views were

rather advanced; he strongly supported the temperance movement and opposed capital punishment. Samuel Edger was accused of being a Unitarian, a Spiritualist, and a secularist, but he rejected these charges. He acknowledged that he favored Spiritualism for its moral values (it had no association with war and eschewed materialism) and its sense of the nearness of the unseen world, but he granted that much nonsense was mixed up with it. He was influenced by Swedenborg and penned a very long essay on the Swedish sage. In the last year of his life, Edger preached a series of sermons published as a pamphlet titled *The One Religion,* in which he argued that religion is one, that all religions are emanations of the divine mind and so indivisible. (Samuel Edger, *The One Religion,* sermons preached in the Lorne Street Hall, April 30 and May 7 and 14, 1882.) It seems clear how a serious and intelligent young woman raised in the atmosphere of such values and attitudes might be predisposed toward Theosophy. Indeed, although he did not join the society, Samuel Edger's sober earnestness, studiousness, and relative intellectual isolation were characteristic qualities of the nineteenth-century Theosophist. See his posthumous *Autobiographical Notes and Lectures* (containing the Swedenborg essay), edited by Kate and Lilian Edger (London: Isbister, 1886).

19. Miss G. M. Hemus, "Early Days of the Theosophical Society in Auckland," *Theosophy in New Zealand* 7, no. 2 (April–June 1946), pp. 49–52.

20. Lilian Edger, M.A., "Memories of Colonel Olcott," *The Theosophist* (Adyar), 61, no. 11 (August 1940), p. 370.

21. Henry S. Olcott, *Old Diary Leaves,* (Adyar, Madras, India: Theosophical Publishing, 1935, 1975), 6:246.

22. Ibid., 6:250–251, 272–273.

23. Edger, "Memories of Colonel Olcott."

24. Olcott, *Old Diary Leaves* 6:240.

25. A. Y. Atkinson, "The Dunedin Theosophical Society, 1892–1900" B.A. thesis, (University of Otago, 1978).

26. Atkinson, "The Dunedin Theosophical Society," pp. 55–57.

27. Ibid., pp. 4–7.

28. Ibid., pp. 53–55.

29. *Christian Outlook, Otago Daily Times, Evening Star* (Dunedin), 1893–1897, *passim.*

30. "Status inconsistent" persons are those whose place in the world, usually imposed by social constraints regarding gender, racial, or class roles, is inconsistent with their talents, education (whether they are schooled or self-taught) and inner disposition.

31. *Christian Outlook,* March 28, 1896, p. 99.

32. Atkinson, "The Dunedin Theosophical Society," p. 47.

33. *Otago Daily Times,* October 7, 1893, p. 2.

34. *Christian Outlook,* February 24, 1894, p. 23.

35. In these writings, as in the Dunedin debates of the previous decade, one is reminded of a comment of J. B. Priestly on the age: "The intellectual Edwardians lived in an atmosphere of hopeful debate. They were ready to argue with one another in private, before an audience, or continually in print. Their disagreements might be wide and deep indeed, but when we look back on

them now we see that they shared a common platform—a belief that men might be converted to a cause, that society might be rationally transformed, if they could win the debate." J. B. Priestly, *The Edwardians* (New York: Harper and Row, 1970), p. 89.

36. *Theosophy in New Zealand,* December 19, 1904, p. 181.

37. Ibid., n.s., 1, no. 1, April 1903, p. 15. Regarding Kipling, the Theosophical poet D. W. M. Burn, of whom more later, writing in a 1905 issue on that fellow poet's "Barrack-Room Ballads," professed to find "philosophical, even Theosophical, meaning in their simple jingly lines."

38. Bertha H. Darroch (principal since 1923), "Vasanta Garden School," *Theosophy in New Zealand* 7, no. 2 (April–June 1946), pp. 56–58.

39. Leadbeater long claimed 1847 as his year of birth, and this date is to be found in many sources. However, Gregory Tillett, in his definitive biography, has established that 1854 is correct, and speculates on reasons for his subject's dissimulation on the matter. See Gregory Tillett, *The Elder Brother: A Biography of Charles Webster Leadbeater* (London: Routledge and Kegan Paul, 1982).

40. For a bibliography of Leadbeater's work and summaries of his teaching, see Tillett, *The Elder Brother.*

41. C. W. Leadbeater, *Australia and New Zealand: The Home of a New Sub-Race* (Sydney: Theosophical Society, 1915). See also Tillet, *The Elder Brother,* pp. 163–164; and Jill Roe, *Beyond Belief,* pp. 216–217.

42. Tillet, *The Elder Brother,* p. 197.

43. Mary Lutyens, *Krishnamurti: The Years of Awakening* (New York: Avon, 1976), p. 155.

44. Roe, *Beyond Belief,* p. 350.

45. The break in practical terms with his Theosophical friends and patrons was gradual, however; Krishnamurti did not establish an entirely separate pattern of life and work until the middle 1930s. It should be noted also that many important Theosophists remained supporters and admirers, and that the Theosophical Publishing House has kept books of his in print.

46. *New Zealand Free Lance* (Wellington) 10, no. 479 (September 4, 1909), p. 4.

47. *New Zealand Free Lance* 10, no. 479 (September 4, 1909), p. 4.

48. The Rev. C. W. Scott-Moncrieff, M.A., "The Coming Christ and the Order of the Star in the East. A paper read to a meeting of clergy and other members of the Church of England, in London, Nov. 27, 1911, by the Rev. C. W. Scott-Moncreiff, M.A., late Warden of St. John's College, Auckland, New Zealand" (Auckland: Lotus, n.d.).

49. *The International Theosophical Year Book, 1937* (Adyar, Madras, India: Theosophical Publishing, 1936, 1937), p. 235.

50. The last appearance of this clergyman I was able to trace is in *Crockford's Clerical Directory* for 1941, which has him living in Winchester and confirms that, after his return from New Zealand, he was officiant at Gatehouse-of-Fleet 1911–1915, and then rector of Lower Stanmore 1915–1930.

51. D. W. M. Burn, *Pedlar's Pack* (Dunedin: Coulls Somerville Wilkie, 1932).

52. See obituary in the *Dunedin Evening Star,* July 7, 1951.

53. *Theosophy in New Zealand* 24, no. 6 (November–December 1926), pp. 165, 169.

54. Ibid. 27, no. 3 (May–June, 1929), p. 82.

55. Ibid. 27, no. 5 (September–October 1929), p. 155.

56. *New Zealand Pictorial and News,* March 13, 1926.

57. *Theosophy in New Zealand* 27, no. 6 (November–December 1929), p. 165.

58. Ibid. 28, no. 3 (May–June 1930).

59. Chiefly in the November–December 1929 issue.

60. Cited in Mary Lutyens, *Krishnamurti: The Years of Fulfillment* (New York: Farrar Straus Giroux, 1983), pp. 27–28.

61. "Broadcast Ban on Krishnamurti," "Not a Messiah," "Indian Teacher," *New Zealand Herald,* March 27, 1934.

62. *The Theosophist* (Adyar) 54, no. 11 (August 1933), pp. 561–567. In view of occasional charges that Theosophy—and Social Credit—contains elements of anti-Semitism or even an ideological relation with German National Socialism, it is worth noting this same issue includes considerable correspondence on an earlier (54, no. 9, June 1933) editorial by Jinarajadasa strongly condemning Nazi persecution of Jews, this only four months after the Nazi seizure of power. *The Theosophist's* subsequent support of the Allied cause during the Second World War was fervent and unstinting. Theosophists, on the other hand, were harshly persecuted in Germany and the occupied territories under the Nazi regime. True, some Nazis writers borrowed and adulterated, often at second or third hand, certain motifs of Theosophy (the root races, Atlantis) as they took from many sources (Wagner, Nietzsche, and even Luther) what was required to form the mishmash that passed for the intellectual expression of a virulently anti-intellectual cause. But Theosophy in its pure form has almost always been most associated politically with the democratic, moderately socialist reformism of Besant's Home Rule League in India or its Labour Party constituency in New Zealand.

63. Correspondence in the archives of the New Zealand Section of the Theosophical Society, Epsom, Auckland.

64. John Marshall, *Memoirs,* vol. 1: *1912–1960* (Auckland: Collins, 1983), p. 261.

65. *The Dominion,* April 4, 1975.

66. David Grant, *Out in the Cold: Pacifists and Conscientious Objectors in New Zealand during World War II* (Auckland: Reed Methuen, 1986), pp. 103, 165 ff. It might be noted, as a point of interest, that Theosophy has always embraced diversity on the issue of pacifism, its ranks including both conscientious objectors and military men. In the period under discussion, the 1930s and early 1940s, prominent Theosophists included the high-principled George Lansbury, who was compelled to resign from leadership of the British Labour Party in 1935 because of his extreme pacifism, and General Maximiliano Martinez, the murderous military dictator of El Salvador 1931–1944; persons influenced by contact with Theosophy range from Mohandas Gandhi to Augusto Sandino, the Nicaraguan mystic revolutionary. However, undoubtedly most Theo-

sophists of that era were idealistic individuals strongly inclined toward non-violence, but (like many others) in agonizing inner conflict between peace and the profound evil they saw emerging in the totalitarian states.

67. "Theosophical Women's Association," brochure (Wellington, n.d., [c. 1940]) and Newsletter of the Association, March 1948 and May 1947.

68. *Theosophy in New Zealand* 15, no. 4 (March-July 1955).

69. John K. Robertson, *Aquarian Occultist* (the life of Geoffrey Hodson) (Auckland: private publication, 1971).

70. *Theosophy in New Zealand* 7, no. 2 (April-June 1946): 39-42.

71. *Light of the Sanctuary: The Occult Diary of Geoffrey Hodson*, ed. Cleo Z. Gregorio. (Manila: Theosophical Publishing, n.d. [c. 1988]). (Available through the Theosophical Publishing House.)

72. *Light of the Sanctuary*, p. 545.

Chapter 5: Magic in the Mind

1. Gregory Tillett, *The Elder Brother: A Biography of Charles Webster Leadbeater* (London: Routledge and Kegan Paul, 1982), p. 168.

2. G. M. Haylock, *History of the Wellington Lodge No. 411, 1917-1972* (Wellington: Wellington Lodge, 1972).

3. This was one of a number of tiny, fluid, and often ephemeral churches of the Old Catholic type, typically headed by grandiosely titled *episcopi vagantes* with minuscule flocks, which have long made up a colorful ecclesiastical underworld in Britain, the United States, and elsewhere. They should not be confused with the more stable and substantial Old Catholic churches of the European continent. However, Mathew, after a varied career in Roman Catholic, Anglican, and Unitarian circles, had managed to obtain consecration as a bishop for England by the Dutch Old Catholic Church on his representation—which turned out to be misleading, though apparently he was innocently deceived—that large numbers of British Roman Catholics disaffected with papalism, and Anglo-Catholics suffering repression in the Church of England, would welcome a British church of Old Catholic type under his leadership. Despite a few inaccuracies and an occasionally condescending tone, by far the fullest and most useful account of this world—including Mathew and the origins of Liberal Catholicism—to date of its publication is Peter F. Anson, *Bishops at Large* (London: Faber and Faber, 1964). For a more recent summary, with exhaustive bibliography, see Karl Pruter and J. Gordon Melton, *The Old Catholic Sourcebook* (New York and London: Garland, 1983). Biographical data on most leading Old Catholic and Liberal Catholic figures, including all New Zealand's Liberal Catholic bishops past and present, may be found in Gary L. Ward, Bertil Persson, and Alan Bain, eds., *Independent Bishops: An International Directory* (Detroit: Apogee, 1990). For a fresh look at the important Australian aspect of Liberal Catholic history, see Jill Roe, *Beyond Belief: Theosophy in Australia 1879-1939* (Kensington: New South Wales University Press, 1986), pp. 244-251 and *passim*.

4. Tillett, *The Elder Brother*, chap. 16, "The Priesthood Recovered," pp. 171-184.

5. C. W. Leadbeater, *The Science of the Sacraments: An Occult and Clairvoyant Study of the Christian Eucharist* (Los Angeles: St. Alban, 1920; 2d ed., 1929; 5th ed., Adyar: Theosophical Publishing, 1967.

6. C. W. Leadbeater and Annie Besant, *Thought-Forms: A Record of Clairvoyant Investigation* (London: Theosophical Publishing, 1901). It might be mentioned that this book, through its seminal influence on such artists as Piet Mondrian and Wassily Kandinsky, had a discernible influence on the development of modern surrealist and symbolist painting. See Tillett, *The Elder Brother*, pp. 261–262.

7. Colin Brown, *Forty Years On: A History of the National Council of Churches in New Zealand, 1941–1981* (Christchurch: National Council of Churches, 1981), pp. 88–89, 194–195.

8. For Krishnamurti's life see Mary Lutyens, *Krishnamurti: The Years of Awakening* (New York: Farrar, Straus, and Giroux, 1975); *Krishnamurti: The Years of Fulfillment* (London: Murray, 1983); and *The Life and Death of Krishnamurti* (London: Murray, 1990), a one-volume distillation of her previous biographical work on Krishnamurti; and Pupul Jayakar, *Krishnamurti: A Biography* (San Francisco: Harper and Row, 1986). Sidney Field, *Krishnamurti: The Reluctant Messiah* (New York: Paragon, 1989) is an informal memoir of a long friendship. A more controversial memoir that brings out some alleged very human characteristics of the teacher is Radha Rajagopal Sloss, *Lives in the Shadow with J. Krishnamurti* (London: Bloomsbury, 1991).

9. Personal letter from Elizabeth Falla to the author, April 10, 1988. I should like to thank Mrs. Falla profoundly for her willingness to undertake the painful yet very helpful task of sharing these memories of her late husband's remarkable and inspiring life.

10. I am indebted to Bill Taylor, secretary of the Krishnamurti Association in New Zealand, for providing new and updated information on the Krishnamurti work in the country, in a personal letter of September 18, 1990.

11. For a sympathetic study of this tradition see John R. Sinclair, *The Alice Bailey Inheritance* (Wellingsborough, Northamptonshire: Turnstone, 1984).

12. Alice A. Bailey, *The Unfinished Autobiography of Alice A. Bailey* (New York: Lucis, 1951).

13. Robert Ellwood, "Making New Religions: The Story of the Mighty 'I AM.' " *History Today* 38 (June 1988): 19–23.

14. Godfre Ray King [pen-name of Guy Ballard], *Unveiled Mysteries* (Chicago: Saint Germain, 1934).

15. "Human Relationships out of Step with Social Conventions: The Beeville Story," *Sunday Morning Post*, July 19, 1955, p. 2.

16. "N.Z.'s Strangest Community," *N.Z. Truth*, August 18, 1959, p. 23.

17. Ibid.

18. This letter and the Young Theosophist material are from the Beeville file in the Turnbull Library.

19. The New York temple of the Order of the Golden Dawn was chartered by MacGregor Mathers; thus—for readers familiar with material that is presented later in our chapter on the Havelock North Golden Dawn—it would pre-

sumably have pertained to the Alpha et Omega sect of the Golden Dawn, one of three branches into which the Hermetic Order split around 1900, not the Stella Matutina which Robert Felkin brought to New Zealand.

20. Much of the foregoing material is based on visits to the Los Angeles BOTA temple and on interviews with Ann Davies, around 1970, and is published in the first edition of my *Religious and Spiritual Groups in Modern America* (Englewood Cliffs, N.J.: Prentice-Hall, 1973).

Chapter 6: The Wizards of Havelock North

1. Attributed by Patrick Zalewski in conversation with the author.

2. Based on Francis King, *The Magical World of Aleister Crowley* (London: Arrow, 1987), pp. 8–9. See also Christopher McIntosh, *Eliphas Lévi and the French Occult Revival* (New York: Weiser, 1974), and Francis King, *Magic: The Western Tradition* (London: Thames and Hudson, 1975).

3. See Ellic Howe, *The Magicians of the Golden Dawn: A Documentary History of a Magical Order 1887–1923* (London: Routledge and Kegan Paul, 1972), chap. 1, for a devastating critique of these texts, including demonstration that the alleged letters of Sprengel contain Anglicisms and other solecisms that would never have been penned by a native German speaker. Fraulein Sprengel has not been identified or traced despite strenuous efforts in Germany by, among others, Felkin of New Zealand fame. See also R. A. Gilbert, *The Golden Dawn Companion: A Guide to the History, Structure, and Workings of the Hermetic Order of the Golden Dawn* (Wellingborough, Northamptonshire: Aquarian, 1986), for the varied views of members of the Golden Dawn and others of the provenance of the founding documents.

4. Gilbert, *Golden Dawn Companion*, p. 2.

5. See Francis King, *Ritual Magic in England* (London: Spearman, 1970), chap. 9, "A Bogus Golden Dawn."

6. Waite's order, after 1915 the Fellowship of the Rosy Cross, continued under his leadership until his death in 1942 and still survives in reduced form. The distinguished Christian mystic and scholar of mysticism Evelyn Underhill, and the remarkable mystical Christian novelist, poet, and critic Charles Williams, were sometime members. Waite himself is perhaps better known as a prolific writer on the history of magic, Freemasonry, Rosicrucianism, etc., than as a practicing occultist. For his life see R. A. Gilbert, *A. E. Waite: Magician of Many Parts* (Wellingborough, Northamptonshire: Thorsons, 1987).

7. For Felkin's medical work in Africa, see *Medical History* 3, no. 1, London, 1959, cited in Ellic Howe, *Magicians of the Golden Dawn*, p. 240 n. 2. Howe mentions the widespread interest and disbelief caused by a paper of Felkin's on a complicated surgical procedure reportedly performed by natives, commenting that "his colleagues' incredulity is of interest because of his later tendency to confuse reality and fantasy"—a judgment of Howe's that, of course, apologists for Felkin reject.

8. Howe, *Magicians of the Golden Dawn*, p. 241.

9. In November 1915 Felkin gave intriguing information to his followers about Christian Rosenkreuz, whom he believed to be the living though hidden

ultimate leader of his tradition, and the higher—i.e., fourth, fifth, and sixth—orders:

> First I will try to explain what I think most of you do not quite realise. The actual as well as the nominal Head of the Inner Order, is our Father in God, C.R.C. himself, who gives us direction and instructions from time to time through Members who are clairvoyant and clairaudient to such an extent that they are able to receive them.
>
> In addition to them there are certain Members who still function on the material plane; most of these live very secluded lives and can only be met with after much difficulty has been overcome. E.O.L. [Neville Meakin] met some of them when he went abroad on pilgrimage before passing over. Q.L. [Harriot Felkin] and myself have also met them at various times and received instructions and help (in 1904, 1909, and 1912).
>
> These members form what has been known to us as the 'Third' Order and it is their business to look after the various Temples and to give advice when required. Most of them live abroad in various countries but one lives in England and I have called him 'The Unknown' or 'Epopt', because for most of you he must remain behind the veil. . . .
>
> Hitherto we have spoken loosely of Three Orders. Now it will be possible to define a little more clearly the different Grades, since during the last three years we have received several of the Higher Grades, which we hope to pass on to those who are ready for them before we leave you" [i.e., for New Zealand].

Cited in Howe, *Magicians of the Golden Dawn,* pp. 274–275. Felkin did indeed impart higher grades just before his departure and also in the New Zealand lodge.

10. Howe, *Magicians of the Golden Dawn,* p. 273.

11. For reasons not fully explained, the initial series of *The Forerunner* ceased after twelve issues, in April 1910. The next issue (no. 13), under a new editor and now published by E. S. Cliff in Hastings, appeared in October 1912. Thereafter approximately quarterly issues appeared until no. 21, December 1914.

12. J. B. Priestly, in his delightful work on the Edwardian age, put the confusing but hopeful new spirit thus: "It was moving in many different directions. It was opening out, not hurrying one way. What it was opening *from,* so leaving behind, was the decaying hulk of middle-class Victorian belief, thought, feeling, taste, customs, habits. It might be reaching out not to Well's scientific Utopia but towards India and Theosophy, Irish peasants and leprechauns, Catholicism and the distributive state, Merrie England and the guilds, a quiet life and a new closeness to Nature, Free Love or no Love but plenty of social service. Where it moved at all, the age—as we say now—was wide open." J. B. Priestly, *The Edwardians* (New York: Harper and Row, 1970), pp. 92–93.

13. John von Dadelszen, "The Havelock Work 1909–39," *Te Mata Times* (Havelock North), September 9, 1983. This long and remarkable article, written in advanced years by a long-time resident of Havelock North and participant in much of that about which he writes, is by far the most complete account of the Havelock work in print, and the source of a good part of the information that follows.

14. Stopford Brooke (1832–1916) was a very liberal clergyman of the era, who had left the Church of England in 1880 to become an independent Unitarian minister; he is also a well-known writer on English literature. See Lawrence Pearsell Jacks, *Life and Letters of Stopford Brooke* (London: Murray, 1917); and Fred L. Standley, *Stopford Brooke* (New York: Twayne, 1972).

15. Emma Richmond (d. 1921), second wife of Henry Robert Richmond, was the first woman elected to the Taranaki Education and Hospital Boards and was an honorary gaol (jail) visitor.

16. S. W. Grant, *Havelock North: From Village and Borough 1860–1952* (Hastings: Hawke's Bay Newspapers, 1978), p. 54.

17. John Chambers (1853–1948) and his brother Mason Chambers (1860–1948), sons of John and Margaret Chambers who immigrated to Australia before 1848 and to New Zealand in 1854, were leading members of a prominent and wealthy local family. See S. W. Grant, *In Other Days: A History of the Chambers Family of Te Mata—Havelock North* (Waipukurau: Central Hawke's Bay, 1980).

18. S. W. Grant, *In Other Days,* p. 130, tells us that "Mason and Johnnie [Chambers] formed a trust, which later became known as the Whare Ra Trust, and Mason and Madge [his wife] gave the land on which the house known as 'Whare Ra' was built in 1913, the architect being Chapman-Taylor, whose style of architecture was then becoming fashionable, not only in Havelock North, but in other parts of New Zealand." James Walter Chapman-Taylor (1878–1958) was not only a prominent architect whose houses are now New Zealand landmarks but also a member of several esoteric orders.

19. Gilbert, *Golden Dawn Companion,* p. 42.

20. Howe, *Magicians of the Golden Dawn,* p. 269. Presumably the three 5 = 6 degree titles are order names of local persons, such as Reginald and Ruth Gardiner, who were thereby appointed to rule the order after the Felkins' return to England.

21. It appears that the Chambers were once again the Felkins' financial "angels." S. W. Grant relates that "in 1916 there is record of Johnnie arranging through Elder and Company to pay the fares to New Zealand of Dr. and Mrs. Felkin and that of a daughter of the doctor by his first marriage, so that they could come to Havelock and live at 'Whare Ra.' " *In Other Days* (p. 130), Grant adds, "The house is on the slopes below Tauroa and there seems to have been much inter-change of visits between the Tauroa and Mokopeka families [branches of the Chambers'] and the Felkins." Yet Grant also notes (p. 131) that "some of the family were influenced by Felkin's theories about life, but others were not impressed," and still others "quite frankly disapproved."

22. Ithell Coloquhoun wonders, perhaps too cattily, how the Felkins "managed the journey since the German U-boat activity of the 1914–18 War was then at its height and civilian travel, particularly by sea, was discouraged," and comments, "Evidently the Doctor had 'friends at Court.' " *Sword of Wisdom: MacGregor Mathers and "The Golden Dawn"* (New York: Putnam, 1975), p. 217. This book, based in part on personal acquaintance with Golden Dawn participants or their families, contains interesting material but must be used with caution; the author is guilty of careless errors, such as putting Robert Felkin's

death in 1922 rather than 1926, and of unfounded speculation, as when she writes (p. 193) that after 1914 the Felkin family's "pro-German sentiments may have put them out of sympathy with their environment and in 1916 they returned to New Zealand and settled there permanently." I am aware of no other suggestion that the Felkins were pro-German so far as the issues of the war were concerned, and in any case New Zealand in 1916 would seem an unlikely choice of refuge for anyone harboring such sympathies.

23. Grant, *Havelock North*, p. 83.

24. Ibid., pp. 83–84.

25. For all that, the remarkable difference in character between the London and Havelock Golden Dawn people, and the nature of their occultism, must be underscored. Consider, e.g., Florence Farr, the actress, companion of G. B. Shaw, and later headmistress in Ceylon (and by some reports then a Buddhist), who was an avid member of the Golden Dawn in the 1890s. On May 13, 1896, she attempted to evoke the spirit Taphthartharath to visible appearance; the ritual entailed boiling a pickled snake in a "hell broth" of various magical ingredients. Her ritual companions were Charles Rosher, a former court painter to the sultan of Morocco and the inventor of a new type of toilet; F. L. Gardner, a stockbroker with a penchant for disastrous investments but who studied alchemy; and Allan Bennett, an electrical engineer with a great magical reputation—he is reported once to have paralyzed a Theosophist, who had allegedly "mocked" him, for fourteen hours with a "magical blasting rod." Bennett later became the first known Buddhist monk of occidental origin (from King, *Magical World of Aleister Crowley*, p. 24). The contrast between such London exotics as these and the sober, churchgoing, prosperous burghers of Havelock North who were nonetheless their occult confreres is marked. Whare Ra doubtless holds its secrets, but it is hard to imagine Reginald Gardiner and his set boiling snakes or blasting Theosophists. But Felkin was an intermediate figure who knew both esoteric worlds well, perhaps all too well, and could shift with an ocean passage or a turn of inner attention from one role to the other.

26. Grant, *In Other Days*, p. 130; and *Havelock North*, p. 84.

27. The success was despite the aforementioned problem; there are rumors of times when the chief appeared in his temple amid a distinct aroma of liquor.

28. Thus R. A. Gilbert, author of two of the very small number of serious scholarly histories of the Golden Dawn, can write, after discussing the 1913 warrant for the Smaragdum Thalasses Temple in Havelock North, "It is to be presumed that Felkin was involved with this temple after 1916 but nothing further is known of its history." *Golden Dawn Companion*, p. 42. Another ostensibly reliable source says that, apparently sometime after 1915, "Felkin went mad and retired to a mental hospital"! Leslie Shepard, ed., *Encyclopedia of Occultism and Parapsychology*, 3d. ed. (Detroit and London: Gale, 1991), p. 678.

29. Patrick J. Zalewski, *Secret Inner Order Rituals of the Golden Dawn* (Phoenix, Ariz.: Falcon, 1988), pp. 8–9.

30. Despite this success, 1926 obituaries of Felkin in New Zealand newspapers, although describing his African adventures in colorful detail, make no mention of the order in connection with his affiliations, speaking of him only as a devout communicant of the Church of England and a prominent Mason. (But

his Masonic work was apparently entirely independent of the Grand Lodge of New Zealand, for there is no mention of him on the "In Memoriam" pages of its 1926–1927 reports.)

31. Patrick and Chris Zalewski, "The Golden Dawn Correspondence Course: A Brief History of Its Origins and Content," leaflet, Wellington: Thoth-Hermes Temple, n.d.

32. Christiana Mary Stoddart, who wrote under the pseudonymn "Inquire Within," was left in charge of the Stella Matutina's principal British center, the Amoun Temple in London. She corresponded at some length with Felkin after the latter's move to New Zealand about the temple's declining state. But she was also plagued by doubts. Eventually switching allegiances to become a devout Christian, she then wrote two often-incoherent books, *Light-Bearers of Darkness* (London: Boswell, 1930) and *The Trail of the Serpent* (London: Boswell, 1936). These sought to warn the world, on the basis of her experience with Golden Dawn groups, of great sinister occult conspiracies. The first work contains, amid much muddle, a firsthand account of Felkin and the S. M. In particular, Stoddart made use of certain "historical notes," which have not otherwise survived.

33. Cited in Howe, *The Magicians of the Golden Dawn*, p. 277.

34. For an account of the advanced rituals, including those of the vault, performed at Whare Ra, together with a brief history of the New Zealand order, see Zalewski, *Secret Inner Order Rituals of the Golden Dawn*. Mr. Zalewski, leader of a Golden Dawn group in Wellington that considers itself a successor to the Havelock Order, presents much previously secret and unpublished material in this remarkable book.

35. Howe, *Magicians of the Golden Dawn*, p. 273.

36. Ibid., p. 274.

37. A booklet by R. W. Felkin, *The Sacramental System* (Auckland: Whitcombe and Tombs, 1918), is the publication of a paper he read at a Church of England Missionary Society conference in Wellington, 1917. Although there are two kabbalistic quotes, it is generally a straightforward Anglo-Catholic statement.

38. John von Dadelszen, "The Havelock Work 1909–39," implies that the three chiefs, whose identity was supposed to be a secret within the order, were these. Patrick Zalewski believes that after Felkin's death they were instead, at least initially, Gardiner, John Chambers, and Mason Chambers. Personal correspondence, March 26, 1990.

39. John von Dadelszen, "Historical Notes," *Tauhara News* 80 (February–March 1988), p. 11.

40. Cited in von Dadelszen, "The Havelock Work 1909–39."

41. Ibid. It must be pointed out that this account of the demise of the Havelock Golden Dawn is not without its dissenters. According to Patrick Zalewski, the closure of Whare Ra left many with bitter feelings toward the chiefs, who were accused of acting high-handedly. Members were simply told, he says, that the temple had closed, and Zalewski also relates that a huge truckload of Golden Dawn and temple documents—which undoubtedly would have been of considerable interest to historians like him and myself—were intentionally

destroyed in a great bonfire. Zalewski goes on to say that just after the closure of Whare Ra he exchanged letters with several ex-members, some of whom offered "cryptic replies about the Order being finished and [that it] should be allowed to rest." But at least one, Jack Taylor, took an opposing view. Although of advanced years and confined to a wheelchair, Taylor helped Zalewski establish the Thoth Hermes Temple in Wellington as a chartered successor. Zalewski also states that "those that had any ability" of the Havelock Golden Dawn group still practice together very quietly. Zalewski, *Secret Inner Order Rituals of the Golden Dawn*, p. 15.

42. Jack Taylor, "The Order of the Table Round," published as app. 4 in Zalewski, *Secret Inner Order Rituals of the Golden Dawn*. Also published (without name of author) as a separate tract distributed by the Order of the Table Round.

43. Patrick Zalewski believes that by the time of his death Felkin personally was actually more involved in the Order of the Table Round than the Golden Dawn and states that he was buried in the robes of this order. Personal correspondence, March 26, 1990.

44. For a fascinating and valuable study of the interlocking Victorian and Edwardian cults of King Arthur, romantic medievalism, chivalry, empire, and gentility, see Mark Girouard, *The Return to Camelot: Chivalry and the English Gentleman* (New Haven, Conn.: Yale University Press, 1981).

Chapter 7: Cults and the Commonwealth

1. Roy Wallis, "Figuring out Cult Receptivity," *Journal for the Scientific Study of Religion* 25, no. 4 (December 1986): 494–503.

2. Rodney Stark and William S. Bainbridge, *The Future of Religion* (Berkeley: University of California Press, 1985).

3. It should be pointed out that Stark and Bainbridge do present data that suggest that New Zealand, as Michael Hill has put it in discussion of this material, "occupies a position of world prominence in current cultic geography" (Michael Hill, "The Cult of Humanity and the Secret Religion of the Educated Classes," *New Zealand Sociology* 2, no. 2 [November 1987], pp. 112–127) Thus the two authors show that in terms of Indian and Eastern cult centers and communities per million population New Zealand, with 5.2, is second only to Australia (5.3) and has four times the rate of the United States. On the criterion of Hare Krishna temples per million, New Zealand with 0.65 leads the world. Other rates are comparably impressive. Stark and Bainbridge, *Future of Religion,* pp. 482–492. This study has been severely criticized for using very small statistical bases (the world-beating Hare Krishna rate reflects two temples in a population of a little over three million) and using the often-dubious membership figures provided by religions themselves. Nonetheless the impression of a lot of minority religious activity is broadly accurate, as is their suggestion it is related to lack of vigor in conventional religion.

4. See Michael Hill and Wiebe Zwaga, "Civil and Civic: Engineering a National Religious Consensus," *New Zealand Sociology* 2, no. 1 (May 1987): 25–35.

5. E.g., ministering largely to their own constituency rather than "sheep

stealing," taking a proper place in interdenominational councils and agencies, in their public rhetoric observing the cardinal civil religion principle of "no offence," conducting business in an open and honest manner, having a core membership that is intergenerational and recognized as comprising sober respectable citizens, having a few institutions and theologians with intellectual *gravitas*.

6. See Sandra Sizer Frankiel, *California's Spiritual Frontiers: Religious Alternatives in Anglo-Protestantism, 1850–1910* (Berkeley and Los Angeles: University of California Press, 1988).

7. The high figure for New Zealand is from Michael Hill and Wiebe Zwaga, "Change in New Zealand Religion: A Comparative Perspective," in James A. Beckford and Thomas Luckmann, eds., *The Changing Face of Religion* (London: Sage, 1989). The low of eleven percent is from Sharon Crosbie, "Why Hast Thou Forsaken Me?" *The Dominion Sunday Times* (Wellington), May 1, 1988, p. 16.

8. Hugh Jackson, "Churchgoing in Nineteenth Century New Zealand," *New Zealand Journal of History* 17, no. 1 (April 1983): 43–54. See also Jackson, *Churches and People in Australia and New Zealand 1860–1930* (Wellington: Allen and Unwin New Zealand, 1987), pp. 115–118. Here he suggests that levels of churchgoing in New Zealand rose during the late 1870s and the 1880s to a peak in 1891 of twenty-five to thirty percent and then declined to a level of little more than half that by the mid-1920s, about where it is now.

9. Kevin J. Sharpe, in his preface to Sharpe, ed., *Religion and New Zealand's Future: The Seventh Auckland Religious Studies Colloquium* (Chaplaincy, University of Auckland, 1982), put it this way: "New Zealand is sometimes described as the most areligious and agnostic country on earth; very few people attend a church or appear interested in organized religion" (p. 5).

10. Social historians have long recognized that many of the Victorian stereotypes really apply only to one segment of society, the middle class, the upper and lower as a rule being neither as conventionally moral nor as religious as the middle. I myself suspect that a figure as high as fifty percent for church attendance in mid-century Britain involves an undercounting of the teeming, anonymous urban and rural poor, never much for churchgoing unless under pressure. By the same token, the common notion that New Zealand was largely settled by middle-class Britons is an exaggeration, perhaps based on the Christchurch model; as we shall see when we look at the case of several immigrants who became Spiritualists or Theosophists, the background was diverse but often working-class, and even those of middle-class or better antecedents were likely to be rebellious, scapegrace youths, mostly male, eager to escape the stuffy, pious world of their parents—hardly the sort likely to start attending church in a new land once they had gotten away from the old.

11. There was a revivalist surge in New Zealand in the 1870s and 1880s, paralleling that of such figures as Moody and Sankey in other parts of the English-speaking world and quite popular especially with the laity. Revivalism had much to contend with, however, in terms of popular indifference and the lack of deep-rooted religious patterns, and its long-term effects were limited. See P. J. Lineham, "How Institutionalized Was Protestant Piety in Nine-

teenth-Century New Zealand?" *Journal of Religious History* 13, no. 4 (June 1985), especially pp. 376–378.

12. For a vivid picture of this largely male immigrant society—e.g., in the 1881 census there were only 656 adult European women in New Zealand for every thousand men—and its cultural legacy, see Jock Phillips, *A Man's Country? The Image of the Pakeha Male—A History* (Auckland: Penguin, 1987).

13. M. R. Sharpe, "Anzac Day in New Zealand: 1916–1939," *New Zealand Journal of History* 15, no. 2 (October 1981): 97–114.

14. See Logie Barrow, *Independent Spirits: Spiritualism and English Plebeians, 1850–1910* (London and New York: Routledge and Kegan Paul, 1986).

15. Erik Olssen, "Truby King and the Plunket Society," *New Zealand Journal of History* 15, no. 1 (April 1981): 3–23.

16. W. J. Stuart, "Secularization and Sectarianism: The Struggle for a Religious Future for New Zealand," in Sharpe, *Religion and New Zealand's Future,* p. 84.

17. Stuart, "Secularization and Sectarianism," pp. 88–89.

18. Wallis, "Figuring out Cult Receptivity," p. 500.

19. Peter Lineham comments that church "pressures were weaker [in colonial New Zealand] than in the 'homeland' because traditional patterns of life had been upset and ecclesiastical institutions were undeveloped," and adds that none other than "Edward Gibbon Wakefield shrewdly observed that the expressions of concern about providing for colonial religious needs were 'nearly all make-believe or moonshine.' " P. J. Lineham, "How Institutionalized Was Protestant Piety in Nineteenth-Century New Zealand?" p. 372.

20. Joachim Wach, *Sociology of Religion* (Chicago: University of Chicago Press, 1944), pp. 17–34.

Appendix 2. The 1960s and After

1. Centrepoint is not discussed here, despite a fascinating and informative day I spent at the commune. But it does not really belong in this book. Centrepoint is only marginally religious in any strict sense of the term and is a world and a book in itself. Fortunately that book has already been written: Len Oakes, *Inside Centrepoint* (Auckland: Benton Ross, 1986).

2. It might be mentioned that some of these groups have a conspicuous political tone. Centrepoint retains the flavor of 1960s radicalism; the Unification Church is strongly anticommunist. British Israel also has a rightist thrust, literature of the John Birch Society type being prominent in its centers. In this connection one might also mention quasi-religious rightist groups like those discussed in Paul Spoonley, *The Politics of Nostalgia: Racism and the Extreme Right in New Zealand* (Palmerston North, N.Z.: Dunmore, 1987), such as Zenith Applied Philosophy, the Church of Odin, the Viking Youth, etc. But because these organizations have been very adequately presented in Spoonley's work they are not treated here.

3. George I. Gurdjieff, *Meetings with Remarkable Men* (New York: Dutton, 1963). Gurdjieff's other major book was *All and Everything: Beelzebub's Tales to His Grandson* (New York: Harcourt, Brace and World, 1950). See also Rafael Lefort, *The Teachers of Gurdjieff.* New York: Samuel Weiser, 1973. The best inde-

pendent work on Gurdjieff and his movment is James Webb, *The Harmonious Circle: The Lives and Work of G. I. Gurdjieff, P. D. Ouspensky, and their Followers* (New York: Putnam, 1980). For further references see Walter J. Driscoll and the Gurdjieff Foundation of California, *Gurdjieff: An Annoted Bibliography* (New York: Garland, 1985).

4. See, e.g., Thomas de Hartmann, *Our Life with Mr. Gurdjieff* (Baltimore: Penguin, 1972); C. S. Nott, *Teachings of Gurdjieff: The Journal of a Pupil* (New York: Weiser, 1962); P. D. Ouspensky, *In Search of the Miraculous* (New York: Harcourt, Brace and World, 1949); and Fritz Peters, *Boyhood with Gurdjieff* (Santa Barbara, Calif.: Capra, 1980).

5. Abdullah Dougan, *40 Days: An Account of a Discipline* (London and Auckland: Gnostic, 1978). This autobiographical work is also the major source for information on Dougan's life prior to 1974.

6. Dougan, *40 Days*, p. 150. The nonstandard transliterations of Arabic words here are as in the original.

7. That discussion was from unpublished copy. Mention should be made, however, of Abdullah Dougan, *Probings* (London and Auckland: Gnostic, 1979). This volume of assorted reflections based largely on Gurdjieff's teachings contains opinions likely to infuriate nearly everyone, from reactionary to radical, especially in the passages on sexuality and marriage. But it is also an interesting philosophical adventure and, in places, a lucid introduction to the complex Gurdjieffian way of thinking.

8. Flyer published by the School of Philosophy, Wellington.

9. Stephen Annett, ed., *The Many Ways of Being; A Guide to Spiritual Groups and Growth Centres in Britain* (London: Turnstone, 1976), p. 255.

10. Michael McIntyre, cited in Annett, *The Many Ways of Being*, p. 143.

11. An Indonesian word meaning exercise or training. The word *Subud* itself was said by Bapak to come from three Sanskrit words, *susila* (morality), which he took to mean right living in accordance with God's will; *budhi* (the inner enlightenment force in human beings), and dharma (which he took to mean submission to the power of God). Bapak himself always remained a Muslim and so interpreted these concepts in monotheistic Islamic categories.

12. John G. Bennett, *Concerning Subud*, New York: University Books, 1959, with much historical and autobiographical material; see also his *Witness: The Autobiography of John Bennett* (Wellingborough, Northamptonshire: Turnstone, 1975, 1983); Anthony Bright-Paul, *Stairway to Subud* (New York: Dharma, 1965).

13. For basic perspectives, see the Society of Guardians, "An Introduction to the Qabalah of the Guardians," booklet (Auckland, n.d.).

14. "$2500 Mystics Meet Competition," *The Dominion* (Wellington), August 30, 1978, p. 2. See also "TM Relaxation," pamphlet (Auckland: The Meditative Relaxation Research Foundation, n.d.); here the title means "Technique of Meditative Relaxation."

15. "Brief Concept of Rosicrucian Christianity," pamphlet (Haarlem: International School of the Rosy-Cross, n.d.).

16. For the colorful story of the OTO and its vicissitudes, see Francis King, *The Magical World of Aleister Crowley* (London: Weidenfeld and Nicolson, 1977; Arrow, 1987).

17. See *Mageia: Thelemic Orgia O.T.O.* (Auckland: Kantharos O.T.O., n.d.) The order practices no great secrecy; this manual, giving the Auckland mailing address, and other OTO publications are available in occult bookshops.

18. Another New Zealand connection with Crowley was in the person of Leila Waddell, a half-Maori violinist who, in England around 1910, was one in the magician's long series of mistresses and coritualists. Known as the Mother of Heaven, she played to great effect as accompanist to certain of Crowley's dramatic public performances of dance and occult rite. See King, *Magical World of Aleister Crowley,* pp. 61–66.

19. "Meditation Is Basis for Life of Peace," *New Zealand Herald,* September 23, 1985.

20. The prominent economist Ravi (Raveendra) Batra, author of the 1987 best-seller *The Great Depression of 1990,* has been deeply influenced by Ananda Marga economic theory. His other titles include *Prout: The Alternative to Capital.*

21. "What Is Ananda Marga?" *The Dominion,* August 1, 1977, Insight.

22. "Dangerous Terrorist Group or 'Potty Sect'? *The Dominion,* August 2, 1977.

23. "Cult Defectors Accuse Leader," *New Zealand Herald,* July 13, 1985, weekend magazine. For a fascinating account of Da Free John's ministry, see Georg Feuerstein, *Holy Madness* (New York: Paragon, 1991), pp. 80–100.

24. Rob Gordon, "A Kiwi Guru's Fall from Grace," *The Dominion,* September 7, 1985.

25. "Narain Guilty of Kidnapping" and "Leader's Power Cited by Judge," *The Dominion,* May 27, 1988.

26. Letter of March 7, 1914; Baughan Papers, Turnbull Library.

27. *The Akaroa Mail,* September 22, 1958.

28. A book by an American anthropologist that offers excellent insights into three of the movements cited here, Radha Soami, the Brahma Kumaris, and the devotees of Satya Sai Baba, in their Indian homeland, is Lawrence A. Babb, *Redemptive Encounters: Three Modern Styles in the Hindu Tradition* (Berkeley and Los Angeles: University of California Press, 1986).

29. *Radiant Living,* April, 1988, p. 3.

30. Joel Goldsmith's books include *The Infinite Way, Practising the Presence, Parenthesis in Eternity, The Art of Meditation,* and others. For a biography see Lorraine Sinkler, *The Spiritual Journey of Joel S. Goldsmith* (New York: Harper and Row, 1973).

31. Although written prior to Hubbard's death or the Australian decision, the best independent book on Scientology remains Roy Wallis, *The Road to Total Freedom* (New York: Columbia University Press, 1977). On Hubbard's life from birth to death Russell Miller, *Bare-Faced Messiah: The True Story of L. Ron Hubbard* (New York: Holt, 1987), can be highly recommended. As Miller states in his introduction, after referring to the "lies, half-truths and ludicrous embellishments" with which the church's official biographies of its founder are allegedly rife, "the wondrous irony of this deception is that the true story of L. Ron Hubbard is much more bizarre, much more improbable, than any of the lies."

32. The classic independent work on the Unification Church is Eileen Barker, *The Making of a Moonie* (Oxford: Blackwell, 1984).

33. See Bruce Ansley, "Witchcraft: Women's Rites," *New Zealand Listener,*

June 8, 1985; and "Power of Inner Wisdom," *New Zealand Herald,* March 3, 1986.

34. For this reason, as the article cited above by Ansley points out, some women have preferred to work in Dianic, or women-only, Wiccan groups. Some are lesbian, some not, but regardless of sexual orientation these women have felt a need, after centuries of male-dominated religious institutions, to explore female spirituality independently of men for a while.

35. For America and England respectively, see Margot Adler, *Drawing down the Moon: Witches, Druids, Goddess-Worshippers and Other Pagans in America Today* (New York: Viking, 1979; rev. ed. Boston: Beacon, 1986); and T. M. Luhrmann, *Persuasions of the Witch's Craft: Ritual Magic in Contemporary England* (Cambridge, Mass.: Harvard University Press, 1989). For Australia, see Neville Drury and Gregory Tillet, *Other Temples, Other Gods: The Occult in Australia* (Sydney: Methuen Australia, 1980).

36. E.g., Nicola Legat, "Transformers," *Auckland Metro,* October 1987, pp. 60–80.

Index

About the Author

ROBERT S. ELLWOOD received his Ph.D. in the history of religion from the University of Chicago Divinity School in 1967. He is the author of numerous books, including *Many People, Many Faiths* and *Alternative Altars*. He is currently professor of religion at the University of Southern California.